The Politics of Regulatory Change

A Tale of Two Agencies

Second Edition

RICHARD A. HARRIS

SIDNEY M. MILKIS

New York   Oxford
OXFORD UNIVERSITY PRESS
1996

Oxford University Press

Oxford   New York
Athens   Aukland   Bangkok   Bombay
Calcutta   Cape Town   Dar es Salaam   Delhi
Florence   Hong Kong   Istanbul   Karachi
Kuala Lumpur   Madras   Madrid   Melbourne
Mexico City   Nairobi   Paris   Singapore
Taipei   Tokyo   Toronto

and associated companies in
Berlin   Ibadan

Library of Congress Cataloging-in-Publication Data
Harris, Richard A., 1951–
The politics of regulatory change : a tale of two agencies
Richard A. Harris, Sidney M. Milkis. — 2nd ed.
p.   cm.
Includes bibliographical references and index.
ISBN 0–19–508191–9
1. Administrative procedure—United States.   2. Trade regulation—
United States.   I. Milkis, Sidney M.   II. Title.
KF5407.H37   1996
342.73'066—dc20   95-32845
[347.30266]

1 3 5 7 9 8 6 4 2

Printed in the United States of America
on acid-free paper

To Eric, Lauren,
Jeffrey, Deborah, David, and Jonathan,
all of whom were born during the time
we worked on this book.

Preface

This project began in the early 1980s, when both of us were completing work on our doctoral dissertations at the University of Pennsylvania. One studied the New Deal period, examining the complex and often conflictual relationship between the presidency and party system that was forged on the anvil of the partisan realignment of the 1930s. The other had centered his research on reform movements of the 1970s, seeking to make sense of the massive change in institutions that was associated with the advent of "social regulation." The long conversations we had, which began largely as a welcome respite from the trials and tribulations of dissertation writing, evolved into fruitful and exciting exchanges on the nature and direction of change in American politics. These conversations marked the beginning of the collaboration that resulted in the first edition of this book.

Our discussions centered especially on the fundamental departures from the regulatory politics of the New Deal that took place during the 1970s. Not only had an important shift taken place in policies, but there also had been significant changes in the institutional arrangements and, most significant, in the governing principles that had characterized the New Deal. Whereas the New Deal focused on economic issues, major initiatives during the 1970s involved the federal government directly in so-called quality of life issues such as safety in the workplace, affirmative action, pollution control, and consumer protection. Moreover, the New Deal emphasis on delegating broad policy responsibility to the president and administrative agencies was replaced by a new institutional arrangement that involved Congress, the courts, and public interest groups in the details of regulatory policy. It seemed to us that these changes, although rarely discussed as such, marked a transformation of the political economy that was similar in magnitude to that of the Progressive and New Deal eras. That is, these changes represented the advent of a *new* regulatory regime—the public lobby regime, as we call it—characterized by a new set of ideas, institutions, and policies.

Our interest in regulatory change was heightened by the 1980 election and its aftermath, which seemed to signal still another major shift in the institutions and policies governing the political economy. Nothing more clearly revealed the aspirations of the Reagan presidency than the vigor with which the president and his aides set about achieving *regulatory relief,* an effort that concentrated on undoing the harm they believed was perpetrated on the American economy by social regulation. The emergence of social regulation in the 1970s was associated with the prominence of ideas that raised fundamental questions about the market economy. The far-reaching effect of this new regulatory regime on the political economy precipitated a strong reaction, which led to a contending set of ideas supportive of building—or rebuilding—a market-oriented regulatory policy.

Especially intriguing about these jarring changes in regulatory policy was their occurrence amid developments in the American political system that many scholars and statesmen viewed as inimical to change. Pundits argued that during the 1970s the American political system was afflicted with a pathological fragmentation, making it virtually impossible to build broad coalitions and subjecting the government to policy immobilism. In our view, however, the reforms of the 1970s, of which the new social regulation was a critical element, fostered a decentralization of institutions that did not paralyze the system but made it responsive to broad ideas and social movements, resulting in dramatic change. It is our interest in these reforms that has animated our inquiries as we have sought, over the past several years, to develop an explanation for the rise of social regulation and the challenge to that regulation posed by the "Reagan revolution." We have learned a great deal in carrying out this study, though we fear that it raises more questions than it answers. Perhaps the best thing we can say about the long hours we put into this project is that our initial enthusiasm has been tempered by the realization of how much we do not know about the complex phenomenon of regulatory politics in the United States.

The questions we have raised suggest that federal regulation should be studied in the context of broader developments in American politics. Indeed, a basic assumption underlying this study is that regulatory politics—the struggle for control over both the administrative levers of power and the policy shaped within government agencies—is central to government activity in the United States. Thus, the study of regulation sheds light on the defining elements of contemporary American politics. Similarly, the development of regulatory politics is best examined from a broad philosophical and historical perspective. In seeking to provide such a perspective, we sought to write a book that will interest not only specialists in regulatory politics but also a more general audience that is concerned with major developments in the American political system. We are grateful that the reviews of the first edition, although not uncritical, acknowledged and appreciated our efforts to analyze the connections between regulatory politics, on the one hand, and broader philosophical and institutional changes, on the other.

That Oxford University Press decided to publish a second edition of *The Politics of Regulatory Change* offers a measure of confirmation that we have also sparked interest among a relatively wide readership. We did not embark on a project of updating this study without a sense of apprehension, however. New editions all too often amount to little more than the inclusion of an additional chapter chronicling events that occurred after the original publication. We hoped to avoid this pitfall and greatly appreciate the support of our editors at Oxford for allowing us to write a second edition that not only takes account of important developments since the publication of the first edition but also offers analysis and evidence that contribute to the ongoing debate about regulation in the United States. With these purposes in mind, we have added three new chapters in this edition (Chapters 7–9) and thoroughly revised the conclusion (Chapter 10).

The first edition necessarily ended on a speculative note, pointing out that the Reagan revolution had failed to eliminate even a single major regulatory law or agency, while acknowledging that the terms of debate and specific policies had shifted in a conservative direction. The Reagan regulatory program stalled somewhat short of its goals, we suggested, because it emphasized executive and budgetary action rather than a broad challenge to the institutional fabric of the public lobby regime. The election of George Bush to the White House in 1988, following a campaign during which he promised a "kinder, gentler" version of the Reagan regulatory program, provided an excellent opportunity to test our conclusions about the resilience of the institutional shifts that accompanied the new social regulation and about the tenuousness of Reagan's administrative strategy for providing regulatory relief. Subsequently, the troubled first two years of Bill Clinton's presidency and the dramatic Republican victory in the 1994 midterm elections brought us full circle, renewing militantly conservative efforts to scale back social regulation. Whether the 1994 election and its aftermath, which gave Republicans majorities in both legislative chambers for the first time since 1954, signal the cresting of the Reagan revolution or another chapter in the fractious regulatory politics of the past two decades is the principal question that we address in the conclusion to the second edition. Thus, we end the second version of our study much as we did the first—with more questions than answers. At the same time, we have been confirmed in our initial judgment that regulatory politics can shed light on the larger questions of government's proper scope in a liberal democracy and the tension between centralized administration and our nation's commitment to the individual pursuit of material satisfaction.

More practically, the writing of the second edition afforded us the chance to respond to some of the helpful critiques of the first. In particular, we tried to expand the scope as well as the number of personal interviews for this manuscript. We built on the strength of the first edition by including over thirty new interviews, which not only renewed our contacts with public lobbyists and officials at the FTC and EPA, but also incorporated the results of conversations with congressional staff members. In a lengthy review of the first edition for *The Journal of Policy Analysis and Management,* Professor John Hird suggested that the introduction of interviews with key congressional personnel might have significantly strengthened the empirical foundation of the book. We sought, in the new edition, to introduce the legislative perspective through extensive discussions with some of those individuals on the Hill who participated in the enactment and oversight of regulatory policy for the FTC and the EPA. Although most of these people, on both sides of the aisle, felt they were in positions too sensitive for us to cite them directly, we believe that the second edition benefited immeasurably from the insights they provided. We are grateful to them as well as to those in Congress who agreed to direct citation.

As with our experience in researching the first edition, we appreciate deeply the fact that the quality of this project is, in large part, attributable to all those who so generously gave of their time and thoughtfulness during the interview process. A central theme of this book is that regulatory politics entails more than the free play of self-interest, that it reflects as well a clash of ideas about government, citizenship, and politics. This aspect of regulatory affairs shone through clearly for us: we were constantly—and pleasantly—surprised at how animated and reflective our respondents proved to be. Certainly this reaction to our inquiries was partly a reflection of the high quality of many of those who serve in government and make up the Washington community. It is also, we are convinced, a commentary on the political times covered in the book. We suspected from the beginning of this project that we were studying developments best characterized as a battle for the destiny of the American polity, and our research confirmed this suspicion. We are indebted to the participants in this battle who took our work seriously and relished the opportunity to enlighten us. Although many of those interviewed will take strong exception to some of our observations and arguments, we hope that in general this volume vindicates the time and effort they so generously contributed to our project.

Both editions of this book benefited tremendously from the critiques of several colleagues who read the manuscript at various stages. A special debt is owed to Michael Reagan, professor emeritus at the University of California at Riverside, who provided us with an extraordinarily rich commentary on the first edition. We also received very discerning critiques on the first version from R. Shep Melnick of Brandeis University and Abigail Thernstrom of the Manhattan Institute, and from two members of the Rutgers-Camden University faculty, Jay Sigler and G. Alan Tarr. For the second edition, Professor Marc Landy of Boston College provided keen insights, especially on the material dealing with the EPA. In addition we want to thank the anonymous readers who improved the manuscript with their constructive criticism, as well as our editor Valerie Aubrey, her successor David Roll, and the Oxford editorial staff for their enthusiastic and skillful help in bringing both editions of this book to fruition. In the middle of our protracted labors to produce the second edition, David Roll decided to pursue a career in medicine. Gioia Stevens, our current editor, coaxed us through the final frantic months of work on this volume; we are grateful for her persistence and patience, and for her tolerance of our temperamental pursuit of a book in which we could take pride.

We would be remiss in not also expressing our gratitude to those who supported our research. We thank the John M. Olin Foundation and the Rutgers University Research Council, who supported the project financially, and Martin Levin, director of the Gordon Public Policy Center at Brandeis, and Jay Sigler, chairman of the Graduate Department of Public Policy and Administration at Rutgers-Camden, who provided us with aid and comfort in the form of office space, research support, and a stimulating environment. Stephen J. Rockwell and Allen S. Kamer provided invaluable research assistance for the second edition.

The publication of this book marks the completion of a long and fruitful period. The time spent on this project has yielded not only two publications, but also all six of our children: Eric, Lauren, Jeffrey, Deborah, and David were born as we worked on the first edition, while Jonathan arrived in the course of our research for the second. In our collaboration we have both grown to appreciate the ongoing vitality of the American political experience. As rewarding as this intellectual journey has been, however, we recognize that it would never have been sustained without the support of our wives, Ellen and Carol, whose love and patience enriched the friendship we and our families share.

Camden, New Jersey   R. A. H.
Waltham, Massachusetts   S. M. M.
August 1995

Contents

The Politics of Regulatory Change

1

Regulation, Deregulation, and the Administrative State

> Although all democratic peoples are instinctively drawn toward the centralization of power, this attraction is uneven. It depends on particular circumstances which may promote or restrain the natural effects of the state on society.
>
> ALEXIS DE TOCQUEVILLE, *Democracy in America*

This is an unconventional book on federal regulation. Its immediate focus is twofold: development of the so-called new social regulation in the 1970s and the concerted efforts of the Reagan administration in the 1980s to deregulate in what most would agree are the two most visible areas of the new social regulation, namely consumer affairs and environmental protection. In terms of this immediate focus, our approach is very much in the mainstream of studies on regulatory policy. We present an in-depth, comparative case study of the Federal Trade Commission (FTC) and the Environmental Protection Agency (EPA), arguably the two critical agencies in these respective issue areas. To be sure, a number of useful lessons about regulatory politics and alternative strategies of deregulation may be learned from this analysis. We also believe, however, that the study of contemporary regulatory affairs offers a distinctive opportunity to grapple with weightier questions of democracy, citizenship, the evolution of an administrative state, and the role of ideas in American politics.

This second set of concerns is a formidable one indeed, especially for a comparative case study. To examine these concerns effectively, therefore, it will be necessary to bolster the case study with a historical and philosophical treatment of regulatory policy. Too often students of regulatory affairs gloss over more profound questions in an effort to arrive at policy-relevant conclusions. In this study, we devote considerable attention to the origins of environmentalism and consumerism in order to illuminate both the broader political implications of these two belief systems and how their underlying ideas helped to transform institutional relations and redistribute power in regulatory policymaking. Accordingly, our analysis of regulation and deregulation in the 1970s and 1980s will encompass an interpretation of the 1960s; in particular, the politics of the New Left and how it was moderated and assimilated into governmental practice via the new social regulation.

Simply appreciating the connection between the New Left and the new social regulation, though, is not sufficient, because the ideological and cultural critiques of the 1960s confronted fairly well-entrenched institutional arrangements established in earlier periods of political ferment and governmental expansion. Moreover, these earlier periods, the Progressive Era and the New Deal, were characterized by their own ideas about regulatory policy, ideas that helped to shape regulatory institutions at the turn of the century and during the 1930s. In the end, evaluating the new social regulation of the 1970s and the deregulation of the 1980s demands an understanding of the relationship between regulatory ideas and institutions as well as the evolution of that relationship through particular historical circumstances. It is impossible, for example, to explain fully either the changes that took place at the FTC in the 1970s or the successes and failures of deregulation at that agency without understanding its creation in the Progressive Era and its role in the New Deal as well as its reinvigoration with the new social regulation. Even for the EPA, established in the 1970s, the legacy of the New Deal is as crucial to our appreciation of contemporary regulatory politics as is the emergence of environmentalism in the late 1960s.

In examining the new social regulation and the Reagan revolution, then, we will have occasion to deal with more general questions about the status and direction of American politics. Indeed, this is entirely appropriate, because environmental and consumer advocates as well as many of Reagan's closest advisors on deregulation raised exactly such questions. The reformers of the 1970s were concerned with far more than ecology and product safety, and the deregulators of the 1980s were concerned with far more than the economic costs of regulation. Ironically, both were deeply troubled about societal ills they attributed to big government. Even more ironically, the actions of both served to erode ideas and institutions that Tocqueville identified as restraints on centralized administrative power in America.

Advocates of the new social regulation insisted on "opening up" government and creating new avenues for citizen participation. To that end, they created a new kind of participatory institution: the public lobby group. These organizations were designed specifically to ensure that the public interest would not be sacrificed or co-opted as policy concerns with environmental protection, consumer affairs, or public health shifted from legislation to administration. Historically, reformers had diminished their efforts after legislative successes only to find that these successes were undermined as the arena switched to bureaucratic implementation. In the view of public interest advocates, the only remedy to this situation was to maintain a permanent watchdog presence with independently operated organizations funded from the grass roots. Public lobby groups were established along these lines (Berry, 1977; McCann, 1986).

Their efforts in this regard did open up regulatory decisionmaking to extensive participation by public lobby groups, and this has had a salutory impact. In fact, we will argue that their success fundamentally altered the regulatory regime put in place during the New Deal, establishing in its stead what we term the "public lobby regime" (see Chapters 2 and 3). For all of the positive institutional change of the 1970s, though, public lobbyists helped to create more federal programs, more government bureaucracy, and a policymaking process that hardly could be called broadly democratic or egalitarian. Proponents of deregulation, on the other hand, sought to reduce drastically the size and reach of the central government's regulatory machinery and to break what they perceived to be reformers' control of the regulatory process. After eight years of the Reagan administration it seemed that, although reformers of the 1970s were not as influential in regulatory affairs as they were a decade ago, deregulators in fact had enhanced the centralized character of regulatory politics. By choosing to use conservative political appointees to harness liberal bureaucrats at the regulatory agencies and by relying on executive orders and the Office of Management and Budget (OMB) to impose draconian cost-cutting policies on those agencies, deregulation actually continued the twentieth-century enterprise of constructing a centralized administrative state in America.

At his inauguration in 1980 Ronald Reagan declared, "Government is not the solution to our problems, government is the problem." That single sentence succinctly captured the essence of what has come to be known as the Reagan revolution. Based on its conviction that the central government had become far too intrusive in American society, the Reagan administration strove to curtail sharply and in some instances even eliminate a great many federal programs. However, nothing more clearly reflected this "revolution" in public policy than the vigor with which the president and many of his advisors set about deregulating the economy. That deregulatory effort, moreover, focused squarely on the so-called new social regulation. Generally, the term new social regulation refers to the numerous federal initiatives in environmental policy, occupational safety, public health, consumer affairs, and equal opportunity that were enacted and implemented during the 1970s.

These initiatives involved Washington, D.C. directly in the quality-of-life concerns which, according to some observers, accompanied the emergence of postindustrial society (Bell, 1957; C. Reich, 1970). Landmark legislation on safety in the workplace, affirmative action, pollution control, and consumer protection profoundly affected business activity in the United States. In addition, billions of federal dollars were committed to these programs, and new bureaucratic entities were empowered to administer them (Lilley and Miller, 1982). Finally, innovative developments in the field of public interest law shifted the battleground of regulatory politics to the federal courts. District and circuit court judges were called on to oversee policy implementation and mediate disputes that previously would have been resolved at the state level or in administrative or legislative arenas. In this sense, the 1970s rather than the 1980s constituted the real revolutionary decade. It is perhaps more appropriate, therefore, to view the Reagan administration's attack on the new social regulation as a "counterrevolution."

Whether we see the 1980s as a revolution or a counterrevolution, though, President Reagan obviously desired a basic reorientation in regulatory policy. His appointments to key regulatory posts, particularly at social regulatory agencies where his most outspoken and controversial assignments were made, signaled a concerted attempt to cut governmental intervention in the private sector. Murray Weidenbaum, his first chairman of the Council of Economic Advisors (CEA), had devoted a number of years to documenting the "excessive" cost of federal regulation, and argued that social regulation was especially wasteful (1979). The antiregulatory views of David Stockman, the director of the OMB, were widely known. More important, the appointments of James Miller to head the FTC, James Watt to direct the Department of Interior (DOI), and Ann Burford to run the EPA, typified a pattern of placing implacable critics of the new social regulation in charge of the very agencies responsible for implementing it. These appointments contrast markedly not only with those of liberal Democratic presidents, but also with those of Richard Nixon who, like Ronald Reagan, desired a reduction in government regulation and a revival of federalism. Nixon sought top-quality, pragmatic administrators; compare for example his appointments of Walter Hickle at DOI or William Ruckleshaus and Russell Train at EPA with Watt and Burford.

The concentration on social regulation was also exemplified by President Reagan's Task Force on Regulatory Relief. In its first report, this special commission chaired by Vice-President George Bush singled out forty-one programs for significant savings to be achieved through deregulation. Of those forty-one programs, thirty-six were in areas of social regulation. Ten of the forty-one were under the jurisdiction of the EPA, and twelve more concerned auto safety rules administered by the National Highway Traffic Safety Administration (NHTSA). The focus on social regulation was unmistakable, but why that focus?

Undoubtedly, the new social regulation had flaws. Perhaps the essentially political character of the processes through which regulatory policy is generated and administered makes such flaws inevitable, because the regulatory process is one of conflict and bargaining rather than clear matching of ends and means. In any event, the notion that social regulation was in need of reform did not originate in the 1980 presidential election campaign. Since the mid-1970s, students of regulatory policy and American politics had been arguing for reform of environmental and consumer regulation. Economists especially were on the cutting edge of the debate over regulatory cost, because both liberals and conservatives among them had agreed that greater efficiencies were possible. In their view, the crucial problem with the new social regulation was what Jimmy Carter's chairman of the CEA, Charles Schultze, labeled the "command–control" formula of these programs. By this, Schultze meant that social regulation directed in great detail the daily operation of business firms.

Critics charged that government intervention in such fundamental areas of business decisionmaking as product and plant design led to unnecessary inflexibility, and even to perverse policy outcomes as agencies came to focus on compliance with arbitrary performance standards rather than attainment of public health or consumer welfare goals. Eugene Bardach and Charles Kagan explain how the new social regulation came to entail these unfortunate results:

> The basic technique of these regulatory programs has been the elaboration of written rules of law setting forth in great detail the protective measures that must be instituted by the regulated enterprises and the enforcement of those rules by government inspectors and investigators, carefully instructed to decide all issues in accordance with the terms of the regulations and not on the basis of *their own potentially arbitrary judgement*. (1982: 187, emphasis added)

These command–control programs, designed specifically to avoid bureaucratic discretion and undue industry influence in the administrative process, created serious problems as uniform federal standards were applied inflexibly in all instances. Not only were extraordinarily high regulatory costs a possible outcome, but ironically strict adherence to highly specific rules tended to stifle technological developments that could achieve desired results more effectively or efficiently (Lave, 1981). This kind of argument prompted Charles Schultze and others in the Carter administration to press for some kind of reform in the various areas of social regulatory policy.

While the Reagan administration's concern about regulatory cost and bureaucratic inflexibility should not be underestimated, deregulation in the 1980s also drew on a deep political conviction that the new social regulation was inconsistent, even antithetical, to the American notion of liberal democracy. Ronald Reagan's rhetoric clearly expressed a fundamental philosophical repugnance toward the new social regulation, a repugnance revealed pointedly in his inaugural assertion that government itself was a problem by virtue of its overly ambitious intervention in society and the economy. President Reagan appeared intent on reducing rather than refining social regulation and the bureaucratic agencies that administered it. He did not want Washington simply to work more efficiently; he wanted it to work less. Consistent with this view, in discussing deregulation, the Reagan administration usually employed the term "regulatory relief" rather than the more traditional "regulatory reform," and this was trumpeted in the title of the presidential commission chaired by Vice-President Bush. This rhetorical shift was significant: whereas in contemporary parlance the word "reform" implies an adjustment of the status quo, "relief" suggests the elimination of certain objectionable behaviors and policies.

Relying heavily on a report prepared by the extremely conservative Heritage Foundation for the Bush task force, Reagan's appointees to key regulatory posts sought to translate rhetoric into action. A major thrust of this report was that the regulatory process had been dominated by liberal reformers and their allies in the bureaucracy. It also concluded that their influence hinged in part on federal subsidies to their participation. A priority in providing regulatory relief, accordingly, was eliminating those subsidies, "defunding the left" as the Heritage Foundation put it. This included cutting not only direct subsidies, but also indirect ones such as low postal rates for nonprofit organizations; public lobby groups depended heavily on these low rates for fundraising efforts. Another aim of the deregulators was to reduce the opportunities for frequent and casual contact between public lobbyists and staff at the regulatory agencies.

The objections that the Reagan administration raised with respect to the new social regulation, then, were rooted as much in politics and ideology as they were in economics and bureaucratic efficiency. Advocates of regulatory relief correctly perceived that the new social regulation not only had altered the substance of national dialogue on federal regulation, but also, to a great extent, had restructured the institutions and processes through which regulatory policy was made. Indeed, if there was anything truly "revolutionary" about the new social regulation, it was this remaking of regulatory politics.

Whereas the consumer and environmental movements brought such issues as automobile safety, asbestosis, air pollution, and toxic waste disposal to the national agenda, government action in these areas did have historical antecedents in the efforts of the Progressive Era and New Deal to regulate product quality, to promote safety in the workplace, and to establish principles of conservation. Undoubtedly the new social regulation entailed a much broader conception of the government's role in the economy, but that conception can be traced to the earlier demands for intervention by the central government. Thus, the new social regulation may be seen as a current manifestation of what some scholars have identified as a twentieth-century reform impulse in the United States (Hofstadter, 1955; Leuchtenberg, 1963). Nevertheless, the new social regulation is markedly different from the earlier varieties, because the institutions through which it is administered are grounded on the observation by contemporary reformers that regulatory institutions of the Progressive Era and New Deal were too susceptible to domination or subversion by business interests (Bernstein, 1955; Galbraith, 1978; Kolko, 1965; Lowi, 1979). It is for this reason that public lobbyists were intent on changing the whole regulatory regime—that is, the system through which regulatory policy is made and implemented—not simply passing new laws. The key to these changes was to develop a permanent organizational presence in Washington through public lobby groups.

Advocates of the new social regulation consciously sought to design regulatory institutions that would minimize the prospects of business exercising undue influence in the administration of regulatory affairs. By the mid-1970s, it was apparent to Carl Bagge, president of the National Coal Association and an experienced participant in regulatory politics, that they had achieved considerable success: "Politically, the consumer movement, the environmental ethic and *the drive toward participatory democracy* . . . are all pushing regulatory agencies to adopt policies that were considered irrelevant a few years ago" (1975: 187, emphasis added). Mr. Bagge could well have added that not only were agencies adopting new rules, but also Congress was passing new laws and creating new agencies. The crucial point, though, is that he was concerned about broad changes in regulatory institutions, especially the emergence of the drive toward participatory democracy, which he perceived as a basis for the new social regulation. Originating in the New Left's critiques of capitalist society, demands for participatory democracy were intended to overcome the privileged political economic position of business. It is important to keep in mind that public lobby organizations and the new social regulation are a considerable distance on the political spectrum from the Students for a Democratic Society (SDS) and truly radical politics. Nevertheless, the connection between the 1960s and the 1970s is central to an understanding of contemporary regulatory affairs as well as broader shifts in American politics. In the context of the new social regulation, it implies a new conception of regulatory politics, one typified by a more open decisionmaking process in which business would have to vie for influence with public lobby groups that functioned as itinerant representatives of the citizenry. Basically suspicious of both government and business, a great many public lobbyists viewed themselves as challenging the establishment, though certainly not as stridently as the social movements of the 1960s did.

The key to achieving any measure of participatory democracy was acquiring an ongoing presence in regulatory institutions. Only in that way, advocates of the new social regulation reasoned, could they avoid the eventual weakening of regulatory policy that befell the supporters of the Progressive Era and the New Deal. Thus public lobby organizations, especially those attempting to represent the consumer and environmental interests of the citizenry, became a hallmark of the new social regulation. Their development and persistence effected a qualitative change in regulatory politics. In addition, the laws and administrative procedures of the new social regulation were specifically structured to facilitate and nurture the participation of public lobbyists. What made the new social regulation "new," then, was the resultant redistribution of influence in regulatory politics. If deregulation in the 1980s was rooted in politics and ideology, it was because the regulatory programs of the 1970s successfully imbedded the concept of participatory democracy in regulatory institutions. The crusading zeal with which the Reagan administration set out to provide regulatory relief indicates a keen perception of how much regulatory politics had changed. The decade of the 1970s brought with it not only new regulatory policies, but also new regulatory ideas and institutions.

Deregulation in Perspective

An important way to distinguish one deregulatory effort from another is by the objectives of those pursuing deregulation (Mitnick, 1981). The Reagan administration's deregulatory program drew its motivation as much from an animus toward the principles underlying the new social regulation as from any desire to increase the cost effectiveness of those programs because the objectives of the president and his advisors were political as well as economic. Consequently, while Ronald Reagan did not invent the issue of deregulation, he did carry it much farther than previous chief executives. In this respect deregulation in the 1980s may be distinguished from earlier attempts to rein federal regulators.

Historically, there have been repeated attempts to streamline the federal regulatory apparatus, to make it more accountable, more efficient, and more responsible. Most of these attempts, moreover, have originated in the White House. Beginning as far back as the Brownlow Committee under Franklin Roosevelt and continuing through the Hoover Commission under Harry Truman and the Ash Council under Richard Nixon, a succession of blue-ribbon panels has sought means to exert presidential leadership over the regulatory bureaucracies. During the 1970s, Richard Nixon, Gerald Ford, and Jimmy Carter all tried, with a variety of measures, to control regulators (Harrison and Portnoy, 1982; White, 1981). Of the three, Jimmy Carter perhaps went the farthest by establishing the Regulatory Analysis and Review Group (RARG). An ad hoc committee including members from the Council on Wage and Price Stability (COWPS), OMB, CEA, the Commerce Department and the Treasury Department, RARG was charged with comparing the costs and benefits of various federal regulatory programs. Although RARG had no formal authority over other actors in the executive branch, its recommendations did carry the imprimatur of the White House.

Despite their distress with the seemingly unmanaged growth of the central government's regulatory bureaucracy, Nixon, Ford, and Carter never exhibited the fundamental skepticism and philosophical antipathy toward federal regulation that characterized the Reagan period. They essentially "kept the faith" with the New Deal principle that federal programs were an appropriate response to socioeconomic problems; their main concern was getting the biggest possible bang for the federal buck. His "new federalism" program notwithstanding, Richard Nixon sponsored central governmental responsibility for environmental protection, and in fact recommended creating the EPA. In spite of his anti-Washington rhetoric and the establishment of RARG, Jimmy Carter presided over the formation of two new cabinet departments.

In contrast, Ronald Reagan was deeply suspicious of federal regulation in principle, especially the social variety. Deregulation was not simply an opportunistic refrain in his administration. Rather, his views had matured over a considerable period of time. For example, at a 1975 symposium on regulatory policy, the then Governor Reagan asserted:

> We are the most regulated society this nation has ever seen, and we are paying for it not only in the coin of the realm, but also in the greater loss of freedom than any of us realize. We have moved a great distance from the system that originated in this country, a system based on the ultimate in individual freedom consistent with an orderly society. (Reagan, 1975: 61)

The alarmist tone as well as the fundamental consistency of his criticisms over time indicate an abiding concern with the political as well as the economic impacts of regulation. Particularly with respect to the new social regulation, he and his advisors felt that there existed an unwarranted and dangerous challenge to basic American political beliefs.

If the Reagan revolution's clarion call for deregulation sets it apart from preceding administrations, its boldness is even more striking when considered in a broader historical and philosophical perspective. As far back as 1787 Americans recognized a need for federal regulation. While the founding fathers saw control of interstate commerce as a means of preserving the Union in the face of foreign threats, they also gave credence to the general proposition that promoting the general welfare might require regulation by the central government. As James Madison pointed out in the *Federalist papers,* ". . . the mild force of reason, pleading the cause of an enlarged and permanent interest, is too often drowned . . . by the clamors of an impatient avidity for immediate and immoderate gain" (Rossiter, 1961, No. 42: 268). Because a society predicated solely on limited government and individual liberty will not satisfy the "enlarged and permanent interest," Madison envisioned an important regulatory role for what he termed a "superintending authority" (Rossiter, 1961, No. 42: 268). This is not to suggest that Madison or his compatriots envisioned the current level of federal regulation, but their arguments and reasoning clearly suggest a rationale for building the contemporary administrative state (on this point, see Rohr, 1987).

In his study of the U. S. Constitution, Sotirios Barber traces a "forward-looking, some say 'positive,' " view of the central government to the founders (1984: 182). In support of this contention, he cites the

Federalist Paper No. 22, in which Alexander Hamilton strongly attacked the claim that extraordinary majorities (e.g., two-thirds) would enhance the general welfare:

> When the concurrence of a large number is required by the Constitution to the doing of any national act, we are apt to rest satisfied that all is safe, because nothing is likely *to be done* . . . but we forget how much good may be prevented, and how much ill may be produced, by the power of hindering the doing of what may be necessary, and of keeping affairs in the same unfavorable posture in which they may happen to stand in particular periods. (emphasis added) (Barber, 1984: 182–83)

The founders obviously perceived a need for a positive aspect to government.

It is important to emphasize these antecedents of positive government, because the Constitution's clear commitment to limited government can easily overwhelm them in our eyes. Indeed, discussions of the Constitution ordinarily stress the classical liberal mechanisms of federalism, separation of powers, and checks and balances which, in the name of liberty, were intended to constrain rather than enhance the central government. Nevertheless, the general rationale of a "superintending authority" promoting the public interest over particular interests was as persuasive to Hamilton and Madison 200 years ago as it was to advocates of federal regulation in the twentieth century. Concentrating on the limiting measures alone yields a one-dimensional and oversimplified view of American government, which none of the advocates of the Constitution held. When the dislocations of first industrial and then postindustrial society evoked broad-based demands for remedial action by the central government, the inherent conflict between these two aspects of American government emerged sharply.

In the twentieth century, then, a serious tension developed between the traditional constitutional emphasis of limited government on the one hand and an emergent public philosophy of positive government on the other. However, it seemed that all important conflicts between these competing principles were resolved in favor of the latter, the result being a tremendous increase in the administrative sphere of the central government. This presented a serious challenge to American democracy, for as Tocqueville had predicted, decentralized administration kept policy close to the people and constrained the state's capacity for tyranny. Conversely, centralization of administrative power, a natural tendency in democratic society, ironically could undermine democratic government.

As early as the 1830s Alexis de Tocqueville had expressed fear of just such a result. He recognized and sought to explain what he saw as an ineluctable tendency toward the centralization of governmental authority in democratic societies. He noted:

> in politics, as in philosophy and religion, democratic peoples give a ready welcome to simple general ideas. They are put off by complicated systems and like to picture a great nation in which every citizen resembles one type and is controlled by a single power. (Tocqueville, 1969: 668)

The natural outgrowth of this democratic propensity is uniform laws and regulations administered by the central government. Citizens legally and politically equal to one another naturally are led to believe that they ought to be subject to exactly the same opportunities and limitations. They will take living equally under the law to mean living under the same laws.

Tocqueville argued further that citizens in a democratic society are concerned primarily with private affairs, especially the pursuit of their material well-being, rather than public affairs. Consequently, he contended,

> It is therefore always an effort for such men to tear themselves away from their private affairs and pay attention to those of the community; the natural inclination is to leave the only visible and permanent representative of collective interests, . . . the state, to look after them. . . . *This naturally disposes citizens constantly to give the central government new powers.* (Tocqueville, 1969: 671, emphasis added)

Particularly in times of crisis or uncertainty, Tocqueville asserted, the citizenry will turn to the central government to protect its material interests.

Crises in American history have always focused the public mind on Washington, D.C., "the only visible and permanent representative of collective interests." In the last half-century, though, the fantastic growth of government, especially of the executive branch, has been accompanied by a marked shift in our political culture, a shift from a predominantly negative and restrictive public philosophy of government to a positive and expansive one. Americans became concerned with what government ought to do rather than with what it ought not do, and governmental responses to democratic pressures have led to an accretion of regulatory power at the center that is difficult to undo after socioeconomic crises have subsided. The development of federal regulation in the twentieth century testifies eloquently to Tocqueville's prescience, because as the socioeconomic dislocations that accompanied industrialization affected society, broad democratic movements, first in the Progressive Era and then during the New Deal, demanded regulatory action by federal authorities.

The new social regulation arose from the same kind of democratic forces. In the late 1960s and early 1970s, a threat to the public's well-being was conceived in terms of postindustrial concerns about the "quality of life" rather than more traditional values relating to economic security. However, the result was the same, democratic demands for federal regulation to protect the public. In fact, since the inception of the Interstate Commerce Commission (ICC) in 1887, Americans have been constructing a huge regulatory edifice, the building blocks of which are the ever-increasing number of regulatory laws and agencies that make it increasingly difficult for ordinary citizens to participate effectively and elected officials to govern.

By any measure, we have devoted more and more resources to regulatory activities by the central government. Yet, regulatory policy in the United States has not developed along a smooth historical line. Rather, it has grown in distinct stages, each stage coinciding with a conscious political effort to redefine the role of the central government in regulating private enterprise (McCraw, 1981). These stages have been characterized not simply by more federal regulation, but by qualitative shifts in the ideas and institutions behind that regulation. In thinking about such shifts, the Progressive Era and the New Deal readily come to mind. In addition, the period of the new social regulation may be seen as a third major shift in the history of federal regulatory policy, the latest episode in the rise of the bureaucratic state (Wilson, 1975). President Reagan and his supporters alleged that the scope of federal regulation had expanded far beyond that envisioned in 1787. It was in part this perception that motivated President Reagan and his supporters to embark on their ambitious program of regulatory relief.

In historical perspective, the attempt of the Reagan administration to deregulate appears truly iconoclastic. Preceding chief executives never challenged the democratic "logic" of increasing the central government's regulatory authority. That is exactly what the Reagan administration set out to do. It is worth reemphasizing, though, that their animus was directed primarily at the new social regulation. President Reagan's frequent references to the necessity of retaining a "safety net" of federal programs demonstrated his acceptance of the shift in public philosophy from a negative to a positive view of government. As ambitious as he was about getting government out of people's lives, he had to acknowledge that our political culture had moved far beyond the original ideas about how much the government ought to do in providing for the general welfare. In his opinion, though, the new social regulation clearly stood beyond the pale. It represented to him an unprecedented increase in the scope and specificity of federal regulation, as reflected in the tens of thousands of pages added to the *Federal Register* during the 1970s. If there was a revolutionary aspect to the Reagan deregulation, it was that a president tried to bring about a qualitative shift that, for the first time since the New Deal, would fundamentally reduce the central government's regulatory role.

The ensuing contest between supporters of the new social regulation and the managers of deregulation in the Reagan administration was of great political significance. The new regulatory programs had dramatically changed not only the substance of the policy process, but its structure and avenues of influence as well. While questions of cost effectiveness and bureaucratic inflexibility had been raised about the new social regulation in the late 1970s, there never was a serious question as to the necessity of the new programs or the legitimacy of the institutions through which they were administered. With his inauguration in 1981, though, Ronald Reagan threw down the gauntlet. Dismayed over the general growth of government since the New Deal, President Reagan and his closest supporters were genuinely alarmed by the new social regulation, which they perceived as misguided liberal attempts to perfect society. More important, in their view these attempts undermined the productivity and sapped the spirit of the American people. The contest, then, was a fundamental confrontation over the character of the American regime that pitted a president with a strong ideological commitment to limited government against the seemingly uncontrollable democratic impulse toward more and more federal regulation. The irony of this confrontation is that Ronald Reagan may have done as much as any president to promote the centralization he denounced even as public lobbyists promoted the big government they mistrusted. A perfect example of this paradoxical tendency is the extraordinary degree to which the Reagan deregulators relied on administrative instruments such as executive orders and the use of the OMB as a regulatory watchdog to accomplish their goals.

Studying Regulation and Deregulation

If Ronald Reagan's call for deregulation impeached the new social regulation, it also posed a challenge, though an indirect one, to the study of federal regulatory policy. For decades economists, political scientists, historians, and students of public administration interested in government–business relations had focused their attention on the expansion of federal regulatory authority (see, for example: Bernstein, 1955; Kohlmeir, 1969; Kolko, 1965; Peltzman, 1976; Stigler, 1971; or Wilson, 1980). There was a good deal of concern about deregulation, but in the context of documenting the problems with extensive federal regulatory programs. This focus on the growth of regulation seemed entirely appropriate—at least until the 1980 presidential election—because American history during the twentieth century ostensibly chronicled the growth of government; the emergence of an expanding federal regulatory apparatus seemed a natural corollary of that growth. However, no social scientific logic dictates that federal regulatory authority must increase always and in all instances. Even if Tocqueville's centralization hypothesis proves correct in the long run, there may be periods of regulatory retrenchment that require explanation. (Mitnick, 1980). As Martha Derthick and Paul Quirk have shown, deregulation and regulation both raise questions of theoretical importance (1985, see especially Chapter 7). Unfortunately, conceptual frameworks devised to explain the rise of regulation or the staying power of regulatory bureaucracies cannot be reconciled with broadbased attempts, such as that initiated under President Reagan, to roll back regulation. In this sense, the Reagan revolution has challenged conventional notions about government–business relations.

Scholarly work that has dealt specifically with deregulation is, for the most part, normative, revolving around economic theory or administrative science (see, for example: Breyer, 1983; Graymer and Thompson, 1982; or Lave, 1981). In this genre, questions about justifications for government intervention in the market and cost effectiveness of regulatory programs have predominated. These "critiques" of federal regulation strongly advocated the elimination of traditional price and entry regulation in many instances. In fact, by the late 1970s regulatory reformers could point to some successes, most notably the airline deregulation, but also significant reforms in trucking and banking regulation. In addition, they built a strong case for employing such policy tools as market incentives and cost–benefit analysis rather than the command–control model of regulation that typified the new social regulation. In the areas of consumer and environmental policy, programs were initiated in the application of cost–benefit techniques and emissions trading, a scheme whereby plants could reduce some pollutants below federal standards in exchange for leaving above the standards, others that would be more costly to clean up.

With the advent of the Reagan revolution, studies of deregulation began to acknowledge the importance of ideology and politics. For the most part they retained a policy-analytic focus, evaluating the deregulatory efforts in terms of the same economic and administrative standards. Like earlier studies, these too ultimately sought to recommend rather than explain regulatory and deregulatory policy (Eads and Fix, 1984). Those studies that did adopt a political focus were usually expository, and eschewed any attempt to develop a larger theoretical or conceptual context for the discussion of deregulation (see, for example, Tolchin and Tolchin, 1984).

In addition, work on deregulation tends to be ahistorical, taking the rationales and institutions of regulatory decisionmaking as contextual variables to be maintained or reformed in order to achieve certain ends. It shows little concern for historical forces that shaped regulatory policy. Regulation, though, is more than a given set of laws and rules; it also entails ideas and institutions that have grown out of particular historical circumstances. Because deregulation is a political as well as a policy-analytic enterprise, deregulators' success depends on an accurate appraisal of regulatory ideas and institutions as much as it does on the simple access to levers of administrative power. That understanding, in turn, depends on a certain level of historical knowledge. As students of deregulation, we must also appreciate the history of the underlying ideas and institutions if we are to understand deregulatory outcomes of the Reagan revolution.

In two respects, then, current approaches to the study of regulation and deregulation are inadequate for analyzing the contest between the new social regulation and the Reagan revolution. First, they do not allow for regulatory decline as well as regulatory growth. Second, their ahistorical and policy-analytic orientation prevents an adequate investigation of the ideological and institutional forces underpinning regulatory policy. Therefore, our first task in this study will be to develop a conceptual framework that can accommodate decreases as well as increases in federal regulation, and that has a strong historical dimension. In studying the new social regulation during the 1980s, we must be prepared to accept, at least in theory, the possibility of a regulatory decline. On the other hand, only by assessing the Reagan deregulation in light of earlier intellectual and institutional developments will we be in a position to judge its "revolutionary" character on something other than a rhetorical level.

Rather than investigating the contest between advocates and opponents of social regulation generally, we have chosen to concentrate on what happened at two key regulatory agencies, the FTC and the EPA. A more general study of deregulation presents the danger of degenerating into a broad and potentially superficial retrospective. In order to avoid that pitfall, it is useful to focus the analysis substantively. Two possible substantive strategies would be to analyze specific areas of regulatory policy or how the Reagan administration attacked the new social regulation in the Congress and the bureaucracy. Neither of these alternatives, though, offers the prospect of a careful historical examination of regulatory policy or of its underlying ideas and institutions. It is for that reason that we decided to study regulation and deregulation at specific institutions.

A number of reasons underlie our choice of agencies for study. First, both the FTC and the EPA administer major elements of the new social regulation, the former in the realm of consumer protection and the latter in the realm of pollution control. Consequently, the Reagan administration singled out these two agencies for special deregulatory attention. Thus, the second justification for studying them is that they were focal points of deregulatory action. Third, these two agencies provide a nice contrast between deregulation at an institution that had existed since the early years of the twentieth century and adapted to the new social regulation, and one that was established in the early 1970s. This contrast offers an opportunity to compare the effects of deregulation on a newer versus an older agency. Finally, the FTC and the EPA allow us to compare the operations of an independent commission and an executive agency, respectively. The political and administrative forces surrounding this difference suggest that deregulators may face different problems and prospects at each type of agency. What emerges from this comparative case study of the FTC and EPA is a revealing "tale of two agencies" during the Reagan revolution.

In order to write these institutional histories and relate them to our conceptual framework, we have relied on a number of sources. In the public record we have examined government reports, congressional authorization and oversight hearings, the *Congressional Record,* and the *Congressional Quarterly.* We have also reviewed the regular and financial press, tracing the debates surrounding deregulation and the new social regulation.

Most important though, we have conducted an extensive series of interviews with officials and former officials at each agency (both at Washington headquarters and at regional offices), with trade association officers, and with public lobbyists. These interviews were open-ended discussions ranging from one to three hours. In a number of instances there were follow-up interviews to clarify points or update information (see pages 407–9 for a list of persons interviewed). While all of the interviews covered the same basic questions, the flexible format permitted the exploration of ideas and insights we had not anticipated. This proved especially helpful in trying to piece together the complex interactions between regulators and deregulators.

Organization of the Book

The remainder of this book is divided into nine chapters, organized around three major tasks. The first two are to develop a conceptual framework and to describe the new social regulation as well as the Reagan deregulation and President Bush's attempt to put his own stamp on regulatory policy. Finally we will concentrate on how the conflict between advocates of social regulation and proponents of deregulation was played out at the FTC and the EPA.

Chapter 2 presents the conceptual framework on which the comparative case study is based. In particular, it explicates two concepts, *regulatory regime* and *inertial forces*. The first of these concepts, by specifying the elements of federal regulation at any particular point in time, provides a means for identifying discontinuities in regulatory politics. The second helps to explain the continuities from one regulatory regime to the next. These concepts and the dynamics of their interaction compose the core of the model of regulatory change. Thinking in terms of regulatory change rather than regulatory growth helps to avoid the theoretical bias that plagues many studies. More important, though, it facilitates a historical perspective on regulatory policy and focuses our attention on the role of ideas and institutions in regulation.

Chapter 3 examines in broad terms the ideas, institutions, and policies of the new social regulation. It demonstrates what was new about them through historical comparisons and by systematic application of the regulatory change model. The argument is developed that certain ideas originating with the New Left in the 1960s played a major role in shaping the character of the new social regulation. Also in this chapter a distinction is drawn between the new social regulation and the more traditional economic variety of government intervention. A clear understanding of the differences between the two is critical to the subsequent analysis. Specifically, we argue that the new social regulation brought about a new regulatory regime, a fundamental departure in regulatory politics and administration tantamount in significance to the Progressive Era and the New Deal.

The fourth chapter offers a general description of the policies and practices of deregulation under President Reagan. His approach to federal regulatory policy is contrasted with those of his immediate predecessors and with the programs of the new social regulation. Along with the third chapter, this one provides the context for an examination of what happened at the FTC and the EPA.

The two case studies appear in the fifth and sixth chapters. These cases further illustrate the character of the new social regulation as well as the circumstances of its emergence in the late 1960s and early 1970s. Again, the model of regulatory changes focuses our attention on the underlying ideas and institutional structures involved. The model also helps to explain the deregulatory successes and failures experienced by the Reagan administration and its appointees to head the two agencies. We will see that the legacy of this deregulation was highly uncertain and problematic.

In Chapters 7, 8, and 9 we assess the resilience of the deregulatory assault on the new social regulation by exploring its fate under the Bush administration. While Vice President George Bush helped to spearhead that assault in the early 1980s, as president he sought, at first, to follow his own somewhat less hostile course on regulatory policy. We examine the extent to which this course represented a departure from Reagan and how it affected social regulation at both the FTC and EPA.

The tenth and final chapter presents our conclusions about the impact of the Reagan revolution in light of not only the Bush administration but also Bill Clinton's regulatory reform efforts and the political sea change wrought by the 1994 congressional elections. Despite the differences in the style and substance of deregulation at the FTC and EPA as well as in the procedures of the two agencies, there are important general lessons demonstrated by these case studies about the enormity of the task confronting those intent on deregulation. These lessons raise what we believe are some challenging questions about citizenship and governance in American politics.

2

The Politics of
Regulatory Change

[W]e still underestimate the extent to which our system was
designed for deadlock and inaction. We look on the current
impasse in Washington as something extraordinary rather than
as the inevitable consequence of a system we accept.

JAMES MACGREGOR BURNS, *The Deadlock of Democracy*

Both the new social regulation and the Reagan revolution were predicated
on concerns about the impact and effectiveness of regulatory policy. Yet
in each instance fundamental criticisms of the prevailing policy process
channeled these concerns into demands for changes in the institutions of
regulatory decisionmaking. Architects of the new social regulation initially were motivated by their conviction that important issues of public
concern had been long neglected. In their attempt to change the focus of
regulatory policy, though, they carried with them an assumption that the
primary reason for the neglect was that big government (the federal bureaucracy) in combination with big business (private corporations) had
come to dominate policymaking at the federal level. Thus, to public lobbyists changes in policy seemed unimaginable without basic changes in
regulatory politics.

For their part, advocates of deregulation in the Reagan administration believed that the new social regulation not only brought about unwarranted encroachments on private enterprise, but also bore responsibility
for a good measure of the economic decline in the 1970s. However, they
too held certain preconceptions about the root causes of problems in regulatory policy. In their view, the new social regulation did change regulatory institutions, but to such an extent that public lobby groups and their
supporters in government wielded undue influence in a new decision process that was effectively shielded from popular pressures.

Thus, the Reagan revolution as well as the new social regulation envisioned fundamental changes in regulatory policy. To view the former as simply a demand for less regulation and the latter for more regulation would be a serious error. Because each ultimately sought to redefine the relationship among government, business, and society, they challenged the regulatory status quo: they shared an aspiration for change in the institutions and processes as well as the substance and direction of federal regulation. In each case regulatory change was to entail not just a *quantitative* shift in policy, but in addition a *qualitative* shift encompassing regulatory institutions.

The purpose of this chapter is to develop a conceptual framework, which will allow us to distinguish qualitative from quantitative shifts in regulatory policy. Changes in regulation, like any politicoeconomic changes, may be studied from a quantitative standpoint, in which case the focus will be secular trends and incremental shifts in policy. They also may be studied from a qualitative standpoint, in which case the focus will be on broad-based social movements and watershed events. While government regulation of business undoubtedly has increased continually over the course of the twentieth century, scholars also have pointed to "waves" of regulatory growth, most notably in the Progressive Era and the New Deal, and these waves may be viewed as qualitative shifts (Wilson, 1975; Stone, 1981). Because our analysis rests on the assertion that the new social regulation constitutes a qualitative shift commensurate in importance with those two earlier periods, it is necessary to establish the conceptual basis for that claim.

Specifically, the conceptual framework will provide two crucial elements of this study: (1) a precise definition of a qualitative shift in regulatory policy, and (2) a schema for systematically comparing qualitative shifts to determine historical continuities as well as discontinuities. With this conceptual framework, we can describe and analyze the new social regulation. In addition, the framework will help to identify the ways in which the Reagan administration has challenged the new social regulation. And, ultimately, it will afford a means of assessing the success of the Reagan revolution. The framework itself is based on two key concepts, *regulatory regimes* and *inertial forces*.

A qualitative shift in regulation will mean a change in the existing regulatory regime. In general, the term "regime" refers to the system of ideas, institutions, and policies that determine how a society is governed. While we believe that the term effectively captures what we wish to express, we must use it with some qualification, because it is a somewhat unconventional usage. Ever since Aristotle, the concept of a regime has been employed to compare alternative systems of power distribution—for example, oligarchy or democracy. By "regulatory regime," we mean the distinct patterns of political intervention throughout American history that have structured government–business relations. To the extent that such distinct patterns have existed, they are characterized by particular *ideas*, *institutions*, and *policies* of regulation. Of course different distributions of power in regulatory politics will also distinguish regulatory regimes. Finally, regulatory regimes exist and change within the context of a larger political regime. Therefore, larger regimes, in the traditional Aristotelian sense, have their particular patterns of governance that set the parameters for regulatory change.

Although the larger regime has always set the context for shifts in regulatory regimes, it is important to note that those changes can have a reciprocal effect as well in reshaping the larger regime itself. Indeed the expansion of government regulatory programs in the twentieth century, especially since the 1930s, has raised serious questions about the possibility of constitutional government being replaced by an administrative state, thereby challenging the ideas and institutions associated with our classical liberal foundations (Lowi, 1979; Milkis, 1987a; Milkis and Harris, 1986; Rohr, 1987). Thus, each regulatory regime may not be simply a reflection of the larger political system, but also may challenge its constitutional arrangements.

Even under the most favorable political circumstances, though, a regulatory regime change is difficult because American politics is encumbered with substantial inertial forces that militate against major shifts. Some of these forces are unique to the United States, deriving from the Constitution. Others, associated with the emergence of bureaucracy, apparently are endemic to most modern states. Yet another variety derives from the prevailing consensus on how society should be governed, the "public philosophy." Although each is a formidable impediment to qualitative shifts in regulatory politics, their combination in the second half of the twentieth century has presented a new kind of bulwork for the status quo. These inertial forces operate whether attempts to change the regulatory regime are designed to increase or to decrease the central government's role.

Notwithstanding the tremendous inertial forces inherent in any regulatory regime, change does occur. Proponents of the Progressive Era, the New Deal, and the new social regulation all overcame inertial forces and established new regulatory regimes. In pursuit of their broad goals, contemporary deregulators confront many of the same obstacles. How, though, do regulatory regimes change? Answering this question is important not only from the academic standpoint of documenting and explaining the emergence of new regimes, but also because it will help to show the enormity of the task faced by deregulators in the Reagan administration.

At this point, it will suffice to note generally that qualitative shifts in regulatory regimes will entail a successful challenge to the ideas, institutions, and policies governing regulatory affairs. Such a challenge requires an active leadership role for political elites and intelligentsia, for they are the elements in society qualified to articulate and effect the challenge. Leadership naturally must be combined with sustained democratic support if inertial forces are to be overcome, and this support grows out of concrete problems confronting society.

Regulatory Regimes

A regulatory regime may be defined as a constellation of (1) new ideas justifying governmental control over business activity, (2) new institutions that structure regulatory politics, and (3) a new set of policies impinging on business. While all three elements—new ideas, new institutions, and new policies—are necessary to the concept of a regulatory regime, no one element is sufficient. Nevertheless, new ideas is the critical element. Most important, the new institutions and policies embody the new ideas. The ideas also give shape to political movements for regulatory change, and provide evidence for the self-conscious involvement of activist reformers in the design of regimes. New ideas, in other words, indicate the leadership role played by intellectual and political elites in establishing a new regulatory regime.

The new ideas of a regulatory regime refer to deep-seated beliefs or principles, a vision of society held by reform-minded elites within the citizenry. In discussing the growth of regulation in the United States, Ellis Hawley has explained that

> ideas and ideology have been important determinants in shaping national regulatory policy and mechanisms for supplementing it . . . *without this ideological dimension it is difficult to explain the mechanisms that emerged or what happened later.* (1981: 120–21, emphasis added)

It is the intellectual elite or "intelligentsia" of society that purveys ideas and ideology. As Joseph Schumpeter (1942) has argued, the intelligentsia, in the modern sense, is not restricted to the artists, poets, and authors, but encompasses journalists, social critics, the professoriate, and political activists. Moreover, the very nature of their professions leads them to critique social, political, and economic institutions, and they are an especially potent force in liberal democratic societies that protect and even encourage dissent. As the intelligentsia becomes more numerous and strategically situated to disseminate their ideas (a natural course of development in modern society), they can more easily assume leadership functions and their ideas become all the more important in shaping political struggles.

While we are interested specifically in new ideas about government control of business, it is important to recognize that these "ideas" are related to the two broader concepts of ideology and public philosophy. In discussing the role of ideas in American politics, it is easy to use these terms interchangeably—and wrongly so. Because we shall be employing all three terms in discussing regulatory change, we must be precise about their respective meanings. Ideas refer to "conceptions existing in the mind as a result of mental understanding, awareness or activity" (Guralnik, 1978: 696). Regulatory ideas, then, are conceptions developed by some intellectual enterprise, which express how and why the government ought to control business. An important Progressive Era idea, for example, was that government had to play a positive role in the economy if monopolistic business practices were to be curtailed.

An ideology means something quite different, specifically, "the body of doctrine, myth, symbol, etc., of a social movement, institution, class, or large group" (Guralnik, 1978: 696). It makes little sense to speak of a regulatory ideology, because ideology entails something much broader and indeed qualitatively different. For example, progressive ideas about positive government action were rooted in the doctrines, myths, and symbols of popular sovereignty and democratic governance. We should understand, however, that the opponents of progressivism could employ the same liberal democratic ideology to arrive at very different conceptions of what government ought to do in relation to private enterprise. Although progressive ideas about regulation are clearly different from progressive ideology, just as clearly the two are interrelated.

Finally, public philosophy, a term coined by Walter Lippman, may be understood as the practical adaptation of ideas and ideology to governance. As a level of abstraction it stands midway between regulatory ideas (concrete understandings about government–business relations) and ideology (broad doctrines, symbols, and myths pertaining to the organization of society). To continue with our example, Progressive Era intellectuals derived their ideas from their ideology but disseminated them to the broad masses in terms of a new public philosophy. This public philosophy included regulatory ideas like "trust busting" that had very specific policy implications as well as ideological elements like the highly charged, symbolic term "robber barons" to refer to industrial or financial magnates; each was a distinct part of Progressive Era public philosophy. It will be convenient to think of ideology as giving rise to regulatory ideas, and public philosophy as giving voice to them. In terms of our conceptual framework, though, ideas are the central concern.

That regulatory politics entails the pragmatic pulling and hauling, bargaining and compromise of the American governmental process should not obscure the importance of ideas. They give shape and direction to the process, even if they are not realized in all their purity. To the extent that the Progressive Era and the New Deal reflect qualitative shifts in regulatory policy, they embodied new ideas about regulation. This is not to say that the supporters of the New Deal completely rejected the ideas of their Progressive Era predecessors or that there are no significant historical continuities between the two periods. However, the ideas underlying New Deal regulation can be easily distinguished from the ideas underlying Progressive Era regulation. Similarly, the ideas behind the new social regulation have departed markedly from those of the New Deal period.

The concept of a new regulatory idea also helps to distinguish deregulation under the Reagan administration. Reagan, in contrast to his predecessors, apparently intended to change the regulatory regime under which we presently live. To do so he had to advance his own ideas. As previous regimes have evolved through conscious political effort, so too deregulators in the Reagan administration had to commit themselves to a political strategy based on coherent ideas about federal regulatory authority, and assume a leadership role in advancing those ideas.

Although new ideas remain the critical defining element of a regulatory regime, the other elements help to characterize it more concretely. Thus, we can distinguish not only the underlying ideas of the Progressive Era, New Deal, and new social regulation, but also the regulatory institutions and policies associated with each regime. Obviously new regulatory institutions refer to regulatory bureaucracies, and each of the three periods was a time in which important new federal agencies were created, or when existing agencies were redirected and given new missions. The FTC, for example, was created during the Progressive Era, but significantly reinvigorated and empowered during the 1970s. The EPA, on the other hand, was established in the 1970s.

Institutions, though, may also be defined as *established and structured patterns of relationships among various organizations involved in regulatory policy*. Thus, institutional change may also involve new legislative and administrative procedures or new channels of participation and power. Historically this has meant shifts in the relations between the executive and legislative branches of government, in the regulatory role of the states versus the central government, in the scope of government–business interactions, and in the methods of interest representation. As we shall see, this broader definition of institutions is especially important for an understanding of the new social regulation.

Finally, new policies help to distinguish a new regulatory regime. Ordinarily this has meant the central government assuming additional responsibilities for the general welfare of society and increasing its regulatory activities, although new policies may just as legitimately refer to a reduction in those responsibilities and activities. The policy differences among the Progressive Era, New Deal, and new social regulation are perhaps more easily discernible than the intellectual or institutional differences. Each period is defined in the public mind by the substance of the policies advocated and enacted. Regulatory policy in the Progressive Era dealt with the impacts of trusts and monopoly on society; it was an attempt to come to terms with the emergence of huge corporate entitites and highly mobile capital in a society that had assumed the economy would be organized by smaller, independent business enterprises closely tied to their geographic bases. During the 1930s, the focus of regulatory policy shifted to protecting labor organization and, more generally, shielding the public from the vicissitudes of the marketplace.

Just as with institutional change, though, the emergence of new policies does not signal a total repudiation of earlier regulation. Nor is it impossible to find antecedents of New Deal policies in the Progressive Era regulatory regime. Nevertheless each regulatory regime reflects a distinct substantive orientation in the policies adopted under it, and this orientation is determined to a great extent by the new regulatory ideas.

While new ideas shape institutions and policies directly, they also shape policies indirectly via institutional change. Regulatory agencies, interest groups, and the three main branches of government all influence policy. Because these institutions transmit or reflect new regulatory ideas, they help to translate these ideas into policy reality. In a sense, institutional shifts serve as intermediary steps in regime change; they are expected to result in policy shifts, although they are also seen as intrinsically worthwhile changes by activist elites. The recognition of institutional effects on policy, in fact, underpins the concept of regulatory ideas and convinces reformist elites of the need for changing the nature of the existing regulatory regime.

This tight conceptual linkage between regulatory ideas and institutions can be a double-edged sword. On the one hand, it promises a richness and subtlety of analysis. On the other hand, it ensures a complexity that can make it difficult to disentangle ideas from institutions when practically applying the conceptual framework. Evidence of new ideas, for example, may constitute evidence of new institutions—and vice versa—because the institutions are an embodiment of the ideas. Similarly, when describing the novelty of regulatory institutions, a discussion of new regulatory ideas is unavoidable. Despite the potential for difficulty, though, we believe that the benefits of a rich and subtle analysis far outweigh the costs of complexity in the concept of the regulatory regime.

A final consideration in employing this concept is that regulatory regimes exist, as we have suggested, in a political environment defined by a larger regime. In the case of the United States this larger regime is defined fundamentally by constitutional principles and mechanisms designed to limit government by dividing authority within and between levels of government. Yet, in the twentieth century, societal problems have militated in favor of a bigger and more centralized regulatory apparatus. The result has been a certain degree of tension between the larger regime and new governmental institutions. This institutional tension, however, only mirrors the constitutional ambiguity on the legitimate scope of government and separation of powers in American politics (Karl, 1983). As a result of this tension and ambiguity, changes in regulatory regimes have always raised questions about governance and the organization of the larger political regime. Indeed, precisely such fundamental concerns about the implications of the new social regulation helped to generate the Reagan revolution.

As the tensions and ambiguities have been resolved in favor of greater government involvement in the private sector, the principles and institutions of the larger regime have been "adjusted." This is not to suggest, as some alarmists might, that the growth of the administrative state amounts to a subversion of the Constitution or an abandonment of limited government and separated powers; our principles and institutions of government are still compatible with the Constitution, because the founders left considerable room for maneuver in developing a government (Rohr, 1987). Madison explained in the *Federalist Papers* that the Constitution sought "the requisite stability and energy in government with the inviolable attention due to liberty" (Rossiter, 1961, No. 37: 226). Regulation, of course, has served as a most important element in providing requisite energy and stability, and in the United States it has functioned as a substitute for direct government control over business. In a sense the growth of the administrative state, especially its regulatory capabilities, may be seen as an attempt to maintain the Constitution and the larger regime in the face of pressures for an even more obtrusive governmental role.

As for separation of powers, John Rohr has ably demonstrated that complaints about the administrative state undermining this principle ring hollow when we consider that the Constitution itself rejects a strict separation (1987). It hardly seems appropriate to decry regulatory bureaucracies for exercising ostensibly legislative or judicial powers when the three main branches of government each play significant roles in the performance of all three functions of government. More important, even though the founders saw distinct virtues in each branch, they clearly envisioned a great deal of latitude in the "blending" of governmental branches, or "departments" as they called them. Interpreting Montesquieu on the separation of powers, *Federalist Papers* No. 47 asserts that "His [Montesquieu's] meaning . . . can amount to no more than this, that where the 'whole' power of one department is exercised by the same hands which possess the 'whole' power of another department, the fundamental principles of a free constitution are subverted."

At a practical level, the historical shifts in regulatory regimes also meant that relations between the central government and the states have been adapted, on occasion, to conform with new realities of regulatory politics. Again, the proponents of the Constitution anticipated such an eventuality, maintaining that if "the people should in the future become more partial to the federal than to the State governments . . . in that case, the people ought not surely to be precluded from giving most of their confidence where they discover it to be most due" (Rossiter, 1961, No. 46). Of course, relations among the branches of government have been altered as well. This all clearly suggests ample scope to accommodate the modern administrative state.

At the same time, we part company with those who would sanguinely aver that the Constitution readily "admits" almost any level of government action in society. The Constitution, as crafted by the founders, may "allow" almost any level of government action, provided all of the obstacles to democratic action can be surmounted, but continual expansion of the state in the United States has necessitated heroic efforts to reconcile big government with the core principles of limited government. An outstanding example of these efforts is the use of the interstate commerce clause to justify environmental regulation and civil rights policy; while this is not preposterous, it surely stretches considerably the original purpose of the central government's authority to regulate interstate commerce. Another bit of evidence on the "malleability" of constitutional principles is the attempt to develop social regulatory programs at the national level, but to return authority to the states eventually under so-called state primacy provisions in the enabling legislation. This arrangement creates a certain messiness, in that the central government has to decide if the states are capable, while often the states would just as soon leave knotty regulatory problems to the "feds." Although many twentieth-century reformers have experienced tremendous frustration with the political system, no reform movement thus far has been able completely to circumvent basic institutions and principles of the Constitution; nor should it if the larger regime is to retain its integrity.

Inertial Forces

While the Progressive Era and the New Deal testify to the mutability of the regulatory regimes (as we have defined them), such qualitative shifts do not come easily, because reformers must contend with the considerable inertial forces inherent in American politics. These inertial forces are generated from three distinct sources: the Constitution, the prevailing public philosophy, and the nature of modern bureaucratic organization. Inertia under the first category derives from the arrangements and relations among governmental institutions set out in the Constitution. The prevailing public philosophy reinforces constitutional inertia because it proclaims the core concepts of the fundamental law. However, public philosophy also inhibits change by elevating ideas about government, including regulatory ideas, to the level of "uncontestable" assumptions, which define the Constitution in practice. Those intent on altering a regulatory regime often must contest certain elements of the public philosophy. For example, supporters of the New Deal had to attack biases against positive government. To the extent that the New Deal remade the public philosophy to legitimate extensive federal regulation of the economy, deregulators in the Reagan administration confront a new impediment to regulatory change.

Bureaucratic inertia is the third variety, and is attributable to the character and behavior of bureaucratic organizations. Changes in the regulatory regime necessarily entail redirecting the activities of the existing government bureaucracies as well as creating new ones, and this can present serious problems as well, even more so if the objective of regulatory change is a reduction rather than an expansion in agency activity.

Inertial Force of the Constitution

A signal feature of the U.S. Constitution is its establishment of an incremental and very deliberate policymaking process. Major policy change is hard to effect, and changing decisionmaking institutions is extraordinarily difficult. The problem (as any U.S. government text reveals) is that, while such change requires the sustained support of a majority of citizens, the Constitution contains a number of devices designed to deny expeditious satisfaction of majority demands. Ours is a system of "minority vetoes" with clear avenues for frustrating majorities.

The most direct majority-curbing devices are the separation of powers and bicameralism. By dividing the government into three distinct branches, and subdividing the legislative branch into a Senate and House of Representatives, the founders ensured that important policy measures could not be enacted easily or quickly. Success would require the consent of the citizenry as represented in the House and the states as represented in the Senate, the support of the president, and, ultimately, the concurrence of the Supreme Court. However, the founders went further in protecting against the rashness and passion of majority factions. Rather than separating the branches of government absolutely, they distinguished them by function, but bound them together through a system of checks and balances. As Madison explained,

> But the great security against a gradual concentration of the several powers in the same department [branch] consists in giving to those who administer each department the necessary constitutional means and personal motives to resist encroachments by the others. . . . Ambition must be made to counteract ambition. (Rossiter, 1961, No. 51: 322)

The whole system of checks and balances (e.g., executive veto, senatorial advice and consent, and judicial review) created a formidable set of obstacles to change on the order envisioned by a new regulatory regime.

In addition, the Constitution established a political system of divided sovereignty, a federal system. Again, the logic of this structure was to reduce the possibility of majority tyranny. The result, as the *Federalist Papers* suggest, was a highly complex political system:

> In its foundation it [the Constitution] is federal, not national; in the sources from which the ordinary powers are drawn, it is partly federal and partly national; in the operation of these powers, it is national, not federal; in the extent of them, again, it is federal, not national; and, finally, in the authoritative mode of introducing amendments, it is neither wholly federal nor wholly national. (Rossiter, 1961, No. 39: 246)

Federalism was to complement the separation of powers and bicameralism to provide, as Madison put it, "a double security to the rights of the people" (Rossiter, 1961, No. 51: 323). Even if state sovereignty is not the potent force it once was under the nineteenth-century Supreme Court doctrine of dual federalism, the general concept of federalism is still to have a residual inertial impact on policy (Elazar, 1972; Sanford, 1967; Wildavsky, 1978: 142–43; Wilson, 1986: 73–75). Welfare is administered largely by the states, which can determine their own level of benefits. Many environmental policies provide for "state primacy" in the implementation of regulations in order to take local circumstances into account. And states continue to have an important voice in the formulation of policy through the traditional mechanism of the Senate as well as newer institutions such as the intergovernmental lobby.

Finally, the Constitution was predicated on the idea of an *extended republic,* the point of which was to minimize the prospect of a majority faction subordinating the policy process to its own interests and against the public interest or minority rights (Rossiter, 1961, No. 10: 83–84). In Madison's view, the most reliable means of securing the rights of individuals against a tyranny of the majority was to extend the sphere of the political system and filter democratic passion through representative institutions. In this manner, the formation and persistence of majorities would be rendered extraordinarily difficult, though not absolutely impossible.

Alexander Hamilton noted, however, that protecting minorities raised the possibility of undermining important policy actions:

> In those emergencies of a nation in which the goodness or badness, the weakness or strength, of its government is of greatest importance, there is a common necessity for action. The public business must in some way or other go forward. If a pertinacious minority can control the opinion of a majority respecting the best mode of constructing it, the majority in order that something may be done must conform to the views of the minority. . . . Hence, tedious delays; continual negotiation and intrigue; contemptible compromises of the public good. And yet, in such a system it is even happy when such compromises can take place: for upon some occasions things will not admit of accommodation and then the measures of government must be injuriously suspended, or fatally defeated. (Rossiter, 1961, No. 22: 148)

Hamilton's misgivings reveal clearly the difficulties that the inertial forces of the Constitution can create.

Hamilton's fears that the inertial forces of the Constitution could immobilize public policy led him to press for an expansive interpretation of the powers granted to the central government, and especially to the executive branch. However, the election of 1800 meant the triumph of the Jeffersonian vision of limited and decentralized government. Even Madison became persuaded that Hamilton's position represented a danger to republicanism. Even more than outright executive usurpation, Jefferson and Madison feared an irresistible tendency to delegate authority to the executive department as the responsibilities of the central government expanded, thereby undermining the division and separation of powers. Madison, who in 1787 defended the idea of a strong national government, wrote a decade later:

> In proportion as the objects of legislative care might be multiplied, would time allowed for each be diminished, and the difficulty of providing uniform and particular regulations for all be increased. From these sources would necessarily ensue a greater latitude to the agency of that department which is always in existence, and which could best mould regulations of a general nature so as to suit them to a diversity of particular situations. And it is in this latitude, as a supplement to the deficiency of the laws, that the degree of Executive prerogative materially consists. (Hunt, 1906, vol. VI: 358)

Although the "Revolution of 1800" did not completely prevent an active presidency (even Jefferson took some extraordinary steps during his tenure), it did firmly implant the concept of limited government as an integral component of our "public philosophy." In fact, Stephen Skowronek has commented that "the absence of a sense of state has been the hallmark of American political culture" (1982: 3). This ingrained bias against big government has been one of the most serious obstacles faced by advocates of regulatory regime change in the twentieth century, and in a sense the history of American regulatory politics since the Progressive Era has been the history of the erosion of that bias.

Clearly, the constitutional foundations of the American political system generate powerful inertial forces that must be overcome if a qualitative shift in regulation is to be accomplished. Since the election of 1800, these forces have acted primarily as a curb on the growth of government. Yet, new regulatory regimes have been created, and as a result the concept of limited government has been steadily weakened. More important, once a new regulatory regime does emerge the inertial force of separation of powers, bicameralism, federalism, and an extended republic that operated against emergence reinforce the new status quo. Also, to the extent that new regulatory ideas supplant the political culture of limited government, the public philosophy becomes supportive of the new regime.

It is important to understand, moreover, that as the new social regulation impelled an adjustment of constitutional principles and governing institutions, the adaptation of the larger regime cloaked the new regulatory regime with a mantle of legitimacy. All of the considerable inertial forces that reform activists had to overcome in establishing their ideas, institutions, and policies operated to inhibit attempts at changing the new status quo.

Inertial Force of the Public Philosophy

In addition to the inertia inherent in the Constitution itself, we can distinguish a second kind of inertia related to, yet analytically distinct from, the founding principles. This particular variety is attributable to the public philosophy. Public philosophy, as we have suggested, is a practical expression of our ideology as well as ideas about how society should be organized and governed. Through public philosophy we integrate grand constitutional principles embodying liberal ideology with our contemporary notion of governance. In effect, public philosophy allows us to reinterpret the grand principles in light of changing socioeconomic conditions. However, once this reinterpretation occurs, public philosophy also endows the new ideas with a constitutional imprimatur, thereby making it extraordinarily difficult to alter them. Once the meaning of liberalism shifted from the classical interpretation of severely restricting the role of the central government to the modern interpretation of enhancing that role in the name of economic stability and material welfare, it was impossible to revive the earlier meaning even by appealing to the Constitution. Indeed, the infamous confirmation hearings of Supreme Court nominee Robert Bork stand as an eloquent testimony to the force of public philosophy in the face of efforts to apply a classical liberal interpretation of limited government. Bork's call for resuscitating the doctrine of original intent ultimately fell on deaf ears; despite the internal logic of his position, even Bork had to allow that our political consensus (i.e., our public philosophy) is so different from the turn of the century that it would be unthinkable to apply original intent in many areas of jurisprudence.

The inertial force of public philosophy, illustrated by Judge Bork's failure before the Senate Judiciary Committee, also raised a serious problem for deregulators in the Reagan administration. We now turn to a consideration of the content of the prevailing public philosophy that they confronted. As we shall see, the nature of this public philosophy presented some unique and prodigious obstacles for them to surmount in their efforts to deregulate.

The current public philosophy has given rise to a policy process in which the lines separating legislation and administration, even the lines separating adjudication and administration, are badly blurred. This system appears to confirm the misgivings about an activist central government that Madison expressed in 1799, in that executive action has indeed become the focal point of public policy. That is not to say that the Hamiltonian vision has finally supplanted the Madisonian one, but rather that expanding the responsibilities of the national government has been accomplished by grafting increasingly centralized authority and institutions onto the constitutional foundation. The result has been an extremely potent set of inertial forces: the dynamics of Washington politics in combination with the prevailing public philosophy.

Theodore Lowi was the first to articulate a trenchant statement of this problem of a public philosophy founded on modern liberalism. In his view, we now live in the "second republic" of the United States. He characterizes this political system as "interest group liberalism," a system in which

> Congressmen are guided in their votes, Presidents in their programs, and administrators in their discretion by whatever organized interests they have taken for themselves as most legitimate; and that is the measure of legitimacy of demands. (1969: 72)

Under interest group liberalism, organized interests are the only effective participants in the formulation of public policy, including regulatory policy. Naturally, organized interests oppose major changes, especially deregulation, because their influence is predicated on the current configuration of regulatory institutions and processes. As Lowi sarcastically concludes, "Besides making conflict-of-interest a principle of government rather than a criminal act, participatory programs shut out the public" (1969: 86). The key actors in each particular participatory program jealously guard their prerogatives. They do so by trying to ensure that the uncertainty and conflict of widespread public participation are minimized.

Students of American politics have long recognized that the context of these relations is policy subgovernments. "Subgovernments," according to Ripley and Franklin, "are small groups of political actors, both governmental and nongovernmental, that specialize in specific issue areas" (1980: 7). Thus, intensely interested nongovernmental actors, in addition to legislators and federal bureaucrats, participate effectively in policy subgovernments. These subgovernments are distinguished by, among other things, fairly technical, low visibility issues, issues in which the media and the general public have only passing or indirect interest. Regulatory policy, moreover, is ideally suited to subgovernment dominance: questions of antitrust, utility rate base formulas, plant design, or suspended particulate content in the air do not attract a great deal of public attention owing to their highly technical nature.

In 1951 Arthur Maas's pathbreaking study, *Muddy Waters—The Army Engineers and the Nation's Rivers,* set the course for a burgeoning literature on subgovernments, policy networks whose operations remained relatively insulated from outside political pressures. Unfortunately this literature has evoked a somewhat vulgar, though widely accepted, view that the activities of all these subgovernments are best comprehended through the so-called iron triangle model. This model suggests that congressional committees or subcommittees, relevant federal bureaus, and private interests (ordinarily a particular industry) are linked in tight tripartite relationships that serve their mutual advantage, usually at the expense of the public interest (see, for example, Bernstein, 1955).

Despite its broad acceptance as a description of subgovernmental inertia, the iron triangle model does not adequately represent the dynamics of Washington politics. Its weakness lies with its failure to capture the richness and complexity of subgovernmental relations. As Hugh Heclo points out,

> Control is said to be vested in an informal but enduring series of "iron triangles" linking executive bureaus, congressional commitees, and interest group clienteles with a stake in particular programs. . . . Looking for closed triangles of control we tend to miss the fairly open networks of people that increasingly impinge upon government. (1978: 57)

Heclo's argument is especially relevant to social regulation, which tends to be characterized by more open issue networks.

The new social regulation was initiated and pursued by activist public lobbies, and those organizations continue to play an important role in the implementation of policy. As Jeffrey Berry concluded in his insightful analysis of public lobbies,

> . . . these organizations are slowly changing the overall environment within which government officials formulate public policy . . . public interest groups have been consistent and enduring actors, aggressively trying to influence governmental decisionmakers. (1977: 289)

In the words of John Gardner of Common Cause, "little by little citizen action began to develop a more professional cutting edge" (1972: 74).

With this professional cutting edge, public lobbyists were able to inject a new set of actors with new concerns into subgovernments. Having carved out a niche for themselves, public lobbies altered subgovernmental relations to such an extent that the iron triangle model fundamentally misrepresents the politics and policymaking of social regulation.

Even though broader issue networks have supplanted iron triangles as a description of policy subgovernments, these issue networks have their own inertial forces that stem from their peculiar dynamics as well as the public philosophy.

In one sense, the newer social regulation contributes to policy inertia by fostering the proliferation of subgovernments. The addition of more issue networks with more policy actors makes fundamental regulatory change that much more difficult. The advent of social regulation, one may argue, has further balkanized the policy process, thereby decreasing the prospects for systemic change. The difficulty of the task confronting the deregulator in any administration is, of course, compounded by the need to compete for political resources required for other objectives of an administration. The White House is unlikely to commit its valuable political resources to the kind of sustained effort that is required to attack the whole array of regulatory issue networks. The fragmented policy process, then, drags a deregulator into a war of attrition that he or she seems bound to lose. A few particular issue networks may be deregulated, but effecting a change in regulatory regime remains a chimerical goal.

Regulatory policy resembles a feudal system in which key legislators may be likened unto local barons, federal bureaucrats unto prelates, and lobbyists unto guilds. Just as in the feudal system, each has a role to play and the legitimacy of those roles is taken for granted by the players. Also just as in the feudal system, it is extraordinarily difficult for the central authority to control these players. Deregulators are in much the same position vis-à-vis legislators, bureaucrats, and lobbyists (public or private) as feudal kings were vis-à-vis barons, prelates, and guilds.

Thus, regulatory issue networks have a strong tendency to maintain the status quo. While they are not as removed from outside influence as the iron triangle model suggests (and this is an important qualification), they do strongly resist political pressures for change. The variety of interests in an issue network may be relatively wide, yet all of them remain organized, and in this respect they promote private interest over the general welfare (McConnell, 1964).

This view of a fragmented and intransigent policy system has prompted Morris Fiorina to write:

> There is a Washington establishment. In fact, it is a hydra with each head only marginally concerned with the others' existence. These establishments are *not* malevolent, centrally directed conspiracies against the American people. Rather, they are unconsciously evolved and evolving networks of congressmen, bureaucrats, and organized subgroups of the citizenry all seeking to achieve their own goals. (1977: 3)

It is the lack of control, communication, and coordination rather than the promotion of private interests over the public interest that most distresses Fiorina. These very qualities of the policymaking process tend to undermine regulatory change.

In order to appreciate fully the strength of political and bureaucratic inertia confronting advocates of deregulation, it is essential to understand that powerful incentives lead the individual subgovernmental actors to support the status quo. By focusing on the structure of the larger political system, it is possible to overlook these individual motivations that lead the participants to eschew wider political forums for the bargaining, logrolling, and infighting of subgovernments. In this environment they can maximize the prospects of achieving their particular goals.

Following Fiorina's line of reasoning that Congress is the "keystone of the Washington establishment," we consider first the rationale for legislators' participation in subgovernments. Representatives and senators promote subgovernmental politics, because it advances their electoral interests. As David Mayhew explains,

> Every member [of Congress] can aspire to occupy at least one piece of policy turf small enough so that he can claim personal responsibility for some things that happen on it. . . . What the Congressional seniority system does is to convert turf into property. . . . And the property automatically appreciates in value over time. (1974: 96–97)

Subgovernments are the means of apportioning the "policy turf." However, the incentives for subgovernmental politics are more subtle than simply claiming credit with the voters at home. Especially in the current electoral environment of media campaigns and political-action committees, it is important to command political resources, and these resources are best mobilized by organized interests.

Prominence in a subgovernment puts a member of Congress in a position to service organized constituencies. Mayhew portrays the kind of exchange relationship that may emerge:

> [M]any congressmen can believably claim credit for blocking bills in sub-committee, adding on amendments in committee, and so on. The audience for transactions of this sort is usually small. But it may include important political actors (e.g. an interest group, the president, the *New York Times,* Ralph Nader) who are capable of both paying Capitol Hill information costs and deploying electoral resources. (1974: 61)

In addition to servicing organized interests in the legislative process, members of congress can intervene on their behalf with the federal bureaucracy. As administration and implementation of policy programs become an increasingly significant part of governmental activity (Lowi, 1979; Dodd and Schott, 1979; Rourke, 1976), this sort of intervention capability also appreciates in value. More to the point, it creates a vested congressional interest in the maintenance of regulatory programs and bureaus in which individual legislators can intervene.

The incentives for organized interests to support subgovernmental politics are easily discerned. It is in this environment that they can most effectively articulate their views. In wider political forums, theirs is simply one more interest in a sea of legitimate concerns. In a subgovernmental setting, however, the expertise they can bring to bear on an issue carries much more weight. Within the confines of an issue network, a business firm or a trade association can present a well-developed technical argument on tariff policy, environmental protection, or worker safety procedures. Public lobbyists can present counterarguments of commensurate refinement and sophistication. Moreover, organized interests on any side of an issue are often unwilling to gamble their goals on a broader democratic process. Environmentalists, for example, are just as fearful as business interests of what a public referendum may reveal about trade-offs between environmental protection and economic growth (Harris, 1985). Both prefer to resolve their differences in a setting in which they exercise more control, and a subgovernment provides such a setting.

Finally, it should be emphasized that subgovernments provide for the establishment of long-term relationships among participants. This is obviously important in the contacts between organized interests and individual legislators. Following the proceedings of a subcommittee over a number of years reveals how alliances are forged and maintained. Just as important, though, subgovernmental politics fosters among all interested parties an incestuous feeling that the issue network is the only legitimate arena for policymaking. They get to know, even to respect, the expertise of one another, and this situation leads to a view that "interference from outsiders" can only undermine good policy. Under these circumstances, it is hardly surprising that organized interests tend to oppose deregulation.

The third major set of actors in subgovernmental politics is, of course, the federal bureaucrats. No less than legislators and the various organized interests, they have powerful incentives for maintaining regulatory issue networks against deregulatory efforts. William Niskanen cogently sets out the rationale for bureaucratic support of the status quo in his study, *Representative Bureaucracy* 1971). Federal bureaucrats are dependent on regulatory programs for their livelihood, because these programs underlie the creation of numerous federal agencies. However, beyond this incentive to maintain programs, Niskanen shows that federal bureaucrats have a positive incentive to aggrandize their departments by seeking out new regulatory missions in much the same way that managers in the private sector maximize their individual utilities by expanding their staff and responsibilities (see, for example, Williamson, 1970). It is important to note that the behavioral model employed by Niskanen to explain bureaucrats' actions is precisely the same as the one employed by Mayhew and others to explain legislators' actions. In the tradition of microeconomics, both sets of actors are viewed as "utility maximizers." This assumption accords closely with the Madisonian political theory that underlies our Constitution. Although this economic model of bureaucratic behavior has been challenged, all students of bureaucracy agree that bureaucrats tend to prefer operating in arenas in which information and technical expertise rather than votes and public opinion are the currency of politics (Kaufman, 1975; Goodsell, 1982). Subgovernments provide such an environment.

The interest that regulatory bureaucrats share with legislators and organized interests in sustaining issue networks provides the basis for a strong opposition to deregulation. While this opposition may not always take the form of a united front, each type of actor contributes to the overall inertia that deregulators must deal with in attacking the vast array of regulatory issue networks. The bureaucrats' control of informational resources, moreover, puts them in an especially advantageous position to defend the programs that they administer (Downs, 1967; Dodd and Schott, 1979; Rourke, 1976).

Another important set of actors worth distinguishing in regulatory subgovernments is the congressional staff. They too have a strong interest in the operation of regulatory issue networks. As regulatory issues become more numerous, more technical, and more complex, congressional staff have played an increasingly important role in drafting regulatory legislation and shepherding it through Congress. In fact, the role of staff in crafting and enacting social regulation has often been critical.

Staff members take on the attributes of policy entrepreneurs. As Michael Malbin explains,

> The staffers improve their position with the boss if they come up with ideas that have a practical chance of going somewhere in Congress and in the press. . . . The aid then becomes known to insiders [members of issue networks] as the person "really" responsible for such and such a program. (1980: 28)

This prestige within the Washington establishment is not necessarily an end in itself, though. Malbin clearly points out that staffers are often genuinely interested in promoting particular policies or programs.

No less than the other actors in regulatory subgovernments, the congressional staff can constitute an impediment to deregulation, particularly with respect to social regulation. Ultimately, all subgovernmental actors favor the politics of an issue network over electoral politics or some other more "democratic" arena, because within the confines of the issue networks their influence is magnified immensely. In the issue networks they become big fish in a relatively little policy pond. Indeed, the individual incentives to maintain regulatory issue networks create powerful inertial forces that reinforce those attributable to the feudal structure of the Washington establishment.

Although the particular dynamics of subgovernmental politics resists major political change, the public philosophy legitimizes and reinforces that resistance by combining it with constitutional interpretation. Over the course of the twentieth century, there has developed a general acceptance of a vigorous central government, and the notion that administration is the main business of government. The new social regulation is the most recent and clearest manifestation of this public philosophy. The irony of the new social regulation is that it is at once more open than traditional forms of regulation, yet is also more insulated from traditional political channels. In this latter sense it is extraordinarily difficult to attack. During the Progressive Era and the New Deal, legislative and electoral politics were important forces of change in overcoming constitutional inertia. However, to the extent that they succeeded in constructing a more potent central governmental apparatus, they fostered a political environment and a public philosophy in which Congress and elections more and more resembled institutions of oversight rather than policy initiation.

It may be true, for example, as Lowi argues, that the emergence of the regulatory state after the 1930s began a change from "Congress-centered government to an executive-centered government" (1979: 274). But since the 1960s the legislature has concerned itself with the details of administration, to the extent that it now plays a leading role in the regulatory state. The rise of issue networks reflects not only Congress' acceptance of the administrative state, but also its rejection of a commonplace feature of the New Deal, namely the delegation of power (Schick, 1976; Wettergreen, 1985). Washington is now a seamless web of institutional relations.

In the traditional constitutional design, governmental institutions were organized so that (as James Madison put it) ambition would counteract ambition, thus checking any unified efforts to extend the sphere of political intervention in society (Rossiter, 1961, No. 51: 322). The issue networks that have emerged, however, constitute "institutional partnerships" that insulate programs from pressures of the traditional political process, including those from the White House and political parties (Melnick, 1985). These partnerships integrate legislative committees and staffs, bureaucratic agencies, public and private interest groups into subgovernments in which regulatory ambitions can effectively resist the vagaries of public opinion and elections. The decentralized nature of issue networks, accordingly, has less to do with balancing political interests through conflict than with circumventing the fragmented power structure of American politics, which has long been viewed as paralyzing reform efforts.

Modern liberalism, expressed by the contemporary public philosophy, has galvanized society behind a more energetic central government, and any effort to moderate that level of energy entails not only controlling the far-flung array of issue networks, but also confronting the public philosophy of positive government that helps to sustain them. The importance of this public philosophy is both reflected and enhanced by the extraordinary role that the federal courts have come to play in the administrative state. The emergence of the courts as a significant actor in regulatory subgovernments during the 1960s was at once interesting and ironic. Before Franklin Roosevelt's court-packing scheme, the judiciary represented perhaps the strongest barrier to federal regulatory authority. However, a subsequent accommodation between the courts and regulatory programs has transformed the judiciary's role from guardian of private rights to promotion of the general welfare of citizens through programmatic regulation. In an extreme view, the courts are now a "managing partner" in the administrative state (Rabkin, 1983). In fact, as our case studies demonstrate, the federal courts have posed one of the primary obstacles to deregulation confronted by the Reagan administration.

This shift in American jurisprudence is a by-product of legislation, public philosophy, and changes in legal doctrine. Many social regulatory statutes specifically provided for a prominent court presence in oversight and implementation (Marcus, 1980; Harris, 1985). Nevertheless, it is clear that the courts' regulatory role began to crystallize prior to legislative authorization. By the late 1960s, the courts had begun to rely on statutory "purpose" to tilt legal interpretation to the advantage of program advocates. As R. Shep Melnick explains:

> All statutes are combinations of purposes and constraints. We want to protect the environment, but not put people out of work. . . . To the extent that the courts increase their emphasis on statutory purpose they strengthen the hands of those who advocate achieving the objectives at the expense of those who seek to impose constraints. (1985: 10)

The judiciary, of course, did not develop this outlook in a political vacuum. It must be seen in the broader context of the emerging public philosophy of positive government.

The transformation of the American judiciary into a force for regulation suggests that subgovernments are not simply coalitions directed to protecting institutional policy turf. The courts' role as an inertial force reveals the extent to which regulatory regimes have a programmatic character. In the last analysis, regulatory programs have become difficult to challenge because they have become part of *a new understanding of rights*. As we recognized that traditional constitutional guarantees of individual rights could not suffice in an age of a national and eventually an international economy dominated by huge corporations, we turned to government, and the executive branch in particular, to secure the blessings of liberty for us and our posterity. Thus, federal programs took on the character of a social contract, and public philosophy imbued it with the force of the Constitution. As one critic of the courts' role in regulatory politics has asked, "What could be more natural than to have the judiciary protect and enforce these new rights, as it had always protected citizens' rights to liberty and property" (Rabkin, 1983: 62).

A recent article in *Judicature* supports this argument by clearly linking an activist judicial posture to the development of the administrative state:

> There is a consistent trend towards administrative rather than legislative action. . . . This trend produces a powerful impetus toward the use of the judicial process to counter administrative actions. As a result, courts are

drawn increasingly into a policymaking role. (Greanias and Windsor, 1981: 400–401)

As we shall see in the next chapter, it is not during the New Deal, but during the era of the new social regulation that the courts became a dominant player in regulatory politics. During the 1930s, there was an attempt to change jurisprudence so that the courts would tolerate a transfer of power to the executive branch. During the 1960s and early 1970s, advocates of regulation looked to the courts to embrace and not simply tolerate programs. In one sense the courts are partners in the administrative state and participants in subgovernmental politics. In a larger sense, though, they have become arbiters of the programmatic "rights" with which the administrative state has endowed organized interests (Melnick, 1988). It is in this light that the courts must be viewed as a roadblock to deregulation. It is also in this light that we can understand how deeply embedded the prevailing public philosophy is in our governing institutions.

Inertial Force of Bureaucracy

In addition to the difficulties associated with the constitutional foundations of politics and the public philosophy, the emergence of a new regulatory regime is made less likely by inertial forces attributable to bureaucracy. Since the writings of Max Weber, social scientists have worried about the responsiveness of bureaucratic organizations to outside political pressures and their general capacity for change. Characteristically, Weber posed the problem in very direct terms:

> Once it is fully established, bureaucracy is among those social structures which are the hardest to destroy. . . . Under normal conditions, the power position of a fully developed bureaucracy is always overtowering. The "political master" finds himself in the position of the "dilettante" who stands in opposition to the "expert." (Weber in Gerth and Mills, 1946)

While he viewed bureaucratic organization as a natural and a desirable development in modern society, Weber also recognized that bureaucracy posed a serious challenge to liberal democracy. Although the two were not irreconcilable, there certainly existed a strong underlying tension between them. The source of this tension is different bases of legitimacy, because rationality and technical efficiency legitimate policy in a bureaucratic setting, whereas popular sovereignty legitimates it in the political system as a whole.

If Max Weber offered a sobering analysis of how the rise of bureau-cracy would affect western society, Robert Michels sounded an alarm about the threat to democratic forms that lay in the evolution of such organizations. In his view, bureaucratic organization was subject to an "iron law of oligarchy," which ensured that democracy would be under-mined. The cruel irony of Michels' theory is that organization and bu-reaucracy are necessary tools of popular expression in modern society:

> Democracy is inconceivable without organization. . . . Yet this politically necessary principle . . . brings other dangers in its train. We escape Scylla only to dash ourselves on Charybdis. Organization is in fact the source from which the conservative currents overflow the plain of democracy. (1959: 1–2)

Michels feared the emergence of a "clandestine demagogic oligarchy pur-suing its ends under the cloak of equality" (1962: 349). The primary aim of this, as in any other oligarchy, would be to preserve and enhance its power. Thus, the evolution of bureaucratic organization would lead to the emergence of powerful inertial forces or, as Michels termed them, "conservative currents."

The fears raised by Weber and Michels were also enunciated by Michel Crozier, another European sociologist. In his analysis, *The Bu-reaucratic Phenomenon,* Crozier concludes that bureaucracy is inherently rigid in its structure and behavioral patterns. Consequently, according to Crozier, "a bureaucratic system will resist change as long as it can" (1963: 196). In fact, he asserted that bureaucracies respond pathologically to pressures for change, becoming more rigid rather than searching for appropriate responses:

> In other words, a bureaucratic organization is an organization that cannot correct its behavior by learning from its errors. Bureaucratic patterns of action, such as the impersonality of rules and the centralization of decision-making, have been stabilized that they have become a part of the organi-zation's self-reinforcing equilibria . . . when one rule prevents adequate dealing with one case, its failure will not generate pressure to abandon the rule, but, on the contrary, will engender pressure to make it more com-plete, more precise, and more binding. (Crozier, 1963: 187)

To be precise, Weber, Michels, and Crozier were interested in bu-reaucracy's ability to resist its own destruction, not in a general inertial tendency attributable to bureaucratic organization. However, it is relatively easy to see how bureaucratic resistance to political challenges results in a more general inertia under the contemporary administrative state. Because the lifeblood of bureaucratic entities is administrative programs, bureaucrats enhance their position by helping to develop new programs and protect their current position by opposing the destruction of existing programs. In fact, it is fair to say that governmental bureaucracies resist destruction by maintaining and promoting programs, especially regulatory programs. In this sense, protecting regulation from political challenge is both an effective means of resisting destruction and a general inertial tendency in governmental bureaucracy.

This pessimistic European view was, at first, disdained in the United States. Advocates and practitioners of administrative science viewed bureaucratic organization as a means of introducing efficiency and sound business practices into government agencies (see, for example: Wilson, 1887; Goodnow, 1900). Moreover, administrative power took on special significance to progressive reformers, given the lack of organizational strength elsewhere in the political system to sustain programmatic change. By the end of World War II, however, the more circumspect European perspective on bureaucracy took hold with American academics, and eventually became enshrined in popular wisdom. Especially the more extreme antigovernment rhetoric of the last twenty years strikes a harmonious chord with Michels' vision of a clandestine demagogic oligarchy pursuing its own ends in the name of democracy. No doubt the emergence of this more critical view of bureaucracy stems at least in part from experience with the fantastic increases in the size and scope of the central government's regulatory apparatus during the 1930s and 1940s.

The optimistic veneer of American writings on bureaucracy, then, became tarnished. Attention shifted from promoting efficiency and honesty in government to the so-called dysfunctions endemic to all bureaucratic organizations (see, for example: March and Simon, 1958; Merton, 1957). Perhaps chief among these dysfunctions was a resistance to change. Anthony Downs summarized this argument as follows in his study, *Inside Bureaucracy:*

> Organizations like individuals are reluctant to accept any change in their environments—whether good or bad—as permanent if such acceptance would require them to make a significant alteration in their customary behavior patterns . . . the costs of readjusting behavior patterns create a certain discontinuity of behavior at the level to which the organization or individual has become accustomed. This characteristic is commonly known as inertia. (1967: 174)

Bureaucratic inertia thus came to be recognized as a potentially serious drawback to the increasing intervention of the government in the private sector. Bureaucracy could not necessarily deliver on its promises of efficiency, and it was inherently unresponsive to democratic forces.

In the conceptual context of a regulatory regime, bureaucratic inertia implies that the regulatory agencies created to administer policy will have a certain staying power, a resiliency, with which deregulators must cope. Demands aimed at reducing or abolishing regulatory policy run headlong into the problems outlined by Weber, Michels, Crozier, and their counterpart American critics of bureaucracy. The character of bureaucracy and of American political institutions combines with the prevailing public philosophy to generate a great deal of systemic inertia. Changing a regulatory regime in the face of these inertial pressures is a formidable task indeed.

Regulatory Change

In assessing regulatory change, it is important to reemphasize that a qualitative shift in government–business relations need not entail an expansion—at least not in theory. In principle, new regulatory regimes may expand or contract the institutional and policy bases of federal regulation; ostensibly the Reagan administration is seeking a contraction.

It is equally important to bear in mind that regulatory regimes cannot shed entirely the institutional and policy relationships of previous regimes, even if the ideas of the new regime directly challenge those older relationships. New regulatory ideas aim to change institutions as well as policies. The questioning of a regulatory regime takes the form of new ideas about the role of the central government in controlling private economic activity. The new ideas may reflect an expansion or contraction of that role, but in either event represent a marked departure from the old ideas underlying the current regulatory regime. In this regard, conflict with the underlying ideas of the existing regulatory regime is unavoidable. Various institutional actors will have developed vested interests in the status quo and seek to maintain it. Naturally they will resist the ideas that challenge the institutional arrangements to which they have become accustomed. This resistance pits the old ideas that support the status quo against the new ideas, and this dialectical clash of ideas can result in either the defeat of the new ideas or the emergence of a synthesis of the new and old. Only with a new synthesis is a change in the regime possible. However, historical circumstances will determine the degree to which the synthesis reflects the new ideas versus the old. Accordingly, the magnitude of change in institutions and policies can only be in proportion to the triumph of new regulatory ideas.

The institutional and policy continuities across regulatory regimes result from the inertial forces inherent in the decisionmaking process that evolves with any regulatory regime. These inertial forces, some of them unique to the American polity, serve to restrict regulatory change whether the change is intended to increase or decrease the central government's regulatory role.

While any attempt to bring about a change in regulatory regimes must entail criticism of the status quo on the level of ideas and institutions, the initial impetus for qualitative shifts derives from a dissatisfaction with regulatory policy. Something must appear obviously wrong with regulatory outcomes in order to generate efforts at change; regulatory policy must be linked to unsatisfactory economic or social outcomes. Liberals, for example, have tended to argue that "market failures" such as the existence of monopolistic situations or externalities require government action. On the other hand, conservatives often object that government regulatory activities have hampered economic development. In either case, there is a connection made between the current state of policy and undesirable regulatory outcomes.

At this level of criticism, particular groups or interests express disgruntlement with regulation policy. Here and there criticism may be couched in more general theoretical terms. On the whole, however, they remain inchoate, ad hoc, and diffuse. This sort of elemental criticism is easily discerned in the very early stages of the Progressive Era and the New Deal (McCraw, 1981). Usually it took the form of objections that unchecked business power was behind unacceptable socioeconomic circumstances. In the late 1960s and early 1970s similar objections may be identified; for example, corporations pollute the environment with no concern for social costs, and the pharmaceutical industry derives unwarranted benefits from Food and Drug Administration (FDA) decisions. Whether there is presumed to be too little or too much regulation, there is no general, systematic critique of regulatory policy. Consequently, dissatisfaction is translated into efforts at incremental adjustment of policy rather than an overhaul of the regulatory regime.

Action directed toward changing regulatory regimes, though, involves not only a very basic dissatisfaction with regulatory policy, but also a conviction that regulatory ideas and institutions must change if policy is to change. Indeed, it is impossible to imagine an attempt at changing regulatory regimes without a strong emphasis on ideology and criticisms of the prevailing public philosophy. Invariably, therefore, attempts to change regimes are accompanied by the active participation of intellectual leaders whose involvement is predicated on a profound concern that regulatory policy is inconsistent with some fundamental principles that ought to govern society. Ordinarily politicians and the citizenry tend to think in terms of adjusting current policy rather than fundamentally redefining the role of the central government in relation to private enterprise. Thinking in such terms, though, is precisely the role of the intelligentsia. Members of the intelligentsia "educate" political leaders and the general public about the shortcomings of a regulatory regime.

While there must be widespread popular disenchantment with regulatory policy for there to be a regime change, politicized intellectuals channel this disenchantment. They articulate it in terms of policy recommendations consistent with a particular vision of society. This ideological dimension is inherent in the regulatory demands advanced by the supporters of the Progressive Era, New Deal, and subsequent proponents of regulatory regime changes. All attempts to change a regulatory regime originate with asymmetries between society's expectations of regulatory policy and its evaluation of that policy. At first, evaluation takes place in terms of policy. At this stage of criticism we find incremental reforms, the enactment of specific pieces of legislation, and minor adjustments in administrative behavior. Action at this level is not intended to change regulatory regimes. Only with the introduction of objections to regulatory ideas and institutions is the regime itself called into question. Thus, the Progressive Era began with efforts to regulate railroads and other large businesses, but eventually entailed profound questions about limited government. Later, the New Deal commenced with a flurry of programs to address the Great Depression, but ultimately entailed an attempt to redesign federal administrative institutions. As we shall see, the new social regulation and the Reagan revolution also involved intellectual and institutional challenges to the status quo. The Reagan revolution, though, had to overcome not only the inertial forces of the Constitution and bureaucracy, but also a public philosophy, developed in the twentieth century, that reinterpreted liberalism in support of an expanding administrative state. Of course, earlier regulatory regimes also had to overcome hostile public philosophies. However, theirs was a job of creating rather than destroying the capacity of the central government. With the shift from a concern with the limits of government to the twentieth-century concern with the responsibilities of government, public philosophy became wedded broadly to vested interests. Attacking this new public philosophy meant asking people to give up something, a much more difficult political problem than asking them, as modern liberalism did, to claim something.

Conclusions

The preceding discussion has laid out a conceptual framework within which we can analyze the attempt on the part of the Reagan administration to institute its program of regulatory relief. A major premise must be that the administration's stated goals were extraordinarily ambitious. It did not simply want to continue with reform of economic regulation, but rather wanted a fundamental reorientation in federal policy, a new regulatory regime with particular emphasis on a real reduction in social regulation.

The pursuit of this reorientation in regulatory politics took place in the face of a complex philosophical and institutional legacy, which posed major obstacles to the Reagan administration's program. For fifty years the American political system had been governed by a public philosophy dedicated to the active intervention of the federal government in the economy. What we term the public lobby regime extended this commitment through institutional changes and policy departures that greatly insulated programs from the regular electoral and legislative processes. The public lobby regime has enhanced the labyrinthine system of issue networks with specific institutional mechanisms that have accentuated the already formidable inertial forces of regulatory politics in the United States. This result is ironic, for, as we shall see in the next chapter, the insulation of the public lobby regime evolved from ideas and institutions expressly designed to democratize regulatory politics. In particular, more "open" procedures were fashioned to increase the role of program advocates and public lobby groups. These democratic procedures undoubtedly have created a more open administrative process, but it is less clear that the public lobby regime has become more accessible to the public per se than the regime it replaced. In fact, the extensive role of the courts in the public lobby regime reflects the tendency of contemporary reformers to conceive of regulatory goals as tantamount to rights, thereby subject to considerations of due process and warranting a status "above politics."

Paradoxically, while the public lobby regime has "opened up" the regulatory process, it also has sheltered regulatory policy from broader democratic influences such as the presidency or electoral politics. This has led Hugh Heclo to note that "[i]t is not easy for a society to politicize itself and at the same time depoliticize government leadership. But we in the United States have managed to do just this" (1978: 124). Thus, it remains to be seen whether or not any president, even one as popular as Ronald Reagan, can significantly alter the regulatory politics that have evolved over the past half century.

The interplay between the Constitution and administration that sustains the regulatory status quo suggests that the traditional principles and practices of American politics have been transformed. The original constitutional design was intended to establish a strong national government, but one that would be limited in the scope of its powers and responsibilities. The extension of the central government entailed coordinating centers of power that, under the Constitution, were supposed to operate at cross-purposes. Since the New Deal and the grafting of bureaucratic institutions onto the constitutional framework, it is no longer clear that ambition counteracts ambition; often it seems that decisionmaking has coalesced in numerous and disparate issue networks to advance programmatic ambition. Deregulation of the public lobby regime, then, will require more than an appeal to reassert the values of the framers. It depends on formulating persuasive ideas with which to challenge the current public philosophy.

In the following chapters we will examine the attempt to deregulate the public lobby regime. This attempt may be traced historically and assessed in terms of its success in overcoming the inertial forces of American politics. To appreciate fully the difficulties of effecting a qualitative shift in regulatory policy, one must carefully delineate the ideas, institutions, and policies of the regime that is the target of demands for change. With this in mind, we now turn to a consideration of the new social regulation, its origins, and the ways it has altered regulatory policy.

3

The New Social Regulation

There is a revolution coming. It will not be like revolutions
of the past. It will originate with the individual and with culture, and it will change the political structure only as its final
act.

CHARLES REICH, *The Greening of America*

A central and perhaps the most significant assertion of this study is that
in the 1970s the emergence of the new social regulation ushered in a new
regulatory regime, the "public lobby regime." In this chapter we delineate
the character of the new social regulation, its distinctive ideas, institutions, and policies that, taken together, define this new regime. The new
social regulation thus represents a qualitative shift in the politics and policy of federal regulation. As we have argued, the key ingredient in any
such shift is the appearance of new regulatory ideas—that is, new conceptions about the relations among government, business, and society.
These new ideas directly challenge the existing regulatory regime, its
efficacy, and even its legitimacy. Of course the emergence of a new
regulatory regime implies that the challenge of new ideas is ultimately
translated into new regulatory institutions and policies, which are the concrete manifestations of any regulatory regime. New regulatory ideas,
though, provide the foundation on which new institutions and policies are
built. In the case of the public lobby regime, the new ideas drew upon
certain elements of the New Left critique.

Unfortunately, researchers interested in regulatory affairs have concerned themselves, for the most part, with the substantive policy shifts
associated with the new social regulation, and have given relatively short
shrift to changes in regulatory institutions and ideas. Along with a different substantive focus, though, the new social regulation has brought
about unprecedented institutional arrangements for making policy decisions. Underlying the changes in both policy and institutions, moreover,

is a deeper and far less appreciated shift in the ideas justifying government regulation of private economic activity.

Economists, as Michael Reagan has observed, have dominated the scholarly literature on the new social regulation (1987). Their overriding concern quite naturally has been the impacts of the new policies, including compliance costs, bureaucratic inflexibility, distortions in economic decisionmaking, and inefficiencies of particular implementation strategies (see, for example: Argyris, 1978; Buchanan and Tullock, 1975; Oi, 1973; Peltzman, 1975; Viscusi, 1979). Policy analysts, intellectual fellow travelers of the economists, have also devoted their attention to the substantive departures of the new social regulation. In particular, they have tried to evaluate the effectiveness of such regulation in achieving stated objectives (see, for example: Bardach and Kagan, 1982; Owen and Brautigam, 1978). Like economists, policy analysts have concentrated on the new regulatory policies as such, and expressed only passing interest in new regulatory institutions and ideas. Their concern with efficiency and effectiveness necessarily entailed some consideration of institutional forms, but such considerations clearly remained secondary. Concern with new regulatory ideas is, for all intents and purposes, nonexistent in this literature.

There are, however, two lines of research that do shed some light, though indirectly, on the ideas behind the new social regulation. The first, associated with the *End of Liberalism* thesis advanced by Theodore Lowi (1979), suggests that the new social regulation represents a logical extension of the ideas of the New Deal. Lowi maintains, in a later edition of his influential work, that the new social regulation of the 1970s represents a more mature and troubling phase of the modern liberalism nurtured by Franklin Roosevelt. In Lowi's view, this latest wave of regulatory expansion has created elitist institutions even more dominated by organized interests and insulated from the people.

To be sure, it is possible to identify a certain insulation of the policymaking process under the new social regulation, because decision making does take place within specific issue networks and outside the realm of public debate. In this political milieu, *organization* becomes a passport to participation. In fact, in criticizing the new social regulation, Lowi portrays its decisionmaking institutions as "socialism for the organized, capitalism for the unorganized," implying that organized interests enjoy a tremendous advantage in influencing regulatory policy (1979: 337). The root of Lowi's criticism is that the new social regulation is a logical extension of interest group liberalism, which he maintains grew out of the New Deal.

The second kind of argument, promoted by neoconservative critics, in effect turns Lowi on his head, suggesting that the new social regulation is antidemocratic not because it extended the New Deal, but because it betrayed the New Deal by supplanting the vision of Franklin Roosevelt with a vision derived from the New Left. Irving Kristol, perhaps the preeminent neoconservative spokesman, asserts that advocates of the new social regulation are

> basically suspicious of, and hostile to, the market precisely because the market is so vulgarly democratic—one dollar, one vote. . . . The "new class"—intelligent, educated and energetic—has little respect for such commonplace civilization. It wishes to see its ideals as more effectual than the market is likely to be. (1973: 26)

The argument that public lobbyists and their supporters constitute such a "new class" echoes Joseph Schumpeter's characterization of the intelligentsia in capitalist democracies. According to Schumpeter, this class develops an independence from, and eventually a hostility toward, the very system that ensures its freedom and autonomy (1942).

Following Schumpeter, neoconservatives see the radicalism of activist reformers in the explicit rejection of the culture and morality of capitalist democracy. In the eyes of neoconservatives, it is this rejection of capitalism, rooted in the New Left critique, that distinguishes the new social regulation from the New Deal. Whereas Kristol and his allies long for the "good old days" of the New Deal, however, critics like Lowi see the new social regulation as the latest stage in the evolution of an administrative state whose decisionmaking processes are highly restricted, and whose cornerstone was laid in the 1930s.

It is our contention that the new social regulation, in fact, neither extended nor betrayed the New Deal. Rather, this regulation, initiated in the late 1960s, amounted to "an uneasy marriage of the New Deal and the New Left." The new social regulation embodied both the insulated institutions that Lowi attacked and the radical ideas that neoconservatives decried. Like any marriage, this union was not a perfectly harmonious match; indeed, it was fraught with tension because the ideas of the New Left directly challenged the legitimacy of New Deal regulatory institutions. Much like Lowi, New Left critics of American politics felt that the legacy of Franklin Roosevelt was a highly insulated administrative state, constructed in the name of liberalism, but in reality little more than a firm foundation for a military-industrial complex that emerged full-blown in the 1950s. Yet, owing in part to the inertial forces of bureaucracy and

American politics, the architects of the new social regulation could never really disentangle themselves from the institutional legacy of the New Deal. Moreover, even though they borrowed and adapted certain key ideas from the 1960s, some public lobbyists continued to feel a kinship with New Deal liberalism and its institutional arrangements that the New Left never did.

Although new regulatory ideas always pose a strong and direct challenge to the regulatory status quo, it is imperative to understand that these new ideas will never be fully realized (short of a bona fide revolution) at the level of regulatory institutions and policies. In the first place, as the discussion of regulatory change indicates, the influence of new ideas may be checked by the existing regulatory ideas. These ideas are part of the "public philosophy." Undoubtedly the commitment to the prevailing public philosophy operated as a constraint on the programs of both the New Deal supporters and more contemporary advocates of regulatory change. In addition, at the level of institutions and policies, inertial forces come into play, constraining the extent of regulatory change. Thus, to some extent, any existing regulatory regime will be sustained when a qualitative shift in institutions and policies occurs.

Of course, to the extent that New Deal policies and institutions presisted, so too did New Deal ideas about regulation. The tide of New Left criticism helped to erode but could never wash away the ideas and institutional forms of the New Deal. In fact, the ideas of the New Deal and New Left clashed dialectically, generating a new synthesis: the public lobby regime. In this new regulatory regime the New Left's suspicion of "the establishment" and its concept of "participatory democracy" were wedded to the New Deal institutional formula of creating federal programs and agencies to deal with public problems. At times this union has promoted some ironical, even anomalous, situations given the discontinuities between the two. Indeed, in the 1970s public lobby activists animated by New Left ideas confronted a paradox. In many respects, they detested the regime of big government fostered by the New Deal, yet because they could not supplant that regime and because they remained committed to national rather than local solutions, they continued to rely on the New Deal formula of creating centrally administered federal programs.

No doubt many will find the argument that the new social regulation reflects a marriage of the New Deal and the New Left a provocative one. Therefore, it is important to be clear about the structure of the argument and the nature of the evidence adduced to support it. The argument is not simply an assertion that the agenda articulated by New Left leaders was realized in the guise of the new social regulation; nor is it an assertion that public lobbyists are, by definition, of the New Left. Rather, the point is that ideas originating with the New Left informed public lobbyists and shaped their demands for institutional change. By the same token, though, recognizing a connection with the New Left permits us to see that the new social regulation is much more than an attempt to protect the environment and to advance the cause of consumer welfare. Even if public lobbyists were not New Left activists—and most never were—the political milieu of the 1960s was a tremendously significant socializing experience for many, especially those in leadership positions.

Evidence for this argument is drawn not only from the public record, but also, just as importantly, from a careful examination of the documentary history of the New Left and from personal interviews with business lobbyists, federal bureaucrats, and representatives of public interest groups, all of whom participate in the politics of the new social regulation. It also should be emphasized that the evidence entails more than merely juxtaposing statements of New Left leaders and contemporary political elites and noting the correlations, although the correlations are both striking and a key element in the argument. Public lobbyists themselves readily acknowledge their political and intellectual linkages with the New Left. In personal interviews, public lobbyists often referred to their experiences in the 1960s or early 1970s when relating the origins of their ideas about government's relationship to business. For example, various individuals cite their experiences at Yale Law School, expecially classes with Professor Charles Reich; their introduction to the writings of Herbert Marcuse and Gunnar Myrdal; their involvement in campus protest; or simply the impact of events such as Watergate, the civil rights marches, and the war in Vietnam on their political views. Some individuals, obviously, were more profoundly affected than others, but then public interest groups cover a range on the left side of the ideological spectrum. Moreover, other actors in issue network politics also recognize the connections. In addition, an emerging body of survey evidence corroborates the influence of New Left on contemporary public lobbyists.

Ultimately, the portrayal of the public lobby regime as a qualitative shift in regulatory affairs is best seen through a systematic comparison with its predecessor, the New Deal regulatory regime. Specifically, a careful application of the conceptual framework should reveal the distinctive character of the public lobby regime by contrasting its ideas, institutions, and policies with those of the New Deal. The framework also requires that we take into account the influence of inertial forces in shaping the public lobby regime. An accurate portrait of the new social regulation, therefore, depends on noting not only discontinuities but also continuities with the New Deal.

Continuities between the New Deal and the New Social Regulation

In thinking about qualitative shifts or historical changes in the federal regulatory role, the New Deal comes to mind most readily. Under the tutelage of Franklin Roosevelt, the New Deal, for the first time, strongly expressed the national government's obligation to ensure the general welfare of its citizens through extensive regulation of the economy. Unquestionably the regulation enacted and implemented during the New Deal signified the emergence of a new regulatory regime. If the new social regulation also marks a regime change, it is a shift away from the New Deal regime. The New Deal, then, is the baseline against which the degree of regulatory change embodied in the new social regulation must be measured.

The experience of the Crash of 1929 and the early years of the Great Depression had destroyed the legitimacy of the old regulatory regime based on a decentralized political system and a general laissez-faire approach to government–business relations (Leuchtenberg, 1963). The earlier political economic order was predicated on the twin assumptions that the general welfare was best served by individuals pursuing their particular economic interests and that those individuals ultimately and justly could be held responsible for their own economic position. However, in the decade before the Great Depression, the economist John Maynard Keynes had maintained that

> it is not a correct deduction from the Principles of Economics that enlightened self-interest always operates in the public interest. Nor is it true that self-interest is generally enlightened; more often individuals acting separately to achieve their own ends are too ignorant or too weak to attain even these. (1926: 12)

Generally this position was adopted by the supporters of the New Deal and employed as a justification for the construction of a new regulatory regime.

Although Keynes was writing in Europe, it is important to point out that this argument for an expanded regulatory role in capitalistic society also had roots in the American Progressive Era (Brand, 1985). Progressives had noted that the rise of corporations essentially changed the rules of the economic game, thereby undermining the assumptions of the old political economy (Hofstadter, 1955). In this sense the seeds of the New Deal were sown in the Progressive Era. Indeed this should not be at all surprising, because the men and women of the New Deal came of age during the Progressive Era.

Notwithstanding that the Progressive Era programs contained precursors of the New Deal, the 1930s did mark a clear departure in regulatory affairs. Even though the ideas, institutions, and policies of the New Deal may be traced to the Progressive Era, it would strain credulity to argue that Franklin Roosevelt was merely emulating his cousin Theodore or Woodrow Wilson.

Discontinuities across regulatory regimes emerge most sharply in terms of ideas. Even at this level, though, continuities exist. These continuities are largely due to the staying power of public philosophy. While the New Deal altered the reigning public philosophy in the 1930s, its contributions became embedded in a new public philosophy, the one that has typified American political culture in the post–World War II era. Similarly, the new regulatory ideas of the 1960s and 1970s altered, but could not eradicate the New Deal public philosophy. In fact, at least four significant ideas of the public lobby regime may be traced directly to the New Deal.

Most important, both the New Deal and public lobby regime had at their core a strong critique of corporate capitalism. Proponents of the New Deal and public lobbyists alike expressed Keynes's sentiments about the end of laissez-faire: even if such a system ever served the general welfare (and in their eyes that was doubtful), the rise of the modern corporation as an oligopolistic and bureaucratic entity made the concept of a truly free market at best a romantic and irrelevant vision, and at worst a rationale for corporate exploitation. For the proponents of the New Deal the experience of the Great Depression completely undermined arguments of political economists that business ought to be given free rein in the pursuit of profits. Public lobbyists' mistrust of corporations is manifest in their recommendations for nationally chartering business firms, and their demands that businesses be locked into rigorous administrative controls under regulatory programs. In the view of public lobbyists, corporations' ability to control information, to employ tools of applied psychology in the age of television advertising, and to despoil the environment require strong measures to ensure the public interest.

A natural corollary of this critique, and a second point of continuity, was that extensive government regulation was not only appropriate, but also absolutely essential if the general welfare were to be even approximated. Thus, both the advocates of the New Deal and public lobbyists also shared a commitment to positive rather than limited government. Unquestionably the most striking continuity between the New Deal and the new social regulation is that both sought to extend the control of the central government over the private economic sector. Although Tocqueville had maintained that democracy and equality would foster a centralization of power, until the New Deal American politics remained committed, even in the sphere of regulatory policy, to a concept of decentralized administration. Although it is true that during the 1912 presidential election, Herbert Croly and Theodore Roosevelt had talked of a "new nationalism" and the possibility of resurrecting the Hamiltonian ideal of government as the "steward of the public welfare" (T. Roosevelt, 1923–1926: 10–30), political discourse continued to equate positive government with unwarranted governmental intrusion.

Prior to the 1930s, modern liberalism, housed primarily in the Democratic party, was associated with its Jeffersonian origins. Even Woodrow Wilson's reform program, which extended the role of the federal government, remained wedded to individual autonomy (Hofstadter, 1955). The New Deal, while not directly rejecting this tradition, raised serious questions about the adequacy of its time-honored ideas and institutions. Franklin Roosevelt's leadership marked a watershed, for the first time closely connecting the concept of equality with the extension of the central government's authority over social and economic processes. The New Deal's establishment of government services as instruments of popular demand gave impetus (as "Hamiltonian" nationalism never had) to the expansion of federal regulatory authority. In the same sense, the new social regulation may be seen as part of the New Deal legacy. Both embodied a powerful commitment to positive government as a guarantor of socioeconomic rights.

Another important continuity between the ideas of the New Deal and the public lobby regime may be seen in their common rejection of the Progressive Era prescription of separating politics from administration. The regulatory initiatives of the Progressive Era established a pattern of placing administrative authority in the hands of "impartial" experts who could arbitrate regulatory disputes and select policy according to rational, scientific principles. With this in mind, most regulatory authority before the New Deal was delegated to independent regulatory commissions (Bernstein, 1955; Cushman, 1972). By the middle of the 1930s, however, regulatory reformers began to realize that this bureaucratic form in fact contributed to the development of a "headless fourth branch of government, a haphazard deposition of irresponsible agencies and unco-ordinated powers" (*Report of the President's Committee,* 1937: 38).

Such a bureaucracy defied any meaningful accountability to the public and precluded the political direction of society envisioned by the New Deal. Accordingly, an important item on the New Deal agenda in the late 1930s was the centralization of bureaucratic control in the hands of the president. The Executive Reorganization Act of 1939 was conceived with this in mind, and it paved the way for more purposeful control of the administrative agencies than had previously been possible in American government. While this politicization of the administration centered on strengthening the presidency, more fundamentally it emphasized a new and more comprehensive regulatory idea; a revamped executive department was to play the critical role in establishing a new "economic constitutional order," as Franklin Roosevelt termed it, a new relationship among government, business, and society. For this reason, New Deal administrative reform included programs that would permanently establish regulatory and welfare agencies and would cover New Deal loyalists in the bureaucracy with merit protection so as to ensure that the New Deal would survive the tenure of Franklin Roosevelt (Milkis, 1985). Political control over the bureaucracy, then, was structured during the 1930s to extend what Roosevelt called the "enlightened administration" of society (Roosevelt, 1938–1940, vol. I: 752).

Contemporary regulatory reform efforts have continued this thrust of politicizing public administration, although obviously the emphasis has shifted from securing presidential control to widening the opportunities for citizen participation in regulatory politics. Underlying attempts to increase federal regulation both in the New Deal and under the new social regulation was a conviction that the progressive ideal of neutral apolitical administration was an oxymoron: the proponents of the New Deal and public lobbyists understood governmental administration to be inherently political, and believed that ignoring the fact simply sacrificed control over public policy to special interests that did recognize it.

The fourth continuity between New Deal and public lobby ideas is that reformers in both periods viewed independent commissions as administrative institutions with an "elitist" character, subject to influences by political and economic interests that do not promote the general welfare of society (*Congressional Study on Federal Regulation,* vol. 1, 1977). In neither period did reformers see the problems of progressive regulation as confined to a certain messiness or lack of coordination, although these concerns were real enough. The more deep-seated issue was that the attempt to achieve neutral administration through independent regulatory commissions was actually undercutting the public interest. Marver Bernstein elaborated this thesis of regulatory "capture" eloquently in *Regulation by Independent Commission* (1955). As he explained, even if regulatory agencies began by vigorously pursuing their mandates to protect the public, with the passing of time and continued interactions with business representatives, dependence on those representatives for information and political support in subgovernmental politics, in addition to the long-term stultification that accompanies most bureaucratic organizations, would result in a condominium between regulators and regulated industries. It is precisely this view that led public lobbyists to seek an active role in the administrative end of the regulatory process.

In many respects, then, the demands voiced in the late 1960s for consumer protection and environmental quality were an extension of the New Deal. Undoubtedly there is a certain historical continuity connecting the two periods of reform, and owing to the forces of inertia in modern American politics, that is to be expected. Even as the precursors of the New Deal may be found in the Progressive Era, so the origins of the new social regulation may be traced to the New Deal.

Nevertheless, the new social regulation also represents a historic shift. The discontinuities distinguishing the regulatory institutions and policies of the 1970s from those of the 1930s outweigh the continuities. As our framework of analysis for regulatory change indicates, moreover, it is at the level of ideas that the existing regulatory regime is most directly challenged, and consequently discontinuities are most obvious at the level of ideas.

New Regulatory Ideas and the New Left Critique

Although the underlying ideas of the new social regulation echo those of the New Deal in a number of important respects, sharp discontinuities definitely distinguish the two. The crucial intellectual point differentiating the new social regulation is that the proponents of the New Deal were essentially conservative reformers, whereas the ideas of public lobbyists reveal a more thorough, some might say "radical," vision of regulatory change. Indeed, the ideas of the public lobby regime, traceable to New Left critiques of the American political economy, often attacked the New Deal itself—at least as it had evolved by the 1960s.

The supporters of the New Deal in general, and Franklin Roosevelt surely, sought to reform the capitalist system in order to preserve it.

According to Frances Perkins, Roosevelt's secretary of labor, Roosevelt "took the *status quo* in our economic system as much for granted as his family" (1946: 328). Having diagnosed a serious economic disorder with potentially convulsive social and political repercussions, the framers of the New Deal prescribed an enhanced central government with significantly expanded regulatory and macroeconomic responsibilities. Notwithstanding Roosevelt's extraordinary efforts to shift the burdens of social welfare and economic security to Washington, D.C., the New Deal aimed to revitalize private enterprise. In his discussion of the intellectual foundations of the "Roosevelt revolution," William Leuchtenberg, one of the foremost authorities on the New Deal, concluded:

> Roosevelt's program rested on the assumption that a just society could be secured by imposing a welfare state on a capitalist foundation. Without critically challenging the system of private profit, the New Deal reformers were employing the power of government not only to discipline business, but to bolster unionization, pension the elderly, succor the crippled, give relief to the needy, and extend a hand to the forgotten man. (1963: 165)

Thus, although the supporters of the New Deal attacked the conventional economic wisdom of the time (because it did not work) the intellectual and ideological underpinnings of their program revealed an attempt to save capitalism by giving it a human face.

The ambivalence of the New Deal with regard to free enterprise was especially apparent in the area of regulatory policy. Undeniably they tried to exercise "discipline," as Leuchtenberg termed it, over a frequently recalcitrant and hidebound business community. This effort gave rise to much of the antibusiness rhetoric of the New Deal. For example, in excoriating many businessmen as "economic royalists," Roosevelt attempted to portray their resistance to the New Deal as the equivalent of Tory opposition in the American Revolution. Such dramatic proregulatory rhetoric was linked to landmark legislative achievements like the Wagner Act, and some of Roosevelt's closest advisors in the early years of the New Deal hoped to translate this rhetoric into much more sweeping socioeconomic change. Nonetheless, Roosevelt and the overwhelming majority of his supporters never abandoned their basic confidence in capitalism. For example, William O. Douglas, an ardent supporter of Franklin Roosevelt, described regulatory agencies under the New Deal in the following terms: "They have become more and more the *outposts of capitalism;* they have been given increasingly larger patrol duties, lest capitalism by its own greed, avarice, or myopia destroy itself" (cited in Bernstein, 1955: 251, emphasis added).

Public lobbyists, on the other hand, professed regulatory ideas that were much more directly critical of the capitalist system. These new ideas cannot be explained as a response to economic problems, though. Indeed, the early 1960s appeared to fulfill the New Deal dream of relatively stable economic growth. The ideas behind the new social regulation, nevertheless, were more "radical"; they went much further than the New Deal in challenging the fundamental assumptions of a capitalist economy. These more radical ideas of the 1960s were never mechanically transformed into social regulation, but they did play a role, shaping the demands for institutional reform in the 1970s.

Whereas the New Deal reflected an intent to redeem capitalism, or rather to save it from itself, public lobbyists raised basic moral questions about the political economic order, sometimes implicitly, sometimes explicitly. Although some "radical" New Deal advocates shared this deep skepticism about capitalism, they did not typify the Roosevelt program, nor did they exercise much influence by the second half of the 1930s. As unprecedented a regulatory change as it was, the New Deal never emphasized a need for moral regeneration of American society, and it is in this respect that the ideas of the new social regulation were more "radical." The public lobby regime's underlying ideas aimed at a cultural reformation, rather than an economic reform, which characterized the New Deal. In contrast to those in the New Deal who concentrated on smoothing out the capitalist road through regulation and welfare policies, public lobbyists frequently make arguments either asserting or implying that capitalism may in the long run be destructive of the human condition. As a result, their ideas pose a more fundamental challenge.

The tension between capitalist culture and the new social regulation emerges most clearly in terms of demands for environmental regulation. Consumerism also reflects this tension, but somewhat less stridently. Environmentalism, as it developed in the late 1960s, stressed the ideas of holism, interdependence, limited resources, and the sanctity of nature. These ideas were represented in toto by the metaphor, "spaceship earth," an image that poignantly expressed the notions that natural resources are finite and that the human species must be seen as part of rather than apart from the ecosystem. Capitalism, in contrast, embodied the view that mankind could harness nature and exploit its resources in the name of progress and with no consideration of limits; as limits were approached, presumably the market's price mechanism would reflect the increased scarcity. At a more profound level, capitalism, linked so intimately with science and technology, reflected a reductionistic logic rather than a holistic one articulated by environmentalists. Thus, the culture and ideas of capitalism were challenged by environmentalism, and this suspicion of capitalism provided an ideological bridge between the environmental movement and the New Left. Beyond that, environmentalism's accent on interdependence and holism echoed the New Left's communitarian aspects.

A British socialist, Hugh Stretton, interestingly concurs with the neoconservatives that environmentalism represents a radical new departure:

> What resources should we use? What goods should we produce? Who should get them and who should pay for them? Those are the minimal environmental questions without which there can be no environmental policy; but as surely as Karl Marx ever did, they question the foundations of social policy. (1976: 4)

Environmentalism and other forms of new social regulation appear more threatening to capitalism than the New Deal ever did, because its advocates raised serious questions not only about capitalism's practical operation and consequences, but about its moral and cultural assumptions.

While not as profoundly opposed to capitalism, consumerism also challenged the prevailing political economic system. This challenge was muted by the consumer advocates' self-perception as upholders of the culture of individualism and self-reliance out of which capitalism developed. Their objections were not to capitalism per se as was the case with environmentalists. Rather, they contended that advanced capitalism was dominated by huge private bureaucracies, multinational corporations, against which individual consumers were nearly impotent. Thus, they tended to see the capitalist system as ironically anti-individualist. This populist perspective created a certain kinship with the views of the New Left, which, as we shall see, retained both collectivist and individualist tendencies, although very few members of the New Left dealt explicitly with this apparent contradiction.

Environmentalism and consumerism, each in its own way, reflected a deep suspicion of capitalism, and this common feature linked them with the New Left. Again, this is not to say that environmentalism and consumerism were simply products of the New Left, because both can trace their historical roots to the Progressive Era, environmentalism to the conservation movement at the turn of the century, and consumerism to progressive concerns about adulterated foods. However, as they developed in the 1960s, they had a natural affinity with the ideas professed by New Left activists. Therefore, the reformers socialized in the 1960s could readily translate their own suspicion of capitalism into environmental and consumer activism. It would be simplistic to infer that the new social regulation is strictly anticapitalist; yet it is surely more confrontational with capitalism than the New Deal ever was, clearly reflecting new regulatory ideas. Perhaps more important, the influence of the New Left meant that public lobbyists, unlike their New Deal predecessors, felt extremely uncomfortable about relying on big government to regulate big business. This discomfort distinguished them from even the more "radical" supporters of the New Deal.

While it is true that public lobbyists were far more dubious of capitalism's ultimate virtue than those in the New Deal, it is somewhat ironic and even unfair to suggest, as Irving Kristol (1973) does, that this may be traced to their antidemocratic bias. By calling them a "new class," he alludes to Milovan Djilas' derisive characterization of the technocrats who were brought to power in Stalinist Russia (1957). Even as a rhetorical device, this seems to go a bit too far. As we have suggested, public lobbyists never completely disengaged themselves from the New Deal.

Outstanding examples of this so-called new class include such prominent public figures as Ralph Nader, Mark Green, Barry Commoner, and Morton Mintz. Neoconservatives correctly maintain that it also includes public lobbyists and their supporters, in the federal bureaucracy, in the media, and even on the bench. Undoubtedly these reform advocates are an "elite" in the sense that they are among the most politically active of citizens, but they also are, as a group, extraordinarily concerned about democracy and the ultimate worth of the individual.

The new regulatory ideas of the 1970s actually challenged the insularity and elitism of regulatory politics as it evolved from the New Deal. Taking a broad philosophical perspective, Samuel Beer (1978) has suggested that environmentalism and consumer activism derived from the early New Left views of Paul Goodman and Theodore Rozak. While this observation is essentially correct, it is important for our purposes to elaborate the connections more specifically and to identify the elements of New Left thought that helped to shape the new social regulation. Accordingly, we shall trace the ideas underlying the new social regulation back to their precursors in the New Left critiques of American society, which were put forth in the 1960s. In doing so, we shall see that the new social regulation borrowed more than a critique of the establishment from the New Left, although the importance of that critique should not be underestimated. To varying degrees, the new social regulation also reflects more positive institutional recommendations of the New Left, especially the demand for participatory democracy.

The central element of the New Left critique was a deep concern that people in modern American society had been stripped of their human dignity and, by extension, their sense of political efficacy. Charles Reich expressed this position in *The Greening of America,* noting that New Left activists saw a profound failure in the New Deal:

> Neither New Deal reforms, nor earlier Progressive reforms restored any power to the individual, or limited power that could be applied against individuals. . . . What reformers did, so far as individuals were concerned, was to take some of that lost power and turn it over to "public" organizations—government, labor unions, farmers' groups. Nothing came back to the people. . . . What reform assumed was that *its* power would be good for individuals, whereas previous power had been bad. (1970: 56)

Progressives and New Deal supporters had attempted to shield the individual from private organizational (i.e., big business) exploitation. However, New Left representatives, much in the same spirit as Lowi, perceived that the "forgotten man" of the New Deal era remained shut out and exploited, only now the individual confronted big government as well as big business. To the extent that the public lobby regime embodies this New Left concern for the individual, it is as much an error for Lowi to view the new social regulation as an extension of the New Deal as it is for Kristol to view it as a renunciation of the New Deal.

In order to appreciate the profoundness of this accent on the individual, it is important to understand that it did not grow out of a political program. Rather, the original concern that emerged in the 1950s was social and cultural; only in its later stages of development did the New Left clearly link social critique with political critique. One of the earliest and best portrayals of this social critique is found in Norman Mailer's *Advertisements for Myself.* Mailer describes the beatniks and hipsters of the 1950s as "white Negroes." With that label, he suggests pointedly their rejection of mainstream culture and institutions epitomized by corporate business and New Deal government:

> The white rebel borrows the risky lifestyle of the negro, always living in the present and refusing the security of those institutions which are part of white society, security which the negro never had. His search is directed entirely toward the pleasures his body can enjoy "here and now." (1959: 27)

According to Mailer, the utter rejection of capitalist democracy at the social and cultural level naturally led to an emulation of the one group that was obviously excluded from that society and culture: black Americans. They were seen as retaining their individuality in the face of technocratic society. The accuracy of that perception is irrelevant for our purposes. The key point is that in the 1950s the view was adopted by that group Jack Newfield called "the prophetic minority." They in turn gave rise to a movement that, informed by existential questions about the meaning of life, increasingly viewed the outcomes of American society as "absurd" (Goodman, 1961). However, even this broad rejection of society was expressed in individualistic terms. For example, Newfield claimed that the 1960s generation perceived that "logic, rules and order explained less and less about a society [that] puts Martin Luther King, Joan Baez and Ken Kesey in jail and Lester Maddox, General Hersey and Ronald Reagan in power" (1966: 25).

Looking back on the development of the New Left, Susan Sontag (1969) noted at the end of the 1960s:

> The view is that the power structure derives its credibility, its legitimacy, its energies from the dehumanization of the individuals who operate it. The people staffing IBM, General Motors, and the Pentagon and United Fruit are [the] living dead. . . . The answer on which everyone is, miraculously, in agreement is subversion—subversion of the culture which produces heartless bureaucrats of death and empty affluence. . . . The American revolutionary vision in the '60's has been preeminently a psychic one.

It is this overriding concern for the individual and conviction that bureaucracy, both public and private, were destroying the individual that underlay the New Left critique and ultimately informed regulatory reform in the 1970s.

If the activism of public lobbyists pales in comparison with that of campus radicals and civil rights leaders of the 1960s, a strong intellectual and ideological connection still remains. As Sontag (1969) reminds us, the accent on the individual was unique to the American left, and ultimately could lead to a "compromising" of its radicalism:

> But [the New Left] is also . . . more provincial, more excruciatingly American. If the main struggle at this moment is to establish an alternative or adversary culture, it is entirely American that the struggle flourishes around the goal of *freedom* (not, for instance, justice). And even more specifically American is what is understood as the content of freedom—the guarantee of freedom to the individual. . . .

> The majority American culture itself reinforces the prevailing New Left belief that there is no necessary conflict between individualism and radical politics.

This "excruciatingly American" character of the New Left is significant, because it helps to explain how environmentalists and consumer activists could at once bitterly attack the establishment and seek to play a role in national political institutions. In a sense, they were intent on restoring integrity to American politics by resuscitating traditional American values of freedom and individualism, but in a national administrative context. There was never a mechanical translation of the New Left program into social regulation; the process was more subtle and evolutionary.

In the 1970s public lobbyists attempted to integrate New Left ideas of participatory democracy and suspicion of the establishment with the New Deal emphasis on administrative professionalism and responsiveness. They envisioned both an extensive federal bureaucracy that was to be more open to citizen participation, and the moral regeneration of the American political economy through citizen activism.

Thus, the New Left concern for the individual logically implied a thorough social and cultural critique, though one that in the context of American political culture left open the distinct possibility of accommodation with the establishment. When this critique elicited unsatisfactory responses from the political system, it eventually expanded to incorporate politics explicitly. Thus, the focus of animus for the New Left became the "establishment," the combination of social, political, and economic institutions that defined American society. The New Left became deeply suspicious of what President Eisenhower had called the "military-industrial complex." Even more important, it became increasingly suspicious of the New Deal and liberal Democrats. The establishment came to be viewed as a system of "corporate liberalism," an unholy alliance of big business, big government, and the permanent military inimical to the dignity of individual human beings.

Given the focus on individualism and freedom, it is not surprising that the civil rights movement of the early 1960s attracted the attention of activists and served as a formative political experience. This experience, followed almost immediately by the escalation of the war in Vietnam, seemed to confirm the suspicions of the New Left. The civil rights movement began by presenting demands to the political system. However, slowly but surely the tentative responses, especially of liberal Democrats, led younger activists, both black and white, to question the efficacy of working through traditional political channels. Even as the mainstream civil rights leaders were approaching the zenith of their prestige, organizers within the Student Nonviolent Coordinating Committee (SNCC) were adopting a more strident line. For example, during the 1963 March on Washington at which Dr. Martin Luther King commanded so much attention, a young SNCC leader, John Lewis, in a speech to the marchers, expressed his deep misgivings about relying on the establishment:

> The party of Kennedy is also the party of Eastland. The party of Javits is also the party of Goldwater. Where is our party?
> We all recognize that if any social, political and economic changes are to take place in our society, the people, the masses, must bring them about. (cited in Teodori, 1969: 162)

These misgivings seemed to be borne out the following year at the Democratic National Convention in Atlantic City. SNCC, aided by a number of young white volunteers, had undertaken a massive voter registration drive in Mississippi, the intent of which was to challenge the regular delegates selected by the white-controlled party machinery. These alternate delegates came to Atlantic City under the banner of the Mississippi Free Democratic Party (MFDP). SNCC and the MFDP were convinced that they had the votes to force a floor debate on delegate credentials. However, Lyndon Johnson and Hubert Humphrey, the party's standard-bearers, interceded to work out a compromise that would allow two token MFDP delegates to be seated. This compromise was supported by Dr. King and Bayard Rustin, the two most prominent civil rights leaders of the day. However, to those who had confronted angry crowds and police harassment during the registration drive, the compromise was at once an unbelievable betrayal and confirmation of Lewis's argument raised the year before.

Attacking Rustin for advocating politics within the Democratic party over protest in the streets, Staughton Lynd argued that coalition politics would be both disastrous and immoral. To Lynd the Democratic party was not only the party of civil rights legislation, but also the party that betrayed the MFDP and was prosecuting the war in Vietnam. Lynd held that "the coalition [liberals, labor and blacks] [Bayard] Rustin advocates turns out to mean implicit acceptance of the Administration's foreign policy, to be a coalition with the marines," and "the style of politics he advocates turns out to mean a kind of elitism . . . in which rank-and-file persons would cease to act on their own behalf and be *merely represented*" (Teodori, 1969: 186, emphasis added). In these comments we can see how the concern for the individual was translated into a suspicion of the establishment. We also can see that the Vietnam War reinforced the New Left conclusions derived from the civil rights struggle.

These "lessons" shaped the ideas of the campus radicals of the 1960s, many of whom had worked with SNCC. However, they carried the analysis even further, defining the system they labeled corporate liberalism. In an antiwar speech in 1965, Carl Oglesby, president of Students for a Democratic Society (SDS), the most recognizable New Left student organization, articulated this position.

> We are here again to protest against a growing war. Since it is a very bad war, we acquire the habit of thinking that it must be caused by very bad men. But we only conceal reality, I think, by denouncing on such grounds the menacing coalition of industrial and military power, or the brutality of the blitzkrieg we are waging against Vietnam or the ominous signs around us that heresy may soon no longer be permitted. We must simply observe that this coalition, this blitzkrieg and this demand for acquiescence are creatures . . . of a Government that since 1932 has considered itself to be fundamentally liberal. (Teodori, 1969: 217)

In a 1966 article for *The New Republic,* Richard Flacks, a leading New Left activist, spelled out the radical view of what had gone wrong with liberalism and the New Deal. In that article, sarcastically titled "Is the Great Society Just a Barbeque," Flacks argued,

> In both its rhetoric and its practice, *liberal corporatism* implies a political structure in which principal policy issues are worked out at the federal level, formulated with the active participation of experts, and ratified—not in the legislative arena—but through a process of consultation among a national elite representing those interests and institutions which now recognize each other as legitimate. (1966: 263, emphasis added)

This portrait of American politics, anticipating almost exactly Theodore Lowi's analysis in *The End of Liberalism* (1969) reveals the essence of a highly developed New Left critique of the establishment, which had emerged by the beginning of the 1970s. This critique retained its influence and appeal as campus activists, moving from their twenties to their thirties, shifted their attention from civil rights and the war to environmental and consumer issues.

While the commitment to individualism and suspicion of the corporate liberal establishment are the central ideas that link the New Left to the public lobby regime, and distinguish it from the New Deal, it would be a mistake to overlook a more practical idea adapted from the New Left by public lobbyists. This idea, "participatory democracy," is widely acknowledged to characterize the new social regulation. It also marks a crucial discontinuity between the New Deal and the public lobby regime.

The commitment to individualism combined with the rejection of the establishment gave rise to the concept of participatory democracy. Participatory democracy envisioned a system of political decisionmaking in which individual citizens rather than organized interests would predominate. Citizens had to become active; otherwise they would be, in Staughton Lynd's words, "merely represented," and thereby subject to manipulation by big business in league with big government. Demeaning the concept of republican government by rejecting the notion of "mere representation" highlights the extent to which activists of the New Left were at odds with American political culture. This view of democracy drew upon the vision of Rousseau rather than that of Locke, the one that predominates in American political culture. The first clear statement on participatory democracy is found in the manifesto of the SDS, *The Port Huron Statement:*

> As a social system we seek the establishment of a democracy of individual participation, governed by two central aims: that the individual share in those social decisions determining the quality of his life; that society be organized to encourage independence in men and provide media for their common participation. (Teodori, 1969: 285)

All in all, this hardly seemed a revolutionary proposal. Indeed, the language is reminiscent of Tocqueville's description of democracy in America. And this should not be terribly surprising considering Beer's argument that there is a strong romantic flavor to the New Left, a longing to reinstate individuals rather than organizations as the focus of public policy. The same political romanticism can be traced to the antifederalists who, although they lost the contest with the federalists, contributed a strong dose of Rousseauean individualism and suspicion of centralized authority to American political culture (Brand, 1988). Still, participatory democracy seems to bear out Sontag's characterization of the New Left as "excruciatingly American" in its radicalism.

This concept of participatory democracy was refined by the SDS from the experience of its members with SNCC and the civil rights activities of the early 1960s. SNCC pioneered a sort of antibureaucratic organization in which the core members (leaders would be an inappropriate term) purposely eschewed any fixed bureaucracy and any grand vision to be imposed on those they attempted to organize. SNCC wanted to educate common people about their political rights, to inculcate them with a sense of political efficacy, and to cultivate activists at the grass roots level who could define and pursue their own issues. Ultimately this brought them into conflict not only with white racists but also with "establishment" civil rights leaders. The means of achieving these aims, first for SNCC and later for SDS and other New Left groups, was "parallel institutions," grass roots organizations that identified issues of concern to members and attempted to monitor and challenge the activities of establishment institutions involved in those issues. As Staughton Lynd explained,

> participatory democracy cherishes the practice of parallelism as a way of saying NO to organized America, and of initiating the unorganized into the experience of self-government. The SNCC or SDS worker does not build a parallel institution to impose ideology on it. He views himself as a catalyst, helping to create an environment which will help the local people decide what they want. (Teodori, 1969: 328)

These parallel institutions served as rough blueprints for the public lobby organizations that emerged in the 1970s. Although neither SDS nor the public lobbyists ever achieved the ideals expressed in *The Port Huron Statement* or Lynd's portrayal of participatory democracy, the basic idea of parallelism influenced both and set them apart from earlier twentieth-century reformers.

Another important element of participatory democracy adapted to the new social regulation was the idea of focusing on a single issue. This related to the New Left notion of "direct action." A natural outgrowth of participatory democracy, direct action meant that, because the establishment could not be trusted to promote the public interest, it was often necessary for citizen organizations to press an issue through irregular political activities. Frequently this meant protest, civil disobedience, or confrontation. While none of these ideas was new, never before had they been put forth as an institutional approach to challenge the establishment regularly. The New Left embraced direct action because it concluded that working exclusively "within the system" was immoral and counterproductive.

A corollary of direct action was attention to single issues rather than adherence to a grand political economic vision. In an essay entitled "The Ideology of the Campus Revolution," Dale Johnson claimed to see an analogy between campus radicals and Cuban revolutionaries. The questionable accuracy of the connection notwithstanding, he does correctly portray the essence of direct action:

> Both Cuban and Campus rebels are strong dissenters, firm in their convictions and willing to speak out and act militantly. . . . Both are pragmatic, always putting first things first, with rarely an eye to ultimate ends. . . . Here at home the pragmatic outlook is manifest in *the multitude of single-issue groups devoted simply to getting things done in the most effective manner possible.* (Teodori, 1969: 196, emphasis added)

While American environmentalists and consumer advocates are surely a far cry from "Fidelistas," Johnson's characterization is an uncanny anticipation of the modus operandi for public lobbyists.

The legacy of participatory democracy, though, has even more important implications for the nature of the public lobby regime. Participatory democracy not only aimed to achieve specific policy ends, but also sought to alter the decisionmaking process itself. Norman Fruchter and Robert Kramer, two prominent SDS organizers, explained this in a discussion of their experience in the Economic Research and Action Project (ERAP):

> The crucial point is that the project [ERAP] is committed to two kinds of change at once: the specific remedying of individual, aggravating grievances, and basic structural changes which would replace present systems of production, authority, administration and control with far more egalitarian and participatory institutions. (1966: 37)

Fruchter and Kramer could just as well have been describing the new social regulation in its simultaneous commitment to policy and process reforms, because direct action aimed at both.

In sum, the New Left activists developed ideas that were highly critical of the established order and embodied some specific programs for institutional change. These ideas—suspicion of the establishment and participatory democracy—helped to shape the public lobby regime and distinguished it as a unique historical episode in the development of federal regulation. When contemporary public lobbyists describe their activities and motivations, they do so in the language of the New Left. In fact, they frequently cite the political experiences of the 1960s as both a source and a model for the public interest movement. Many public lobbyists came of age politically during the civil rights and antiwar struggles, either participating directly or witnessing events from the vantage point of college campuses where the ideas of the New Left were openly discussed (Beer, 1978; Haefele, 1978). As their attention shifted to the issues of the 1970s, they naturally drew on those experiences and ideas.

The foregoing review of New Left ideas makes it clear that activists of the 1960s presented a very basic challenge to American society. They rejected not simply the outcomes of political and economic processes, but the very nature of those processes. Indeed, their critique was based on an assertion of the immorality of American culture. The questions, however, remain, how relevant is this critique to the new social regulation and to what extent did public lobbyists of the 1970s adopt and bring to fruition the demands of 1960s activists?

Adapting New Left Ideas to the New Social Regulation

While it is hardly a simple matter to establish a positive impact of New Left ideas on public lobbyists, it is possible to construct a persuasive argument that some important New Left ideas ultimately were reflected in the new social regulation and that public lobbyists were the conduit for those ideas. Two kinds of evidence may be adduced. First, an emerging body of survey data indicates not only that the 1960s generation, or at least elements of it, sympathized with the New Left view of American society, but also that this radical ideology persisted among activists and channeled their political involvement into consumerism and environmentalism. Although not all public lobbyists fall into this category of 1960s activism, a significant number do, and they often acquired leadership positions in public interest groups. Second, personal interviews provide evidence that leading public interest groups are staffed by individuals sympathetic to New Left ideas. Even more important, they are self-conscious about the linkages between their political views or those of other public lobbyists and the New Left.

There is little question that, in their youth, many members of the 1960s generation—that is, the segment of the population that attended high school and college in the 1960s—held a highly critical view of American society, or that this view reflected the ideas of the New Left (Whalen and Flacks, 1984; Hoge and Ankey, 1982). However, the gross, aggregate data also show that this generation voted overwhelmingly for Ronald Reagan in 1980. As M. Kent Jennings points out in a recent study, we can make sense of this "paradox" by adopting Karl Manheim's more sophisticated view of generations as political entities (1987). In this view, the political or ideological color of a generation is set not by an entire age cohort, but by an active and influential subset of that cohort. Following Manheim, his analysis reveals that as a whole the 1960s generation did indeed become more conservative, but the minority of real activists, those who were genuinely committed to social change during the 1960s, remained remarkably consistent in their views and remarkably active in politics:

> [C]ontinued manifestations of a political generation may be quite localized but nevertheless quite potent . . . if one listens to contemporary debates or observes political influentials in action, the imprinting of generational experience is often patent. Because of their influence, elites and near-elites can continue to represent the orientations of a political generation even when those orientations are not widely shared by mass publics. (Jennings, 1987)

Public lobbyists obviously fit Jennings's notion of an influential cohort within a generation. It is true that the differences between them and less activist members of the 1960s generation narrowed over time, but a statistically significant gap remained.

In another relevant study, Stanley Rothman and Robert Lichter analyzed the relationship between elite ideology and perception of risk in the use of nuclear energy (1987). The significance of this research for our purposes is that nuclear energy is an issue area that bridges the environmental and consumer movements; it entails risk to the environment as well as public health and economic issues of concern to public utility customers. Rothman and Lichter specifically identify public lobbyists as a political elite. They conclude not only that the ideology of public lobbyists is rooted in the New Left, but also that it explains their perception of nuclear risk and their preference for social regulatory policy. According to Rothman and Lichter, public lobbyists, even in the 1980s remained far to the left of mainstream American politics: 51 percent of the public interest activists they surveyed believed that the United States should move toward socialism, and 34 percent revealed a favorable approval rating of Fidel Castro (1987: 396; perhaps public lobbyists were Fidelistas after all). Even more intriguing is their conclusion that environmentalism came to serve as a surrogate for direct criticism of American society:

> The environmental issue was among several on which those hostile to the dominant values of the society could focus. These problems were real and they could be used to mobilize a much larger number of individuals looking for a meaningful cause to express their hostility to "corporate capitalism." (1987: 396)

The argument is not that a handful of radicals sought to manipulate issues to subvert society, but rather that the New Left ideology of public lobbyists inclined them naturally toward the environmental (and consumer) causes in the 1970s as the issues of civil rights and Vietnam receded on the national agenda. While these survey studies are hardly conclusive, they do clearly suggest an influential role for New Left ideas in the programs of public lobbyists. The Jennings and Rothman–Lichter findings are much more persuasive, however, when combined with the views of public lobbyists themselves on the origins of the new social regulation.

The most easily recognized idea of the New Left that seemed to shape the perspective of public lobbyists was their commitment to participatory democracy. In this regard, they employed exactly the same language as the radicals of the 1960s. For example, Alan Morrison, the director of litigation for Public Citizens, expressed a deep commitment to "the democratic participatory aspect" of public interest activity, and saw this as a major difference between regulation of the 1970s and early efforts at controlling business:

> A framework was established in which people other than industry have a significant role to play, and this is true not only in the [regulatory] agencies, but also in terms of going to court to assure compliance with the law. . . . In the mid-sixties agencies essentially could do anything not strictly prohibited by law. (personal interview, June 12, 1986)

Similarly, in words strikingly reminiscent of *The Port Huron Statement,* Daniel Becker, legislative counsel for Environmental Action (EA), related that

> One of the most significant achievements brought about by public interest groups has been the development of the grass roots. . . . EA is concerned with how to get people involved in the movement and to learn how to help themselves, equipping local citizens to protect their interests against corporate power. (personal interview, June 11, 1986)

Finally, the director of legislation at Common Cause, Kathleen Sheekey, saw all public lobby groups as part of a coherent reform effort directed at energizing the citizenry:

> The common thread among all concerned groups is activism. . . . What we are trying to do is develop citizens as lobbyists, to bring citizens into

the decision-making process. Our work is much less advocacy than education. (personal interview, July 23, 1986)

The commitment to participatory democracy among public lobbyists
is both deep and widespread, and this commitment surely distinguishes
them from New Deal supporters. It also raises serious questions about
the neoconservatives' characterization of them as an elitist group, a "new
class." While the concept of participatory democracy has not been translated precisely from theory to practice, the idea is not simply a rationalization for their self-aggrandizement.

It is easy to distinguish activists of the 1960s, especially the more
militant ones such as the members of the SDS, the Weathermen, or
SNCC, from the Friends of the Earth, the Sierra Club, or Public Citizen.
However, the differences are basically at the level of strategy and tactics;
this does not preclude the possibility that they share some fundamental
criticisms of American society. Our contention is that all of these groups
were informed by a common set of ideas that derive from the New Left.
To be sure, it was easier for SNCC than for public lobby groups to ap-
proximate the ideal of participatory democracy in its internal organization. Yet public lobbyists do seek to follow the precepts of participatory
democracy. They are intent on "energizing" the citizenry and on involving them in decisions that affect their lives; it is harder, though, if the
decisions are made on the federal level as opposed to the local level
where SDS operated its community action projects.

The pragmatic focus on single issues provides an even closer parallel
between New Left activists and public lobbyists. Single-issue politics is
almost a given for those interested in participatory democracy, because
concrete problems and solutions are the best way to arouse the interests
and passions of citizens. It is important to establish institutions and
frameworks through which the people can participate in decisionmaking,
but in the 1960s and the 1970s activists recognized that real issues were
necessary to induce people to avail themselves of these new opportunities. Participatory democracy is the first idea any public lobbyist will
raise in discussing his or her goals. Moreover, our examination of the
institutions and policies of the new social regulation will reveal that participatory democracy is not simply hoary rhetoric, but a real blueprint for
institutional design.

The antiestablishment perspective of the New Left is more difficult
to discern among public lobbyists. One can get a sense of it, though,
simply by walking into the offices of a public lobby organization. The
links with the politics of the 1960s are revealed in a variety of ways,

some subtle, some explicit. The style of dress, the cartoons and posters on the walls, the bicycles parked in the offices, the sense of urgency among the staff, all create a sense of déjà vu with the tumultuous times and counterculture of the previous decade. This sense is heightened when one compares it to the atmosphere prevailing at regulatory agencies or business lobby organizations, the institutions of big government and big business. At these offices dark suits and ties are the order of the day, in contrast to open shirts and slacks, or even blue jeans; the walls are likely to be adorned with pictures from photo opportunity sessions with high-ranking politicos, in contrast to cartoons attacking business and government leaders or posters decrying nuclear weapons, world hunger, and pollution. These echoes of radical criticism and contrasts with the office culture of the "establishment" are suggestive, but hardly conclusive evidence of a connection with the antiestablishment views of the New Left.

In part it is difficult to discern public lobbyists' suspicion of the establishment, because they have more immediate policy and process concerns in the forefront of their thinking, and the idea of participatory democracy relates to these concerns directly. Still, suspicion of the establishment does lurk behind their emphasis on citizen activism. For example, Brent Blackwelder, vice-president of the Environmental Policy Institute, punctuated a discussion of deregulation under the Reagan administration by noting that "the history of the American political process is one of special interests predominating except in cases of far-sighted individuals and Presidents" (personal interview, July 22, 1986). Like the New Left activists, Blackwelder had little confidence that "the system" (a synonym for "the establishment") would serve the general welfare in the long run.

The basic reason for rejecting the establishment, as Blackwelder explained, was a sense that the individual was shut out of politics and manipulated by organized interests. Redressing that situation was the whole point of participatory democracy. On this point, Kathleen Sheekey of Common Cause explained that group's formation with the following assertion: "Everyone had a voice but the people. . . . In the late sixties the timing seemed right for people to want a say. There was a feeling of powerlessness" (personal interview, July 23, 1986). The sense that there was a need for the people to assert power harks back directly to the New Left. And, Sheekey notes, the late 1960s are generally perceived as the period that spawned public lobby activism. American society was seen as dominated by corporate liberalism, and this view provided a raison d'être for Ralph Nader as well as Abbie Hoffman.

Naturally big business was a primary target of this antiestablishment sentiment inherited from the New Left. The corporation was seen as the primary beneficiary of corporate liberalism, and as such commanded the attention of radicals. They did not want simply to discipline business, but wanted to alter fundamentally the way business decisions were made; the point of participatory democracy was to involve the people directly in decisions that affected the quality of their lives, because the establishment could never be trusted to take their interests into account. It is in this respect that the closest kinship between public lobbyists and the 1960s radicals can be found. Joan Claybrook, the president of Public Citizen, described how the new social regulation attempted to redistribute power from big business and big government to the people:

> Social regulation took decisionmaking out of the hands of corporate managers and *socialized it*. . . . There were a whole number of changes in the way business did business, but decisionmaking was the key. Public interest groups essentially democratized the decision process and put something other than profit into the equation. (personal interview, June 11, 1986, emphasis added)

The critical point is that, like New Left activists, public lobbyists simply did not trust the establishment, even when it was controlled by liberal Democrats. Consequently, they saw a need to develop alternate ways of making public decisions.

Richard Ayers, senior attorney for the Natural Resources Defense Council (NRDC), noted the clear connection between the activism of the 1960s and public lobby activity: "Historically public participation can be traced to the idea of participatory democracy. . . . Direct expression as a form of participation came from the civil rights movement and the Vietnam experience" (personal interview, July 22, 1986). As in the 1960s, participatory democracy in the 1970s meant the involvement of citizens in deciding specific issues of clear concern to them.

As the college students of the 1960s became the public lobbyists of the 1970s, they carried with them the ideas of the New Left. However, in practice the issues of environmentalism and consumerism never aroused the passions that civil rights or the antiwar movement did. Consequently, the challenges to the establishment became less strident and activists seemed less radical in their demands. Mark Silbergeld, an attorney for Consumers Union, pointed out that these days "The public interest movement scans at least half the ideological spectrum" (personal interview July 23, 1986).

In fact, there was never a complete triumph of New Left ideas. To an extent, a total triumph was prevented by the lack of any grand vision for society among the radicals of the 1960s. In addition, the impact of these ideas was also limited by the ambivalence of the New Left noted by Susan Sontag: the commitment to the individual linked directly with the prevailing political culture. Thus, it was not difficult for these ideas ultimately to become assimilated, especially as the energies of the activists shifted from the highly charged issues of racial equality and Vietnam to environmental quality and product safety. Finally, the forces of institutional inertia checked, to some extent, the impact of participatory democracy. While the public lobby regime brought with it new regulatory ideas traceable to the New Left, the ideas and institutions of the New Deal were never completely abandoned.

Nonetheless, participatory democracy and suspicion of the establishment remain important to our understanding of the public lobby regime. They separate the new social regulation from the New Deal regulation. Together, these ideas form a coherent perspective on regulation, a perspective Andrew McFarland has protrayed as a "theory of civic balance":

> This system of beliefs implies that widely shared interests are not adequately represented . . . unless citizens form new institutions for representation, American government will have an elitist character, in that economic, political, and bureaucratic leaders will control public policy for their own benefit. (1976: 7)

This theory of civic balance draws directly on the New Left critique, and as such reflects important discontinuities with the New Deal regulatory regime, because it calls for the construction of new policymaking institutions.

New Institutions

The impact of new regulatory ideas must be measured by the degree of change in regulatory institutions. Although the public lobbyists of the 1970s were definitely influenced by the ideas of the New Left, the extent to which those ideas were translated into institutional reality remains to be seen. Without establishing that linkage between regulatory ideas and institutions, it is impossible to sustain the argument that the new social regulation coincided with the emergence of a new regulatory regime. However, as distinctive as the institutions of the public lobby regime are from those of the New Deal, it is important to reemphasize that there are continuities as well. The continuities stem from the inertial forces set

TABLE 3.1.   Federal Regulatory Agencies by Date of Establishment

1932–1945	1970–1978
Federal Home Loan Bank Board (1932)	Environmental Protection Agency (1970)
Commodity Credit Corporation (1933)	Federal Railroad Administration (1970)
Federal Deposit Insurance Corporation (1933)	National Highway Traffic Safety Administration (1970)
Securities and Exchange Commission (1934)	National Oceanic and Aeronautic Administration (1970)
Federal Communications Commission (1934)	Postal Rate Commission (1970)
National Labor Relations Board (1934)	Consumer Product Safety Commission (1972)
Federal Maritime Commission (1936)	Mine Safety and Health Administration (1973)
Agricultural Marketing Service (1937)	Occupational Safety and Health Administration (1973)
Civil Aeronautics Board (1940)	Economic Regulatory Administration (1974)
	Nuclear Regulatory Commission (1975)
	Securities and Federal Grain Inspection Service (1976)
	Office of Surface Mining (1977)

forth in our model of regulatory change. The dialectical interaction of new and old regulatory ideas yields a synthesis less radical than new ideas themselves. Even after the clash of ideas, though, bureaucratic and political inertia constrain the degree of change in regulatory institutions.

Because both the New Deal and the public lobby regime contain a commitment to positive government, it is reasonable to expect that both periods would be characterized by the creation of federal regulatory agencies. Indeed, both are, and this is the most visible institutional parallel between them. Table 3.1 lists the federal regulatory agencies created in the 1930s and the 1970s. In the era of the new social regulation as well as the era of the New Deal, reformers turned to the central government to address public problems. Moreover, reliance on Washington meant not neutral administration, but politicization of the bureaucracy. As Lowi has pointed out, this politicization, in combination with the New Deal-type growth of regulation, created a balkanized policy environment dominated by organized interests. Subgovernments define the institutional environment in which regulatory politics occurs for the new social regulation too. Although the new social regulation envisioned a different kind of subgovernment, one in which regulatory politics would be "opened up" through participatory democracy and direct action, organized interests continue to enjoy advantages in such an institutional setting. Reformers in the 1970s never presented an alternative to the New Deal formula of addressing public problems through federal programs. Rather, they grafted their ideas of participatory democracy and direct action onto federal programs and bureaucratic procedures. In this sense the public lobby regime is truly an "uneasy marriage of the New Deal and the New Left."

Although both New Deal supporters and public lobbyists sought to politicize the regulatory bureaucracy, they each followed different institutional strategies. Like public lobbyists, supporters of the New Deal saw the inadequacy of the regulatory process, particularly with respect to independent commissions (Report of the President's Committee on Administrative Management, 1937). In response to these inadequacies, the New Deal sought to extend the control of the president over the bureaucracy through such institutional mechanisms as the White House Office (WHO), the Bureau of the Budget, and executive reorganization authority (Milkis, 1985). This attempt to establish "presidential government" was limited to a great extent by congressional opposition during Franklin Roosevelt's second term. Yet, the New Deal attempts to strengthen the hand of the president vis à vis the bureaucracy were designed to make the White House into the primary institution through which the public interest could be represented.

On the other hand, those pressing for social regulation in the 1970s intended to create institutions for interest representation that would be independent of traditional powers, including the president. This discontinuity between the 1930s and the 1970s reflects the evolution of reformist ideas about regulatory policy. Just as the New Deal supporters had "learned" that the Progressive Era ideal of neutral administrators impartially overseeing regulatory policy in the public interest was a chimera, public lobbyists "learned" about the pitfalls of politicizing public administration through the White House. Perhaps most important, it became clear that the Oval Office might not be occupied at all times by an individual of Franklin Roosevelt's vision and commitment to executive action. No doubt for advocates of the new social regulation, this was the message of the Eisenhower years. More ominously, though, the chief executive might be hostile to the goals of public lobbyists. Whereas the institutions of the invigorated presidency, such as the Budget Office, emerged under Roosevelt as agencies committed to a more energetic and rational regulation of the economy, these institutions were further honed and transformed during the Nixon administration as tools of "conservative" administration (Nathan, 1983; Moe, 1985). Thus, from the standpoint of public lobbyists, White House alliances can be valuable political resources, but should not be counted on as a bulwark of the public interest.

However, the rejection of the presidency as the institution through which the public interest could be pursued runs deeper than the simple insight that the president might not always be receptive to progressive programs. The legacy of the New Left made public lobbyists suspicious, even cynical, about American politics in general. This cynicism, importantly, extended not only to conservative Republicans. Beginning surely with Lyndon Johnson, and for some with John F. Kennedy, activists were unwilling to trust liberal Democrats either. To the extent that political parties were viewed as elements of the establishment, they could not be entrusted with the general welfare of society. As for regulatory agencies, even under the New Deal system of "presidential government," they were perceived as ineffectual at best. Still worse, New Deal liberalism was seen as tending toward corporate liberalism, the alliance of big business, big government, and the military against the interests of individual citizens. While most public lobbyists never adopted the extreme radicalism of SDS, the New Left critique of the establishment did incline them to seek alternative regulatory institutions.

The fundamental institutional strategy of public lobbyists was to promote the public interest through participatory democracy, and the new social regulation does embody specific institutional mechanisms to ensure wider citizen participation than was found in subgovernmental networks, which grew up around New Deal programs (McFarland, 1976). What the public lobbyists were intent on doing was penetrating these subgovernments to establish their own organizational presence in the policy process as a counterweight to business and entrenched bureaucrats. Richard Ayers of the NRDC explained the logic of this institutional approach:

> The motivating and animating idea of the NRDC was the realization that in the twentieth century, and especially since the New Deal, the executive branch is the most powerful of the three [branches], and the interests of the public get lost for lack of expertise and knowledge in the administrative process. In the past, environmental and other citizen groups won victories in the legislative branch only to lose in the executive branch. It is clear that the administrative process is where the action is. (personal interview, June 11, 1986)

Apparently Ayers and other public lobbyists, along with Theodore Lowi and New Left critics, found out that the "presidential government" of the

New Deal had shifted the locus of interest representation substantially from the Congress and elections to subgovernments and administrative processes. Unlike Lowi, though, their response was not to advocate the rule of law, but to promote participatory democracy. Paradoxically this meant extensive use of bureaucracy and the courts to advance democratic ends. In a sense, public lobbyists took dominance by the executive branch as a fait accompli and tried to infuse this centralized form of government with the ideal of participatory democracy. Thus, public lobbyists had one foot in the establishment and one foot outside of it; they participated in the enhancement of the administrative state, yet drew their political and spiritual sustenance from attacking it.

Public lobby organizations were created with the idea in mind of establishing a permanent presence for citizens in the regulatory process. In this sense, these organizations were, themselves, an important institutional innovation. In the late 1960s and early 1970s the United States witnessed a burgeoning of national public lobby organizations. According to Jeffrey Berry, of the eighty-three public interest groups at which he conducted interviews in the early 1970s, nearly half (47%) were formed between 1968 and 1972. The Nader group, Public Citizen, Common Cause, and Friends of the Earth are some of the more renowned organizations formed in this period. Just as important, though, traditional groups such as the Sierra Club, the Audubon Society, and Consumers Union adopted a more activist posture, lending their considerable prestige to the struggle for social regulation (Allaby, 1971).

In the parlance of the New Left, they served the function of "parallel institutions," organizations through which ordinary citizens could monitor and challenge the actions of regular (i.e., establishment) decisionmaking institutions. Public lobby organizations reflected the ideas of the New Left in other respects as well.

Not unlike SNCC and SDS, public lobby groups attempted to rely on a grass roots structure (Berry, 1977). Although only a small nucleus of activists actually participated regularly in subgovernmental politics, their clout was enhanced considerably by their success in building huge memberships through which they generated financial support. For example, between 1967 and 1977 the membership of the Sierra Club grew from approximately 55,000 to almost 180,000. Similarly, the Audubon Society increased its membership from about 54,000 to over 280,000 in that period (Sandbach, 1980). This membership was important for two reasons. First, it provided an independent financial base that public lobbyists felt was essential to the legitimacy of their claim to represent the citizenry. Explaining that a grass roots base was critical to public lobby activity, Joan Claybrook held that

> Funding is the key. As long as public interest groups maintain their virginity and get their money from the public they will remain democratic. The real danger is in accepting funding from business. Once you sell yourself you no longer can claim to represent the people. (personal interview, June 11, 1986)

Second, the large memberships gave public lobbyists a base from which to draw future activists and issues. As with New Left organizations, public lobby groups relied on grass roots membership to become active at the local level and to help press local or regional concerns at the federal level. They also sought to educate and involve local citizens who were not official members. This point was made by Daniel Becker:

> All congressmen support a cleaner environment in their public statements, but we [EA] have to be able to go into their districts and educate the people, tell them this congressman voted against the environment in this instance. And we have been very successful in this kind of activity. It's [EA] not just a bunch of left wing yahoos on the Hill, but we involve chambers of commerce and garden clubs. (personal interview, June 11, 1986)

Echoing the ideas of the New Left, he went on to argue that the "development of the grass roots" was one of the most significant achievements of the public interest movement. In fact, he characterized environmentalism and consumerism as "mass movements at their base," clearly implying that public lobbyists conceived of their activity as much more than interest representation. Public interest groups were a "necessary compromise" with the establishment to accomplish policy ends, but activists never renounced their suspicion of big government and big business or their commitment to grass roots democracy.

Similarly, Kathleen Sheekey was convinced that the success of Common Cause was also linked to "grass roots activism" (personal interview, July 22, 1986). In fact, Common Cause reserves one-third of the seats on its board of directors for grass roots members. In addition, each state chairman attends two board meetings per year, and there is an annual state leadership conference. Moreover, the national organization not only seeks to educate citizens about particular issues, but also seeks to respond to local concerns. As Sheekey explained, Common Cause's recent involvement in the nuclear freeze movement was a radical departure from its traditional concerns such as freedom of information and campaign finances. However, this issue percolated up from the grass roots. Like environmental and consumer lobbies involved in the freeze movement, Common Cause supported protests and marches—in other words, direct action on a specific issue.

Public lobby groups also reflected the New Left concept of participatory democracy in that they attempted to be as "antibureaucratic" as possible. Organizationally, public lobby groups were designed to promote the individual by imbuing him or her with a sense of worth and political efficacy. It is too easy to dismiss this aspect of public lobby activity and to view them, as some critics do, as just another interest in the hurly-burly of pluralist politics. Even if they have not achieved the ideals of citizen participation—even if the exigencies of subgovernmental politics led Washington activists to play a stronger leadership role than *The Port Huron Statement* envisioned—they did take seriously the notion that bureaucratic organization undermined human dignity and creativity. Describing Public Citizen, Joan Claybrook noted that it was structured on Ralph Nader's "theory of organizations." By this she meant that the objective was to keep them small and not to let them outlive their usefulness. Nader kept shifting and changing organizations, as new issues developed. From the standpoint of "national" organization this seems ill-advised; ordinarily organizations seek a structure with which to deal with a variety of issues, but the Nader strategy was to shift structures in response to issues. The deeper motive behind this seeming confusion was to avoid "the deadening effects of bureaucratization" (personal interview, June 11, 1986). This highly pragmatic view of institutional structure resonates with the New Left ideal of participatory democracy.

While the public lobby organizations, themselves, constituted new regulatory institutions, reformers also sought to change the other institutions that traditionally constituted regulatory subgovernments. As Douglas Costle, EPA administrator under Jimmy Carter, noted, "Public interest lobbyists were more interested in the process of regulation than the substance (personal interview, April 8, 1985). This shift in attention from substance to process reflected an understanding that the business of modern American politics had as much to do with administration as with legislation. As Bruce Ackerman and William Hassler point out in their excellent study of air pollution policy,

> [Environmental] Statutes passed in the 1970's did more than commit billions of dollars to the cause of environmental protection. . . . They also

> represent part of a complex effort by which *the present generation is revising the system of administrative law inherited from the New Deal*. (1981: 5, emphasis added)

The intent of social regulatory laws to change the administrative process along with the substance of regulatory policy is reminiscent of the New Left's dual objectives of redressing grievances and altering decision structures (Fruchter and Kramer, 1966). Specifically, public lobbyists sought to create institutional means by which they ensure their participation in the implementation as well as the enactment of regulatory policy. The idea behind these efforts, as Joan Claybrook related, was to make the regulatory politics into a truly adversarial process:

> Public interest groups have opened up decisionmaking. They acquired expertise; learned the technical material and subject matter. . . . *I analogize the situation with a courtroom: you can't have a trial with an advocate on just one side,* and that is what decisionmaking was like before the *institutionalization of public interests groups*. They are a counterforce to the self-interest of just industrial giants. (personal interview, June 11, 1986, emphasis added)

This adversarial approach to regulation was rooted in a mistrust of the establishment that was voiced originally by the New Left.

The means of institutionalizing the participation of public lobbys were intended to make the regulatory process more and more like a courtroom. Alan Morrison, Public Citizen's director of litigation, pointed out, for example, that neutral principles governing discovery, evidence, and public notice were an important basis of the "new regulatory framework" established in the 1970s (June 12, 1986). By creating a highly formal decision process analogous to a regular court of law, public lobbyists hoped to gain access to subgovernmental politics, which had evolved into a set of informal relations among business interests, legislators, and bureaucrats.

A number of measures put in place by the new social regulation were designed to carve out such a permanent niche for public lobby organizations. One of the most important of these measures was the establishment of citizen lawsuits. In particular, a number of regulatory statutes of the 1970s granted automatic standing to "interested parties" in civil suits. In some instances, interested parties also could initiate regulatory enforcement actions (Galloway and Fitzgerald, 1981; Harris, 1985). Based on case law, "interested parties" was constructed to include citizens with other than direct economic interests. Environmentalists successfully claimed an "aesthetic" interest in natural scenery subject to economic development plans (*Sierra Club* v. *Morton,* 405 U.S. 727, 1972). The use of class action suits also afforded public lobbyists a means of taking advantage of the citizen suit provisions of the new laws. These measures guaranteed public lobbyists a role in implementation and, more important, a tool for monitoring enforcement of the new social regulation.

Morrison noted: "An important effect of the new regulation is that agencies think twice before acting; they consider the possibility that they may be sued" (personal interview, June 12, 1986). Richard Ayers, Senior attorney for the Natural Resources Defense Council, elaborated on that interpretation:

> Writing the Air and Water Acts really broke new ground in providing for suits against polluters and the EPA. These laws also broke new ground in providing for fee awards to public interest lawyers. . . . In fact, the NRDC could even receive fees if it didn't prevail. This was crucial because it enabled environmentalists to challenge corporate polluters directly or through suits against the EPA even though their resources were no match for the legions of lawyers industry could throw into a contest. This kind of public participation strengthened the enforcement machinery. (personal interview, July 22, 1986)

The ability to sue the EPA or other regulatory agencies on issues of enforcement was an especially important innovation, because it allowed public lobby groups to pursue enforcement against a great number of firms or industries without having to commit resources to suing them individually.

An institutional development related to citizen suits was the creation of public permitting procedures whereby public lobby groups could play a direct role in overseeing implementation. This was particularly important in environmental regulation as Ayers noted:

> The permitting process was also an important institutional change. Opening it up to the public denied polluters a key means of weakening the laws' impact. The agencies had to commit to paper, and the record could be the basis of enforcement suits. . . . Congress and the bureaucrats probably didn't envision the litigation that followed. (personal interview, July 22, 1986)

Public permitting, then, was a double-barreled weapon. In the first instance, public lobbyists could play a role in making business decisions that directly affected ordinary citizens; this addressed *The Port Huron Statement*'s goal of involving the people in quality-of-life decisions and fit Claybrook's characterization of the new regulation as "socializing" business decisions. However, if public lobbyists felt there was a lack of compliance, the records of the permitting process provided a paper trail that could be followed into court under citizen suit provisions.

Thus, the courts became a key ally of the public lobbyist, because they were instrumental in prying open subgovernments, and subsequently in overseeing implementation. Dan Becker of EA bluntly stated that

> We [environmentalists] have been using the legislative process and the courts to establish structures, to get timetables for bureaucratic action which can serve as the basis for future litigation, to get right-to-know principles, all aimed at affecting administration. (personal interview, June 11, 1986)

This direct and regular participation in administration was an essentially new role for the federal courts. In this sense they too must be considered new institutions under the public lobby regime, although it is somewhat ironic that participatory democracy should be pursued through ostensibly the least democratic of the three branches of government. While the Constitution never absolutely separated the administration from adjudication, the active involvement of the courts in implementation has blurred the distinctions between executive and judicial functions more than the founders ever intended.

Finally, the public lobby regime changed regulatory institutions by opening up administrative rulemakings. Perhaps the most controversial measure adopted was the so-called intervenor funding program at the FTC. Under this initiative, the federal government subsidized public lobby participation in agency proceedings, thereby helping to promote a regular voice for consumers in administrative affairs. In a de facto way, though, the acquired expertise and extensive participation of public lobbyists in other arenas of regulatory politics assured their inclusion in rulemaking proceedings. Even under the Reagan administration, most agencies at least maintained the pretense of consulting with public lobbyists.

While the rise of public lobby groups and the restructuring of subgovernmental decision processes were critically important to realizing the new regulatory ideas, the most easily identified new institutions were the federal agencies created in the late 1960s and early 1970s. These bureaucratic organizations were established to administer the programs of the new social regulation (see Table 3.1). It is equally important to bear in mind, however, that older federal agencies and cabinet departments often were redirected and infused with the new regulatory ideas. An outstanding example of this redirection is the Department of Interior (DOI).

Historically, the DOI had perceived its primary mission as assisting in the discovery and exploitation of the natural resources of the United States. Its various divisions, such as the Geological Survey and Bureau of Mines, had faithfully executed this mission into the 1960s. However, with Secretary Stewart Udall's strong assertion in 1964 of the department's responsibility to ensure environmentally sound mining practices, the DOI began a slow but steady shift toward an environmentalist perspective. The transformation was completed in 1977 when public lobbyists argued that the Office of Surface Mining (OSM), the agency created to implement the national surface mining law, should be placed within the DOI, because they felt the EPA was "too soft" on some key strip mining issues (Harris, 1985). As we shall see, a similar metamorphosis took place at the FTC during the 1970s.

In conclusion, although the new social regulation brought with it a number of different institutional changes, they are tied together by a common bond: the ideas that public lobby organizations brought to the policy process. These ideas incorporated the fundamentals of the New Left critique: a devotion to the individual over organization; a deep suspicion of the establishment, especially big business; a commitment to participatory democracy; and a bias for direct action and single-issue politics. To a great extent these ideas were brought to fruition. After more than a decade of experience with the new social regulation, in both the public and private sectors, William Ruckleshaus described contemporary regulatory politics in words that testified to the legacy of the New Left:

> Today the debate on public participation is over. The new regulatory process reflects the public take-back of delegated power following Vietnam . . . this led to the War Powers Act. . . . On the domestic side there was a similar phenomenon reflecting a lack of faith and trust in the executive branch. This lack of faith and trust was also fueled by the disjunction between promise and performance in the Great Society. . . . There must be guarantees for citizen participation. The question is how to make it work? (personal interview, June 5, 1985)

The institutional changes brought on by the new social regulation have enabled public lobbyists to speak for the public interest, at least their version of it, in subgovernmental forums that had previously been closed to such views. In this sense, the 1970s reflected the New Left revolt against traditional (i.e., New Deal) political ideas and institutions.

Yet, the civic-balance theory's continued focus on federal programs as a means of redressing grievances ultimately frustrated the New Left vision. There was a certain irony in, as Joan Claybrook put it, "institutionalizing" participatory democracy; to a radical of the 1960s this might even seem a contradiction in terms. Nevertheless, the regulatory institutions of the the public lobby regime are different. New Left ideas were, to some extent, translated into institutional reality. There is no question that public lobbyists enjoyed considerable success in changing the regulatory process in the 1970s.

New Policies

The final element in the concept of a regulatory regime—new policies— is no less evident in the new social regulation than new ideas and new institutions. The scholarly attention to the new social regulation is itself testimony to the important new policies that emerged in the 1970s. Table 3.2 provides a list of the most significant social regulatory programs enacted under the public lobby regime. Impressive as it is, this inventory of new social regulation only begins to tell the story of how the public lobby regime reshaped public policy. Each of these new laws brought about an expansion of rules and regulations through which federal agencies specified performance and compliance standards for American business. A crude measure of this fantastic increase in regulations is the growth of the *Federal Register* from approximately 60,000 pages in 1969 to over 70,000 by 1977.

Naturally some agencies had more pronounced impacts than others, and not all new regulations of that period pertained to social regulation. However, the bulk of the increase is attributable to the activities and demands of public lobbyists. They succeeded in remaking the relationship of government to business. As one staff attorney at the FTC put it, "There has been a sea of change in the marketplace. The Commission [FTC] forced business to clean up its act in the 1970's" (personal interview, July 23, 1986).

The impact of these efforts is indicated not only by the enactment of new laws and the writing of new regulations, but also by the societal costs and benefits they have generated. It is particularly important to be mindful of the benefits, however hard they may be to analyze, because it is easy to be seduced into focusing on the more easily quantifiable costs. The effect of the new social regulation is revealed in both costs and benefits.

One estimate developed by Murray Weidenbaum and Robert DeFina

TABLE 3.2.   Major Social Regulatory Measures
Enacted Between 1969 and 1977

Law	Year
Mine Safety and Health Act	1969
National Environmental Policy Act	1969
Poison Prevention Packaging Act	1970
Clean Air Act Amendments	1970
Cigarette Advertising Act	1970
Railroad Safety Act	1970
Tire Safety Act	1970
Water Quality Improvement Act	1970
Occupational Safety and Health Act	1970
Consumer Product Safety Act	1972
Bumper Standards Act	1972
Ocean Dumping Act	1972
Pesticide Regulation Act	1972
Federal Water Pollution Control Act	1972
Noise Pollution and Control Act	1972
Safe Drinking Water Act	1973
Hazardous Materials Transportation Act	1974
Clean Air Amendments Act	1974
Federal Trade Commission Authorization	1974
Safe Drinking Water Act	1974
Seat Belt and School Bus Standards	1974
Magnuson–Moss Warranty Improvement Act	1974
Energy Policy and Conservation Act	1974
Coal Leasing Amendments Act	1974
Hart–Scott–Rodino Anti-Trust Amendments	1976
Federal Rail Safety Act	1976
Toxic Substances Control Act	1976
School Bus Safety Act	1976
Medical Devices Safety Act	1976
Department of Energy Organization Act	1977
Clean Water Act Extension	1977
Clean Air Act Amendments	1977
Safe Drinking Water Extension Act	1977
Surface Mining Control and Reclamation Act	1977
Saccharin Study and Labeling Act	1977

pegged the annual cost of social regulation at $19.48 billion by 1976
(1978): These cost estimates have been severely criticized by other observers of regulatory affairs. In particular, Litan and Nordhaus point out
that blending energy and environmental matters into a single category can
seriously distort the impact of social regulation since energy policy in

TABLE 3.3.   Annual Cost of Social Regulation for 1976 (millions of dollars)

Area	Administration	Compliance	Total
Consumer affairs	$1,516	$5,094	$6,610
Worker safety	483	4,015	4,498
Energy–environment	+ 612	+ 7,760	+ 8,372
TOTAL	$2,611	$16,869	$19,480

Source: Weidenbaum and DeFina, 1976.

the seventies was tied in with price controls. Thus, the costs derived by Weidenbaum and DeFina are probably magnified. In addition, the Weidenbaum and Defina estimates may well exaggerate the costs by employing a methodology of linear extrapolation with respect to paper work burdens. They took measures of paper work costs in the early 1970's when firms were just getting accustomed to the new regulations and projected the costs from these early years to arrive at their estimates (Litan and Nordhaus, 1982). Despite these important qualifications, it seems certain that the new social regulation had a tremendous effect on business, especially at the level of the individual firm. Although the combination of energy and environment into a single category may exaggerate social regulatory costs to some extent, because some energy programs were related to price control regulation, the Weidenbaum–DeFina data do give an idea of the profound impact of the public lobby regime. Even students of regulation, who have severely criticized their data, readily admit that compliance costs alone make the new social regulation a significant factor in business behavior (Eads and Fix, 1984).

In a more refined attempt to evaluate regulatory cost at the microeconomic level, the Business Roundtable commissioned a study by the public accounting firm, Arthur Anderson. This analysis focused on forty-eight major corporations, and tried to estimate the "incremental costs" imposed on these firms by specific social regulatory programs. Incremental costs are the difference between what a firm would have spent on environmental, consumer, and safety problems in the absence of federal programs, and the actual expenditures under the programs studied. Thus, the estimate is biased downward by using incremental as opposed to gross costs. Table 3.4 summarizes the findings of the Business Roundtable study. From a firm-level perspective as well as a microeconimic perspective, then, the new social regulation has had a tremendous policy impact.

As for the benefits of the new social regulation (while they are more difficult to measure), it seems clear that they too have been significant.

TABLE 3.4. Incremental Compliance Costs for Three
Social Regulatory Agencies (millions of dollars)

Agency	Incremental Costs
EPA	$2,018
OSHA	217
FTC (Consumer Regulation Only)	+ 26
TOTAL	$2,261

Source: Business Roundtable, 1979.

The findings of a 1982 Massachusetts Institute of Technology (MIT) study on regulation showed, for example, that air pollution laws had benefited Americans at the rate of between $5 billion and $58 billion per year, OSHA regulations saved as much as $15 billion annually in work-related accident expenditures, and Consumer Product Safety Commission standards on infant cribs reduced serious crib-related injuries by 44 percent. Considering both the costs and benefits of the new social regulation, one is left with the inescapable conclusion that its overall policy impact has been significant. Moreover, these effects are part of a coherent effort to change the process as well as the substance of regulatory policy; they help to define the public lobby regime.

Conclusion

The new social regulation embodied new regulatory ideas, restructured existing regulatory institutions, and put in place an impressive array of new policies that have had a tremendous impact. Taken together these new ideas, institutions, and policies define a new regulatory regime. Yet, while the public lobby regime does not represent a faithful continuation of the New Deal, neither does it reflect an outright betrayal. The New Deal extended the central government's obligation to provide for the general welfare of society; it legitimized extensive federal regulation of the private sector. The public lobby regime also seeks to expand the regulatory role of government. However, the public lobby regime departs from the New Deal in being decidedly more critical of capitalism and traditional political decisionmaking. This more critical perspective underlies the emphasis placed on creating institutional mechanisms for participatory democracy in the 1970s.

Currently we are still in the process of answering William Ruckleshaus's query: How can we make citizen participation work in American politics? The difficulty in devising an adequate response derives from the idea of participatory democracy as being rooted in the ideals and suspicions of the New Left and as being practiced in an institutional environment established during the New Deal. The dilemma for public lobbyists is to remain true to their belief in citizen action, from which their political influence grew, while tackling problems of social regulation that, in a modern society, appear amenable only to national responses; they must operate effectively in the Washington establishment, while not becoming a real member of it. Thus the public lobby regime was born of an uneasy marriage between the New Deal and the New Left.

This ambivalent situation accounts for public lobbyists' penchant for detailed regulation and due-process provisions. Not unlike a partner in a "modern" marriage who works out contractually the responsibilities of the other partner in advance, public lobbyists seek to specify with great care the responsibilities of the governing institutions to which they are wedding themselves: in both instances the relationship is based on a minimum of trust. Also, like the hypothetical spouse, public lobbyists clearly retain their right to "divorce" if, in their opinion, members of the Washington establishment violate the terms of the contract by not vigorously enforcing regulations or by being lax in assuring administrative due process. Finally, like the modern marriage, courts play a key role in negotiating and overseeing agreements. It could hardly be otherwise in such an uneasy marriage.

If the administration of Ronald Reagan wanted to bring about another major regulatory shift, it had to address the ideas and institutions as well as the policies of the new social regulation. Moreover, it had to deal with the aspects of the New Deal that have persisted. The Reagan deregulators had to confront a half century of political economic tradition. They had to persuade the American people that regulatory relief was an idea whose time had come. Perhaps more important, though, they had to cope with the inertia inherent in subgovernmental politics.

In the following chapter, we shall examine the broad program conceived by the Reagan administration to change the character of federal regulation. We shall then examine how deregulators fared in their efforts to transform two of the most important social regulatory agencies, the FTC and the EPA.

4

The Regulatory Program of the Reagan Administration

> The only public men in democracies who favor decentralization are, almost invariably, either very disinterested or extremely mediocre; the former are scarce and the latter powerless.
>
> ALEXIS DE TOCQUEVILLE, *Democracy in America*

The policy program initiated by the Reagan administration raised regulatory relief to a status unprecedented in our recent political history. The New Deal rooted the modern administrative state in American politics, setting the foundation for nearly five decades of growth in government regulations. As we noted in Chapter 3, with the rise of the public lobby regime there was a dramatic increase in regulatory activity during the 1970s. To be sure, regulatory reform became an important issue during the latter part of the 1970s, and significant *economic* deregulation occurred during the Carter presidency. Yet, not until the election of Ronald Reagan was there a concerted and far-reaching commitment to reduce government intervention in the American economy. As noted in earlier chapters also, a signal feature of this effort to reduce government intervention was the sharp focus on *social* regulation.

This program of regulatory relief, so dramatic in the context of recent history, was undertaken in what seemed to be a favorable environment for a major shift in regulatory politics. The governing philosophies of the New Deal and public lobby periods were challenged by the advent of a renewed celebration of the marketplace among intellectuals, think tanks in Washington, and elected representatives. Moreover, recurring economic problems were associated with the burdens of the regulatory state. In December 1980, two of the president's closest allies—David Stockman, who was selected to direct the Office of Management and Budget (OMB), and Jack Kemp (R-New York)—urged on him an emergency program intended to head off what they described in a lengthy memo as an "economic Dunkirk," threatening to overwhelm the new administration. Coming to terms with this crisis required, in addition to tax cuts and firm long-term fiscal discipline, an immediate and far-reaching program of regulatory relief.

The 1970s, Stockman and Kemp argued, had created a "ticking regulatory bomb," which they warned would result, without corrective action, in a "quantum scale-up" of regulatory burden during the next eighteen to forty months. The grave tones of this memo reveal that regulatory relief was viewed not merely as an exercise in sound economic policy, but as a critical battle in a war against ideologues and policies deemed to be hostile to the vitality of a free-enterprise system:

> [T]he basic dynamic is this: during the early and mid-1970s, Congress approved more than a dozen sweeping environmental, energy, and safety enabling authorities, which for all practical purposes are devoid of policy standards and criteria for cost–benefit, cost-effectiveness, and comparative risk analysis. Subsequently, McGovernite no-growth activists assumed control of most of the relevant Cabinet policy posts during the Carter Administration. They have spent the past four years "tooling up" for implementation through a mind-boggling outpouring of rule-makings, interpretative guidelines, and major litigation—all heavily biased toward maximization of regulatory scope and burden. Thus, this decade-long process of regulatory evolution is just now reaching the state at which it will sweep through the industrial economy with near gale force, preempting multi-billions in investment capital, driving up operating costs, and siphoning off management and technical personnel in an incredible morass of new controls and compliance procedures. (printed in Greider, 1982: 146)

Lest business become mired in such an intrusive set of policies, which would cripple the American economy, the memo called for a program of regulatory "ventilation," beginning with a "well-planned and orchestrated series of unilateral administrative actions to defer, revise, or rescind existing and pending regulations where clear legal authority existed," as well as a one-year moratorium on new rulemaking by the government (Greider, 1982: 156–58).

Thus, the stage was set during the early days of the administration for a dramatic assault on the regulatory status quo. In his first State of the Union message the president identified the need to reduce regulation as one of the central ingredients for the restoration of economic growth:

> American society experienced a virtual explosion in governmental regulation during the past decade. . . . The result has been higher prices, higher

unemployment, and lower productivity growth. Overregulation causes small and independent business men and women, as well as large businesses, to defer or terminate plans for expansion. And since they're responsible for most of the new jobs, those new jobs are not created.

Now, we have no intention of dismantling the regulatory agencies, especially those necessary to protect environment and ensure public health and safety. However, we must come to grips with inefficient and burdensome regulations, eliminate those we can and reform the others. (*Public Papers of the Presidents,* Feb. 18, 1981: 113)

Measures were then quickly taken on several fronts to put a program of regulatory relief into effect. These measures included strengthening the authority of the OMB to screen regulations promulgated by the regular bureaucracy, carefully selecting personnel who would support the administration's program to staff agency and department positions, devolving regulatory authority to the states, and initiating legislative reform to constrain regulatory programs. In effect, the administration pursued regulatory relief by executive administration and legislative initiatives.

For several reasons, the greatest emphasis was placed on administrative efforts, leaving the Reagan presidency with no major legislative achievements. This suggests an ambiguous legacy of Reagan's regulatory program. In the short term, notable achievements were made in reducing government intervention in the economy. Yet the failure to obtain significant legislative changes makes the future of such achievements uncertain, particularly because the Reagan regulatory program further enhanced presidential authority over social regulation. It may be, as Eads and Fix suggest, that "ironically, this will leave future presidents better equipped to reconstruct the regulatory edifice Ronald Reagan promised to dismantle" (Eads and Fix, 1985: 294).

Nevertheless, in some respects the actions by the Reagan administration can be viewed as a logical extension of long-standing developments in the political system. Since the New Deal, presidents have increasingly employed the administrative tools available to them in the pursuit of their policy goals. The long-standing development of what Richard Nathan calls the "administrative presidency" marked the Reagan domestic program as the most recent expression of this historical process (Nathan, 1983; Moe, 1985; Milkis, 1987a). Yet, the consequences of this development—the politicization and centralization of the executive department— reached a new stage of development during the Reagan years, due to the ideological character of the Reagan presidency and the unprecedented assault that ideology inspired against prevailing domestic programs. The regulatory program of President Reagan illustrates especially well how his domestic initiatives entailed both a continuation of and departure from prevailing public policy. It is the purpose of this chapter to review the Reagan regulatory program in general terms, and to provide an explanation for why this program developed as it did.

Deregulation by Executive Administration

Executive Oversight of Regulatory Policy

The most significant part of the Reagan administration's program of deregulation was the series of steps to consolidate regulatory decisionmaking in the White House. A month after taking office Reagan signed Executive Order (EO) 12291, which required agencies to examine the costs and benefits of all proposed major rules and to pick the least costly alternative. Major rules were defined as those that would cost industries $100 million or more to comply. The order authorized the OMB to ensure that agencies followed these procedures.

At the same time that EO 12291 was issued, Reagan appointed the Presidential Task Force on Regulatory Relief, headed by Vice-President Bush, to apply cost–benefit analysis to existing rules. This review included a consideration of the so-called midnight regulations of the Carter administration, on which the President imposed a sixty-day freeze on January 29, 1981 (*Public Papers of the Presidents*, 1981: 56). Before disbanding in August 1983, the task force issued a report that claimed "these reviews [would] save the consumer, businessman, universities, and state and county officials some $150 billion over the next ten years" (Presidential Task Force on Regulatory Relief, 1983: 5).

Such claims were vigorously disputed by opponents of the administration's regulatory program. Representative John Dingell (D-Michigan), chairman of the House Energy and Commerce Committee, for example, attacked the executive orders, arguing such administrative procedures circumvent the regular mechanisms of the Constitution and "ignore the benefits lost by the protection to the American people's health and safety those regulations would have provided" (*Congressional Quarterly Weekly Report*, Aug. 10, 1985: 1603).

The concerns of Dingell and other critics of the administration's program were further aggravated by additional oversight measures taken in January 1985. In order to establish a closer review of regulation, Reagan issued EO 12498, which required agencies to give their agenda for the year to the OMB. It also mandated that they indicate how the proposed policies, goals, and objectives were consistent with the administration's regulatory principles. This mechanism, which resulted in an annual report outlining the regulatory program of the administration, was compared by Vice-President Bush to the budget process in which agency requests go to the OMB for review (*Congressional Quarterly Weekly Report*, Aug. 10, 1985: 1603).

Critics, however, said there were important differences, most significantly the lack of review by Congress as a final step in the regulatory process. Whereas Congress was responsible for final action on the president's budgetary program, EO 12498 established the OMB as the final arbiter of the regulatory process. This executive agency, specifically the Office of Information and Regulatory Affairs (OIRA) within the OMB, reviewed regulatory plans to determine if they met the administration's objectives and guidelines. Even though agencies could appeal an OMB decision to the president, the final version of the regulatory program was determined within the White House, undermining, critics claimed, the regulatory authority delegated to executive agencies by congressional statutes (*Congressional Quarterly Weekly Report*, Aug. 10, 1985: 1602–3).

Responding to the criticisms lodged against its executive oversight program, the Reagan administration claimed that such efforts at controlling the bureaucracy were deeply rooted in constitutional principles and historical developments (Presidential Task Force on Regulatory Relief, 1983: 3; Miller, 1986). To be sure, the concern with presidential control over the bureaucracy has long been a focus of regulatory experts in both political parties. We have noted that efforts to extend presidential influence over the executive department can be traced back to the report of the Brownlow Committee of 1937. The 1930s marked the advent of administrative politics as a focal point of government activity; consequently, thereafter, the pursuit of control over the bureaucracy and regulatory activities was not simply an "intramural" squabble between the White House and the bureaucratic agencies that are nominally under its jurisdiction, but directly related to control over the direction and character of American public life (Rourke, 1984). Moreover, presidents, as chiefs of state, have viewed such control as central to their constitutional responsibilities, as well as their personal and programmatic ambitions.

The rise of the new social regulation greatly accentuated the concern of presidents to exercise influnce over "their domain." The previous chapter indicates how laws and administrative mechanisms were put in place as part of the public lobby regime that challenged the New Deal pattern of regulatory politics. The regulatory channels developed during the

1970s established a loose coalition of bureaucratic agencies, congressional subcommittees and staffs, courts, and public advocacy groups that considerably eroded the discretion of presidents and executive officers to shape public policy. These channels posed a direct threat to presidential governance. Moreover, the explosion of regulation and the recasting of administrative institutions coincided with, and to a degree contributed to, increasing public doubt about the expansion of government. Since the early 1970s, therefore, presidents have been compelled to undertake the difficult task of controlling the expanding and increasingly disparate activities of the bureaucracy.

Beginning in the 1970s administrations have, accordingly, instituted increasingly formal review requirements (OMB, 1986, XI). Nixon established in the executive office of the president a "quality-of-life" review of regulations pertaining to environmental controls, consumer protection, and occupational and public health and safety. For certain categories of regulation, agencies were instructed to provide the OMB a summary description indicating the principal objectives of programs, as well as evidence that some consideration was given to the costs of, and alternatives to, the proposed actions. The Ford administration, in turn, required agencies to prepare, and the OMB to review, "inflation impact statements" for major agency rules. This process was mandated by EO 11821, issued on November 27, 1974, which initiated for the first time a cost–benefit policy evaluation program. In implementing cost–benefit analysis, Ford's advisors emphasized a policy of reduced regulation of the workplace and environment, reflecting the administration's position that social regulations, rather than those bearing directly on the impact of supply, were the most damaging to the economy (Fuchs and Anderson, 1984). Carter continued this emphasis on systematically comparing the costs and benefits of regulatory programs, requiring detailed analysis of regulatory actions and review by the executive office of the president. As noted in Chapter 1, in early 1978, he established the Regulatory Analysis and Review Group (RARG) to manage the policy evaluation process mandated by EO 12044. As was the case with the Nixon and Ford administrations, the focus of executive oversight centered on social regulations, especially those issued by the EPA and the OSHA. Thus, during the 1970s, presidents established elaborate administrative mechanisms to control the expansion of government interference in the marketplace, with special emphasis on reducing the heavy costs generated by health, safety, consumer protection, and environmental regulations.

These precedents notwithstanding, as we have suggested, the Reagan administration's regulatory oversight program represented a marked departure from past policy. This program's commitment to centralize review processes and to clamp down on the expansion of regulatory authority far surpassed that of previous administrations. Whereas previous attempts to review regulations distributed authority among several executive branch offices and departments, such as the Council of Wage and Price Stability and the RARG, the Reagan program has been carried out exclusively within the Office of Information and Regulatory Affairs (OIRA) of the OMB. Moreover, for the first time cost–benefit analysis was made mandatory, except where prohibited by law, thus ensuring that the Reagan administration's review program would have a much greater impact than that of previous administrations on the regulatory activities of line departments and agencies. In the Ford and Carter administrations, in fact, compliance with OMB decisions was voluntary; therefore, the task of performing cost–benefit analysis remained "little more than a presidential recommendation" (Fuchs and Anderson, 1984).

The distinction between the Carter and Reagan regulatory review programs was especially significant. While Carter was considered a moderate Democrat in terms of his commitment to traditional social welfare programs, he was far less equivocal in his support of social regulation. The lament in the "economic Dunkirk" memo about the regulatory power of "McGovernite no-growth activists" alluded to the Carter administration's appointment of over sixty public lobbyists to executive posts, many posts involving considerable influence on the shaping of public policy (Cameron, 1977). Carter's appointees included Michael Pertschuk, an ardent consumer advocate, who became chairman of the FTC; Joan Claybrook, from the public interest group, Congress Watch, who was named to direct the National Highway, Safety and Transportation Administration; and Eula Bingham, an advocate of strict health and safety regulations, who was selected to direct the Occupational Safety, and Health Administration (OSHA). Because of his strong support for social regulation, Carter's review program was patterned after the permeable administrative channels that emerged with the rise of the public lobby regime. Not only did the RARG include ranking members from several agencies outside of the executive office of the president, such as the EPA, but EO 12044 also contained provisions designed to "maximize public participation in rule formulations" (Fuchs and Anderson, 1984). For example, Section 2C, entitled "Opportunity for Public Participation," read:

> Agencies shall give the public an early and meaningful opportunity to participate in the development of agency regulations. They shall consider a variety of ways to provide this opportunity, including (1) publishing an

> advance notice of proposed rule-making; (2) holding open conferences or public hearings; (3) sending notices of proposed regulations to publications likely to be read by those affected; and (4) notifying interested parties directly. (*Federal Register*, vol. 43, no. 58, March 24, 1978: 12662)

In order to ensure meaningful public participation in informal rulemaking, Carter's EO 12044 set a sixty-day minimum comment period in certain cases.

In contrast to the Carter program, the regulatory review mechanism established by the Reagan presidency subordinated open procedures and public participation to the political goal of reducing the role of government. As such, it represented a severe challenge to the principles of the public lobby regime in which regulatory reform was viewed largely as a matter of process. The oversight programs of the Nixon, Ford, and Carter presidencies were used primarily as a check on the quality of decisionmaking and the consistency of regulations with macroeconomic objectives (Rosenberg, 1986). The Reagan regulatory review program, on the other hand, was focused on transforming the principles of governance, which gave rise to the new social regulation. The final report of the Task Force on Regulatory Relief insisted that the president's executive order was not intended to establish "abstract accounting standards for regulations"; rather, the principles of these procedures were based on a commitment to private economic solutions. The primary inquiry engaged in by OMB was, accordingly, "whether government regulation was needed" (Presidential Task Force on Regulatory Relief, 1983: 14–15). The commitment to regulatory relief was emphasized by the authority given to the OMB to waive the cost–benefit requirement when deregulatory rules were proposed (Fuchs, 1988: 92).

Thus, whereas the regulatory program set up by the Carter administration established elaborate procedures for public participation and open deliberations, Reagan's executive orders have been applied to concentrate authority within the OMB, making the conservative regulatory staff within that agency virtually the only point of access for parties seeking to influence the formulation of a proposed rule (Fuchs and Anderson, 1984). Moreover, the procedure established for screening regulations was not part of the public record, shifting the process away from the courts, and facilitating "ex parte contacts" with businesses seeking a reduction in government intervention in the economy (*National Journal*, Jan. 16, 1982: 93).

The highly centralized and "secretive" nature of the executive order system led to the most persistently and urgently voiced concerns about the Reagan regulatory review program (Rosenberg, 1986: 229). Critics of the administration claimed that in its zealous commitment to reducing the burden of regulation on industry, the OMB was giving business lobbyists an exclusive, off-the-public-record opportunity to reargue issues they lost at the agency level (*National Journal*, June 14, 1986: 1339). It was discovered, for example, that James Miller, the first OIRA director, conducted a number of private sessions with trade groups, corporate leaders, and industry lobbyists. In April 1981, Miller gave the House Oversight and Investigations Committee a list of thirty-six meetings that OMB officials had with business and consumer groups. Of the thirty-six meetings, all but four were with major industry lobby groups, from the Chamber of Commerce of the United States to the Garbage Compactor Manufacturers Association, which wanted to discuss noise standards. Of greatest concern to members of Congress was that some of these private meetings were followed by administration decisions to delay or review rules affecting groups that met with Miller. For example, soon after Miller met with the representatives of the American Mining Congress, a rule of the Department of the Interior on the extraction of coal was postponed indefinitely (*National Journal*, Jan. 16, 1982: 93). Direct industry lobbying in the OMB was also documented by the *Washington Post* in its report on the efforts of Miller's successor at the OIRA, Christopher DeMuth, to obstruct the issuance of OSHA grain dust regulations. Even though the Supreme Court upheld the issuance of such standards in 1981, DeMuth successfully persisted through 1983 in holding up the OSHA action in this matter (*Washington Post*, Nov. 11, 1983, A15; Newland, 1985: 162).

These instances of business influence, it was claimed, undermined the integrity of the governmental decisionmaking process, as well as the court's ability to engage in effective judicial review. Noting that there had been few court cases directly challenging instances of OMB interference, a 1986 report prepared for the Senate Committee on Governmental Affairs made the point that "one reason for the paucity of litigation is the inability of potential plaintiffs to gain access to the information they need to bring a successful suit, an ironic Catch 22" (Rosenberg, 1986: 232).

The centralization of oversight responsibility in the OMB not only ran counter to the movement during the 1970s to provide full and meaningful public participation in agency regulatory decisionmaking, but also impinged on administrative procedures designed to strengthen the hands of those who advocated programmatic objectives. The use of cost–benefit analysis as a principal tool of public policy shifted the burden of proof to program advocates, because the "benefits" of government intervention were more difficult to calculate concretely than the "costs." In fact, the House Energy and Commerce Subcommittee on Oversight and Investigations Hearings of early 1981 disclosed that the regulatory analysis worksheets of the OMB (the forms used to review new rules) contained no space to list the benefits of those rules. There were two spaces for costs, however—one for government and one for the private sector (*National Journal*, Nov. 16, 1982: 98). Because many environmental, health, and safety laws either prohibited or deemphasized the calculation of costs, critics of Reagan's OMB claimed it had "usurped statutorily assigned policy functions of agencies" so as to enforce the Reagan agenda (Newland, 1985: 163; also see Morrison, 1986: 1063).

Clearly, then, the consolidation of regulatory authority in the White House, though ostensibly an extension of the prior system of presidential control over agency rulemaking, departed dramatically from past regulatory practices. The subordination of participatory processes to the goal of relieving the economy from the burdens of federal regulation marked an especially sharp departure from the public lobby regime. These processes were considered by President Reagan and his conservative supporters as beneficial to a small number of program advocates who did not truly represent the public; moreover, supporters of regulatory relief believed that the influence of these advocates in administrative channels threatened, as Howard Phillips, executive director of the Conservative Caucus, put it, "to render irrelevant the election returns" of 1980 (*National Journal*, Aug. 1, 1981: 1374).

Yet the Reagan challenge to regulatory policy, emphasizing executive orders and OMB review mechanisms, was carried out for the most part on the level of administration. In effect, the procedures governing regulation were transformed from an institutional setup that favored program advocates to one that benefited those who were avowedly hostile to regulatory initiatives. We noted in Chapter 2 that the development of the public lobby regime emphasized procedural reforms that circumvented or replaced traditional channels of policymaking. In their endeavor to expand the programmatic responsibilities of the national government, advocates of social regulation supported reforms that simultaneously reduced the discretion of bureaucratic agencies and fixed the business of government more on administration. This merging of programmatic and administrative reform took place in response to an understanding that policy implementation was critical in determining the integrity of reforms. The expansion of public administration starting with the New Deal created a situation by the 1970s whereby the channels in which programs were actually put into effect were viewed as the heart of political action. And the emergence of the public lobby regime marked an era in which reform emphasized more open implementation procedures not only as a means to advance the goals of consumer and environmental activists, but also as legitimate ends in their own right. It was not surprising, therefore, that the Reagan administration sought to seize control of these procedures and put them in the hands of those who would seek a new direction in public policy. Nor was it surprising that such efforts would be viewed harshly by the administration's political opponents. The battle over what often seemed to be obscure procedural details veiled a struggle over fundamental principles of government. In this sense, the regulatory review process established by the Reagan administration was not simply a response to business influence, but also a principal element in a comprehensive philosophical challenge to the prevailing role of administrative agencies and public lobby groups in economic life.

The result of the OMB review process imposed by EO 12291 and EO 12498 was a significant decrease in the number of regulations issued, and, though to a lesser extent, a reversal of prior rules (OMB, 1985: 581–84; 1987: 627–36; Rosenberg, 1986: 210–13). Yet, it remained to be seen if the changes in executive oversight of regulatory activity carried out by Reagan would be permanent. The Presidential Task Force on Regulatory Relief argued that the reconstructed executive oversight mechanism had been so successful that it would in all likelihood become a "permanent" program, much like the federal budget review process adopted in the 1920s (Presidential Task Force on Regulatory Relief, 1983: 4). But, unlike the budgetary process, the newly established regulatory process was not made part of statutory law. Moreover, the regulatory channels set up by the Reagan White House raised serious legal and constitutional questions. Article II of the Constitution does establish the president as the locus of executive power, and since the 1930s there have been repeated efforts to enhance White House control over the bureaucracy. But these efforts have been limited by the long-standing commitment in the American political system that the ultimate power to define and direct the action of executive officers rests with the Congress (Rosenberg, 1986: 226). As Louis Fisher writes,

> Although it is sometimes thought otherwise, the Constitution does not direct the president to carry out the laws. Instead, he "shall take care that the Laws be faithfully executed." If a statute creates an independent officer and makes the officer's judgement final and conclusive, and the officer faithfully executes the assigned statutory duty, the President's responsibility is at an end. Of course Congress cannot vest in such officers duties that

would usurp the President's constitutional authority, such as the power to pardon or to nominate, but many executive duties can be delegated to officials who function beyond the president's control. (Fisher, 1986: 19)

Therefore, it has been argued that the president's constitutional obligation requires that he uphold the regulatory scheme enacted by Congress, a scheme that was reaffirmed over the Reagan administration's legislative efforts (Morrison, 1986: 1063). Yet, the regulatory power granted the OIRA, critics charged, circumvented, if it did not directly violate, procedures guaranteed by the Administrative Procedures Act (APA), as well as many enabling statutes. Alan Morrison, director of the Public Citizen litigation group in Washington, argued that the procedural obligations established in administrative statutes were rendered ineffective as a result of the authority of OMB to reject a regulation without giving any reason, leaving an agency head the job of devising an acceptable de facto reason for refusing to proceed with a regulation or for deleting a particularly offensive requirement. And, because this process often operated behind closed doors, Morrison asserted, "there is no way for the public, the Congress, or the courts to know precisely what OMB has done and what the real basis is for decisions issued under the nominal signature of the agency head" (Morrison, 1986: 1067–68).

Opponents of the OMB also noted that historically rulemaking in the federal government was an essentially decentralized, agency-oriented process. Prior to 1981, the vast bulk of administrative lawmaking authority was vested formally in agency heads, making unilateral presidential intervention in regulatory activity appear to be arbitrary and capricious. The APA, in fact, which deals with the manner in which regulatory rules are to be promulgated, focuses exclusively on *agency* rulemaking procedures and does not appear to contemplate a formal role for the president. Furthermore, the legislative history of the APA shows that Congress "rejected a proposal for a central oversight body to monitor and coordinate agency performance" (Rosenberg, 1986: 228). It may, indeed, be true that there are serious flaws with the statutory base of the regulatory status quo, as well as the constitutional interpretation that supports it, but it is inconceivable that the elaborate statutes and conventions that have given rise to administrative politics can be effectively challenged by executive fiat.

The aggressive use of White House oversight as a tool of regulatory relief, then, faced serious political and legal challenges that made its long-term impact very uncertain. For example, in *Environmental Defense Fund* (EDF) v. *Thomas,* the EDF filed suit over the delay by the OMB of an EPA regulation to control the underground storage of hazardous wastes. In January 1986, the district court ruled that the ability to delay or force changes in agency regulations by the OMB "is incompatible with the will of Congress and cannot be sustained as a valid exercise of the president's Article II powers" (Civil Action No. 85-1747, District Court of D.C., January 23, 1986, Slip Opinion: p. 9). This decision, which the administration did not appeal, was decided narrowly on the merits, but a broader judicial ruling was expected to come from another case, *Public Citizen Health Research Group* v. *Rowland,* which, came before the U.S. Court of Appeals for the District of Columbia in early 1986. In this case, which for the first time directly raised the question of the constitutionality of EO 12291, Public Citizen charged that the OMB forced the OSHA to delete from a final rule a controversial standard limiting workers' brief, high-level exposure to ethylene oxide, a sterilizing chemical widely used in hospitals (*Congressional Quarterly Weekly Report,* June 14, 1986: 1340). The OMB approved another standard in the final rule that set a limit on the cumulative exposures an employee may receive in one day, but argued the standard restricting short-term, high exposures was not adequately supported by health effects data and that the OSHA failed to qualify the risks that were to be addressed.

The decision of the OSHA to go along with the reservations of the OMB and drop the short-term standard was so sudden that there was not enough time to produce a clean copy of the final rule prior to the deadline that was worked out with the U.S. Court of Appeals for the District of Columbia. The copy submitted to the *Federal Register* was the original document, with the deletions simply blacked out, an interesting example of the problematic nature of the role of the OMB in regulation. That role often did not lead to careful deliberations between the OMB and regulatory agencies, but to extensive, and occasionally heavy-handed, weakening of standards. The OSHA acknowledged that its decision to delete hastily parts of the ethylene oxide rule was based "largely in response to reservations expressed" by the OMB. This type of incident reinforced the perception among supporters of social regulation that the regulatory review process was not attuned to making government intervention in the marketplace more cost effective, but to the complete triumph of economic principles that were anathema to the zealous protection of health, safety, and the environment. A suit was filed, accordingly, challenging the adequacy of the ethylene oxide standard, a challenge supported by a large part of the scientific community, and the role of the OMB in weakening the final rule (Rosenberg, 1986: 217–18). Furthermore, five house committee chairmen added their support to the suit, filing a friend of the court (amicus curiae) brief on behalf of the plaintiffs. They charged that the ethylene oxide case was "part of a pervasive and persistent pattern of intrusion and interference that has shifted the locus of discretionary decision-making authority from the agencies designated by Congress to OMB" (*Congressional Quarterly Weekly Report*, June 14, 1986: 1340).

The U.S. Court of Appeals for the District of Columbia circuit issued its decision on the *Rowland* case in July 1986. The court ruled that the OSHA had failed to accumulate substantial evidence to support its decisions not to issue the short-term standard for ethylene oxide, and ordered the agency to start a new rulemaking. But the court refused to take up the constitutional challenge posed by Public Citizen. While granting that the participation of the OMB in the ethylene oxide regulation presented "difficult constitutional questions concerning the executive's proper role in administrative proceedings and the appropriate scope of delegated power from Congress to certain executive agencies," the court cited a long-standing precedent in support of the judiciary's reluctance to decide questions pertaining to the separation of powers. Having determined that the decision of OSHA on the short-term standard did not withstand its statutory review, the court side-stepped "the difficult constitutional questions presented by OMB's participation in this episode" (*Public Citizen Health Research Group* v. *Tyson*, 796 F.2d 1479, D.C. Cir. 1986: 1507).

To this point, it seems unlikely that the controversy surrounding the OMB and the OIRA will be resolved in the courts. The issuing of EO 12291 and EO 12498 greatly accentuated the long-standing tension between an agency head's statutory responsibilities and his or her accountability to the president. But this tension appears to be an inevitable consequence of the expansion of administrative power in American politics, and is not resolved in any statute or the Constitution itself. As Christopher C. DeMuth and Douglas H. Ginsburg, both former directors of the OIRA, argue, the battle for control over public administration that gives rise to the controversy surrounding executive oversight of regulation "is a political question that can be 'answered' only through the tension and balance between the president and Congress—that is, the political branches—in overseeing the work of agencies." (DeMuth and Ginsburg, 1986: 1083).

In the playing out of this political controversy, of course, advocates of social regulation were hardly powerless. Indeed, by the end of Reagan's first term, public advocates and their allies in Congress had mounted a strong political assault on the regulatory review program. This assault was aided in two ways: first, the authority of the OMB to screen agency regulations had not been written into law; and second, the administration had not managed to influence change in the organic statutes that were supportive of social regulation. Although consumer and environmental activists had not been successful in getting the courts to rule on the general question regarding the constitutionality of the authority of the OMB to oversee regulation, they were successful, as the *Thomas* and *Rowland* examples reveal, in getting the courts to declare in particular cases that OMB action conflicted with statutory requirements. The relative paucity of the public record on OIRA activities might have reduced the prospects for public lobby organizations to use the federal courts as successfully as has been the case with regular-line agencies, but clearly legal challenges were still possible in certain important cases.

Furthermore, congressional oversight committees frequently imposed effective political pressure on the OMB by revealing several instances of what seemed to be especially imprudent executive interference with agency responsibilities. For example, as the case study of the EPA will show, a firestorm of criticism deflected an attempt by the OMB to pressure the EPA into abandoning asbestos regulation. Similarly, the House Government Operations Subcommittee on Human Resources and Intergovernmental Relations prevented the OMB from influencing the Food and Drug Administration (FDA) to change its proposed rule pertaining to the availability and sale of experimental drugs. As originally drafted, the proposal would have required drug manufacturers to provide evidence that a "treatment investigational new drug" was effective and safe. But after the OMB got hold of the draft, the standard required the FDA to allow the use and sale of a drug unless the FDA could prove it was clearly ineffective or unreasonably dangerous. This change shifted the burden of proof from drug manufacturers to the FDA, without spelling out whether the manufacturer had to provide the FDA with data to support its application. As a result of congressional pressure, however, the final standard marked a return to the more cautious approach of the FDA, and an acquiescence by the OMB (*National Journal,* May 30, 1987: 1407).

Congressional resistance to the Reagan administration's attempt to assume control over the regulatory process culminated in 1986, resulting in efforts to impose legal restraints on the authority of the OIRA. Most significant, the House in passing the FY 1987 appropriations bill for the Department of the Treasury, U.S. Postal Service, and executive office of the president, deleted all funding for the OIRA. The hostility underlying this action in the House was not absent in the Republican-controlled Senate. In fact, the staff of the subcommittee on Toxic Substance and Environmental Oversight issued a report in February 1986, detailing the influence of the OMB on agency regulations, which, according to its Chairman David Durenberger (R-Minnesota), suggested decisions made at and by the OMB were "not subject to either public scrutiny or effective Congressional oversight," because none of the many laws created to assure fairness and openness applied to the White House regulatory review process. While granting that there was no concrete evidence that either these or other laws were violated, Durenberger added: "neither can there be any assurance to the contrary because of the cloak of secrecy and executive privilege which protects OMB officials and their decision-making processes" (U.S., Senate, 1986: V).

In order to stave off efforts in both congressional chambers to block the 1987 budget request of the OIRA, the OMB announced new policies in the summer of 1986 designed to increase public disclosure of the office's involvement in the federal rulemaking process. A June 13 directive from Wendy Lee Gramm, director of the OIRA, detailed eleven new steps to give the public greater access to the regulatory review activities of the OIRA. These steps ensured that the OIRA would make available upon written request drafts of proposed and final agency rules submitted for review under EO 12291; copies of all written correspondence between agency heads and the OIRA concerning rules; drafts of agency submissions of planned regulatory activity (Gramm, Memorandum for the Heads of Departments and Agencies Subject to Executive Orders Nos. 12291 and 12498, printed in OMB, 1987: 605–7).

Gramm's memo dampened Senate enthusiasm for joining the House in its effort to eliminate the OIRA funding, and the Senate Appropriations Committee eventually allocated $5.4 million from the OMB. But House critics of the OMB such as Representative John Dingell continued to press their efforts to cut off the funds of the OMB, arguing that Gramm's directives were limited in scope, and failed to address what the critics of the OMB considered to be the fundamental unfairness of the regulatory review program, that is, the "undue leverage available to OMB under this program and the absence of a statutory mandate for such a program" (*Congressional Quarterly Weekly Report,* June 21, 1986: 1410).

Eventually, the House and Senate worked out a compromise that took effect in the 1987 omnibus fiscal spending bill, which imposed potentially severe curbs on the power of the OMB to review and revise the regulatory actions of line agencies. It made future administrators of the OIRA presidential appointees subject to confirmation by the Senate. Moreover, it restricted the use of the funds of the OIRA to the "sole purpose" of reviewing information–collection requests contained in another agency's rule or regulation (*Congressional Quarterly Weekly Re-*

port, Oct. 25, 1986: 2660–61). Interestingly, this was the task originally assigned to the OIRA when it was created by the Paperwork Reduction Act of 1980. This is certainly not a trivial task; indeed, nearly every proposed regulation contains paperwork requirements, allowing the OIRA considerable review of regulation under the Paperwork Reduction Act. Furthermore, the OIRA could still use general OMB funds to conduct regulatory review, funds that continued to be provided as long as Ronald Reagan was president (*OMB Watch,* Nov. 1986). Nevertheless, these restrictions were symptomatic of persistent congressional pressure on the OMB, which had a dampening effect on the executive branch, easing somewhat its stranglehold on the regulatory agencies. Such a reaction to a critical pillar of the Reagan regulatory program reflected the deep resentment generated among legislators of both parties by the administration's unilateral assault on regulation. Given the legacy of the public lobby era, neither Congress nor the courts were prepared to suffer easily any president's attempt to seize control of the regulatory process. It is not difficult to see why the Reagan administration felt justified in imposing a forceful review process, but, as we argue in more detail in subsequent chapters, the short-term impact of the OMB oversight may have jeopardized the prospects for long-term change in the substance of regulatory policy (also see Rabkin, 1986).

Personnel Policy

Another important part of the Reagan Administration's management strategy involved paying very careful attention to the appointment of loyal and determined policy officials to departments and agencies. The appointments process was particularly cricial to clamping down on regulation in the independent regulatory commissions such as the FTC and the FCC, which were not covered by EO 12291 and EO 12498. Within these commissions, political appointments were made so that the Reagan zeal for the free market infused agency policy even in the absence of the OMB ministrations. For example, James Miller, a conservative economist, was selected to head the FTC in early 1982, after having served both as the head of the OIRA and coordinator of the Task Force on Regulatory Relief. He had long been recognized in academic and government circles for his opposition to government regulation. Shortly after his appointment to the FTC, Miller expressed his support for the Reagan administration's view that most things will work best if government leaves them alone:

> Most economists have a substantial appreciation for what the market can do, and a realization that government intervention cannot accomplish what

> its proponents maintain. Among the spectrum of economists, I tend more toward the free market than most. (*National Journal,* Dec. 5, 1981: 2149)

Similarly, Mark Fowler, a conservative attorney for radio and television stations, brought a deep and abiding commitment to regulatory relief when he assumed the chairmanship of the FCC. He immediately undertook an effort to eliminate those broadcast regulations with social purposes, such as the requirement that operators of TV stations broadcast twenty-eight hours of free television weekly and that they ascertain the needs and interests of their markets. In effect, Fowler sought to displace what he viewed as the "public trustee concept" of the agency with a "marketplace approach":

> The public trustee concept doesn't relate to reality. Because a broadcaster was a public trustee, the commission had an excuse to burden that public trustee with certain obligations on programming. When the commission starts to dictate programming, to me, that is an impermissible encroachment on the first amendment.
>
> The requirements it imposed in effect made this commission a national program director. I think, ideally, what we should do is go back to what we were originally, and that is a traffic cop. Make sure everyone's on the right frequency; no protectionist philosophy. Let the marketplace decide what goes out over the airwaves. (*National Journal,* Aug. 14, 1982: 1412)

Despite Fowler's deregulatory philosophy, however, the FCC was willing to impose a more stringent regulation of "obscenity" and "indecency" on the airwaves. In April 1987, the commission, with the chairman's support, announced an expanded concept of indecency, promising a more muscular enforcement of acceptable standards for public broadcasting. It went beyond a 1975 decision that proscibed seven "dirty words" dealing with sex and body functions. Now the FCC would punish the use of any "patently offensive language"—a more comprehensive phrase—that was broadcast at any time when "there is a reasonable risk that children are in the audience." Critics of this more stringent regulation of the media predictably accused Mark Fowler of rank hypocrisy. For example, Andrew Schwartzman, the head of the Media Access Group, a consumer advocacy organization, complained: "Mark Fowler has claimed to be a champion of free speech, but he's left a legacy of censorship" (*New York Times,* April 17, 1987: A1, A17). In general, this view was echoed by the communication industry, which argued that the new standards of the FCC were inconsistent with the Reagan-era promotion of expanded First Amendment rights and a free-market approach for all broadcasters, much like that enjoyed by the print media. In his defense, Chairman Fowler claimed the FCC "acted carefully" in deciding to expand the scope of indecency, and added that the regulation of such standards touched on principles so fundamental as to be more important than free-market forces, that is, the obligation of the government to prevent programming that might "damage young minds" (*National Journal,* Aug. 1, 1987: 2004).

The ambiguous push for marketplace solutions at the FCC underlined a serious dilemma for the Reagan administration in seeking to create a new regulatory regime. While President Reagan pointed to government as "the problem" in the crisis portrayed in his first inaugural address, the solutions proposed to solve that crisis frequently involved the forceful use of government. Not only did the Reagan presidency feel the need to make aggressive use of centralized administration in the form of executive orders and to pull back regulations it opposed, but it also espoused a conservative philosophy that presupposed the use of the state to strengthen—or rebuild—the moral fabric of the nation. Indeed, the greatest triumph of modern conservatism, according to President Reagan, was "to stop allowing the left to put the average American on the moral defensive" (Reagan, 1985).

It is important to note, in this regard, that upon his appointment as secretary of education in 1985, William Bennett became one of the administration's most important cabinet members. Rejecting marketplace solutions to educational reform in favor of using his office to cultivate "traditional values," Bennett was described in a *National Review* piece as a "neocentralist" in his approach to educational reform. The neocentralist is a conservative who supports "governmental action to ensure high standards of content and performance," and is distinguished thereby from "neopluralists," who favor private schools, local control of public schools, and parental authority, and whose favorite reforms are education vouchers and tuition credits (Wagner, 1987). In defense of traditional values, Secretary Bennett used his office more as a "bully pulpit" than as a source of programs and experiments. For example, he denounced "value-neutral" sex education in schools, calling for courses that would "teach children sexual restraint as a standard to uphold and follow" (Bennett, 1987: 38). While this approach showed respect for the presumption of "neopluralist" conservatives against centralization, in another sense, Bennett's approach greatly centralized educational reform. As David Wagner put it,

> Previously, conservative reformers concentrated primarily on the question, "who decides?" They were concerned with returning educational power to

parents and communities, and reversing the flow of such power toward
higher levels of government and professional educators. But now, for the
time being, at least, vouchers have taken second place behind values.
(1987: 31)

The Reagan administration had promised upon assuming office to
eliminate the Department of Education, viewing this most recent addition
to the bureaucracy as a perpetrator of federal intervention into matters
that should be decided at the local level. Yet the Department of Education's eventual role as a leading force in a government-sponsored crusade
for moral regeneration suggests that the task of the Reagan regulatory
program was not to dismantle the state, but to put it to new uses. In
addition to the efforts by the FCC and Department of Education, the
Reagan administration imposed regulations discouraging abortions and
enforcing the development of welfare policy that gave agencies greater
power over welfare clients in the determination of eligibility. Such an
approach prompted Theordore Lowi to argue that "William Rehnquist,
not William Simon or David Stockman, is the correct personification of
the Reagan administration: the free market comes second to a strong state
capable of exercising moral leadership, moral education, moral mobilization and moral authority" (Lowi, 1985: 315–16). This may exaggerate
somewhat the Reagan administration's commitment to *conservative*
"statism"; in its assault on social regulation, at least, the administration
emphasized rolling back rather than applying new regulatory programs.
But surely it is misleading to view the Reagan regulatory program simply
as an assault on a large discretionary state. Moreover, the moral tenets of
the president's conservatism explain why, in the mounting of an assault
on social regulation, the marketplace approach of James Miller and Murray Weidenbaum often took a back seat to a more ideological brand of
regulatory change pursued by appointees such as James Watt and Ann
Burford.

The effort by the Reagan administration to select department and
agency heads who would be ideologically in tune with the president represented a sharp departure from the practices of recent administrations.
In mid-1981, the *New York Times* reported "a revolution of attitudes involving the appointment of officials who in previous administrations
might have been ruled out by concern over possible lack of qualifications
or conflict of interest, or open hostility to the missions of the agency they
now head" (*New York Times,* July 3, 1981: 1, 8).

Although individuals such as James Miller had impressive credentials, enabling them to carry out effectively the administration's program,

serious problems arose when the administration selected people based on their antiregulation attitudes without regard for their political and managerial expertise. For example, the original appointment to the NHTSA was Raymond Peck, a former lobbyist for the coal industry and foe of regulation, who had virtually no experience in the transportation or automotive industry. Peck had considerable experience in government, having served during the Nixon and Ford years as the Department of Commerce's environmental counsel, director of the Department of Treasury's office of energy regulatory and legislative policy, and deputy assistant interior secretary for energy and minerals. He was selected for the NHTSA post because his experience was in fields other than highway safety and, more fundamentally, he was on record as a foe of regulation, a record he developed as an aggressive advocate for mineral producers, while he was vice-president and director of regulatory affairs for the National Coal Association (*National Journal*, Jan. 28, 1981: 737). The Reagan administration believed, it seems, that someone like Peck, with a long-standing commitment to regulatory relief and an outsider to the highway safety field, would bring an uninhibited and unequivocal free-market approach to the agency.

Yet, Peck's inexperience in transportation policy and poor management proved to be serious liabilities to the administration, and he was forced out of his position in 1983 (Tunstall, 1985: 13). He was extensively involved in one of the Reagan presidency's biggest regulatory setbacks: the failed effort to rescind the passive-restraint rule for automobiles as not cost effective. This regulation sought to achieve automatic crash protection by requiring automobile manufacturers to install either of two passive-restraint devices: air bags or automatic seatbelts. The Supreme Court overturned the Reagan administration's effort to rescind the automobile safety rule in July 1983, in a decision that characterized this deregulatory action as "arbitrary and capricious." The Court unanimously found that the agency had acted arbitrarily in not considering the obvious option of mandatory air bags, the effectiveness of which the NHTSA never challenged, and by a vote of five to four, decided that it had also acted arbitrarily in dismissing a detachable automatic seatbelt requirement (*Motor Vehicle Manufacturers Association of the United States, Inc., et al., v. State Farm Mutual Automobile Insurance Company, et al.*, 463 U.S. 29, 1983). Harvard economist Robert Leone, who served as a Council of Economic Advisors staff member early in President Reagan's term, blamed this defeat for the administration on Peck and his staff, whom he claimed scored a "paper victory" by revoking the air bag rule without adequate research (*National Journal*, July 23, 1983: 1536).

As we shall discuss in Chapter 6, the appointments to the EPA were the most damaging of the administration's first term. Ann Burford, selected as director of the EPA, was a conservative attorney from Colorado. An outspoken opponent of environmental regulation, she was appointed on ideological and political grounds, even though she lacked the expertise and government background essential to running a complex agency like the EPA (Tunstall, 1985: 14). Burford's disastrous management of the agency alienated not only public lobbyists but business interests as well, who felt her actions created an unpredictable and hostile political climate that militated against constructive changes in environmental controls.

Although the personnel policy of the Reagan administration often led to severe criticism and, on occasion, damage to the president's regulatory program, it reflected a commitment to establishing control of the executive branch in the interest of lessening regulation on business enterprises. Moreover, senior White House officials pointed out that Reagan's appointments were in many respects simply the mirror image of the Carter administration's appointments of environmentalists, consumer activists, and civil rights figures to positions in which they could convert strong commitments to social regulation into government policy. As one of Reagan's advisors put it, the strategy of placing hostile personnel in key department and agency positions was "not unlike putting Carol Foreman [an aggressive public interest lobbyist] in the consumer affairs division at the Agricultural Department," naming an appointee criticized by the president for putting shoppers' interests ahead of those of farmers (*New York Times,* July 3, 1981: 8).

While the Reagan administration's emphasis on ideology in key appointments was in certain respects merely the "mirror image" of Carter's personnel policy, it was perceived nevertheless as a fundamental challenge to past administrative practices. The Carter administration's appointment of many public lobbyists to important executive posts was in a sense the culmination of a decade-long development, which, as we noted in the previous chapter, brought about a new regulatory era. Yet the "public lobby regime" was an extension and radicalization, rather than a rejection, of the New Deal. The Reagan program, on the other hand, posed fundamental challenges to the philosophy of government that had prevailed for a half-century, based on the idea that expansive supervision of business activity was in the public interest. It is also significant that President Reagan, unlike President Carter, envisioned a comprehensive recasting of regulatory politics, leading to personnel practices that made the Carter administration's appointment process appear to be quite temperate by comparison. Similarly, in challenging the "liberal establishment," the Reagan administration was prepared to go much further than its recent Republican predecessors.

The pursuit of a "whole new ball game" in regulatory politics, as E. Pendleton James, the first White House personnel director, put it, inclined the administration to make appointments such as Raymond Peck and Ann Burford who were put in unfamiliar policy circles. At least such individuals would not "go off and marry the natives," becoming advocates for their agencies and departments, as occurred so often in the Nixon administration (Nathan, 1983: 30). According to James, on critical appointments to the regulatory agencies, the president's top advisor, Edwin Meese III, often "interjected himself" into the interviewing process in order to assure conformity to Reagan's goal of ending the adversarial relationship between business and regulatory agencies (*New York Times,* July 3, 1981: 1, 8).

The Reagan personnel office systematically bypassed more moderate and politically experienced Repbulicans who, they felt, would not work earnestly to undo past programs. For example, Russell Peterson, president of the National Audubon Society, complained in 1981 that, in staffing the Council of Environmental Quality, which environmentalists considered the "conscience of the executive branch," the Reagan administration had not only frozen Democratic activists out of environmental jobs, but had also bypassed Republican moderates, such as Russell Train, former administrator of the EPA, in favor of hard-liners who shared Secretary of Interior James Watt's dedication to increased mining and oil drilling on federal land (*New York Times,* July 3, 1981: 8).

An additional measure taken to assure a loyal group of top political appointees involved setting up "training or indoctrination activities to an unusually high degree" (Nathan, 1983: 75). During the transition period, cabinet members learned about their departments from conservative task forces rather than from the personnel within their agencies. Appointees also met frequently with Reagan in this early period so they could "get used to working with him" before developing close ties with their department staff (*National Journal,* Feb. 21, 1981: 302). Moreover, Meese directed the formation of White House cabinet councils, which were designed "to function as the primary vehicles for the formulation of Administration policies—once again providing a layer of separation from career policy experts in the agencies" (*National Journal,* April 9, 1983: 733).

Much of the personnel policy of the Reagan administration, therefore, focused on the regular bureaucracy as the source of mischievous regulatory activity. Not only were efforts made to insulate political appointees from the civil service, but there were also extraordinary measures taken to rein in the career civil servants. Reagan appointees took every advantage of opportunities to transfer and remove career officials in domestic agencies felt to be unsympathetic to the administration's objectives (Nathan, 1983: 77). "Reductions in Force" (RIFs) were carried out in many agencies, and where such tactics proved inadequate, owing to the limits set by civil service protection and seniority rules, personnel were transferred to break up old loyalties and vested interests (Kristol, 1985: 64).

In effect, the integrity of the civil service was subordinated to the task of redefining the purposes of government. In some cases this was done so crudely that plans to reshape the activities of departments or agencies were aborted. For example, James Watt sought to break up the professional staff of the Office of Surface Mining's Denver office by proposing that the office be shifted to Casper, Wyoming, an effort that was rejected by agency personnel and congressional oversight committees as an attempt "to gut the agency, by doing it through the back door" (*National Journal,* April 9, 1983: 733).

In other areas of the federal bureaucracy, the civil service was manipulated with more success. For example, Thomas Pauken, the Reagan choice to head ACTION, the new federal umbrella for the Peace Corps, VISTA, and other service organizations, successfully neutralized the opposition of his professional staff in his effort to reorient VISTA, the agency's most prominent component, away from supporting various community organizing and advocacy groups to support for more traditional local volunteer groups. He did so by using "Schedule B" appointments— a civil service shortcut to hire people with special skills—to bring in loyalists, and hiring and transferring a large number of civil servants. Pauken avoided the type of political backlash that occurred at the Interior Department by resisting ACTION being used as a dumping ground for loyal, though unqualified, "Reaganists," and appointing a topflight group of associates, "many of whom had little or no government experience and little in the way of political connections, almost all of whom eventually moved onward and upward in the Reagan Administration" (Kristol, 1985: 65).

While the management of James Watt and Ann Burford demonstrates the pitfalls of manipulating the civil service for policy goals, the actions of Thomas Pauken and James Miller suggest how such manipulation can be part of a successful redirection of a government agency. The cases of Miller and Burford will be examined in detail below. It is important to realize, however, as the administration's directors of personnel policy claimed, that the politicization of the bureaucracy did not begin with Ronald Reagan. In fact, the Civil Service Reform Act of 1978 passed under the Carter administration as a device to make the bureaucracy more responsive to political leadership was an effective instrument under Reagan to change the activities of the federal government (Nathan, 1983: 76, 77–78). This act replaced the bipartisan Civil Service Commission with the Office of Personnel Management (OPM), an agency headed by political appointees, and subjected some 1500 Schedule C positions and 700 senior executive service appointments to explicit control by a presidential administration through demotion, transfer, or removal. Hailed by many as an important reform of management, this act facilitated a significant politicization of the bureaucracy. For example, the Civil Service Commission had kept the number of Schedule C positions, which generally provided administrative and staff support for higher-level political appointees, under 1000. But the Carter administration drove the number up to 1566, and Reagan, as of mid-1983, had 1615 exempt appointees on his payroll (*National Journal,* April 9, 1983: 736). The number of political appointees added to a bureaucracy of some 2.1 million federal employees was small in absolute terms. But these changes have generally occurred at the top levels of the civil service, accentuating their importance, and took place at a time of reduction in overall federal employment. In addition, the Reagan administration enhanced its influence on the bureaucracy by subjecting all of its political appointments to extraordinarily tight control—insisting, for example, on White House clearance of each noncareer appointment in the government (Pfiffner, 1986: 4–6).

Whereas some proponents of civil service reform argue that the Reagan assault on the career staff was a perversion of the system, more sympathetic observers saw such actions as a logical development. As Richard Nathan has written, "it can be argued that the [1978 Civil Service Reform] law is working exactly the way it should, despite the pain involved for persons removed from office" (Nathan, 1983: 78).

But the use of the new law by the Reagan administration was far more ambitious in challenging past civil service practices than the utilization of the statute by the Carter presidency. Reagan's choice to direct the OPM, Donald J. Devine, vigorously reduced the distance between politics and administration, taking aggressive steps to ensure "a response to what the elected officials want" (*National Journal,* April 9, 1983: 733). In effect, Devine transformed the role of the OPM from an oversight agency to an arm of the administration, permitting an unchecked circumvention of civil service protection. The erosion of the status of the senior civil service was especially devastating. The Senior Executive Service was envisioned by the authors of the 1978 reform bill as a buffer between political appointees and program specialists; yet few who were in this status were kept under Reagan, and the politicization of the OPM by Devine undermined any prospects for a corps of neutral and competent civil servants to be established at the top of the federal bureaucracy. Devine's predecessor, Alan K. Campbell, dean of the graduate school of public administration at Syracuse University, took a more conventional approach to the civil service; as principal architect of the bill that created the OPM, he provided a vehicle for greater political involvement in personnel matters, but his approach was far less partisan and ideological than that of Devine (*National Journal,* April 9, 1983: 734).

The management of the OPM itself was particularly heavy-handed during the Reagan presidency. While the total employment at the agency dropped from 6400 to 5700 during Devine's reign, the number of political appointees (noncareer senior executives and Schedule C positions) grew to over forty, nearly three times as many as there were during the Carter presidency (U.S., Senate, 1985: 38). Moreover, these political appointees were not chosen for their expertise in public administration; on the contrary, the Reagan appointments to the OPM suggest a strong disinclination to accept public administration as a distinct and worthwhile sphere of activity. Indeed, as Frederick Mosher observed, "the principal qualification of many of these senior-level OPM appointees appears to be their experience in political campaigns" (Mosher, 1985: 409). To the chagrin of the Republican Chairman of the Senate Committee on Governmental Affairs, Ted Stevens (Alaska), Devine himself actively participated in the 1982 and 1984 election campaigns (U.S., Senate, 1985: 102–4). Furthermore, one OPM executive, who headed the Senior Executive Service, resigned in 1982 to manage an unsuccessful GOP senatorial campaign in Maryland, then, a few days after the election, came back to his post, which had been held for him, in open defiance of the spirit of the Hatch Act (U.S., Senate, 1985: 38–39; Mosher, 1985: 409).

The unchecked political activities of the Reagan team at the OPM eventually self-destructed. Devine was denied a second four-year term as director when it came to light during his confirmation hearings that he had secretly attempted to delegate himself authority to continue to run the agency after his original term expired. In what a White House official appropriately described as an "incredible manner of behavior," Devine was exposed not only as having maneuvered behind the back of his deputy and acting successor, Loretta Cornelius, but as having asked her to lie about it (U.S., Senate, 1985: 338–423; *National Journal,* June 15, 1985: 1419). In part, this incident reflects a failure of statesmanship and, in part, it is symptomatic of an unprecedented rejection by the Reagan administration officials of the understanding that there were benefits to be gained by using the knowledge of their career staffs (Campbell, 1985: 412).

Thus, although the politicization of the bureaucracy did not begin in the Reagan administration, the political intervention in personnel matters during the 1980s sharply departed from precedent. Since the New Deal, civil service reform had been employed as an instrument of programmatic policy; however, the Reagan administration's use of personnel tactics challenged long-standing political arrangements that favored program advocates. It was one thing to provide an opportunity for political intervention to generate more creative and energetic policy, and quite another to use this opportunity to put an ideological harness on federal departments and agencies. The former intention gave impetus to the 1978 Civil Service Reform law; the latter suggests how the Reagan personnel program represented an unintended and ironic legacy of civil service reform.

The Reagan administration's departure from past personnel practices and its assault on the civil service were viewed as necessary to bring about a single-minded commitment to reducing the regulatory burden on the economy. At the same time, the long-term consequences of such personnel practices were unclear. One scholar, for example, while sympathetic to the administration's commitment to changing regulatory policy, questioned the benefits gained from relying so heavily on "outsiders," who were so clearly alienated from the agencies they served:

> That the new appointees all shared President Reagan's concern to reduce regulatory burdens was quite plain. That they had the capacity to reorient policy within their own agencies in effective ways was much less clear in many cases, however. Blocking new regulations and accommodating sizable budget cuts require no great skill. But appointees with no prior experience in their agency's policy field may fail to recognize the most promising—and politically viable—opportunities for reforming existing rules and procedures. Appointees with a hostile or suspicious attitude toward their own agency's programs may fail to develop the trust and cooperation of their civil service staffs, thus forfeiting the expertise and experience they might offer to reform initiatives. And appointees who seem too sensitive to immediate industry pressures may fail to build public trust and confidence, thus strengthening the hands of their critics in Congress. (Rabkin, 1986: 230–31)

Although appointees such as James Miller and William Bennett had rather well-developed visions of reform, and were able to enlist, at least to an extent, the career staff in their efforts to redirect the agencies they led, many other Reagan appointees were inadequately prepared for such a task. Subsequent chapters will compare Reagan appointees in terms of their ability to bring about regulatory change, and offer some conclusions about the overall impact of the leadership selected to direct the Reagan regulatory program. We have stressed that ideas are the central element in regulatory change. Yet, as our case studies reveal, ideas are not enough; strategically situated people who can eloquently promote these ideas and make them politically effective are also essential.

Budgetary Politics

The administrative strategy of the Reagan presidency was further supported by budgetary politics. Prior to the election of 1980, regulators had grown accustomed to routine increases in staff and funding. Reagan, however, proposed a staff reduction of at least 10 percent for all agencies and a slashing of agency appropriations. Reductions in force and budget cuts were directed especially at the agencies and programs that served as the foundation of the new social regulation. For example, in terms of total percentage reduction from FY 1981 to FY 1985, two aggressive consumer agencies, the FTC and the Consumer Product Safety Commission (CPSC), lost 11 and 16 percent of their funding, respectively. These agencies were more severely affected by reductions in staff. The number of permanent positions at the FTC declined from 1665 in 1981 to 1075 in 1985, while the staff was reduced at the CPSC during this period from 855 to 502 positions (OMB, 1981–1987).

Because budget austerity could not be imposed unilaterally by the administration, but required the support of Congress, there were limits to this aspect of the Reagan administrative program. But Congress was generally more receptive to legislative changes in budgetary matters than it was to more direct assaults on the legislative basis of the regulatory state. After Reagan took office, it became clear that agencies could no longer expect increases in staff and funding, a change in expectations that became politically significant (Tunstall, 1985: 19). The cuts seriously weakened morale at those agencies most affected, and contributed to the confusion that characterized the regulatory environment of Reagan's first term. This reversal in expectations was a complement to the executive orders that temporarily halted the activities of the public lobby regime, inasmuch as it resulted in significant change but did not necessarily ensure a long-term transformation of regulatory politics. In fact, congressional support for imposing fiscal restraints on federal regulators waned after 1983. Although budgetary appropriations and personnel levels were not restored to pre-1981 levels for most agencies, by the end of the president's first term Congress began to slow the decreases and in some cases to approve increases in funding and positions. Within the EPA especially, as Chapter 6 reveals, there was a strong congressional reaction to the administration's fiscal program after 1983.

One of the Reagan administration's more important budgetary battles in the "war" against the public lobby regime involved a campaign to "defund the left." When Reagan assumed office in 1981, a coalition of some eighty conservative activist groups urged him to eliminate the power of the federal bureaucracy to subsidize public advocacy organizations, arguing that such action was necessary for the success of the administration's deregulatory agenda (*National Journal,* Aug. 1, 1981: 1374–78). The incoming administration shared this assessment; indeed, President Reagan himself once referred to public interest litigators as "a bunch of ideological ambulance chasers doing their own thing at the expense of the poor who actually need help" (quoted in Greve, 1987: 91). Subsequently, strenuous efforts were made to prevent federal agencies from providing grants, contracts, or consultant fees to interest groups. In collateral moves, the OMB sought to change regulations concerning the political activities of federal contractors and the Internal Revenue Service (IRS) sought to redefine the meaning of "charitable" organizations, making it more difficult for public interest groups to engage in anything resembling partisan political activity (Peterson and Walker, 1986: 163).

The Reagan program to "defund the left" met with mixed success at best (see, for example, Greve, 1987). One of the reasons for the administration's inability to constrict public lobby access was that most of the groups were far less threatened by proposed cutbacks in federal money than conservatives appeared to believe. A 1981 *National Journal* survey of liberal advocacy groups indicated that, while some groups got a substantial share of their revenue from federal sources, most were prepared to survive without it. For example, while the Planned Parenthood Federation of America, one of the targets singled out by the conservative coalition for defunding, got slightly more than half of its $24 million budget from the federal government, many other public interest groups, including several environmental and consumer protection groups, received very little direct assistance from the federal government (*National Journal,* Aug. 1, 1981: 1376). Furthermore, the public interest movement displayed some ingenuity in diversifying its financial base. A 1985 survey of citizen groups by Mark Peterson and Jack Walker revealed that to compensate for the losses they anticipated from Reagan's budgetary policy, public interest organizations were able to increase significantly the revenues they received in 1985 from business firms, churches, and unions. They also earned more by selling the services of their staffs, gaining greater returns on investments and staging other fund-raising events (Peterson and Walker, 1986: 175). One of the more creative methods employed by several mass-membership organizations was to persuade major banks to issue credit cards that carried a public interest group's name and logo. A small percentage of the cardholder's financial transaction goes to the group identified on the card (Greve, 1987: 99).

As Chapter 6 will show, some public interest groups, especially those active in environmental policy, were aided in their effort to achieve financial diversification by the Reagan presidency's assault on social regulation. The administration's free-market, deregulatory rhetoric and the controversial administrative activities by the likes of Ann Burford and James Watt (dubbed the "Fort Knox of the environmental movement") reinvigorated what had been a flagging public interest constituency, and led to an increase in private contributions to liberal advocacy groups in the early 1980s. Peterson and Walker found in their survey that some public interest organizations suffered financially during Reagan's first term, but many of the groups from the environmental, peace, and women's movements reported sharp increases in the size of their memberships (1986: 173).

Perhaps the most significant reason for the inability of the Reagan presidency to affect adversely the financial base of citizen groups was its flawed understanding of the public interest movement. Leaders of the conservative caucus pushing for cutbacks in public lobby access viewed activists in consumer and environmental policy as ideological extremists, with virtually no public support and intent on rendering irrelevant the election returns. Such a view badly underestimated the popular support these groups were capable of generating for their causes. To be sure, as we suggest throughout this book, some of the principles underlying the public interest movement were largely unacceptable in the context of American politics, and, when unchecked, capable of eliciting strong political opposition. Yet many of the specific goals of citizen activists— clean air and water, protection of the consumer, a more open political process—were unassailable, and tapped powerful concerns that were deeply imbedded in American politics. Hence, a gathering of consumer and environmental activists at the so-called Coolfant Conference of July 1982 decided that "staying alive under Reagan" would be enhanced by "packaging" information that would "play on 'valence' positions, positions no one disagrees with, such as stopping the 'buying of America,' or controlling bad business" (summary of the Coolfant Conference, July 1982: 3–4). Neither the fear of big business nor the concern that "special" interests dominated American politics was especially new or controversial. As Hugh Heclo has written, the vision of public interest groups was "a thoroughly American vision of a broad good government, citizen's movement led by outsiders who were uncorrupted by established authority" (Heclo, 1988). The genius of public lobby groups was their ability to make use of such "valence" issues in bringing about specific institutional and programmatic reforms. This brand of reform politics created a large source of latent, if not continuously engaged, support that made the goal of defunding the left, as the *National Journal* noted, "another fond dream of conservatives" that would in all likelihood "remain a dream" (*National Journal,* Aug. 1, 1981).

It is also important to note, as Chapters 2 and 3 suggest, that public interest groups had influenced institutional changes that, paradoxically, made these insurgent groups an integral part of the system. Conservatives were not completely wrong in rejecting the liberal advocacy groups' attempt at self-justification—advocacy groups were not all that different from ordinary interest groups. But this fact stemmed less from public interest organizations' attachment to "parochial" concerns than it did from the institutional legacy of the "public lobby regime," which redid the political system in a way that "clasped an inherently disruptive player to its bosom" (Heclo, 1988). As a result, Donald Brand (1988) points out, public interest groups have one foot inside and one foot outside the interest group system. Their influence "within the system" enabled these groups to fend off effectively most of the Reagan administration's efforts to scale back their financial base.

It is most significant that throughout the 1980s the public interest movement continued to enjoy considerable support in Congress. One of its greatest successes in this regard was its protection of funding for the Legal Services Corporation (LSC), the single largest program in support of public interest litigation. The LSC had won the enmity of conservatives by giving grants to legal aid firms that successfully litigated cases that led to a wholesale transformation of the Aid to Families with Dependent Children (AFDC) program, by relaxing state-imposed eligibility criteria and by abolishing residency and work requirements (Melnick, 1986). The Reagan administration's persistent attempts to abolish the LSC, however, were resisted by Congress. Not only did Congress refuse to abolish the agency, but it even prevented significant cuts of the budget

of the LSC and extensively curtailed the agency's discretion by prohib-
iting it from reducing support for any of its grantees (Greve, 1987: 100).

In this and other instances, supporters of the public interest movement had only to prevent congressional action to maintain their budgetary
support; its federal financial stake was deeply rooted in a system in which
public lobby organizations had become part of the status quo. Thus, defunding the left required more than a drive to cut off the funds for a
recalcitrant group of activists; as our analysis of the public lobby era
suggests, it required bringing about a new regime. Nothing demonstrated
this more deeply than the judiciary's support for government funding of
citizen advocacy. In the late 1960s, the courts fashioned the "private
attorney general doctrine," which reimbursed public interest groups for
their law enforcement efforts—without, however, requiring the groups to
pay opponents' expenses for unsuccessful litigation. This doctrine was
derived from a very broad interpretation of congressional fee authoriza-
tions, and the courts refused, as our study of the EPA shows, to go along
with the Reagan administration's efforts to limit such awards.

In effect, public interest groups' funding was expanded and sustained in association with institutional changes and judicial rulings that
were attendant to a new understanding of rights in American politics. On
the view that public interest groups were aiding in the enforcement of
important constitutional objectives, the funding of citizen activists had
come to be viewed virtually as an "entitlement" largely insulating these
programs against budget cuts, even when such reductions were supported
by a popular president (Greve, 103–4). To be sure, some budgetary support for public interest groups was reduced. The elimination of intervenor
funding at the FTC, as described in Chapter 5, is an example. Yet this
action was the exception rather than the rule.

Transferring Regulatory Authority to the States

Another important element of the Reagan regulatory program involved
the delegation of regulatory authority to the states. In his State of the
Union address of January 26, 1982, Reagan proposed an ambitious program to, as he put it, "make our system of federalism work again." This
plan called for "swaps" and "turnbacks" that would give to the states
total responsibility for the AFDC and food stamp programs, as well as
some forty-four programs in the areas of education, employment and
training, social services, public health, transportation, and community
development. In return, the federal government would assume complete

responsibility for the Medicaid program and provide a trust fund to help defray the costs to the states for assuming these additional responsibilities. Furthermore, as the trust fund was phased out gradually after four years, federal excise taxes would be turned over to the states to manage these programs as they saw fit (*Public Papers of the Presidents,* 1982: 75–76).

This program envisioned in one bold stroke a reordering of tasks between the federal and state governments that would reverse a longstanding trend toward centralization of authority. Although the grand vision of the Reagan administration, as laid out in the 1982 message, was never translated into a bill and placed before Congress, the underlying values of Reagan's federalism guided other less publicized, but important, actions by the administration that are likely to have a major impact on federal regulation. And many of these changes affected programs in the area of social regulation.

A report by the Presidential Task Force on Regulatory Relief in August 1982 argued that in order for the administration's "New Federalism" initiative to succeed, "significant attention must also be devoted to correcting excessive intrusion into state and local affairs from programs which remain at the federal level" (Presidential Task Force on Regulatory Relief, 1982: i). The report pointed to twenty-four regulatory actions that it claimed saved state and local governments between $4 billion and $6 billion in total investment costs, and $2 billion in annually recurring costs. Moreover, the report (pp. i–ii) asserted that by reducing paperwork reporting requirements the Reagan administration had freed 11.8 million work hours per year for state and local government employees. Among the actions cited for providing large savings and enhanced flexibility to the states was the Education Consolidation and Improvement Act of 1981, which consolidated twenty-eight restrictive categorical federal programs into one block grant allowing "maximum flexibility to state and local agencies in administering funds and designing programs" (p. 3). Also mentioned were modifications in the administration of the Clean Air Act, allowing for the extension of the emissions trading policy begun under the Carter administration and the facilitation of State Implementation Plans (SIPs), both of which would give states broad discretionary powers in the regulation of air quality standards.

The administration's cost-saving claims were viewed as exaggerated by some independent observers, but even some critics granted that the state and local governments were, as Michael Fix puts it, the "big winners in regulatory relief" (*National Journal,* Aug. 4, 1984: 1464). During the administration's first year in office, several of the ten most burdensome regulations cited by a report of the Advisory Commision of Inter-governmental Relations were drastically modified, giving the state and local governments a lot of the relief they wanted (Fix, 1984; *National Journal,* Aug. 4, 1984: 1464–69).

Most of the changes achieved by the Reagan administration in inter-governmental regulation were carried out administratively, leaving the bulk of the underlying statutes intact. This administrative action was pos-sible because a large number of laws passed in the area of social regula-tion, especially many of those in the environmental area, had been struc-tured in such a way to facilitate regulatory federalism. The basic design—referred to as "partial preemption"—calls for the federal government to set minimum standards, but authorizes the states to assume responsibility for administering programs within these broad boundaries (Fix, 1984: 154; M. Reagan, 1985). But plans for regulatory federalism were badly stalled prior to the implementation of the Reagan administration's pro-gram of regulatory relief. For example, the Clean Air Act requires states to submit SIPs; however, the elaborate rules for putting such plans into effect had created an enormous SIP backlog awaiting review by the EPA. The Reagan administration made procedural changes to expediate state preemption, reducing pending plans by 97 percent from January 1981 to October 1982. These changes did not reflect simply better managerial procedures, but in large part reflected unprecedented deference for state plans in the Reagan administration. It was the push for deregulation and not a reduction in red tape per se that accelerated the acceptance of state administrative discretion (Fix, 1984: 171).

In fact, a close examination of efforts to eliminate the SIP backlog indicates that this policy hardly led to careful systematic analysis or the revitalization of federalism. One EPA staffer termed these efforts as "shoveling out all the garbage in order to get the system current" (quoted in Fix, 1984: 171). Many states simply adopted the programs, regula-tions, and performance standards developed by federal agencies, because they believed in them in many cases or, where this was not so, it was too costly to develop new plans. Moreover, in many instances in which states were not content to let the federal regulators "carry the ball," they submitted poorly conceived inplementation plans, and that, with the envi-ronmental groups' participation in the approval process, ensured their de-feat (Fix, 1984: 171–72).

One might have expected that the most significant difference to fol-low from the devolution of responsibility for regulation in environmental and other social areas would not be in the formulation of the regulations themselves, but in less aggressive enforcement. When students of implementation consider the states, they often view them as potential veto points that impede aggressive regulation. Often the states lack the political muscle, and in some cases the will, to support vigorously these standards.

Nevertheless, the picture of regulatory enforcement at the state level is more complicated than such a pessimistic view suggests. For example, one study of the OSHA during the period of 1977–1981 presents a more mixed picture concerning state performance. Some state programs evinced less enforcement vigor than the OSHA achieved in the areas in which it held direct jurisdiction; many other state agencies surpassed OSHA (Thompson and Scicchitano, 1985a). It would follow, therefore, that the Reagan administration's emphasis on devolving regulatory authority to the states would not always produce de facto regulatory relief; in fact, some of the early evidence suggested that many states resisted the changes in national regulatory policy pushed by the Reagan presidency (Thompson and Scicchitano, 1985b). In some cases, business even faced the prospect of more onerous controls. Many states responded to the situation of a declining federal presence by increasing the number of state regulations, resulting, some former devotees of deregulation feared, in a "50-Headed Hydra" (Foote, 1984: 218; *Business Week,* Sept. 19, 1983: 124).

Thus, at the conclusion of the Reagan administration's first term, it was very uncertain that "New Federalism" would lead to a loosening of the regulatory ratchet. Given the diversity in state responses, Michael Reagan speculated "that a substantial time lag is necessary for changes initiated at one level to permeate through the other levels in the labyrinthine maze that constitutes our regulatory apparatus" (M. Reagan, 1987: 202).

"New Federalism" initiatives might have eventually resulted in an enervation of regulatory enforcement, particularly because the Reagan administration's desire to give the states a larger role in intergovernmental programs was accompanied by a substantial relative cutback in the level of federal grants-in-aid to help the states perform their functions (M. Reagan, 1987: 201). It remained to be seen, however, whether or not the Reagan initiatives to enhance the responsibility of state and local governments in regulatory politics would be enduring. Outside of the few actions by Congress to authorize ten block grants in 1981 and 1982, which consolidated a total of fifty-eight categorical programs in such fields as education, health, social services, and community development, the Reagan federalism program had been carried out by executive order and could be reversed by future administrations. Moreover, in some cases such unilateral action was rejected by the courts as undermining the integrity of statutes. For example, the National Wildlife Federation in 1984 led a successful legal challenge of regulations issued by the Office of Surface Mining that would have improperly delegated to states the power to approve surface mining plans on federal lands [In re: Permanent Surface Mining Regulation Litigation, 21 Env't Rep. (BNA) 1724 (D.D.C. July 6, 1984)].

Industry, in certain instances, also has posed roadblocks to the delegation of regulatory authority to the states. In many cases, as noted, state regulators rushed in where Washington no longer treaded, resulting in fragmented regulation that imposed substantial costs on business. In response, as Susan Bartlett Foote noted, "advocates of deregulation who formerly were opposed to regulation at any government level, have turned with increasing frequency to Washington to ask for centralized regulations that preempt state laws" (1984: 218). For example, in response to concerns over the hazards posed by chemicals in the workplace, many states and municipalities adopted varying regulations addressing this problem. As a consequence, the OSHA promulgated a national standard in 1984. The purpose of a national rule by the OSHA, strongly supported by the chemical industry, was to establish mandatory uniform standards for both manufacturers and employers, thereby preempting more stringent state requirements (Foote, 1984: 221–22; Gray, 1983: 101–3). Business support for uniform federal standards was especially strong in certain areas of environmental regulation in which many firms had established a working relationship with the EPA and had invested substantial amounts of money in compliance.

Where legal conflicts between state and business interests arose over delegation, the Reagan administration frequently demonstrated a willingness to relax its expressed support for federalism and side with business (Eads and Fix, 1985: 310). A case in point is *Pacific Electric Company* v. *State Energy Resources Conservation and Development Commission* (461 U.S. 190), which saw the federal government join the petitioners in an unsuccessful effort to persuade the Supreme Court that a California statute authorizing a moratorium on nuclear power plant construction was preempted by the Atomic Energy Act of 1954.

Therefore, the devolution of regulatory authority faced and in all likelihood will continue to face substantial opposition. It is true that this was one of the most "successful" efforts of the Reagan regulatory program, largely due to the structure of social regulatory statutes and the tolerance of budgetary cuts in grants to state and local governments (Nathan and Doolittle, 1984). Yet, the substantial cuts in federal aid to state and local governments may very well have impeded the devolution process; in the absence of assured federal funds it was unlikely that states would support efforts to devolve regulatory authority (Eads and Fix, 1985: 309–10). In fact, as the 1994 congressional elections have shown, such "unfunded mandates" are a major problem for state government. Furthermore, on several occasions the Reagan administration did not hesitate to impose nationalist views when it furthered substantive goals (*New York Times,* Nov. 16, 1986: E5). The case study of developments at the FTC indicates, for example, that James Miller was hardly reluctant to preempt state and municipal laws in order to promote economic competition in areas such as taxicab rates and eyeglass prices. Where a genuine commitment to decentralization was evident, the need to centralize executive authority in many instances to serve such a cause had ironic and unintended consequences in the long run. Such a possibility is especially important to consider, given the limited statutory achievements of the Reagan regulatory program.

Regulatory Relief and Legislative Reform

The Absence of Statutory Change

Although the administrative actions of the Reagan administration were extensive and significant, these actions were not reinforced by changes in the legislative base of the regulatory edifice. The first chairman of Reagan's Council of Economic Advisors, Murray Weidenbaum, wrote in an assessment of the administration's statutory achievements during the first term, "I must report that the results have been disappointingly few" (Weidenbaum, 1984: 19). This concern was shared by other members of the administration who feared that without legislative reform the Reagan regulatory program would be subject to legal challenges in the short run and administrative reversals in the long run. For example, the aforementioned "economic Dunkirk" memo prepared by David Stockman and Jack Kemp just after the 1980 election stressed the limited administrative discretion allowed the executive in the statutes governing social regulation and urged Reagan to seek a legislative mandate for the centralization of regulatory oversight in the White House:

> [A] fundamental legislative policy reform package to be considered [after the administration's initial 100 days in office] will have to be developed. This would primarily involve the insertion of mandatory cost/benefit, cost/ effectiveness, and comparative risk analysis into the basic enabling acts— Clean Air and Water, Safe Drinking Water, TOSCA [Toxic Substances

Control Act], RCRA [Resource Conservation and Control Act], OSHA, etc. Without these statutory changes, administrative rulemaking revisions in many cases will be subject to successful court challenge. (printed in Greider, 1982: 158)

No such comprehensive program of legislative reform was ever developed. The administration did lend modest support to a broad procedural reform bill that the Congress debated in 1982. This omnibus legislaton would have provided formal statutory authority for the review of regulations by the executive office. The establishment of statutory oversight procedures also would have required agencies to consider the costs and benefits of new regulations and explain in some form why a new rule is or is not cost effective. A bill including such provisions passed the Senate unanimously in 1982, but failed to clear the House. Although the measure seemed to have broad support in Congress, this support eventually faded—in part owing to the controversy that surrounded the Reagan administration's strong executive actions to achieve regulatory relief, and, in part owing to the opposition of the administration to certain parts of the statute. In the end, this piece of legislation stalled over a lack of consensus about which branch of government should administer the legal restrictions on regulation. For example, the members of Congress wanted to increase congressional oversight of regulations by mechanisms such as the legislative veto, but the president was opposed to such provisions (*National Journal,* Jan. 16, 1982: 95) Reagan's resistance to these measures and the limits imposed on congressional oversight measures involving the legislative veto by the Supreme Court in its landmark decision of *Immigration and Naturalization Service* v. *Chadha* (51 LW 4907, 1983) dampened considerably legislators' enthusiasm for statutory restrictions on regulatory action.

The administration's halfhearted assault on the legislative base of regulation more fundamentally reflected "its desire to avoid raising controversial questions that could impede the speedy enactment of its tax and budget initiatives" (Weidenbaum, 1984: 19). The focus on fiscal policy was accentuated by the severe recession that began soon after Reagan assumed office. The Reagan administration argued that regulatory relief, especially in the areas of consumer, environmental, health, and safety protection, would stimulate the economy. Yet, ironically, it estimated that economic exigencies prevented a concerted effort to bring about fundamental regulatory reform. Granting that the administration's record in persuading Congress to revise regulatory statutes was not as good as its record in imposing executive controls, the President's Task Force on Regulatory Relief reported in 1983:

Much of this is attributable to the recession. The economic picture which is now brightening (with the help, in part, of the regulatory reform effort), required that the Administration give the highest priority domestic attention to fiscal policy. Recessions also generally make economic deregulation more difficult because of the stagnating or contracting markets, and this recession was no exception. (Presidential Task Force on Regulatory Relief, 1983: 6)

The easing of the recession, however, did not lead to an emphasis on statutory reform. As Reagan's second term began, regulatory issues were no longer so prominent and "relief" in the form of legislative initiatives was still given a low priority. Regulatory relief in the form of revised enabling statutes was achieved primarily in areas of economic regulation, such as bus transportation and banking, and these initiatives were begun under the Carter administration. In the area of social protection, however, which was especially important to the regulatory program of the Reagan administration, the legislative base remained in place (Weidenbaum, 1984: 19–23).

As Martha Derthick and Paul Quirk note, in successful deregulatory efforts, "the politics of deregulation with respect to health, safety, and the environment—the subjects of the post-1967 wave of regulation—were entirely different from the politics of procompetitive deregulation" (1985: 218). Assaults on economic regulation preceded the Reagan administration, and brought liberals (attentive to consumerism) and conservatives (attentive to free enterprise) together in a broad coalition for reform. On the other hand, efforts to recast the legislative base of social regulation were resisted by public lobby groups and a number of Democrats and Republicans in the Congress (even in the Republican-controlled Senate). Thus, the Reagan administration, reluctant to expend the enormous political capital required to undertake changes in social legislation, pursued its goals through executive action.

The Logic of Administrative Reform

Scholars and practitioners of regulatory politics have strongly criticized the Reagan administration for failing to undertake a full-scale frontal assault on the legislative base of social regulation. In not doing so, both critics and supporters claim, the administration sacrificed long-term for short-term gain. As the *National Journal* noted in an assessment of Reagan's first-term achievements, the president had "tamed the regulatory beast but not permanently broken its grip":

> One popular image of President Reagan's first term portrays him success-
> fully pulling the fangs out of government regulation. But a more realistic
> portrait would show Reagan as tamer, using whip and stool to hold the
> regulatory process at bay. When Reagan folds his whip four years from
> now, most of the regulatory restraints he imposed could be reversed by a
> new Administration. (Dec. 1, 1984: 2284)

As the case studies that follow reveal, the deregulatory "whip" of the adminstration became less effective during the second term. In fact, there were important examples of renewed activism in consumer and environmental regulation, strongly suggesting that the regulatory process was no longer at bay. It may be, then, that the emphasis on executive action rather than institutional reform was a fatal miscalculation by the Reagan administration, dooming its efforts to achieve regulatory relief to ephemeral status. Moreover, as mentioned earlier, scholars such as Eads and Fix suggest that the expansion of presidential control over social regulation during the Reagan years may have had the ironic and unintended consequence of facilitating the revival and expansion of aggressive regulation. As they put it:

> In the absence of legislative change, the Reagan legacy will be broadened
> administrative discretion and greater presidential control over the course of
> social regulation. While this might give deregulation-minded presidents
> like Ronald Reagan an opportunity to reduce perceived regulatory burdens,
> it also gives presidents with differing philosophies the power and the tools
> they need to turn regulation to quite different ends. (Eads and Fix, 1985:
> 318)

Nevertheless, the emphasis on executive action rather than statutory reform in the Reagan administration represents in many respects a logical reaction to historical shifts in presidential politics (Milkis, 1987a; Moe, 1985: Arnold, 1986). Beginning with the administration of Franklin D. Roosevelt, the imperatives of policy action have encouraged presidents to stress the institutions of the White House as a means to supplement (or circumvent) the formal procedures of American politics. In effect, the reforms proposed by the Brownlow Committee and subsequent presidential panels to study executive management have been conceived to enable presidents to assume more effectively the leadership burdens of an active state within the constitutional framework designed to limit the reach of government. The Brownlow Committee's assertion, "the president needs help," reflected the clashing of governing philosophies that had been a part of American political life throughout the twentieth century and became particularly acute during the development of the New Deal. From that time, the administrative capacity of the president was expanded (with Congress' grudging acquiescence) to overcome the inertia of American politics. Accordingly, the institutionalization of the presidency has gone hand in hand with a politicization of the executive department, which has established executive administration not simply as a foundation for more effective implementation of programs, but as a tool of policy that could supplant the enactment of formal statutory authority (Lowi, 1985).

This development has not only fundamentally reordered the system of checks and balances in American politics, "relegating" Congress and the courts to participation in the specifics of administration, but also has impeded the development of a capable and effective governmental apparatus (Pfiffner, 1986; Heclo, 1987). The presidential policy apparatus has been increasingly structured around personal loyalists, largely excluding professional expertise in the executive office and the bureaucracy (Newland, 1985). Even organizations created with the notion of equipping the presidency with neutral and competent staff support, such as the Bureau of the Budget and the Council of Economic Advisors, have been shaped by presidents to secure "responsive competence," not "neutral competence" (Moe, 1985: 239).

Thus, although the convergence of executive action and public policy (and the concomitant politicization of governmental institutions) has been criticized by scholars and public servants, these developments have been driven by powerful historical and institutional forces. As Terry Moe argues, the institutional fragmentation of American politics, the growth in the complexity of social problems, and the expectations surrounding presidential performance have compelled modern presidents to pursue their programs through unilateral executive leadership:

> In the American separation of powers system, the president is the only politician with a national constituency and thus with an electoral incentive to pursue some broader notion of the public interest, even if restricted to the interests of the coalition that supports him. . . . [T]he president has always been a convenient governmental focus, and, as government has taken a more positive role over the years in addressing a wide range of social problems—and as Congress has shown itself quite incapable of institutional coherence and political leadership, the president has increasingly been held responsible for designing, proposing, legislating, administering, and modifying public policy, that is, for governing. (Moe, 1985: 239)

All modern presidents have been driven to seek control over the structures and processes of government, but this compulsion has been particularly powerful for presidents who have sought extensive programmatic changes. The expansion of presidential capacity initially went hand in hand with the development of liberal reform. During the presidencies of Franklin D. Roosevelt and Lyndon Johnson especially, there were major efforts made to exalt administrative action and institutions as a substitute for regular policy channels. The limited prospects for party government in the United States, requiring ongoing cooperation between the president and Congress, reinforced institutional developments that increasingly made politics and policy a matter of administrative management as the government took on a more positive role in solving social and economic problems (Milkis, 1987b).

The imperatives of policy reform, then, within a political system designed to constrain the expansion of government programs, gave birth to what Richard Nathan terms the "administrative presidency" (1983). Moreover, the emphasis on executive administration by those presidents who have sought policy departures in a conservative direction, such as Nixon and Reagan, was consistent with a long-standing pattern of institutional development.

Conclusion: Regulatory Change and the Limits of Administrative Action

The case studies developed in the next two chapters suggest that energetic and carefully conceived administrative action can bring about substantial alterations in regulatory policy. In this sense, the Reagan administration did not simply continue historical trends in administrative arrangements. Building on some incipient developments during the Nixon years, it reoriented executive institutions into a coherent framework that served an unprecedented commitment in recent American history to reducing the responsibilities of government (Nathan, 1983). The substantial success in making that commitment effective marks the political administration of the Reagan presidency as a dramatic departure in American politics.

Nevertheless, there are limits to administrative action. The development of the administrative presidency depends on the willingness of Congress and the courts to delegate broad authority to the president and executive agencies to govern. In effect, such discretion was part of a broad commitment to the understanding that such an institutional development would facilitate the creation of a positive state in American politics. In a sense, a conservative program of executive action as intended by a Nixon or a Reagan violates this understanding. Indeed, the rise of the public lobby regime, as described in Chapter 3, was a response in part to what contemporary reformers viewed as the failure of the modern presidency to fulfill the expectations that shaped the administrative reforms of the New Deal and Great Society (Melnick, 1985).

Consumer, environmental, and health regulations were accordingly established on an institutional coalition of courts, bureaucratic agencies, congressional subcommittees, and public lobby groups that establishes a formidable barrier between the presidency and social policy. Moreover, many of the recast regulatory channels of the public lobby era were created by statutes and cannot be transformed by executive actions alone; rather, they represent a form of post–New Deal administrative politics, which are based on legal requirement rather than presidential and bureaucratic discretion. Perhaps, therefore, without a comprehensive commitment to revise the legislative base of the public lobby state, the institutional legacy of programmatic liberal politics makes a regulatory realignment unlikely. The major obstacles of long-term change may not be, as Eads and Fix suggest, that future presidents will use the regulatory control apparatus of Reagan's administration to reconstruct and expand the regulatory edifice he was seeking to dismantle. Rather, the limits of administrative action may be the structured insulation of that regulatory edifice from the president's influence in the first place. The studies that follow of the FTC and the EPA reveal that the Reagan administration, with the use of executive initiatives, was able to gain extensive control over regulatory agencies and to change many regulatory policies. It is much less clear, however, that these efforts fundamentally altered the basic structure of the public lobby regime.

5

The Federal Trade Commission, Consumer Protection, and Regulatory Change

> Consumption is the sole end and purpose of all production; and the interest of the producer ought to be attended to only so far as it may be necessary for promoting that of the consumer.
>
> ADAM SMITH, *The Wealth of Nations*

During the 1970s, the Federal Trade Commission (FTC) was one of the most controversial public agencies in Washington. As the government organization largely responsible for patrolling the excesses of American business, the FTC became one of the leading centers of consumer activism during the development of the public lobby regime. In fact, the commission became so controversial that even before the election of Ronald Reagan, strong political opposition was mounting against its ambitious program of consumer protection. Moreover, unlike the Environmental Protection Agency, which we discuss in the next chapter, the FTC became the target of the Congress, as well as the Reagan administration.

In the case of the FTC, then, the Reagan program of regulatory relief continued an attack on consumer activism that began in the late 1970s. This assault was so severe that it prompted Michael Pertschuk, the activist and controversial chairman of the Carter era, to recount in detail, as he put it, the "pause" of the consumer movement after a decade of remarkable triumphs (Pertschuk, 1982). The election of Ronald Reagan appeared to represent a fitting conclusion to this tragic tale. Whereas the Carter administration had fought against the Congress's efforts to strip the FTC of its statutory authority, the Reagan administration seemed poised to join in the rout of the commission. The Reagan transition team singled out the FTC as a prime example of the ill effects of government meddling; and after naming one of the leading architects of the president's regulatory relief program, James Clifford Miller III, as the FTC chairman in the latter part of 1981, the Reagan administration seemed intent on using the commission as a "textbook case" of how to reverse government intrusions into the marketplace (*National Journal,* Dec. 5, 1981: 2149).

The attempt to redirect the FTC is of interest not only as an important example of the rise of, and subsequent challenge to, social regulation. The case of the FTC is also of interest because the commission's historical development indicates how a bureaucratic agency can be modified as regulatory regimes shift. Unlike the EPA, the FTC was not created during the advent of the public lobby era. As a product of the Progressive Era, this independent regulatory commission, which was originally created in 1914 to enforce antitrust laws, seemed ill-suited to become a leading force for the consumer protection. Indeed, the transformation of the commission into an activist consumer agency between 1969 and 1978 was a remarkable metamorphosis. Although, with the passage of the Wheeler–Lea Act, the FTC was authorized to protect the consumer as well as the competitor in 1938, this statute represented mainly latent potential until the late 1960s. It is not inaccurate to suggest that the New Deal passed the FTC by without affecting it extensively.

In this chapter, we shall examine the transformation of the FTC into a consumer protection agency during the development of the public lobby regime. In turn, we consider the assault by the Congress and the Reagan administration on the commission, investigating specifically whether the FTC, having been so fundamentally reshaped during the 1970s, was redirected once again a decade later. As the discussion of recent developments at the agency suggests, the effort to curtail consumer protection at the FTC during the late 1970s and 1980s was especially strong because of certain historical and institutional factors not present at most other agencies responsible for social regulation. Yet, the pattern of regulation and deregulation at the commission over the past two decades is remarkably similar in significant ways to the situation in other areas of regulatory politics. These parallels testify to the comprehensive influence the public lobby regime has had on the American political system. Indeed, it remains to be seen (given the pervasive influence of this regime) whether or not it can be displaced, even at an agency such as the FTC, where programs dedicated to consumer activism became the focus of such a severe political backlash. While the Reagan appointees to the commission brought a well-considered framework to reshape the agency, legislators, favoring a more ad hoc, problem-solving approach to regulatory reform, eventually balked at comprehensive institutional reform.

The history of the FTC exemplifies both the intransigence and malleability of the American bureaucracy. The commission's evolution indicates, most essentially, that at certain critical historical junctions when regulation undergoes fundamental shifts it is possible to redefine the mission and organization of certain parts of the "permanent" government. The future of the FTC, then, depends on whether or not the Reagan revolution indeed ushered in a new regulatory regime.

The Creation and Early History of the Federal Trade Commission

The FTC was created to control the consolidation of business that began during the latter half of the nineteenth century. Declaring unfair methods of competition illegal, the Federal Trade Commission Act was passed with the intention of correcting the deficiencies of the Sherman Antitrust Act (1890), which empowered the government to intervene after a monopoly actually existed. The enabling statute of the FTC established an agency that could act against an incipient monopoly, thereby obviating the weakness of the Sherman Act, which only authorized government to react to a fait accompli (Jaenicke, 1978: 478). In reviewing the early history of the FTC, one is struck by the complex and confusing series of events that led to the creation of a commission endowed with broad statutory authority, though one lacking the political support to exercise consistently its considerable powers. Neither Woodrow Wilson nor his most important economic advisor, Louis Brandeis, initially supported the concept of a strong interstate trade commission. Wilson's message to Congress in January 1914, proposed an agency that would serve "as an indispensable instrument of information and policy," one that would moderate but not be unduly restrictive of business methods (McCraw, 1984: 118). Accordingly, the administration pushed a bill introduced by Representative James J. Covington (D-Maryland) that did not contemplate an enforcement agency but one that squared with the preference of Wilson and Brandeis for an information agency. The commission would secure and publish information, conduct investigations as directed by Congress, and suggest methods of improving business practices and antitrust enforcement (McCraw, 1984: 119).

Yet, this proposal that went to the Congress in the form of a bill to create a weak advisory commission came out in the form of a statute setting up a strong commission endowed with broad regulatory powers (Cushman, 1941: 188). This turn of events took place as a result of the inability of Congress and the president to reach final agreement on the terms of the Clayton Antitrust Bill, which was proposed with the intention of specifying in detail the meaning of unlawful trade practices. This would have left the primary responsibility for enforcement to the Department of Justice and the courts. When such precise definition proved impracticable, the president, in consultation with congressional leaders, decided to pursue a different strategy, that is, to formulate a broadly worded prohibition against "unfair competitive trade practices" and to give to the proposed trade commission the "quasi-judicial" job of applying this law to particular cases (Cushman, 1941: 186–87).

Thus, a statutory solution was abandoned for an administrative one, a strategy reinforced by the influence of George Rublee, a former member of the Progressive party. Called in by the White House to help draft antitrust legislation when Brandeis was occupied by an Interstate Commerce Commission (ICC) rate case, Rublee persuaded the president, and eventually Brandeis as well, to support the concept of a strong trade commission, which was an important plank in Theodore Roosevelt's 1912 presidential campaign. Wilson opposed the Progressive party's proposal and his "New Freedom" was originally conceived in conformity with the traditional Democratic commitment to decentralization of power; however, the deadlock over the Clayton bill and Rublee's timely intervention in the drafting of the FTC statute encouraged the president to change direction. This development marks a watershed in the development of regulation as the principal tool for policing the excesses of business (McCraw, 1984: 122–26).

Echoing the consensus of modern scholars, the historian Thomas McCraw has written that "the FTC has been a singularly unsuccessful agency during most of the seventy odd years since its creation" (McCraw, 1984: 81). This undistinguished history is largely attributable to the ambiguous ideas and policies that have governed the agency. Unlike those regulatory bodies, such as the EPA, established during the public lobby era, the broad mandate of the FTC did not reflect a conscious understanding about the virtue of agencies overseeing several industries so as to avoid "capture" and schismatic policy. Rather, the broad authority granted by the organic statute of the FTC reflected the strong disagreement that existed during the early period of the twentieth century about the appropriate role for a trade commission. For example, as Robert Cushman notes, "business, desiring a mild and benignly helpful administrative body to aid them in the solution of their problems, had nothing but antagonism for the powerful commission advocated by the enemies of trusts and big business" (Cushman, 1941: 181). Furthermore, the supporters of a strong commission included the likes of Louis Brandeis, who expressed an "antibigness ethic" and envisioned the FTC as the guardian of the small producer and shopkeeper, and those such as Herbert Croly, who wanted a trade commission as a means of avoiding the dismemberment of large firms—by regulating and thereby legitimating them (Cushman, 1941: 181; McCraw, 1984: 126–28).

The disagreement about the mission of the FTC extended to questions about the relationship of the agency to the political process. Consistent with the organizational principles of the Progressive Era, the FTC was established as an independent regulatory commission. The enabling statute provided for a board of five members, no more than three of whom would come from the same political party. The commissioners would serve terms of seven years and be paid a salary of $10,000 each, "a high figure for 1914, intended to give prestige to the new agency" (McCraw, 1984: 124). The architects of the commission believed that this prestige would be enhanced by the qualities of nonpartisanship, expertness, and stability that were expected to characterize the work of an independent commission. It was felt that the FTC should be modeled after the ICC, which commanded widespread respect, as a "means for correcting what many believed to be the partisan and pressure-controlled administration of the antitrust laws by the Department of Justice" (Cushman, 1941: 188). As Senator J. T. Morgan (D-Alabama) argued during the course of debate on the FTC statute:

> Whatever we do in regulating business should be removed as far as possible from political influence.
>
> It will be far safer to place this power in the hands of a great independent commission that will go on while administrations may change. This is one reason why I believe in having all these matters placed, so far as they can be, in the hands of a commission, taking the business matters out of politics. (*Congressional Record,* 51, 8857; quoted in Cushman, 1941: 190)

Yet, the broad authority granted the FTC ensured that its nonpolitical status would be violated constantly. The enabling act not only left it to the FTC to define "unfair methods of competition," but also gave the commission the discretion to apply the standard of unfairness, however defined, according to its estimation of whether "a proceeding by it in respect thereof would be in the interest of the public" (Section 5). Given that no consensus existed about the agency's mission, such a broad delegation of authority left the FTC exposed to shifting political winds. Furthermore, perhaps sensing that the tasks before the commission were impossible, distinguished figures such as Louis Brandeis declined President Wilson's invitation to serve as a member. Consequently, the agency got off to a woeful start, a beginning that foreshadowed a troubled history. As McCraw notes, "The FTC lacking strong leadership, drifted aimlessly from this task to that, making little impact. And on those few occasions when the commission did try to do something important, Congress or the Supreme Court intervened" (McCraw, 1984: 126; Cushman, 1941: 241).

Ironically, however, the greatest vulnerability of the commission has also been its greatest strength. The diffuse regulatory authority of the FTC, while a liability in important respects, has at least left it free from narrow interest group capture. The absence of captors has allowed the FTC to be buffeted by persistent and significant political forces, but also to be influenced from time to time by broad ideas and political movements (Katzmann, 1980; Wilson, 1980: 393). The strength and weakness of the FTC in this respect help to explain how it become a vanguard of consumer protection, but one that fell prey to a powerful political backlash.

The New Deal and the Advent of the Consumer Movement

The Wheeler–Lea Act

The FTC became an explicitly consumer protection agency for the first time in 1938 with the passage of the Wheeler–Lea Act. To be sure, the responsibility of the FTC to prevent "unfair methods of competition" involved it in consumer affairs prior to the passage of this statute. Before the Wheeler–Lea Act, however, the commission could not undertake a trade proceeding on behalf of the consumer per se, but had to demonstrate that the trade practice in question harmed the offending business's competitors. Thus, if the FTC wanted to act against a company that engaged in false or deceptive advertising judged to be injurious to the consuming public, it was necessary for the commission, before issuing a formal complaint, to document actual competition and the injurious effect on competitors.

The Supreme Court rendered a decision in 1931 that imposed such a limitation on the legal authority of the FTC and precipitated the changes brought by the Wheeler–Lea Act. In *Federal Trade Commission* v. *Rala-*

dam Co. (282 U.S. 829) the Court reversed the commission's order against the respondent to cease from representing its "obesity cure" as a scientific method of treating obesity, and from representing the preparation as a remedy for obesity, unless accompanied by the statement that it could not be taken safely except under medical direction. Justice Sutherland's opinion for the Court, while granting the claims of the agency that the acts and practices of the company involved "dangerously misleading advertisements of a remedy sold in interstate commerce," held that the commission had no power to ban these "antifat" pills on the ground of their harmfulness to the health of consumers. This was so inasmuch as the duties of the FTC did not include protecting the health of citizens, but extended only to unfair practices among business competitors.

The Wheeler–Lea Act was passed in 1938 to remedy this rigid restriction the courts applied to the regulatory activities of the FTC. This amendment to the agency's organic statute ameliorated what commissioners and members of Congress believed to be a crippling jurisdictional condition. As the bill's Senate sponsor, Burton Wheeler (D-Montana), noted in the course of debate on the legislation,

> [t]he Commission spent most of its time and most of its money allotted to it by the Congress, in running down the question of whether or not one man has lost some money by reason of unfair trade practices on the part of another. After all, Congress is not interested in whether John Smith lost some money as the result of the advertising complained of, but the question is whether or not the general public has been deceived or injured by reason of it. We are here to legislate with respect to that question. (*Congressional Record*, 80, 6593)

The legislative action taken by Congress in 1938 amended the organic statute of the FTC so that "unfair or deceptive acts or practices in commerce" were declared to be unlawful and brought within the commission's reach. This clearly gave the FTC responsibility to police trade practices that harmed the consumer as well as the competitor. The Wheeler–Lea Act amended the commission's organic statute for the first time since it was passed in 1914. That the limited authority of the FTC did not become a serious political issue until the 1930s is primarily attributable to consumer protection not being an important area of public policy prior to the depression. The Wheeler–Lea Act was one of the products forged on the anvil of the consumer movement that emerged during the 1930s. Yet an examination of the politics of consumer protection during the creation of the New Deal reveals the great limitations of this movement. Indeed, as the ensuing discussion indicates, the placement of primary responsibility for consumer protection in the FTC was, in fact, symptomatic of the weakness of consumer advocacy during the regulatory regime of the New Deal.

Consumerism in the 1930s

Although individuals such as Thorsten Veblen and Wesley Mitchell had made theoretical contributions to consumerism early in the twentieth century, widespread popular concern about this subject did not begin until the late 1920s. The National Consumers' League began in 1899, but its concern (and that of the various state affiliates) was not to provide consumer information or protection but to ensure fair treatment for workers in industries producing consumer goods (Smith, 1979–1980: 104). The activities of the league during the first two decades of the twentieth century emphasized encouraging voluntary efforts on the part of retailers to institute better working conditions for their employees. For instance, the Rhode Island League's minutes of its annual meeting in 1908 reveal that discussion centered on "moves in other cities toward influencing department stores to close at 9:00 instead of 10:00, allowing girls and women, especially those living outside the city, to reach home earlier" (Consumers' League of Rhode Island, *Minutes of the Annual Meetings,* vol. 1, Nov. 27, 1908, John Hay Library, Brown University.)[1]

Given the lack of attention to consumer issues prior to the 1930s, most of those who participated in the creation of the FTC did not consider the consumer to be part of the agency's constituency. In fact, an important, if not principal, responsibility of the FTC was to protect small business against giant competitors, even though such protection in certain cases impeded the formation of more efficient firms that, by charging lower prices, would have benefited the consumer. Reformers such as Louis Brandeis saw themselves as engaged in a "crusade against bigness," which they felt threatened autonomous individualism, a condition critical to the vitality of the polity (McCraw, 1984: 108). Such a crusade was driven by a political judgment that tended to be either indifferent or even hostile to the consumer.

It is important to note, however, that the support for the small producer expressed by many progressive reformers went hand in hand with an antipathy toward *consumption,* an antipathy that, ironically, became

---

[1] The authors thank J. Shank Gilkson of Middlebury College for bringing this material to their attention.

an important foundation principle of the consumer movement. Brandeis, for example, was repelled by "conspicuous consumption," a sentiment prevalent among significant contributors to the consumer movement during the New Deal, as well as the consumer advocates who became so prominent during the public lobby era. As McCraw notes, however, the celebration of a decentralized economy during the Progressive Era prevented reformers of that period from linking criticism of big business with support for consumer protection:

> Brandeis angrily denounced conspicuous consumption. But in so doing he drifted imperceptibly into an attack on consumer preference, a principle that lies at the very core of a market economy. Consumers had in effect betrayed him; they had refused to follow his precepts against bigness; they had revealed their true nature by passively buying the endless stream of goods that flowed from the center economy. In that way, consumers had guaranteed the success and permanence of the center firms Brandeis detested. And for such a mistake, he would never forgive them. (McCraw, 1984: 107–8)

The animating principle of the consumer movement that arose during the New Deal reflected a similar distaste for excessive materialism, but was motivated by the hope that the consumer could be encouraged to act more sensibly. While Brandeis "detested" the consumer, consumer advocates of the 1930s such as Frederick Schlink and Robert Lynd sought to protect consumers from, and educate them against, the pathologies they felt afflicted modern capitalist society.

This attention to consumer reform was encouraged by dramatic developments in the American economy during the first three decades of the twentieth century. From 1900 to 1930 the population of the United States increased by 65 percent, while from 1899 to 1930 the volume of the manufacturers increased by 151 percent, with a peak in 1929 representing an increase of 208 percent from 1899 (Lynd and Hanson, 1933: 857). This development signaled a transition whereby the great bulk of things consumed by American families was no longer made in the home, and the efforts of family members, as Lynd put it, "focused instead on *buying* a living" (1933: 857, Lynd and Hanson's emphasis).

According to a growing number of social reformers, such a change dictated a focus on consumption rather than production. It was imperative to recognize, they felt, that social factors ranging from increased urbanization to more immediate considerations involving the techniques of production and marketing had made "intelligent consumption" virtually impossible (Lynd, 1936). In the wake of such developments, consumers, who were the target of increasing and more manipulative advertising, had become "Alices in a Wonderland of conflicting claims, bright promises, fancy packages, soaring words, and almost impenetrable ignorance" (Chase and Schlink, 1935: 2; Smith, 1979–1980: 105).

The onset of the Depression amplified and focused these criticisms, which hitherto had appealed almost exclusively to a college-educated, middle-class audience (Smith, 1979–1980: 105; Lynd, 1936: 498). As frenetic efforts by business "to put its house in order" failed to precipitate an upswing, attention focused on the consumer as a critical factor in getting the economy moving again. Consumer advocates argued that previous economic policy had been seriously flawed in only considering producers' interests and that prosperity could only return if attention was paid to the needs of the consumer. Hundreds of consumer organizations and agencies sprung up on a local as well as a national level (Smith, 1979–1980: 105).

In recognition of the emergence of the consumer as an independent agent whose needs had to be considered in dealing with business and labor, a Consumer Advisory Board (CAB) was established in 1933 as part of the National Recovery Administration (NRA). Though given meager power, the CAB played a significant role in challenging the business-oriented price and production policies of the NRA. Moreover, it tried to develop a consumer constituency that would support a change in policy. A Bureau of Economic Education was established, which was headed by Paul Douglas of the University of Chicago and responsible for a limited experiment in the organization of county consumer councils. About 150 of these councils were eventually established, but, as Ellis Hawley notes, "they never developed into the effective consumer pressure group that their creators had in mind" (Hawley, 1966: 76).

The failure to establish a strong constituency remained the major weakness of the consumer movement during the 1930s. Whereas industry and labor could turn to their well-organized constituencies to provide political pressure, the consumer as such remained relatively inarticulate, indifferent, and unorganized, and therefore unable to wield economic and political power (Hawley, 1966, 198–204). As a result, consumer advocates played a marginal role in the New Deal.

In the last analysis, this status reflected the consumer movement's attack on certain core principles of a market economy that were deeply ingrained in American culture. There was, to be sure, a moderate group of consumer advocates, composed of such organizations as the American Home Economics Association, the General Federation of Woman's

Clubs, and the American Association of University Women, who did not criticize consumption patterns in American society but favored increased consumer information. A more militant group, however, represented by Frederick Schlink's Consumer's Research and academicians such as Robert Lynd and Rexford Tugwell, likened consumer behavior to a pathology bred by a confusing and manipulative marketplace, which undermined values expressing deeper and subtler ways of viewing human experiences (Smith, 1979–1980; 105–6; Lynd, 1936: 492–93; 1957: 31–32).

Consumer advocates were quite conscious of the challenge their movement represented to the American way of life, and, accordingly, were not optimistic about the prospects for the development of a powerful consumer lobby. As Lynd wrote in a 1936 *Political Science Quarterly* article, "Democracy's Third Estate: The Consumer,"

> [I]t is small wonder that one's role as private consumer leads the furtive existence that it does. Nor does it appear likely that "the consumer" will become more self-conscious and coherent or less hypnotized by his preoccupation with his role as producer in the near future. The undertow of the culture sets heavily in the direction of the individual's struggling to earn more money rather than to maximize the purchasing power of such income as he has. The latter course of action smacks too much of the penny-pinching mode of life which the more articulate element of American life likes to think of itself as escaping from; and reacknowledgement of it as a permanent personal design for living still feels too much like a denial of one's heritage as an American and the admission of personal defeat. (Lynd, 1936: 514)

The strong forces in American culture that obstructed advances in consumer consciousness led advocates to look to government as "a surrogate responsible for the public interest." They resorted to the hope that the role of consumer could rise to public attention through "the action of the agencies of public administration in Washington" (Lynd, 1936: 515). Yet the proposal of such individuals as Lynd and Leon Henderson, both of whom played active roles in the aggressive, though politically ineffective CAB, for a department of the consumer failed to make much of an impression on Roosevelt and members of Congress (Hawley, 1966: 200). Franklin Roosevelt was not unsympathetic to consumerism, but the exigencies of the Depression focused reform efforts on economic security and better conditions for the laborer. The 1937 Executive Reorganization bill proposed a Department of Public Welfare that might include a consumer's bureau, but this possibility disappeared after the president's initial administrative reform program was defeated (Hawley, 1966: 200). The economic crisis of the 1930s simply did not provide a very suitable environment for New Deal public administration to attend closely to the needs of the consumer.

In many respects, then, the consumer remained the "forgotten man" of the New Deal. The 1930s witnessed the birth of a consumers' movement, but this movement and the challenge it posed to the American political economy were of limited significance until the late 1960s.

The passage of the Wheeler–Lea Act symbolized the weakness of the consumer movement during the New Deal. This act established the FTC as the most important federal agency for consumer protection, but by default. The responsibility to regulate advertising was granted to the commission only after efforts, which were supported by consumer groups, to place that power in the Food and Drug Administration (FDA) were blocked. In fact, a bill sponsored by Senator Copeland (R-New York) in 1933, granting the FDA authority to regulate advertising was widely considered overdue and appropriate, for the lack of that power had long been recognized as a defect in the organic act of the federal agency charged with protecting the public from unsanitary and dangerous products.

Although the FTC had shown an interest in protecting the public from deceptive advertising prior to the *Raladam* case, consumer groups preferred to place such responsibility in the FDA. The FDA enjoyed much greater enforcement powers relative to the FTC. According to the provisions of the Copeland Bill, the FDA would have powers of factory inspection under certain circumstances, could seek injunctions to deny a company the right to make interstate shipments, and could impose heavy fines and prison terms. The FTC, in contrast, could only enter a cease-and-desist order (Stone, 1977: 159–61). Moreover, the Department of Agriculture, in which the FDA resided at this time, was staffed, at least during the early days of the New Deal, with enthusiastic consumer advocates such as Rexford Tugwell and Jerome Frank; the FTC, on the other hand, in the view of those who favored strong regulation, was controlled by individuals who were all too friendly with business interests (*Business Week,* April 8, 1937: 42).

In this respect, the passage of the Wheeler–Lea Act in 1938 represented a defeat for consumer groups and a victory for those interests who wanted a less onerous regulation of advertising than they expected from the FDA. The authority to regulate unfair or deceptive acts or practices in commerce was granted to the FTC, while the Copeland Bill, as finally passed, virtually stripped the FDA of authority over advertising of food and drugs, unless such advertising could be tied directly to health problems.

Although dismissed as virtually worthless by consumer groups, proponents of the Wheeler–Lea Act saw it as an effective compromise between the need to allow for flexibility in commercial practices, on the one hand, and the need to strengthen the confidence of the public in advertising claims, on the other hand. Noting the elimination of numerous time-honored slogans and themes, as well as a marked toning down of claims in advertising copy soon after the passage of the Wheeler–Lea Act, John Benson, president of the American Association of Advertising Agents, claimed that the law was "the best thing that has happened to the advertising field." That companies could no longer make fraudulent claims, such as hair tonics would cure dandruff or baldness, was accepted as both fair and beneficial by most executives in fields affected by the new trade legislation (*New York Times,* Aug. 14, 1938: section III, 8).

At the same time, this legislation fell far short of the expectations expressed by militant consumer advocates. The elimination of blatant fraud in commercial practices did little to reform consumption patterns or rectify the position of great disadvantage advocates believed the consumer occupied relative to business. Yet the FTC was unlikely to engage in a zealous pursuit of the consumer interest. The ambiguous mission that had always hampered the FTC was, if anything, further confused by the passage of the Wheeler–Lea Act. This law enabled the commission to make consumer protection an important new area of concern for public policy; however, the agency's commitment to the consumer was tempered by its continuing responsibility for dealing with the competitive process. In fact, the responsibility of the FTC to protect small businesses was extended in 1936 with the passage of the Robinson–Patman Act, authorizing the commission to forbid certain types of price discrimination practices especially harmful to small retailers. The continuing responsibility to police competitive practices was not necessarily incompatible with the agency's new authority to protect the public from unfair and deceptive business practices, but it deflected attention from the *consumerism* supported by individuals such as Robert Lynd and Leon Henderson. As a result, consumer advocates continuously criticized the FTC for lacking a strong sense of direction in the organization of its regulatory activities.

This desuetude was aggravated by the lack of attention paid to the FTC during the 1930s, which meant it played a very limited role in the regulatory regime of the New Deal period. During the early days of his presidency, Roosevelt sought to put a New Deal stamp on the FTC by removing the most conservative of its commissioners, William E. Humphrey. The appointment of Humphrey by President Coolidge in 1925 signaled a significant change in commission policy, which, according to its critics, transformed the FTC into an agency that "served not as an overseer but a partner of business" (Cushman, 1941: 225–26; Leuchtenburg, 1967: 278). Roosevelt, however, was rebuffed in his effort to terminate Commissioner Humphrey's service prior to the expiration of his seven-year term in the 1935 landmark case of *U.S.* v. *Humphrey's Executor* (295 U.S. 602, 1935). Justice Sutherland's decision granted constitutional legitimacy to independent regulatory agencies, proclaiming that a commissioner could not be removed on the basis of political disagreement:

> The power of removal here proclaimed for the President . . . threatens the independence of a commission, which is not only wholly disconnected from the executive department, but which . . . was created by Congress as a means of carrying into operation legislative and judicial powers, and as an agency of the legislative and judicial departments. (*U.S.* v. *Humphrey's Executor,* 295 U.S. 630, 1935)

This decision and the failure to bring independent regulatory commissions under firmer presidential direction through administrative reform legislation during Roosevelt's second term encouraged his administration to use regular executive agencies and newly created independent agencies, such as the National Labor Relations Board (NLRB), to spearhead the New Deal program. Consequently, the FTC became a source of patronage for southern congressmen who held influential positions on the commission's oversight committees in the House and Senate (Cox et al., 1969: 140). Thus, the FTC not only suffered from rather weak enforcement powers and the incipient state of the consumer movement, but also from a lack of professional competence that afflicted its staff until the late 1960s.

In light of this history, the evolution of the FTC into a vigorous agent of consumer protection between 1969 and 1978 is remarkable. Yet the Wheeler–Lea Act and other developments during the New Deal did endow the agency with a rich source of potential. The change in the organic statute of the FTC significantly broadened the powers granted in the original trade commission act. Section 5 of the original statute, which extended only to "unfair acts of competition," was now amended to make unlawful "unfair or deceptive acts or practices in commerce," thus giving the commission an unlimited regulatory license to patrol the marketplace. Although most trade associations were very receptive to FTC regulation, a few did express concern about granting an executive agency such unlimited legal authority. Hugo Mock, counsel for the Toilet Goods Association, warned his colleagues soon after the Wheeler–Lea Act was passed "that the language has the merit of simplicity, but also the defect of indefiniteness, which means that it gives a great deal of latitude to the Trade Commission to decide what is an unfair or deceptive act or practice" (*New York Times*, May 25, 1938: 32). During the New Deal, the FTC became, as another legal advisor to trade organizations put it, a "director of national business conduct," in theory only (*New York Times*, March 20, 1938: section III, 8). Yet the emergence of the public lobby regime was to actualize this legal authority to an extraordinary degree.

The Federal Trade Commission and the Public Lobby Regime

The FTC underwent a dramatic change beginning in 1969 that transformed an agency known to its critics as "the little old lady of Pennsylvania Avenue" into an aggressive consumer advocate. The metamorphosis of the FTC occurred amid the broad developments in the American political economy that ushered in the public lobby regime. One important indicator of the advent of a new reform era was the rise of environmentalism and the creation of the EPA. Yet, just as important was the emergence of the consumer movement from the decidedly marginal status of the New Deal to a central place in the regulatory regime of the public lobby era.

According to Ellis Hawley, consumer activists during the late 1920s and 1930s offered a critique of economic behavior that was "somehow un-American." Indeed, we have seen that consumer advocates themselves granted as much. Because of this strident rejection of certain fundamental American values, Hawley claims, "the advocacy of the consumer causes was left largely to eccentrics, nonconformists, misfits, dilettanti, and amateur enthusiasts; to such groups as college professors, clubwomen, social workers, recent immigrants, and a few professional agitators, none of whom could wield much political power or speak for any well-organized constituency" (Hawley, 1966: 200).

Similarly, Ralph Nader and a handful of supporters began their consumer advocacy in Washington as seemingly powerless "gadflies and outsiders." Yet "Nader's raiders," as they were dubbed by the Washington press corps, went on to become the core of a large community wielding great influence in Congress and through the courts (Armstrong, 1971). As noted in Chapter 4, after the election of Jimmy Carter in 1976, the last major center of resistance to their influence—the executive branch—was "occupied" by some sixty former activists in the public interest movement, many of them closely associated with and recommended to the president by Ralph Nader. In fact, it was at the suggestion of Nader that Carter appointed Michael Pertschuk as chairman of the FTC (personal interview with Michael Pertschuk, July 20, 1982). As *Fortune* reported in 1977, "clearly Nader's invaders were inside the gates" (Cameron, 1977: 252). By the late 1970s, then, the once-forlorn consumer movement had become a major part of the establishment, though a reconstructed one.

The development of consumerism during the 1960s is usually attributed to the "entrepreneurial politics" of Ralph Nader and a small circle of supporters who managed to translate a narrow base of expert knowledge and meager funds into a flourishing nationwide movement (see, for example, Pertschuk, 1982: 1–45). The surge of "the consumer," however, was related to the broad ideological and institutional changes we discuss in Chapter 3. One critical factor was the emergence of a middle class with loose ties to American industry. The emergence after World War II of a large group of articulate, relatively affluent individuals, who, through employment in education, government, and the social services, were largely independent of business influence, was a necessary condition for the development and support of consumerism. (Stone, 1977: 232–33.) Unlike the New Deal, which not surprisingly was dominated by the exigencies of economic deprivation, postwar conditions in the United States provided a far more favorable environment for attention to the problems associated with what Robert Lynd called "buying a living."

A departure from the New Deal in this respect began during the Kennedy and Johnson administrations. Although the New Frontier and Great Society were focused primarily on extending the New Deal commitment to economic security, both Kennedy and Johnson began to address issues that related to the "quality of life" in American society. Kennedy, in fact, was the first president to give specific support and sympathy to the consumer's cause (Creighton, 1976: 43). Following the tradition of Roosevelt in associating programmatic liberalism with an extension of rights, Kennedy's first special message to Congress on the consumer identified a consumer's "bill of rights." These rights included:

(1) The right to safety—to be protected against the marketing of goods which are hazardous to health or life.
(2) The right to be informed—to be protected against fraudulent, deceitful, or grossly misleading information, advertising, labelling or other practices, and to be given the facts he needs to make an informed choice.

(3) The right to choose—to be assured, wherever possible, access to a variety of products and services at competitive prices; and in those industries in which competition is not workable and government regulation is substituted, an assurance of satisfactory quality and service at fair prices.

(4) The right to be heard—to be assured that consumer interests will receive full and sympathetic consideration in the formulation of government policy, and fair and expeditious treatment in its administrative tribunals. (*Public Papers of the Presidents,* March 15, 1962: 236)

Yet, the notable recognition of the "consumer's rights" during the Kennedy administration proved to be nearly as insignificant as the creation of the Consumers' Advisory Board during the 1930s (Creighton, 1974: 43). In the last analysis, the New Frontier envisioned an important extension but not a fundamental departure from the regulatory politics of the New Deal. Certainly there was no challenge during the Kennedy presidency to the institutional formula of the New Deal tradition. That is to say, the architects of Kennedy's program readily accepted the leading role of the president in public policy and the broad delegation of authority to administration tribunals. In general, Kennedy's attention to consumer affairs emphasized strengthening rather than remaking existing regulatory patterns.

The view of consumerism as a significant, yet minor, area of public policy was also characteristic of the Johnson administration. The architects of the Great Society reaffirmed Kennedy's proclamation of "consumer rights" and developed further a reform vision dedicated to "quality of life" issues.[2] In January 1964, Johnson established a Committee on

---

[2] In an August 1965 memo, White House aide Douglas Cater urged the president to demonstrate that he was "deeply concerned with the 'quality' as well as the 'quantity' of life in America," by "proclaim[ing] a number of specific noneconomic goals toward which [the president was] striving" (Memorandum, Douglas Cater to LBJ, Aug. 3, 1965, *Office Files of Horace Busby,* Box 51). Johnson approved of this idea and made this theme a major part of his 1966 State of the Union address:

> A great people flower not from wealth and power but from a society which spurs them to the fullness of their genius. That alone is the Great Society . . . Yet slowly, painfully, on the edge of victory has come the knowledge that shared prosperity is not enough. In the midst of abundance modern man walks oppressed by forces which menace and confine the quality of his life, and which individual abundance alone will not overcome. (*Public Papers of the Presidents,* Jan. 12, 1966: 6)
>
> In laying out the obligations of the government to ensure "the good life," Johnson explicitly mentions the obligation to protect the environment and consumer.

Consumer Interests, an action, he promised, "assured that the voice of the consumer will be loud, clear, uncompromising, and effective in the highest councils of the Federal Government." So as to fulfill this promise, Johnson appointed Esther Peterson, an assistant secretary of labor, as the chairman of the committee and his special assistant for consumer affairs. Thus, the president announced, "[f]or the first time in history, the American consumer interest—so closely identified with the public interest—will be directly represented in the White House" (*Public Papers of the Presidents,* Jan. 3, 1964: 108).

But this position never fulfilled the potential its close relationship to the White House promised, and Ms. Peterson returned to her job in the Department of Labor in early 1967. The administration's reaction to her departure suggests how consumer issues were considered to be of symbolic importance alone—window dressing, if you will, for the major initiatives of the Great Society. Upon hearing of Ms. Peterson's desire to return to the Department of Labor, White House aide Bill Moyers wrote in a memo to Johnson:

> This leaves us—if you approve of this step—with the question of what to do about the consumer role. For political reasons, I doubt the wisdom of leaving it unfulfilled. While it does little substantively, it does fill a political need. For the President to be concerned with consumer affairs is important. (Memorandum for the President, Bill Moyers, March 30, 1966, *Office Files of Bill Moyers,* Box 11)

This tepid support for consumer issues notwithstanding, the Great Society was an important way station to the activism that characterized government programs in this policy area during the 1970s. The vacated position of special assistant for consumer affairs was filled by Betty Furness, a onetime television personality. Although this appointment was considered to be a worthless one at the time by consumer advocates, Furness did become, during her time in office, progressively more outspoken on matters of the consumer's interest (Creighton, 1976: 44). Moreover, as the Vietnam War escalated during 1966 and 1967, imposing a serious burden on the federal budget, consumer issues, which entailed little direct government expenditure compared to more mainstream New Deal–Great Society social welfare programs, appealed increasingly to the president's agenda setters. Into this proconsumer environment entered the policy entrepreneurs in the Congress and public interest lobbies, leading to a flurry of consumer protection legislation during the late 1960s (Pertschuk, 1982: 19–26).

Although the support of the Johnson administration was a significant factor in the rise of the consumer movement, the devastation of his presidency brought on by the national reaction to urban riots and the Vietnam War may have been even more important. The virtual collapse of Johnson's popular support initiated an assault on the presidency and political parties that sharpened and focused consumer advocates' criticism of the American political economy. The decline of the institutional regime forged by Democratic liberalism proved to be a great opportunity for public interest groups and their advocates to alter the shape of American political life.

This insurgency had a powerful influence on the FTC, which remained a "neglected" agency, as it had been throughout the New Deal period, until 1969. Yet, by 1977, with the appointment of Michael Pertschuk as chairman of the commission, the agency had come to reflect to a remarkable degree the same ideas of consumer advocates that had long been spurned as "un-American." Indeed, as the Democratic leaders of the Senate and House commerce committees expressed to President Ford in the fall of 1975, consumer regulation had become "as American as hot dogs, baseball, apple pie and Chevrolet" (quoted in Pertschuk, 1982: 20).

Nevertheless, the sudden and forceful attack on the FTC that began in 1978 attests to the severe limitations of the seemingly triumphant consumer movement. In part, this "backlash" illustrates the resurgence of business influence on regulatory politics in the United States during the late 1970s. It also reveals, however, serious weaknesses in the consumer movement. These shortcomings are best reflected in the philosophy of consumerism itself, which in turn gave shape to changes in institutions and policies during the public lobby era. It is to these changes that we now turn our attention.

New Ideas

The emergence of the consumer movement as a powerful national influence on regulatory policy was a response to a new set of ideas in the late 1960s advocating aggressive government intervention in the economy on behalf of the consumer. To be sure, these ideas were not a complete departure from the past. The consumer movement and the FTC have a long history, and those reforms that were put in place during the public lobby era owed much to this past. Unlike the environmental movement and the development of the EPA, which directly reflect the regulatory politics of the public lobby era, the resurgent consumer movement and the revitalized FTC continued to display certain traits reminiscent of regulatory reform during the Progressive Era and the New Deal.

In particular, the surge of consumerism brought into the mainstream the strong criticisms of American consumption patterns that consumer advocates of the 1930s had articulated from the periphery of the New Deal. The more aggressive consumer advocates of the public lobby era reveal the same ironic distaste for consumer preferences expressed by Frederick Schlink and Robert Lynd earlier in the twentieth century. Ralph Nader and those who share his views are motivated by more than a desire to educate consumers about the obligations companies have to their customers; in addition, they seek to reform the consumer's values and behavior. Echoing the concerns of consumer advocates during the 1930s, contemporary activists charge that business and market forces have enslaved the consumer to false idols. Nader, for example, charges that "corporations, by their control of the market and economy, have been able to divert scarce resources to uses that have little human benefit or are positively harmful." Corporate abuse, in effect, creates a massive "involuntary subeconomy" that severely vitiates the quality of life in American society:

> By [involuntary sub-economy] I mean the billions that consumers would not have paid if they knew or could control what they were getting, or if corporations observed elementary standards of honesty, safety, and utility in producing and selling things that are bought. Consumers are now spending billions of dollars for products under false pretenses: meat and poultry that are adulterated with fat and water; patent medicines, mouthwashes and "aids" to beauty and diet that do far less than they are said to do or nothing at all. (Nader, 1973a: 5)

In Nader's view the abuses of the market economy are sufficiently damaging and pervasive to justify a challenge to the basic principles and achievements of advanced capitalist society. As he wrote in 1971:

> This year the gross national product of the United States will exceed one trillion dollars, while the economy will fail to meet a great many urgent human needs. . . . Indeed, the quality of life is deteriorating in so many ways that the traditional statistical measurements of the "standard of living" according to personal income, housing, ownership of cars and appliances, etc., have come to sound increasingly phony. (Nader, 1973a: 4)

The consumer advocates of the public lobby era continued a tradition, which could be traced back to the Progressive Era and reformers such as Louis Brandeis, whereby criticism of market forces led indirectly to a rejection of consumer preferences that were at the foundation of a market economy. But following consumer advocates of the 1930s, contemporary critics of the political economy have chosen to save rather than heap scorn and derision upon the American consumer.

The consumer movement of the 1970s, however, was also extensively influenced by the civil rights and antiwar movements in a way that sharply distinguished it from previous defenders of the consumer's interests. Their marginal status during the New Deal notwithstanding, consumer advocates of the 1930s readily accepted the New Deal emphasis on presidential leadership and benign public administration as a solution to the injustices that afflicted the marketplace. They supported Roosevelt's efforts to reconstruct the executive department into a vehicle of reform, believing, as Robert Lynd put it, "that if man's role of consumer [was] to rise to public attention, it [would] probably have to be through the action of agencies of public administration in Washington" (Lynd, 1936: 515).

While supportive of strengthening government agencies responsible for guarding the rights of consumers, the more critical advocates of the public lobby era were driven by a passion for change that far surpassed the goal of strengthening the FTC or establishing the department of the consumer in Washington. The animating principle of consumer advocacy was direct citizen activism, an objective that reflects the social vision of other reformers who shaped the public lobby regime. Decrying "a citizenship of wholesale delegation and abdication to public and private power systems," Ralph Nader argues for a structural change in society that will achieve participatory democracy in economic as well as political matters:

> Building a new way of life around citizenship action must be the program of the immediate future. The ethos that looks upon citizenship as an avocation or opportunity must be replaced with the commitment to citizenship as an obligation, a continual receiver of our time, energy, and skill. And that commitment must be transformed into a strategy of action that develops instruments of change while it focuses on what needs to be done. This is a critical point. Too often people who are properly outraged over injustice concentrate so much on decrying the abuses and demanding the desired reforms that they never build the instruments to accomplish their objectives in a lasting manner. (1973b: 369)

For many consumer advocates of the 1970s, then, federal regulatory power *on behalf* of the consumer was at best a partial solution. Consumer activists have, to be sure, supported a vigorous regulation of industry. Nader, in fact, has supported the federal chartering or licensing of corporations, proposing the establishment of a federal chartering agency with the responsibility of licensing all companies in interstate trade. The formation of corporations with massive national or international power required, at the least, a strong national authority (Nader, 1973c: 358). Yet it was necessary, consumer advocates stressed, that administrative agencies responsible for controlling corporate abuses not become as unresponsive and inefficient as regulatory agencies typically had in the past. Regulatory bodies, therefore, should not be delegated responsibility to act for consumers but be governed by administrative mechanisms, such as liberal provisions for citizen suits, "so that agency lethargy or inefficiency could be checked by interested citizen activity" (Nader, 1973: 365). In the last analysis, the achievement of a viable participatory democracy—one that could realistically challenge corporate power—required the infusion of public administration with democratic ideals and action.

It is important to recognize that not all of those active in the consumer movement endorse this grand vision. Many consumer advocates, in fact, argue that the religious fervor that drives Ralph Nader and his associates is not particularly relevant to protecting consumers. For example, influential organizations like Consumers Union have a primary interest in testing products and informing the consumer, which, from Nader's point of view, is too limited an agenda for the consumer movement. Accordingly, Nader resigned from the Consumers Union board of directors in mid-1975, arguing that consumer education was worthless without more forceful action to change the system that perverted and oppressed consumer choice (Creighton, 1976: 63). Therefore, the consumer movement is a diverse one with different philosophical understandings about the appropriate role of government and advocacy. As Mark Silbergeld, director of the Washington office for Consumers Union, notes:

> Some [consumer advocates] feel that there need only be a modicum of health and safety guaranteed by regulation; others feel that government should regulate everything that breathes. For example, the Consumers Union does not feel there should be a ban (prohibition) on tobacco. This position may prompt some elements of the consumer movement to consider us traitors to consumer health. We do support full disclosure of the risks of using tobacco and control of smoking in public places. . . . Nader and Pertschuk are idealists. They feel that the role of government and advocates is to directly reform people's lives and values. My feeling is that people should know what they are getting into. (personal interview, July 23, 1986)

In a sense, the burning morality of the more forceful consumer advocates represents both the greatest strength and weakness of the consumer movement. The "passion that rules Ralph Nader" enabled him to capture the attention of the American people, especially the young. Nader inspired thousands of students in law, medicine, engineering, and every other field to work for him. Indeed, at the height of his influence in the early 1970s, it was said that getting a job with Nader was "tougher than getting into Yale Law School" (Armstrong, 1971: 147). The young and talented amateurs who formed the mass base of Nader's movement exemplify the vitality and compelling "underdog" quality of public interest advocacy that put consumer reformers, to use Pertschuk's phrase, "on the side of the angels" during the late 1960s and early 1970s (Pertschuk, 1982: 44). As the economic historian Lucy Black Creighton wrote in 1976:

> Nader has been able to do what the consumer movement has not been able to do—he has raised money to support the cause and has brought about change. Probably even more important, Nader has been able to generate a level of enthusiasm and publicity for the consumer that is far greater than at any time before he came on the scene. The consumer movement is dependent on Nader for its continuing vitality. (Creighton, 1976: 63–64)

Yet, the uncompromising idealism at the basis of the most aggressive consumer advocacy has taken its toll on the consumer movement as well. The religious fervor with which militant advocates have attacked corporate power has in certain respects sacrificed consumer reform on the altar of rhetorical excess. Richard Armstrong noted in his 1971 profile of Nader:

> If, on the one hand, Nader has advanced the cause of consumer protection, by his skillful marshalling of facts in support of specific reforms, he has, on the other hand, made reform more difficult through his habit of coating his facts with invective and assigning the worst possible motives to almost everybody but himself. By some peculiar logic of his own, he has cast the consumer and the corporation as bitter enemies, and he seems to think that no reform is worth its salt unless business greets it with a maximum of suspicion, hostility and fear. (Armstrong, 1971: 145)

Robert Reich, who headed the Office of Policy and Planning at the FTC during the time Michael Pertschuk was chairman, characterized such an ideological position as a "David and Goliath" view of the world. Although, as we have noted, there were competing philosophies within the consumer movement, this polarizing vision had a powerful influence on the institutional network of the consumer movement, including the FTC (personal interview with Robert Reich, Nov. 20, 1984). As a result, the FTC became the principal actor in an extraordinary burst of creative consumer reform during the 1970s, only to find itself at the center of a political controversy that severely challenged the viability of consumerism in American politics.

New Institutions

Although the influence of the ideas discussed in the previous section on regulatory institutions was not direct, there is no doubt that consumerism did have a strong impact on the decisionmaking process. For all their visionary rhetoric, consumer advocates centrally concerned themselves with influencing institutions. In fact, as Chapter 3 notes, the public interest movement integrated the revolutionary ideas of the New Left with the more pragmatic and institutional emphasis of the New Deal. In a sense, the consumer movement sought to harness the revolutionary vision and fervor of the civil rights and antiwar movements as an agent for change "within the system." As one of Nader's close associates, Lowell Dodge, noted about his colleague's open disdain for the "counterculture":

> There's a conflict between living life on a level of feeling on the one hand and Ralph's product ethic on the other. To produce, to have an impact— that's what Ralph admires. Consciousness III doesn't give a damn about the FTC. Ralph does. (Armstrong, 1971: 147)[3]

It is interesting in this regard that a 1969 Nader report on the FTC is widely regarded as a first cause in influencing dramatic changes at the agency. As a result of these changes, the commission became the principal fomenter of consumer activism during the public lobby area. Accordingly, the Nader report's effect on the FTC illustrates how the broad

[3] "Consciousness III" is a form of thought that Charles Reich associated with the youthful rebellion of the 1960s. In his widely read book on the counterculture, *The Greening of America* (1970), Reich claimed that this intellectual orientation had emerged from earlier stages of American consciousness that inhibited, rather than encouraged, the development of human potential. "Consciousness I" is the consciousness behind the American dream: a mixture of individual dignity and greed. "Consciousness II" is the dominant consciousness of the corporate state, the New Deal solution to the abuses of capitalism. "Consciousness III," which Reich felt had begun to emerge from all this in the youth of the 1960s, is one of self-actualization, "of openness to any and all experience." For a sympathetic but critical analysis of Reich's thesis see Peter Marin's review of *The Greening of America* (*New York Times,* Nov. 8, 1970: VII, 3).

ideas of consumerism were explicitly applied in remaking regulatory institutions during the 1970s.

The report was issued in January 1969 by seven volunteers organized by Nader, six of whom were students, or recent graduates, of Harvard and Yale law schools. Its central theme was that mediocre leadership and personnel constituted a "malignant cancer" that debased the integrity of the commission. As a result, the agency was mired in trivia and unable, and apparently unwilling, to enforce its statutes. Special disdain was expressed for the chairman of the FTC, Paul Rand Dixon, who, the report charged, viewed the resurgent consumer movement with skepticism, if not disdain. A Tennessean, Dixon was also derided for sustaining the long-standing practice of using the FTC as a source of patronage plums for southern congressmen, such as Joe Evins another Tennessee native, who held important seats on the agency's oversight committees. Politics intruded on the commission in such a way that lawyers from prestigious law schools were actually discriminated against, prompting the report to conclude that "bright men need not apply to the FTC" (Cox et al., 1969: 150–58).

Beyond the effort to expose the lassitude of the commission, the Nader report asserted the existence of a "crisis" for the consumer that transcended individual personalities and capabilities. The regulation of unfair competition and the credo caveat emptor (let the buyer beware) may have once served the American public. By the 1960s, however, the Nader report argued, a "new marketplace" had developed "which indicated it was no longer wise for government to rely solely on fostering competition to do the job" (Cox et al., 1969: 16–19). The conditions that defined the new economy were: the rise of the corporate state through the growth of conglomerates and shared monopolies into an oligopolistic structure; the communications revolution, including use of nationwide television and the rise of cost of access to the medium; the information explosion, including increasing use of mass data-handling techniques to attack the privacy and autonomy of the consumer; and the growing sophistication of the science of applied psychology, involving influence by suggestion, subtle deception through image manipulation, and the creation of the demand through associations with sex, fear, and power fantasies. These new developments demanded that the government, particularly the FTC, direct its energies toward active protection of the increasingly vulnerable consumer.

The FTC, though, in 1969 seemed woefully negligent in responding to the growing consumer crisis. Although Congress increasingly since the 1930s had recognized the deceptions suffered by the American public, the FTC had not fulfilled its new role as protector of the consumer. Said the Nader report:

> There is a piece of heroic statuary in front of the Federal Trade Commission's building in Washington, D.C., that symbolizes the purpose of the agency as set forth in its founding statute. The statuary depicts an unruly and powerful horse—American business, a danger and a menace unharnessed—being restrained by a strong and determined young man, the FTC. But the FTC is neither young nor young-thinking, it is not strong nor does it seek to be strong, and it has no desire to restrain. Indeed, the commission does not view American industry as a horse at all, but rather as a docile beast who now and then needs a mild "whoa." (Cox et al., 1969: 37)

The Nader report concluded by calling for a series of measures that might reorient the agency to its proper role—protection of the consumer. It recommended increased regulation of modern advertising techniques, better commissionwide planning, new programs for the ghetto consumer, more information disclosure to mobilize maximum support of consumers, more statutory authority to seek preliminary injunctions and criminal penalties for violations of FTC law, and the uprooting of political and regional cronyism that had for years undermined the agency's professional competence (Cox et al.: 163–173).

Such criticism of the FTC was not especially radical or novel. Indeed, similar assaults documenting mismanagement and demoralization had been directed at the FTC since the 1920s (see, for example, Henderson, 1924). The direct impact the Nader report had on the FTC, however, was surprising. It sparked a series of political actions that eventually revitalized the agency. Later that year further criticism was directed at the FTC by the American Bar Association (ABA) in a report prepared at the request of President Nixon (ABA, 1969). Though more moderate in tone and scholarly in approach, the sixteen practitioners and scholars who composed the special ABA commission essentially shared the Nader report's criticisms of the FTC. For example, in its analysis of the agency's consumer protection programs, the ABA report found "the agency [had] been preoccupied with technical labelling and advertising practices of the most inconsequential sort" (ABA, 1969: 2). Noting the long history of the failure of the FTC to fulfill its promise—to live up to the potential of its broad statutory authority—the ABA report concluded:

> [T]his Commission believes that it should be the last of the long series of committees and groups which have earnestly insisted that drastic changes

were essential to recreate the FTC in its intended image. The case for change is plain. What is required is that changes now be made, and in depth. Further temporizing is indefensible. Notwithstanding the great potential of the FTC in the field of antitrust and consumer protection, if change does not occur, there will be no substantial purpose to be served by its continued existence; the essential work to be done must then be served by other governmental institutions. (1969: 129)

The authoritative ABA report served to reinforce the criticisms of the Nader group, precipitating strong efforts on the part of Congress and President Nixon to remake the commission from the ground up. In September 1969, just as the ABA report was issued, the agency became the target of hearings before the Senate Subcommittee on Administration Practices and Procedures, which was chaired by Edward Kennedy. After two days of hearings, Senator Kennedy closed the proceedings by admonishing the FTC to model its activities after ardent consumer advocates in the public interest movement and Congress:

The Federal Trade Commission should be a household word on the Main Streets of America, not because of what it has not done, but because of what it can do and will do for our citizens. The name Paul Rand Dixon should bring the same associations to the average newspaper reader as the name Ralph Nader. [FTC Commissioner] Mary Gardiner Jones should be known as well as Betty Furness; and [FTC Commissioners] Everitt McIntyre, Phil Elman, and James Nicholson should get the same attention from consumer groups and publications as Phil Hart, Bill Proxmire, and Gaylord Nelson, for the FTC Commissioners are also meant to be protectors of the little man, advocates for the people, and sources of power for the consumer and small businessman. (U.S., Senate, 1969: 109)

This sentiment was echoed by President Nixon in his special message to the Congress on consumer protection of October 30, 1969. In a remarkable demonstration of bipartisan support for consumerism he called for the adoption of a "Buyer's Bill of Rights," which in its particulars was very similar to those pronounced by the Kennedy and Johnson administrations. Unlike these earlier presidencies, however, Nixon took direct action to strengthen the commitment to consumer protection at the FTC. Endorsing the recommendations of the ABA report, Nixon announced that "the time [had] now come for the reactivation and revitalization of the FTC." Accordingly, he promised that his appointees to the commission would take measures "to initiate a new era of vigorous action" to protect the consumer (*Public Papers of the Presidents,* 1969: 887).

With the support of the White House, two Nixon-appointed chairmen of the commission—Casper Weinberger and Miles Kirkpatrick (who served as the chairmen of the ABA commission)—began in 1970 to institute a top-to-bottom overhauling of the organization and personnel of the FTC. Taking advantage of the lack of civil service protection of the FTC attorneys, who compose about 75 percent of commission professional employees, Weinberger discharged eighteen of the thirty-one top-level staff members. Upon replacing Weinberger in September 1970, Miles Kirkpatrick, with the able assistance of his executive director, Basil Mezines, began transforming the remainder of the professional staff; in all, Kirkpatrick replaced nearly a third of the middle and lower-level staff (Muris and Clarkson, 1981: 4–5; Clarkson, 1981: 55). Due to the efforts of these Republican chairmen, a step considered essential by the Nader report and other agency critics was dramatically undertaken: the "deadwood" in the FTC was replaced by younger attorneys, most of whom came from the nation's more prestigious law schools. Furthermore, for the most part, these attorneys brought to the agency a strong commitment to consumer protection; consequently, an immediate push began in the commission for more aggressive control of advertising and antitrust action against large corporations.

Another contributing factor to the revitalization of the FTC was an organizational renovation, initially carried out by Weinberger and subsequently refined by his successors. Weinberger consolidated the heretofore-disparate organizational apparatus into two principal operating bureaus—competition and consumer protection. The Office of Policy, Planning and Evaluation was also created to aid the commission, which was mired in an ad hoc case-by-case approach to law enforcement, in determining priorities. Among its main effects, this reorganization plan reduced the number of levels of review channels between the staff and commission members, greatly expediting the aggressive pursuit of deceptive and unfair business practices (Kovacic, 1980: 158–160).

Also noteworthy was the strengthening of the regional offices of the FTC between 1969 and 1980. Long considered a dumping ground of inferior personnel, the regional offices, beginning with Chairman Weinberger's efforts, were greatly upgraded. This extended the aggressive reach of the commission throughout the country. In fact, much of the commission's increased activism during the 1970s was attributable to these revamped offices. For example, they were responsible for 99 percent of the total dollars in consumer redress collected by the FTC in 1980 (*FTC: Watch,* Oct. 23, 1981: 9).

Although these changes in organization and personnel greatly contributed to the rise of consumerism in the FTC during the 1970s, other developments were critical as well. As noted at the outset of this chapter, the FTC, though formally an independent agency, has always been severely buffeted by political forces. The transformation of the commission during the 1970s was no exception to this pattern. The evolution of the FTC was in important respects due to a loosely organized, but influential, coalition of consumer advocates among Senate and House members, a talented and programmatically ambitious congressional staff, an aggressive core of investigative and advocacy journalists, and an elaborate network of consumer public interest groups.[4]

In the absence of such a coalition, which constantly prodded the commission to expand its activities on behalf of the consumer, it is unlikely that the agency would have followed the course that it did. According to Robert Reich, the FTC was governed by two competing regulatory paradigms during the 1970s. (personal interview, Nov. 20, 1984). On the one hand, it was influenced by what Reich calls "microeconomic efficiency," which entailed a circumspect view of regulation. According to this view, consumer protection programs were needed but *only* to correct market imperfections. The other competing paradigm was what Reich calls the "David and Goliath" approach, which we referred to earlier in discussing the ideas of consumerism. This involved a more militant commitment to consumerism, one governed by the understanding that the market was debased by disproportionate corporate influence on government and the economy. In this view, a steadfast public interest commission, with the strong support of "external" professional advocates for the consumer, had to act as an adversarial, countervailing force against what was perceived to be the domination of special interests over the American political economy.

The revitalization of the commission by Casper Weinberger, according to Reich, was carried out by "straddling these two perspectives," a strategy continued by the three Republican chairmen who followed Weinberger from 1970 to 1977: Miles Kirkpatrick, Lewis Engman, and Calvin Collier. This approach entailed a commitment to upgrading the

---

[4] An interesting description of the "entrepreneurial coalition" that gave impetus to the expansion of consumer protection is given by Michael Pertschuk in his account of the "rise and pause" of the consumer protection movement (Pertschuk, 1982: 13–36).

quality of agency personnel and expanding its activities. At the same time, however, careful attention was paid to the economic consequences of regulatory action. Thus, the Bureau of Economics, which was responsible for applying economic analysis to agency activities, was upgraded along with the policy bureaus. The competition between these regulatory paradigms in the agency played itself out in an ongoing "dialogue" between economists and lawyers about the degree to which the marketplace required corrective measures (Katzmann, 1980). This dialogue harnessed considerably the enthusiasm for regulation brought by the many young, talented, and ambitious attorneys, who were recruited to upgrade the commission during the early 1970s. One attorney, who came to the FTC in 1970 with a degree from a prestigious law school and experience in Ralph Nader's Public Interest Research Group, noted:

> I had a gut feeling that it would be fun to go to Washington and help the underdog (i.e., the consumer), and when I first got there, it was fun—we were winning. I came to the Federal Trade Commission with the same feeling. Before long, however, I was in the position of having to defend what we were doing (as a member of a Commission bureau in 1972). Then we got into economics, especially market failure—our concern was how to make the market work. I was and am committed to the market system, but I see a strong role for regulation. (personal interview, July 22, 1986)

The commitment to a strong role for regulation among many FTC staff attorneys was checked until 1977 by Republican control of the White House and their choices for chairmen of the commission. As a result, the revitalization of the FTC during that period did not involve adventuresome regulatory initiatives, affecting broad sectors of the economy, but a heightened commitment to ensuring fair business practices. Lewis Engman who was chairman of the commission from 1973 to 1976, likened the FTC at the time to "a tough but fair policeman walking the beat." As he told members of the Western region convention of the American Association of Advertising Agencies:

> I don't view the FTC as a regulatory agency. Whether others have in the past or not, I view our function as a law enforcement agency and will challenge unfair and deceptive advertising as it appears. (Quoted in U.S., Senate, 1974: 152)

This view of the responsibilities of the FTC was severely criticized by consumer advocates in the public interest movement and Congress. In their view, a case-by-case approach, even one pursued by the more determined and talented FTC staff of the 1970s, did not sufficiently challenge the asymmetrical relationship that existed in the marketplace between buyer and seller. Consumer activists argued for a much more systematic assault on market forces, involving broadly conceived regulations, having the force of law, and far-reaching enforcement measures, which would impose a serious financial burden on violators of such rules. Judy Jackson, speaking on behalf of the Consumer Federation of America, joined with a number of consumer groups at a 1974 commerce committee hearing in blistering the commission and Chairman Engman for failing to become "a real zealot in terms of consumer affairs." In response to the chairman's characterization of the FTC as a "cop on the beat," Jackson told the members of the commerce committee:

> I think it is horrendous for the Chairman of the FTC to tell business groups that he does not consider his agency as a regulatory agency. He is telling business, "Don't worry too much about us, until you have actually put out a deceptive ad."
>
> In other words there is no preventative law. We are concerned that the FTC use its trade regulations rule in terms of defining parameters. You can do far more with that then trying to go against each individual deceptive ad.
>
> I think it is important to enforce the law, of course. But if you tell business you are going to be the cop on beat, that is essentially ad hoc. (U.S., Senate, 1974: 755)

Of course, consumer advocates had been hurling criticism at the FTC for failing to live up to the potential of its far-reaching consumer protection powers since the late 1930s without having the desired effect. Yet, the consumer movement had become both better organized and more politicized by the 1970s (Vogel, 1981: 171). The Consumer Federation of America was formed in 1967 by a group of activists as an umbrella organization representing a number of organizations, including the President's Consumer Advisory Council. Furthermore, Ralph Nader was able to parlay his "uncompromising and dark idealism," which he displayed with a remarkable understanding of the "uses and needs of the media," into a large and well-funded network of lobbyists and litigators based in Washington (Vogel, 1981: 171; Pertschuk, 1982: 30–33). The surge of the consumer movement also influenced older organizations that traditionally eschewed direct political involvement. For example, the Consumers Union, founded in 1936 as an organization dedicated to educating the consumer, established an advocacy office in Washington in 1972.

Finally, as David Vogel notes, the position of consumer lobbyists was strengthened in the 1970s by an alliance they were able to develop with organized labor:

> While particular trade unions have at times differed with the positions taken by environmental groups, organized labor has been an extremely active and effective part of the consumer coalition. By contrast, organized labor did not exist as an important national force during the Progressive Era and was preoccupied with fighting—successfully to be sure—for its very existence during the New Deal. (1981: 171)

No longer was it the case, then, that the consumer interest was mute. To be sure, the consumer consciousness Robert Lynd hoped to see arise among the average individual was still inchoate. Yet the well-organized professional consumer advocates were able to arouse the public, if only episodically, with dramatic examples depicting motorists "skewered like shish kabob on non-collapsible steering wheels," babies burned to death by flammable fabrics improperly labeled, and regulatory agencies "chattled to business and indifferent to the public" (Armstrong, 1971: 219). The outrage induced by such appeals was not sufficiently sustained to build an organized grass roots effort, but the American public did become supportive enough of consumer issues for activists to reshape the administrative process at the FTC and other agencies very much in their own image.

Of course, this would not have been possible if Congress was not receptive to such a reconstruction of the consumer regulatory apparatus. Many members of Congress, however, recognized the appeal consumer issues had and chose to "market" them through the media as champions of the public interest. The Senate Commerce Committee, especially, became a shelter for advocates of energetic consumer protection. Its chairman, Warren Magnuson, pursued a strong proconsumer record as a means to revitalize a flagging political career. One of Magnuson's first acts in this regard was to make Michael Pertschuk consumer counsel for the Commerce Committee in 1964, charging him with the task of developing the senator's consumer record and building a knowledgeable and committed staff of consumer advocates. Over the next ten years, Pertschuk oversaw the writing and passage of considerable consumer legislation. These efforts culminated between 1973 and 1976 with the enactment of statutes that virtually completed the decade-long refurbishing of the FTC.

When Pertschuk was rewarded for his service to the consumer cause with his appointment as chairman of the commission in 1977, the full potential of this institutional reconstruction was realized. During his volatile term as chairman, Pertschuk committed the agency to the "David and Goliath" regulatory paradigm in a far less tentative fashion than had his Republican predecessors.

Two congressional statutes were especially significant in enabling the commission to assume this more aggressive posture. First, the Alaska Pipeline Act of 1973 greatly increased the agency's enforcement powers, doubling the penalties for violating FTC cease-and-desist orders to $10,000, empowering the U.S. district courts to grant mandatory injunctions and other equitable relief to enforce commission orders, and granting the commission greater powers to appear on its own behalf in federal court. In addition, this act expanded the commission's information-gathering power, removing the requirement that the agency had to submit its reports to the OMB for its approval (Muris, 1981a: 14).

Even more significant was Congress's passage of the Magnuson–Moss Act of 1975, which further expanded the enforcement powers of the FTC and confirmed the commission's authority to issue industrywide rules. This piece of legislation remedied what had been cited since 1969 as the most glaring structural deficiencies in the commission's authority. It was now possible for the agency to sue in federal district court for redress to consumers who had been injured by acts or practices that the commission had found to be unfair or deceptive. Furthermore, the commission was freed from the necessity of having to enforce its statutes with the use of the cease-and-desist order, which consumer advocates since the fight over the Wheeler–Lea Act had dismissed as a useless tool of enforcement. Violators of the FTC law were now made subject to strong civil penalties of up to $10,000 in certain instances, even if they were not themselves subject to a commission cease-and-desist order.

Finally, the Magnuson–Moss Act enacted a strong mandate for industrywide rulemaking. The commission had in a few cases issued trade regulation rules prior to the Magnuson–Moss Act; and the 1971 regulation requiring octane ratings to be posted on gasoline pumps led to the first judicial recognition of the asserted rulemaking authority of the FTC (*National Petroleum Refiners Association* v. *FTC*, 482 F 2d 672, D.C. Cir. 1973). Yet Congress's passage of this legislation in 1975 eliminated lingering doubt about the legitimacy of this authority, and, more important, expressed Congress's support for the commission to exercise what, in effect, amounted to wide-ranging legislative power. With this authority firmly established by congressional action, the FTC became, as one former staff member put it, "the fourth most powerful body in Washington" (personal interview with Terry Latanich, Dec. 17, 1982; also see Muris, 1981a; 14–15; and Ellis, 1981: 161–63).

This power, however, was accompanied by a number of procedural obligations which, in effect, restricted the administrative discretion given to the FTC. These provisions were characteristic of legislation passed during the public lobby era. In addition to following the "notice and comment" requirements of the Administrative Procedures Act, the FTC was also obligated to conform to procedural safeguards such as publicizing proposed rules, stating with particularity the reason for the proposed rule, and allowing interested persons to submit written data, views, and arguments, all of which were to be made public (Ellis, 1981: 162).

The procedural obligations established by the Magnuson–Moss Act were a response to, as the 1969 ABA commission report had put it, "Commissioners' [having] been criticized for making themselves available to those representing respondents or potential respondents on a *ex parte*, off-the-record basis" (ABA, 1969: 3). Public procedures were crafted accordingly to allay the possibility of the agency's "capture" by the targets of its activities, as well as to facilitate the participation of public interest groups in the rulemaking process.

The goal of enhancing the participation of public interest advocates was addressed specifically in the Magnuson–Moss Act with the establishment of an "intervenor funding program," thus making the FTC the first major federal regulatory agency possessing explicit statutory authority to fund public participation in agency proceedings.[5] This program provided funds to support the participation of individuals who demonstrated:

(1) . . . that they represent an interest that would not otherwise be adequately represented in the proceeding for which assistance is sought;

(2) . . . that representation of this interest is necessary for a fair resolution of the proceeding;

(3) . . . that the persons seeking funding would be unable to participate in the proceeding without it. (U.S. Senate, 1979: 168)

In practice, these funds overwhelmingly went to public interest groups supportive of the ambitious proconsumer policies that were increasingly pursued by the FTC after the enactment of the Magnuson–Moss Act. The list of grants made under the public intervenor program read very much like an honor role of staunch consumer advocates, includ-

---

[5] For a thorough description and analysis of the intervenor funding program of the FTC, see Boyer (1981).

ing Americans for Democratic Action (ADA; $177,000 in grants to participate in five separate rulemaking proceedings), Action for Children's Television (ACT; $84,614 to participate in the children's advertisement proceedings), and the Consumers Union ($132,257 to participate in four separate rulemaking proceedings).[6]

Although the amount of monies expended was small in terms of the total budgetary outlays of the FTC, the public participation program became one of the most controversial aspects of the commission's new activism. The targets of rulemaking proceedings and critics of the commission in Congress accused the FTC of utilizing these funds to enhance the intervention of groups who, as Senator Simpson (R-Wyoming) told a 1979 Senate Commerce Committee hearing, "echoed" the views of consumer advocates within the commission (U.S., Senate, 1979: 156–57). Opponents of the program were also critical of the grants that were awarded to professional public lobby groups that had ample resources and hardly seemed in need of taxpayer's support to participate in rulemaking. For example, the ADA received substantial funding, yet this group had a national membership of nearly 75,000 people and an annual budget of $1.6 million (U.S., Senate, 1979: 157). Similarly, Consumers Union also received substantial FTC grant support, yet had an annual budget in FY 1979 of $23.7 million. Consequently, the FTC was accused of failing to achieve a proper balance of interests in its compensation decisions: "Too many Washington-based organizations, too many 'repeat' players appearing in multiple proceedings, and too few small businesses had received support" (Boyer, 1981: 71). One survey indicated that from the start of the compensation program through January of 1979, approximately 65 percent of all compensation funds obligated by the FTC went to only eight groups (Boyer, 1981: 131).

But supporters of the program argued that the intervenor funding program opened the policy process to interests that otherwise would have been rendered ineffective. To be sure, public interest groups had substantial membership support and funding; however, the resources of these organizations available for advocacy still paled next to those of the large corporations and trade associations that were the target of FTC rulemaking. According to advocates such as Esther Peterson, the director of the U.S. Office of Consumer Affairs during the Johnson and Carter administrations, public participation funds were necessary to remedy a situation

---

[6] For a list of grants made under the FTC public intervenor program, see U.S., Senate, 1979: 158–60.

in which, "large corporations and well-heeled trade associations can readily deploy the resources needed to prepare technically proficient and analytically sophisticated presentations . . . ," while "other parties . . . often find the costs of meaningful participation in agency proceedings to be prohibitive." She argued that simply to *permit* participation in public proceedings to take place, without providing financial support to certain groups, would subjugate public interest organizations to an expensive war of attrition that would invariably benefit regulated interests and harm consumers (U.S. Senate, 1979: 167).

Advocates of intervenor funding grants also argued that groups that qualified for support because they otherwise would not have been able to participate, were not only groups that had no money—that is, which met a poverty or near-poverty test. Although many public interest groups had substantial revenues, these revenues might not have been available for advocacy. For example, Mark Silbergeld, director of the Consumers Union Washington office, noted that a very small portion of his organization's revenue was set aside for advocacy activities. This support for lobbying, Silbergeld argued, could only "supplement, but never possibly replace [Consumer Union's] function of providing advice and counsel to consumers about the expenditure of family income through *Consumer Reports*" and other publications. Thus, to apply an in forma pauperis test in the dispensation of public participation funds would make it impossible for virtually any membership organization to receive the funds it required to take part effectively in regulatory proceedings (U.S. Senate, 1979: 195–203).

Moreover, public lobbyists argued, applying a test for intervenor funding grants that precluded well-established advocacy groups would have a deleterious effect on the *quality* of public lobbying. Some consumer groups that participated in a number of different proceedings and sought funding to take part in all stages of the proceedings in which they were involved claimed that without this continuity of representation the consumer advocates could not achieve equality with business and trade group respondents. Although the FTC was criticized for concentrating awards among a relatively few organizations and law firms that composed a specialized "pro-consumer FTC bar," Barry Boyer argued that "the agency might well have provoked equally strong criticisms . . . had it emphasized 'grass roots' participation and distributed funds to participants less technically competent to address issues raised in the proceedings" (1981: 71).

The underlying dilemma of striking an acceptable balance between technical competence and "participatory democracy" was inevitable, given the statutory obligations established by the Magnuson–Moss Act. This statute required attention not only to "fairness" but also to "adequacy of representation" in the implementation of the intervenor funding program. In fact, the problems of managing an acceptable trade-off between expertise and grass roots participation were endemic to the task of combining expansive administrative power with republican government. Administrators of the public participation program at the FTC were well aware of the difficulties they faced in recasting rulemaking proceedings that would genuinely be open to "public" participation. An Assistant Director of the Bureau of Consumer Protection, James V. Delong, who played an important role in administering intervenor funding, expressed the view in 1977 that "the public participation program, like rulemaking proceedings themselves, [had] two aspects that [did] not always mesh smoothly": a "technical inquiry into what is going on in a particular industry and what steps may be taken by the Federal Trade Commission to alleviate consumer inquiry"; and "a large component of participatory democracy," which, unlike technical studies, asked "consumers and consumer groups directly whether they [felt] a need for [regulatory action]" (quoted in Boyer, 1981: 70, note 69).

In the final analysis, the public participation program became a controversial issue, because it symbolized an emergent commitment to remake the administrative procedures that governed the American political economy. It was one of several mechanisms established during the 1970s that greatly increased the role played by public interest lobbies in the development of regulations. In the face of such a challenge, corporations and trade associations lashed out at institutional reforms like the intervenor funding programs, recognizing that imposing such procedural changes represented a fundamental, though incipient, challenge to business' influence on rulemaking proceedings.

The controversy surrounding public participation programs was especially great at the FTC (Boyer, 1981: 40). First, the agency's activism during the latter period of the 1970s emphasized industrywide rulemaking that threatened to restructure large parts of the economy and provoked powerful opposition. Second, the consumer activism that characterized the aggressive use of the rulemaking power of the FTC seemed to make compensation for public interest lobbies unnecessary. As Boyer notes, "if direct funding is intended to counterbalance the persuasive powers of the regulated industry," it hardly seemed necessary to develop such a program in an agency like the FTC, where Chairman Pertschuk admitted publicly in 1979 that "staff attorneys had conducted antibusiness 'vendettas' in rulemaking proceedings" (Boyer, 1981: 140; see also *Washington Post,* Oct. 6, 1979: D9).

But what made the FTC intervenor funding program seem especially beneficial to consumer activists and egregious to business concerns was that those groups compensated with public funds did not simply reinforce staff positions. In a few important rule proceedings, the original staff attorneys left either the rule or the commission before a final decision was issued, and the initial agreement between the staff and compensated consumer representatives vanished. This was the case in the funeral practices ruling, in which the original staff was widely considered zealous in its pursuit of an antiindustry rule, but was eventually replaced by a new group of staff attorneys who were less committed to the original rules than their predecessors had been, as well as more sensitive to the antiregulatory climate that prevailed by the time the FTC was prepared to render a final decision (Boyer, 1981: 136–37). Michael Pertschuk asserts that the potential of the intervenor funding program was indicated in cases such as this one, when compensated consumer groups, which participated in every phase of a rulemaking procedure, were able to persuade the commission not to follow the recommendation of the staff that substantial reductions be made in a controversial rule that was developed during earlier stages of the proceedings:

> In terms of money [the intervenor funding program] was not that important. But it was a very important ideological issue for change. That is why there was strong opposition to it all along. It was a very important first step in allowing consumer interests to be heard more effectively. . . . The consumer groups influenced such proceedings by the weight of their arguments rather than political heat. In the funeral home situation, the staff . . . negotiated a compromise on the proposed rule which cut below the bone. The public interest groups effectively argued before the Commission that this compromise would undercut the rule. But it was the merit of the consumer advocates' testimony and not really political heat that influenced the Commission's decision. After listening to business groups, consumer people, and staff, the Commission adopted a rule which was less stringent than the original but stronger than the one proposed by the staff. . . . One thing the public participation funding did was to bring skilled advocates before the Commission. (personal interview, July 30, 1982)

Much of the controversial action of the FTC during what we call the public lobby era surfaced during Michael Pertschuk's reign over the commission. He did not initiate most of these actions—they were initiated under previous Republican chairmen at the prodding of Congress and public interest groups—but Pertschuk sharpened the commission's commitment to consumer protection. According to one former FTC staff member, Pertschuk aroused controversy by associating its activities with a public interest crusade:

> Every policy that became controversial was in the pipeline before Pert-schuk became chairman, but he made the controversy more acute. He was on T.V. constantly—he made the agency's work glamorous and took credit for its activities. (personal interview with Terry Latanich, March 30, 1984)

Although some felt he was going too far, Pertschuk was able to engage the staff so that it participated enthusiastically in this crusade. At first the staff, which hitherto had been subjected to the more circumspect managerial style of Republican leadership, was confused by Pertschuk's more flamboyant leadership. Eventually, however, they became support-ive of the new chairman's consumer advocacy. Not only were many of the FTC staff members favorably disposed to consumer protection in the first place, but they were also young and talented attorneys who found it in their political and bureaucratic self-interest to support a regulatory pro-gram that allowed for creativity, expansion, and discretion in their day-to-day responsibilities (R. Reich interview, November 20, 1984).

Furthermore, Pertschuk made an effort to recruit new staff who were committed advocates and had experience in the public interest movement. Whereas chairmen like Weinberger and Kirkpatrick had sought to up-grade the quality of the staff by recruiting topflight law students, Pert-schuk more than previous chairmen made an effort to bring aboard law-yers of the highest caliber who were committed activists. As one staff attorney who came to the Commission in 1975 put it:

> Kirkpatrick and Weinberger actively sought out the best talent, as they viewed it. Under Pertschuk the best talent was also sought out. Where the approaches differed was on the premium placed on academic performance. For example, who is better, a 4.0 graduated from Harvard who engaged in no "public service" programs, or a 3.85 graduate from Harvard who ran the legal aid program or was otherwise actively involved in proconsumer programs. Under the earlier chairmen, I am confident that the 4.0 student would have been chosen. Under Chairman Pertschuk, I am confident that the latter would have been chosen. (personal correspondence with Terry Latanich, March 30, 1984)

By selling the FTC as a "large public interest firm" that "embodied consumer interest," Michael Pertschuk virtually completed a transforma-tion of the FTC that ended with this institutional product of the Progres-sive Era looking very much like those created during the public lobby regime. The commission had long been admonished for failing to restrain American industry, which was depicted by the unruly and powerful horse in the heroic statuary adorning the front of the main FTC building. By the 1970s, however, it was the commission that had become the horse, and its corporate and trade association antagonists who were seeking restraint.

The transformation of the FTC was one element of the far-reaching institutional developments that took place during the late 1960s and 1970s in the area of consumer protection. The pattern of these developments were generally characteristic of the changes in regulatory politics during the public lobby era; but the effect of these changes on the FTC was limited in certain important respects. That the FTC, unlike the EPA, was not created during the advent of the public lobby regime affected the degree to which it could be infused with the mission and institutional mechanisms of that regime. For example, the original mission of the FTC was to police unfair and deceptive business practices with a view to ensuring fair competition, a commitment that was weakened but never fully displaced by the revitalization of the agency during the 1970s. Indeed, as the ensuing discussion of deregulatory efforts at the commission indicate, the continuing commitment to the traditional mission of the agency facilitated the efforts of James Miller to rein in the consumer activism that evolved during the public lobby period. Reagan-appointed officials at the EPA could not make use of such long-standing tradition in their efforts to redirect environmental policy.

Perhaps the most significant difference between reform of the FTC and other public lobby institutions has to do with the role of the courts. We have noted how the courts played a critical role in the rise of social regulation. At the FTC, however, the judiciary, while surely important, was not the critical point of access for public lobbyists that it was at agencies such as the EPA. In fact, laws passed by the Congress and decisions rendered by the courts during the 1970s accorded considerable discretion to the commission in carrying out its additional responsibilities. This discretion was granted in deference to the status of the FTC as an independent regulatory commission, entitling it to act as a court of equity in defining and enforcing public values. As noted, Congress and public interest groups prodded the commission to become increasingly involved in consumer protection, but the FTC was not subjected to the same extensive judicial oversight as the EPA.

Public interest groups, to be sure, pushed for mechanisms, such as automatic standing to sue, which made litigation a critical element of environmental regulation. Although consumer advocates supported efforts to revitalize the FTC, they argued that agencies of public administration alone would fail to achieve the goals of the consumer movement. As John Banzhaf, chairman of the public interest group, Legislative Action on Smoking and Health, told the Consumer Subcommittee of the Senate Committee on Commerce in February 1970:

> If we look only at government to do something about consumer problems—and only the Government—we can never win. We could line Pennsylvania Avenue with Federal Trade Commissions and not have enough manpower to police one-tenth of the misleading ads and deceptive trade practices, and the same holds true of the Justice Department. No matter how you slice it, there will always be problems of bureaucracy, red tape, political pressures, incompetence, understaffing and other problems if we rely principally on the government or condition other actions upon their decisions.
>
> Why not encourage some of that self-determination we hear so much about today and let the consumer do some suing for himself. The purpose of consumer suits and class actions is to encourage the consumer to do the job because there are so many of them. They are collectively immune from a wide variety of pressures, and, best of all, they work for free. . . .
>
> I therefore say to you, let us sue too; just give us the tools we need and then get out of the way if you want to see a real customer revolution and a real war on consumer problems. (U.S., Senate, 1970: 157–58)

The granting of these tools, however, would have required more radical surgery on the organic statute of the FTC than Congress was willing to undertake. The character of this statute, crafted during the Progressive Era, and the lack of such action-forcing mechanisms in consumer laws as timetables, has meant fewer public citizen suits in consumer protection than has been the case in environmental regulation. This has deprived the consumer movement of an important instrument of influence. The relatively limited role of the courts in consumer protection became especially significant during the 1980s when the Reagan appointees to the FTC were able to exercise administrative discretion in redirecting the commission that was not available to their counterparts in most other agencies responsible for social regulation. The broad discretion granted the FTC in one sense was a tremendous asset to social reformers, as the revitalized commission of the 1970s had the will and authority to review virtually every consumer protection problem (Muris, 1981b: 35–49). At the same time, however, this lack of legal restraint on the FTC exposed the agency to a severe political reaction against its participation in wide-ranging social policy.

New Policies

The rise of the consumer movement led to a veritable explosion of new policies that greatly expanded the role of government in consumer affairs. These additional government responsibilities can be divided into two general policy areas. The first includes legislation and regulations regarding the consumer's right to be properly informed about products and market transactions. To guarantee such a "right," major initiatives were undertaken during the 1960s and 1970s to protect the consumer from fraudulent and misleading packaging, advertising, and financial practices. The second policy area involves government action to protect the health and safety of the consumer. Statutes and regulations in this arena brought a multitude of new controls on the manufacture and sale of automobiles and consumer products, and led to the creation of two new government agencies: the NHTSA (1966) and the Consumer Product Safety Commission (1972).

The FTC, with its newly acquired enforcement powers and wide-ranging legislative mandate, became an especially important agent in the expansion of consumer protection in both of these policy areas. One study of the FTC during the 1970s noted the agency's foray into a seemingly unlimited number of ambitious programs:

> In 1970, its budget of approximately $21 million was used to enforce 11 statutes. By the end of 1979, with its budget approaching $70 million, the Commission had enforced 16 new statutes and had created or proposed more than 60 programs and 40 rules to regulate American business. Further, the Bureau of Consumer Protection had taken bold measures to regulate advertising, credit practices, and warranties, as well as attempting to remedy problems that state regulation caused in the eyeglass and funeral industries. The Bureau of Competition had initiated the largest case in the Commission's history to break up the nation's largest oil companies. (Muris and Clarkson, 1981: 6)

This expansion occurred in two stages. In the first, which began in the late 1960s and lasted until the passage of the Magnuson–Moss Act, the agency undertook more active enforcement of the tasks delegated to the FTC by Congress. In areas such as flammable fabrics, truth-in-lending, and deceptive advertising the commission instituted more aggressive case-by-case enforcement of business practices. During this period, the agency's policies were characterized by an aggressiveness that Lewis Engman likened to the "tough but fair policeman walking the economic beat."

The second stage of policy expansion at the FTC began with the enactment of the Magnuson–Moss Act. After this, the commission began to invest a considerable amount of its resources in the development of trade regulation rules, which involved it in activities that affected broad segments of the economy and entailed deliberations about broad social policy. The first trade rule, dealing with the easing of restrictions on the advertisement of ophthalmic goods, was issued in 1978. By 1979, the FTC had promulgated two more and had under consideration seventeen additional proposed rules, including an extremely controversial regulation to curtail extensively children's advertising.

In effect, whereas prior to the Magnuson–Moss Act, the commission's enforcement of policies impinged on individual companies, by the late 1970s, the agency was pronouncing programs that had the breadth and force of major pieces of legislation. This more ambitious regulatory approach also extended to the Bureau of Competition, which began during this period to experiment with innovative industrywide programs. Major initiatives were undertaken against the automobile, oil, and food industries that looked well beyond traditional antitrust policy. For example, unable in many concentrated industries to find direct evidence of anticompetitive practice, the FTC during the early 1970s decided to prosecute large companies in major industries for a "shared monopoly"—that is, for tacit collusion to drive up prices and keep out competitors. This initiative, which focused on ready-to-eat breakfast cereals as a test case, had involved the commission by the late 1970s in a direct assault on the "oligopolistic" structure of the American economy.

Thus, the evolution of policy at the FTC resulted in a program that reflected many of the ideas of the public lobby regime. This program, governed by the mixture of New Deal liberalism and New Left economics that gave impetus to social regulation during the 1960s and 1970s, eschewed a commitment to competition and consumer protection, narrowly conceived. Instead, as Michael Pertschuk put it in an address to the 1977 New England Antitrust Conference, the goal was to take "the broad view . . . , attempting through enforcement initiatives and the power of information to bring the structure and behavior of major industries, and, indeed, of the economy itself, more into line with the nation's democratic political and social ideals" (quoted in Foer, 1979: 2).

An interesting aspect of the expansion of consumer protection during the 1970s is how policy issues and programs dovetailed with efforts to strengthen regulatory institutions. As we note throughout this book, the public lobby era involved a conscious attempt to reform the policy *process* in order to better ensure a long-term, staunch commitment to programmatic reforms. Consumer activists, however, confronted the problem that specific policies, and the politics of outrage elicited by these policies, were easier to "sell" on the Hill and to the public than the less dramatic institutional proposals, although the latter were considered more critical by activists to the enduring vitality of the consumer movement. To a degree, this problem was overcome by harnessing concern about specific issues to comprehensive reform efforts. For example, consumer activists created a National Commission on Product Safety to hold hearings around the country with the purpose of exposing design shortcuts and flaws in consumer goods. This was done with the expectation that these well-publicized hearings would lay the political groundwork for the creation of a permanent Consumer Product Safety Commission, having full authority to set product safety standards and to order recalls (Pertschuk, 1982: 42–43). As noted, this goal was achieved in 1972.

Similarly, the widespread public concern over "nonperformance and exculpatory fine print" in product warranties was used as a platform for the institutional reforms of the Magnuson–Moss Act. Recognizing that proposals for change in FTC procedures, lacking the dramatic appeal of flammable fabrics or product safety, had fallen rather flat since they began surfacing in 1969, Commerce Committee staffers decided to couple such reforms to a consumer complaint that had registered widespread indignation. As Michael Pertschuk reports:

> To take advantage of the energy behind warranty reform, in the bill, which came to be known as the Magnuson–Moss Act, we married warranty reform (Title I of the act) to a series of FTC Act amendments . . . (Title II). Though many factors aided in the nuturing and passage of that legislation (including the virtuoso lobbying performance by Congress Watch and the Consumer Federation of America), the ease with which consumers (and senators) could relate to the warranty provisions of the bill and their genuine popularity provided a critical legislative loft for the more significant, but emotionally unprepossessing, FTC reforms. (1982: 44)

As consumer advocates hoped, these institutional reforms eventually led to a more systematic and aggressive approach to social regulation on the part of the commission. This approach to consumer protection, however, made the FTC many powerful enemies. Under Pertschuk's reign, especially, the commission began to antagonize, among others, the organized bar, the American Medical Association, and the insurance, television, advertising, automobile, and drug industries (*Congressional Quarterly Weekly Report,* Aug. 11, 1979: 1649). The mobilization of this

opposition was not solely attributable to Pertschuk's penchant for charac-
terizing the commission's work as a public interest crusade, but also to
the tremendous impact the emerging trade regulation rules had on large
and powerful sectors of the economy. As Pertschuk noted during part of
a lengthy *apologia* to the Commerce Committee in 1979:

> [T]here are those who consider themselves friends of the Commission who
> counsel us to "cool it." Rulemaking, they point out quite correctly, galva-
> nizes the political opposition of whole industries at a time, while case by
> case adjudication picks off companies one by one, often to the barely dis-
> guised delight of competitors. They counsel us to turn back to the old
> standbys that kept the Commission out of the limelight and out of trouble—
> isolated frauds and deceits by marginal firms—too often one step ahead of
> the criminal law and effective Commission actions.
>
> Yet Congress enacted the Magnuson–Moss Act, in the conviction that
> rulemaking is the fairest and most effective means of delivering the benefits
> of marketplace rules to honest competitors and consumers alike. . . . No
> doubt we have committed our share of sins, both of omission and commis-
> sion. . . . But I think . . . the outcry you are witnessing is in large part
> a reflection of the effectiveness, of rulemaking, the "rules are beginning to
> bite." (U.S., Senate, 1979: 510)

The rule proceeding that caused the FTC the greatest political difficulty was the children's advertising case. In 1978, the FTC staff recommended and the commission agreed to consider imposing major restrictions on television advertisements aimed at young children. The rule
proceeding was based on the consideration of three options: a complete
ban on television advertising for programs aimed at children under eight
years old; a ban on advertising directed at children under twelve years of
age "for sugared food products, the consumption of which posed the most
serious dental risks"; and a requirement that television advertising for
sugared food products be balanced by nutritional disclosures funded by
advertisers (*FTC Staff Report on Advertising to Children,* 1978: 345–46).

What distinguishes this case is that it galvanized opposition that
went well beyond the powerful television and breakfast cereal industries.
In fact, on March 1, 1978, the "liberal establishment organ," the *Washington Post,* issued a devastating assault on the children's advertising
proceeding, entitled "The FTC as National Nanny." The most damaging
aspect of this attack was that the *Post,* rather than raising serious questions about the First Amendment implications of the contemplated advertising ban, chose instead to dismiss it as uncommonly silly:

But what are the children to be protected from? The candy and sugar-coated cereals that lead to tooth decay? Or the inability or refusal of their parents to say no? The food products will still be there, sitting on the shelves of the local supermarket after all, no matter what happens to the commercials. So the proposal, in reality, is designed to protect children from the weaknesses of their parents—and the parents from the wailing insistence of their children. That, traditionally, is one of the roles of a governess—if you can afford one. It is not a proper role of government. (*Washington Post*, March 1, 1978: A22)

Richard Leighton, serving as a special counsel for the Grocery Manufacturers of America, argued before a Senate Commerce Committee hearing in 1979 that "[t]he Children's Advertising proceeding [was] a good choice for legislative oversight because it contain[ed] the seeds of FTC's own destruction" (U.S., Senate, 1979: 417). Indeed, the controversy surrounding this case was a lightening rod, which led eventually to efforts by Congress and the Reagan administration that halted, at least for a time, consumer activism in the commission. Had the FTC proceeded more cautiously on this and other issues, perhaps the devastation signaled by the reaction to "kid-vid" could have been avoided. Not only were measures proposed by the agency that smacked of censorship, but the proceeding was also run in such a way that affected business interests could claim, with considerable justification, that they were not granted a fair hearing during the commission's deliberations (U.S., Senate, 1979: 418–20). Michael Pertschuk himself admits that if he had seen the signs of surging resistance to the activities of the FTC, "there would have been no proposal to ban advertising." He and his staff would have gone after the issue, "albeit in less threatening ways" (M. Pertschuk interview).

That an astute political observer like Pertschuk, who spent fourteen eminently successful years in the Senate Commerce Committee, did not see such a broadside coming is perhaps less revealing of a lack of political savvy on Pertschuk's part than it is of the moral imperative of the consumer movement to which he was committed. This movement was inspired by the view that "irrational" behavior on the part of the consumer was due to responses conditioned by an immoral society, an immorality bred primarily by powerful business interests. It was this view that gave rise to the consumer movement in the 1930s and thrust it to the forefront of political reform during the public lobby era. Thus proceedings such as children's advertising were not pursued for the attainment of competition or economic efficiency, but to free the oppressed and manipulated consumer from the throes of corporate immorality. The FTC staff suggested that advertising directed to children for certain foods containing sugar was "unfair" to parents, because it could produce intractable family conflict—putting "parents to the hard choice of allowing their children to take those health risks [associated with the excessive consumption of sugar] or of enduring the strife that can accompany denial of requests induced by television advertising" (*FTC Staff Report on Television Advertising to Children,* 1978: 34). Consumer activists would surely grant that untoward familial conflicts were inevitable, but situations of this sort were unacceptable and demanded public attention when viewed as an example of corporate immorality (Pertschuk, 1982: 154). To deny the power of corporations to wield influence through advertising and other business practices, to proceed more pragmatically, might take the consumer advocate down the path of accepting the existent patterns of consumer preferences. Yet given the commitment of contemporary social reformers to "participatory democracy," they could not readily follow a path that would have involved a recognition of possible tensions between such a commitment and the reform of capitalist society.

The last section of this chapter demonstrates that the FTC did not simply self-destruct during the late 1970s. In important respects, the attack on the commission resulted from a sudden and widespread shift in political wind that was not directly attributable to its regulatory activities. Moreover, although this reorientation in political ideas and actions during the 1980s has had an important impact on the FTC, it is far from certain that the consumer movement and the agency's commitment to it is dead. To a degree, however, the problems that have recently plagued the consumer movement, as well as other movements of the public lobby era, do stem from tensions within the governing principles and institutional strategies that gave shape to reform over the past two decades.

The Federal Trade Commission and Deregulation

The appointment of James Clifford Miller III as chairman of the FTC in September 1981 was indicative of the Reagan administration's strong interest in redirecting the agency. By the time of Ronald Reagan's election to the presidency, Miller had earned a reputation as an ardent critic of social regulation who shared the president's view that most things will work best if government leaves them alone. An economist with vast experience in academia and government, Miller headed the staff of Reagan's Presidential Task Force on Regulatory Relief during the early days of the administration. He was the president's point man in designing a program to transform regulatory politics, playing a principal part in writing EO 12291, as well as implementing that order as the administration's first director of the Office of Information and Regulatory Affairs (OIRA).

Thus, Miller's appointment to head the FTC ensured that the commission would become a major target of Reagan's regulatory relief program. In fact, Miller became interested in the agency as a member of Reagan's transition team in an effort to examine and influence a situation that best represented what he considered to be the abuses of social regulation. He was originally called by the Reagan transition people and asked about heading the transition team for another agency, but declined and suggested heading the team for the FTC instead. Miller knew little about the detailed operation of the commission, but was well aware of its extensive powers and controversial activities, which made the agency an attractive challenge for one who advocated a new vision for regulatory politics (personal interview with James Miller, July 15, 1983).

The FTC transition report clearly revealed Miller's philosophy and the policies he would seek as chairman of the commission.[7] The report shows the Miller administration was committed to toning down the more ambitious initiatives of consumer protection on the basis of an intellectual framework that acknowledged a legitimate role for social regulation. This framework, while reflecting a generally hostile view of government intervention in the marketplace, did recognize an important difference between "economic" and "social" regulation. Economic regulation, which has largely to do with restrictions on price, entry, and exit, should for the most part be eliminated, because it restricts competition and inhibits the effective working of the marketplace. Social regulation, however, which protects the public from market externalities like health hazards and fraud, should not be eliminated but reformed with a view to making it less costly. Miller and his top advisors expressed the view that for the most part FTC regulation was social and that its excessive activism should be curbed by more carefully integrating economic analysis into agency action (J. Miller interview).

As we noted in Chapter 4, the promotion by the Reagan administra-

---

[7] The introductory sections of the *Transition Report* are reprinted in Senate, *Congressional Record*, 127, S10162–S10169. The conclusions and recommendations sections are reprinted in *Daily Executive Report* (BNA), Jan. 29, 1981: G1–G3. The text of the Reagan administration's FTC *transition Report* was made available to the public by *FTC: Watch*.

tion of economic analysis as a means of restraining regulation represented more than an effort to slow the growth of social regulation. In fact, the support of economic analysis was the linchpin of a philosophy envisioning a fundamental departure from the institutions and policies of the public lobby regime. In the first instance, a commitment to this philosophy involved a rejection of those programs pursued by the FTC during the 1970s that were directed to challenging the basic principles and structure of the American political economy. Consequently, in the area of antitrust policy, the transition report called for the termination of the innovative industrywide programs, such as the "shared-monopoly" case, which embarked the FTC on the "objectionable" course "to reshape the structure of American industry" (*Transition Report,* Introduction, S10163).

Similarly, the transition team recommended that the commission terminate all those cases in the area of consumer protection based on "social theories." While not mentioning any cases specifically, this criticism was clearly directed at initiatives such as children's advertising, which challenged the underlying morality of a market economy:

> The role of the Commission in the area of consumer protection should be to replicate, to the degree feasible, the workings of an efficient marketplace. Whatever the merits of various "social goals," we believe that Congress is the appropriate forum for addressing these issues and deciding whether and how they should be achieved. (*Transition Report,* Conclusions and Recommendations, G1)

In effect, the philosophy James Miller brought to the FTC resurrected the notion that economic efficiency and a competitive marketplace were equivalent to the interests of consumers. This assumption had been challenged by consumer activists throughout the twentieth century, but was embraced by conservative economists such as Miller who sought to cultivate a renewed faith in the rationality of consumers and the benefits of a market economy. In the last analysis, this faith led to a fundamental reconsideration of the value of consumer protection. Accordingly, even the more circumspect view of past Republican FTC commissioners such as Lewis Engman, who saw the agency's work as entailing strong law enforcement, was seriously questioned by the FTC transition report. As noted above, Engman had eschewed the view of the commission as a forceful agent of regulation, advocating instead the "cop on the beat" approach to consumer protection. The Miller approach to the FTC, however, downplayed the law enforcement approach, proposing instead that the commission be an "economic agency," out to achieve consumer protection by emphasizing efficiency and competition. In this understanding of the agency's role, the FTC would not give up law enforcement entirely, but would subject this activity to thorough economic analysis:

> We believe that in allocating its scarce resources to various programs and activities, the Commission should be guided by the effects on economic efficiency. Obviously, this means that a decision to take issue with a particular business practice transcends the question of legality. One must ask whether the probable effects of the agency's actions would be to improve the functioning of the economy, bring about greater efficiencies, and increase consumer welfare. (*Transition Report*, Introduction, S10162)

Whereas even the more moderate activities of the FTC during the 1970s were governed by a skeptical view of business practices and market forces, the Miller approach to consumer protection redirected that skepticism to regulation itself. Consequently the vision of the FTC as an economic agency implied not only a more important role for the commission's Bureau of Economics, but also a significant reorientation of this role:

> In their role of supporting the Bureaus of Competition and Consumer Protection, the agency's economists in recent years have spent most of their time identifying imperfections in the marketplace. Government intervention is justified only when imperfections in the marketplace exceed imperfections associated with intervention. Consequently, an analysis of the imperfections of governmental intervention is absolutely essential to informed decisionmaking. (*Transition Report*, Conclusions and Recommendations, G2)

Many of Miller's critics viewed his intellectual framework as a recipe for undermining consumer protection. They asserted that the effort to be more economically rigorous in selecting targets for regulation resulted in an endless dissection of cases that only resulted in paralysis. While granting that it was right for the commission to be sensitive to the imposition of excessive regulatory burdens on free enterprise, Michael Pertschuk accused Miller of carrying this concern "to irrationality and excess," thereby "crippl[ing] the Commission's law enforcement mission" (Pertschuk, 1984: 9).

Such criticism of Miller's regulatory program did not go unheeded, yet his formulation of an intellectual alternative to the public lobby regime contributed greatly to the substantial success Miller had in redirecting the commission before he became director of the OMB in 1985. As the next chapter indicates, the lack of a defensible framework for regulatory change severely damaged the efforts of the Reagan administration to redirect the activities of the EPA. But Miller's framework provided a basis for attacking past FTC policy, as well as grounds for sustaining a commitment within the commission to significant regulatory action. Consequently, the Miller administration was willing to undertake aggressive law enforcement in those areas in which such action was consistent with its governing philosophy. In fact, the transition report advocated expanding the agency's activities in certain areas that were designed to eliminate explicit collusion. For example, it praised the commission's efforts "to expose guildism in the professions," arguing that the agency's work in this area was in the public interest and should be expanded (*Transition Report*, Introduction, S10162). This view was reflected in the Miller administration's strong resistance of efforts by the AMA and ABA to eliminate the commission's authority to challenge anticompetitive professional self-regulation. In this respect, the intellectual framework of James Miller and his top advisors at the FTC provided a foundation for a systematic reconstruction of the agency that could not simply be dismissed by consumer advocates as catering to special interests.

Another important factor in the Reagan administration's attempt to remake the FTC was Congress's assault on the commission. Unlike the situation at the EPA in which there was strong bipartisan support for environmental policy in the House and Senate, a political backlash formed in opposition to the FTC after 1977. This resulted in a congressional mood that was inhospitable to further expansion of the commission's authority and more disposed to scrutiny of the ambitious ventures the FTC already had under way (Kovacic, 1980: 183; Weingast and Moran, 1982: 35–37). The development of congressional opposition to the FTC was not simply attributable to what were widely perceived as the regulatory excesses of the Pertschuk administration. We have noted that most of the rules directed at entire industries and professions that were so controversial were begun with the passage of the Magnuson–Moss Act in 1975; indeed, deliberations about many of these regulations began in 1971 and 1972. Given the elaborate process required to promulgate a final rule, the proceedings for many issues being investigated moved slowly, so that most rules did not come to a head until Pertschuk became chairman. This created the impression in Congress that there had been an unusual burst of activity, reflecting unrestrained activism at the commission, after 1977. In fact, however, all but two of the nineteen rules that were either completed or under consideration during Pertschuk's reign had developed over a decade at the behest of the Congress, the ABA commission, public interest groups, and the press (U.S., Senate, 1979: 512–13). Pertschuk's militant rhetoric and personnel policies accentuated the controversy that surrounded the agency's work. But the reaction to the FTC must also be understood as an accident of time; just as a number of long-standing measures were coming to fruition, Congress and the nation were moving in the opposite direction.

This situation ultimately led to a sharp confrontation between Congress and the FTC in 1979, culminating in legislation that sought to establish greater congressional control over the agency. It is important to recognize that this confrontation was aggravated by the open and highly decentralized issue networks that composed the institutional foundation of the public lobby regime. It was not really Congress that the FTC responded to during the 1970s, but rather its oversight committees in the House and Senate. In fact, during this period substantial legislative authority devolved to subcommittees, leaving the FTC dependent on the ministrations of subcommittees responsible for consumer affairs within the House and Senate commerce committees. These subcommittees tended to be quite unrepresentative of Congress as a whole. For example, one study of the Senate Subcommittee on Consumer Affairs shows that the average ratings that the Americans for Democratic Action (ADA) computes for measuring support for its program were in the case of subcommittee members well above the average for the full Senate throughout most of the 1966–1976 period, but significantly below that average by 1979.[8] While the full Senate's average score, which was very stable over the entire decade, fell only a modest eight points (from 46 to 38) between 1977 and 1979, the subcommittee score plunged thirty-one points (from 57 to 26) and the subcommittee chairman's dropped eighteen points (from 50 to 32). This suggests why the FTC was subjected to an especially violent shift in political climate during the late 1970s; apparently, the growing opposition to social reform in American politics was magnified in the case of the FTC by the extraordinarily sharp shift in the commission's oversight subcommittee's preferences away from consumer activism (Weingast and Moran, 1982: 35–38).

The tension between the Congress and the commission resulted in the Federal Trade Commission Improvements Act of 1980. This act im-

---

[8] Weingast and Moran found that ADA scores were a very accurate predictor of Senators' votes on FTC issues: the higher the ADA scores, the greater the probability of voting for an activist FTC (1982: 35).

posed many restrictions on specific trade rule proceedings at the commission. For example, the children's advertising proceeding was allowed to go forward, but the commission could only address itself to "deceptive" practices, and was forbidden to exercise its broader general authority to police "unfair" practices in this particular instance. This imposed a much greater burden of proof on the agency, requiring it to demonstrate that alluring advertising directed at children was false rather than simply unfair. Consequently, this proceeding was closed by the agency. Several other activities of the agency were also either prohibited or restricted, leaving only the funeral price disclosure rule, which addressed widespread commercial abuses by funeral homes, essentially unobstructed (Pertschuk, 1982: 113). As part of negotiations directed at heading off more damaging surgery on the organic statute of the FTC, the commission agreed to accept a termination of funding for the controversial intervenor funding program (interview with FTC staff member, Aug. 12, 1987). No funds were requested for this program in President Carter's budget proposal for FY 1981. In turn, the direct funding authority survived the numerous 1980 amendments to the Federal Trade Commission Improvements Act with only a few additional limits on the agency's discretion.[9] Although the FTC managed to preserve its legislative authority to disperse public participation funds, that it agreed to forgo a 1981 appropriation to do so "reflected the shadow of suspicion the legislative oversight process had cast not only on the FTC's administration of the program, but also on the concept of compensating public participants in administrative proceedings" (Boyer, 1981: 57).

In order to ensure ongoing congressional control over FTC activities, the 1980 Federal Trade Commission Improvements Act contained a two-chamber legislative veto—the first permitting Congress to veto any actions of an independent agency, without the approval of the president (*Congressional Quarterly Almanac*, 1980: 233–36). The importance of this provision became apparent in May of 1982 when Congress vetoed the controversial used-car rule that would have required dealers to dis-

---

[9] The amendments stipulated that no person could receive more than $75,000 for participation in any single rule-making proceeding, and no more than $50,000 in any fiscal year. The Federal Trade Commission Improvements Act also required that 25 percent of the appropriated compensation fund be set aside for small business, and directed the commission to create a special small business outreach program (Boyer, 1981: 57, note 26; The Federal Trade Commission Improvements Act of 1980, PL 96–252, Section 10, 94 Stat. 374).

close major defects in used cars and state the extent of any outstanding warranties. The rejection of this rule by overwhelming numbers in both congressional chambers (the House voted 286 to 133 and the Senate 69 to 27 to approve the veto) was a dramatic indication of Congress's willingness to impede the commission's activism (*New York Times*, May 27, 1982: 1). Used-car dealers hardly made for popular allies, and Congress's support of this provision was clouded by the substantial campaign contributions distributed by the National Automobile Dealers' Association. To a point, this action by the House and Senate can be explained by the structure of the used-car industry: used car dealers, after all, are located in virtually every congressional district. Fundamentally, however, this incident indicated that the consumer activists were no longer viewed as champions of the public interest. Rather, they were now frequently chastised as purveyors of excessive bureaucracy and government intrusion, and, as such, vulnerable to virtually any industry's effort to free itself from the commission's activities.

The enactment of the Federal Trade Commission Improvements Act of 1980 indicated that the reining-in of the FTC preceded the election of Ronald Reagan. In fact, Michael Pertschuk, who was chastened somewhat by the attack on his agency, told a 1979 hearing before the Senate Subcommittee for Consumers that the commission had to assume "a greater responsibility for making sure that . . . industries who will be affected by proposed rules feel that they can get heard and will be heard" (U.S., Senate, 1979: 532). Toward the end of Pertschuk's term as chairman, the agency, accordingly, began to tone down its more aggressive activities, a trend that continued when David Clanton became acting chairman after the 1980 election. Prior to Miller taking over as chairman of the commission, a *Wall Street Journal* editorial celebrated what it called the "FTC Metamorphosis." Pointing to the agency's dropping of its lengthy and controversial antitrust suit against the major oil companies and the curtailment of its investigation of the automobile industry, the *Journal* concluded that the FTC was "undergoing a transformation from its activist role in the 1970's" (Sept. 18, 1981: 30). In many respects, then, James Miller only continued fundamental regulatory "reform," which had led to considerable retrenchment of consumer activism after 1978.

Nevertheless, Miller's efforts to redirect the FTC did not simply reinforce a broader attack on the commission. In fact, his leadership played a critical role in focusing what had been a rather ad hoc approach to regulatory reform at the FTC into a more systematic effort to redefine the mission and reconstitute the institutions of the agency. As the FTC transition report noted, opposition to FTC activities was directed primarily at the curtailment of investigations or rulemakings of particular industries rather than the development of institutional reforms (*Transition Report,* Introduction, S10166). The enabling statute of the commission, for example, was essentially left intact. Moreover, most of the specific restrictions or prohibitions contained in the 1980 Federal Trade Commission Improvements Act were temporary. And the most significant mechanism in the statute—the legislative veto—was declared unconstitutional by the sweeping 1983 decision of the Supreme Court in *Immigration and Naturalization Service* v. *Chadha* (103 U.S. 2764). The federal courts made clear that this decision applied to the commission in *Consumers Union* v. *FTC* (691 F. 2d 575, D.C. Cir., 1982; aff'd 103 S. Ct. 3556, 1983), which overturned Congress's veto of the used-car rule, declaring that the provision of the 1980 Federal Trade Commission Improvements Act, giving the legislature authority to reject unilaterally agency initiatives, was a violation of the separation of powers. By 1983, then, Congress's actions to restrain the commission had not amounted to a fundamental challenge to the agency's authority; Congress intervened to protect certain interests, but had not really curtailed in a comprehensive fashion the broad authority of the FTC to police deceptive and unfair business practices.

The Reagan administration and James Miller's stewardship of the FTC represented a much more systematic challenge to the commission's past activities. The attempt by Miller to question the underlying assumptions of consumer protection led to efforts on the part of his administration to pursue a thorough revamping of the FTC, an effort that included proposals to curtail the agency's enabling statute. Ironically, in certain instances this led Miller to resist congressional efforts to restrict agency programs. Because he was committed to an intellectual framework that celebrated economic analysis and the virtues of the marketplace, Miller resisted congressional initiates to protect particular interests that were engaged in price-fixing arrangements. For example, when lawyers sought to free themselves from agency action to break up arrangements that amounted to price-fixing, he scolded the members of the ABA for seeking "special privilege" that would place them "above the law." His administration felt, Miller insisted, that "competition [was] the order of the day in the professions and elsewhere" (*Washington Post,* Aug. 1, 1983: All). In such matters, Miller was not prepared to go as far as Congress in restricting agency activities.

Yet, inasmuch as he was willing to challenge the underlying philosophical assumptions of regulations directed at protecting the consumer, Miller sought changes in the FTC that, if they had been fully implemented, would have brought about a far more enduring and systematic transformation of the commission than Congress was willing to accept. By 1978, Congress was prepared to keep a tighter rein on the FTC with a view to checking certain of its activities that it found politically untenable. But legislators were far less enthusiastic than Miller about making the commission into an "economic agency." For all their fulminations about particular FTC practices, most members of Congress remained committed to the notion at the basis of reform since the Progressive Era that regulation served the public interest. Moreover, in the last analysis, the members of Congress, especially those on the oversight committees of the FTC, have a political *self-interest* in preserving an active commission capable of pronouncing programs for which they can take credit. The controversy stirred by the FTC under Pertschuk caused legislators considerable uneasiness and created uncertainty about what the commission should do, but did not lead to serious efforts to reduce the virtually unlimited statutory authority of the agency. As James Carty, vice-president and manager of regulation and competition for the National Association of Manufacturers (NAM), noted after the *Chadha* decision:

> We would hope that [the Supreme Court's decision] would lead to changes in legislative authority. But although the FTC is an agency they love to hate, Congressmen still want an active Commission. They really do not know what the FTC should do. (personal interview, July 28, 1983)

Congress' ambiguous relationship with the FTC during the late 1970s defined the possibilities and limitations of the Reagan administration's influence on the commission. In many respects, Miller's efforts to tone down the commission's activism were appreciated and supported by the Congress and business interests. Yet, when Miller's program touched on fundamental propositions about the value of regulation or the legislative authority of the commmmission, he was less successful, raising serious questions about the enduring legacy of his chairmanship. It is to the particular elements of the Miller program that we now turn our attention.

Regulatory Relief and Executive Administration

We have noted that the Reagan program of regulatory relief involved executive administration and legislative initiative, and that for several reasons, the greatest emphasis was placed on administrative efforts. This was characteristic of reform efforts at the FTC, but Miller, more than most other Reagan appointees, did make an effort to modify the organic statute of the agency he headed. The transition report attributed a large part of the commission's problems to "the extremely broad discretion granted by the enabling statutes" (*Transition Report,* Conclusions and Recommendations, G1). In Miller's view both "unfair" and "deceptive" trade practices needed to be defined more carefully not only "to contain the agency over the long run, but also to insulate it from political abuse" (J. Miller interview).

In the short run, however, Miller chose to use administrative power to begin the process of reorganizing the commission so that it conformed with the president's basic philosophy. The chairmen's influence on the agency was limited in important ways by the autonomy of the FTC as a regulatory commission independent from the president. The agency is governed by a bipartisan body of five members who serve for seven-year terms, and during the first two years of his presidency Reagan made only one appointment, James Miller. Nevertheless, the chairman of the commission has important powers that extensively affect the day-to-day operations of the agency. This control is largely a product of New Deal administrative reforms, which, the Humphrey's Executor decision notwithstanding, eventually eroded considerably the autonomy of the independent regulatory commission from presidential influence. Especially significant in this regard was Truman's Reorganization Plan 8 of 1950 that provided for the chairman of the regulatory commissions to be "appointed by the president and serve at his pleasure." These chairmen have been delegated considerable administrative discretion, providing the opportunity for the president to give some direction to independent regulatory bodies (Derthick and Quirk, 1985: 61–74).

The FTC, more than any other regulatory commission, has given general executive powers to its chairman and thereby increased his powers (Stewart and Cromartie, 1983: 542). For example, he appoints the bureau directors and sets the overall direction of the Bureau of Competition, Bureau of Consumer Protection, and the Bureau of Economics. The chairman's authority is still formally limited in important ways. The appointed bureau heads must be ratified by the commission; moreover, administrative responsibilities exercised by the chairman are generally subject to the policy positions adopted by the commission. Nevertheless, the chairman's executive authority provides the opportunity to emerge as the dominant figure in the agency, an opportunity forcefully seized by the Miller regime. Upon assuming control over the agency, Miller focused his efforts on exercising tighter control than his immediate predecessors over all the FTC staff, whom he viewed as generally committed to an "activist" regulatory philosophy (J. Miller interview).

An important ingredient of this administrative clampdown on staff was to burden them with very demanding standards of evidence in order to pursue regulatory initiatives. This created a tremendous amount of conflict for a large part of the staff during the early days of Miller's tenure; although they were not as ideological as Miller believed, they generally supported the efforts during the 1970s to encourage attorneys in the policy bureaus to take full advantage of the agency's broad legislative authority. As a result, they viewed the standards of evidence employed by the Miller administration in litigation and rulemaking matters as an attempt to shut down rather than reform the agency. Not only were market surveys and other forms of economic research required that provided precise quantitative evidence that industry abuses were widespread, but also substantial information about the probable effect of proposed remedial measures on the target of a rule proceeding.[10] By rejecting much of the accumulated evidence acquired prior to his arrival and demanding additional, more empirically precise, evidence before he would accept a rule, Miller and his top advisors were able to impede or kill off many of the eleven rules still pending at the commission before he arrived.

The difficult standards of proof required to complete rules were extremely frustrating to staff attorneys who had worked over a long period of time gathering substantial, if not empirically precise, evidence of market abuses. Staff members were especially resentful of the Miller regime's standards of evidence for remedial measures that often seemed to require in their view an impossible threshold of empirical precision in order to sustain a regulation. For example, staff attorney Terry Latanich, who played a leading role in formulating the Funeral Practices Trade Regulation Rule, told the House Subcommittee on Consumer Affairs that the administration's rejection of the remedy proposed by the staff during that proceeding illustrated that Miller's remedial standards were "excessive, [fostering] delay at best, inaction at worst" (Latanich, 1984: 143). This remedy, which would have required funeral homes to provide itemized price lists to consumers at the funeral home, and to inform consumers who called the funeral home that price information on these lists was

---

[10] For a discussion of the Miller administration's view on standards of evidence for rule-making, see Muris (1982).

available over the telephone, was rejected by the Miller administration on the grounds that it would impose undue cost burdens on the industry, that the case for the rule had not been made, and, most important, that the remedies proposed were highly unlikely to solve the problems. The rulemaking staff argued that the remedy imposed minimal costs and cured the unfair practices. In effect, staff members argued that the standards of evidence for remedial measures obscured the need to make a fundamental choice about what the role of government ought to be. As Latanich put it:

> In my judgment, the standard of proof for the remedial requirements of rules required by the Miller Administration is often not achievable, at least not at a cost that can be borne by the Commission. Good market research can readily identify the frequency and effects of acts and practices that occur day-to-day in a market. It is much more difficult, however, to predict the effect of a remedy. In many cases it is difficult, if not impossible, to simulate actual market conditions and analyze empirically the likely effect of a remedy that has been proposed. If the role of the Commission is to be that of an agency at the cutting edge of consumer protection law at the federal level, it will not always be feasible to have the level of certainty that the Miller Administration would like to see. (1984: 134)

Whether or not the standards of proof established by the Miller administration were onerous or "impossible" was in the eye of the beholder. According to Timothy Muris, who served as director of both the Bureau of Competition and Bureau of Consumer Protection during the time Miller chaired the agency, it was not only possible, but essential for commission rules to be based on "systematic projectable evidence," such as surveys of consumers and econometric studies of industry behavior. The past practice of the commission to rely primarily on "anecdotal" evidence was inappropriate for rulemaking, which after all involved the commission in "generalization" of economic conditions:

> The problems in FTC rulemaking have stemmed not from too much evidence but from the wrong kind. A survey, after all, is little more than a systematic method of collecting anecdotes so as to project them to the population as a whole with proper statistical safeguards. The records of the commission's proceedings are voluminous indeed, but they are collections of trees from which the size and shape of the forest can seldom be determined.
> Survey evidence is easy to obtain. Indeed, the commission routinely conducts systematic surveys to establish a "baseline" for later evaluation of the impact of its rules. The problem is, however, that it conducts the

surveys only *after* it has closed the rulemaking record. . . . [T]he baseline study of the funeral rule cost $65,000, and substantially undercut a major factual premise of the rule—namely, that funeral directors refused to discuss prices over the telephone.

At the very least, the commission should consider the findings of its baseline surveys when it makes final decisions. [Yet] in the funeral proceeding, the commission declined even to seek comment on the baseline survey and went ahead with its preliminary decision to regulate the industry. . . . More important, however, the commission should conduct surveys at the beginning, not the end, of its proceeding. (Muris, 1982: 23)

Underlying the debate within the FTC about standards of evidence was strong disagreement about the appropriate role for the commission. The requirements imposed on the agency for rulemaking under Miller were hardly impossible, yet surely the need to acquire more exacting information, particularly in regard to remedial measures, would inhibit the agency from launching ambitious consumer protection programs. But, of course, the political leadership of the Miller administration wanted to pull back the FTC from the "cutting edge" of consumer protection. We noted that the FTC transition report reflected a strong animus against the commission's more ambitious industrywide proceedings. In the place of such activities, the Miller administration preferred a case-by-case approach and a greater reliance on industry self-regulation. Such an orientation no doubt fostered a less adversarial relationship with business, but was anathema to many career people, especially those recruited during Pertschuk's chairmanship, who were devoted to a mission of aggressive consumer protection. Many of these individuals, whose principles and talent were frustrated by Miller's more cautious approach to regulation, left the agency soon after he assumed control over the commission.

Many personnel, however, who did not leave the agency were resigned to a quieter role for the commission. The FTC was heavily dominated by lawyers whose legal training inclined them to express a professional, if somewhat reluctant, recognition that there was a broad concern in the country to tone down the activism of the federal government. Their admiration for Pertschuk's commitment to consumer protection notwithstanding, they granted that the agency went too far under his leadership. Indeed, when Miller first came to the commission, many career staff claimed that they were frustrated not so much by Miller's attempt to make changes, as they were by his apparent unclear signals about the sorts of concerns he wanted to address (personal interview with assistant regional director, March 29, 1982).

This sense of uncertainty was perplexing to Miller, because he spoke in detail about priorities in the transition report, and in many speeches and testimony (personal correspondence with James Miller, Oct. 12, 1983). Perhaps, however, the FTC staff resented having to read Miller's writings to find out what his views were on the commission. Many complained that Miller and his top advisors were extraordinarily insulated, that an impenetrable wall existed between the chairman and the staff. As Chapter 4 pointed out, this was generally characteristic of the relationship between Reagan appointees and civil servants, who were viewed by the administration as the enemy.

In part, however, the uncertainty and hostility felt by the staff was an inevitable consequence of Miller's efforts to redirect the agency. This was especially so, because this reorientation entailed an overall reduction in staff activity. This was not only a threat to the principles and professional ambitions of many FTC attorneys, but also to their job security. By reducing the size of the agency and pursuing less adversarial techniques, Miller's programs reduced opportunities for attorneys both within and outside the agency.

In this respect, morale at the commission's regional offices was especially devastated. Although Miller made an effort to exercise tighter control over all the staff, this effort was felt more strongly by the regional offices. The policy bureaus severely slowed their activities, which hitherto had been a central part of the agency's consumer activism. In fact, feeling they "were often a source of hare-brained initiatives and [were] very difficult to control," Miller stated publicly his preference to eliminate all of them (J. Miller interview). Although Miller's intention to close the regional offices was blocked by the whole commission (which only agreed to close four offices) and eventually Congress (which refused to terminate any of them), the uncertainty while all this was going on was very damaging to morale. Moreover, though ultimately allowed to stay in business, all the regional offices endured a hiring freeze and reduced resources. One regional staff attorney described the forlorn state of the regional offices during the early period of Miller's reign as follows:

> The regional offices are struggling for survival. There is a feeling of paranoia evident—a feeling that the more active the agency, the more it will be looked at unfavorably by the Washington office. Many people feel that the offices which are most effective will be closed. . . .
>
> To give you an idea how bad morale is—how all the regional offices feel a sense of impending doom: People in the L.A. office feel that they

will be closed down [rather than the San Francisco regional office] because San Francisco is a nicer place to visit. (personal interview, March 29, 1982)

The morale of the career staff at the FTC was probably damaged more than was necessary in order to redirect the agency. To be sure, some conflict between the Reagan appointees and the staff was inevitable, given the fundamental departure Miller envisioned from the agencies' past activities. Uncertainty and hostility, however, were greatly accentuated by the Reagan appointees underestimating the professionalism of the staff. As Miller himself admitted in 1983:

> . . . let me say that I was wrong about the staff. When I came here, I thought 80 percent of the staff was sufficiently ideologically zealous that their professional performance would be impaired. I have found, however, that 80 percent of the staff is really very professional and responds well to the new leadership. About 20 percent is not as responsive as I would like: a few are terribly disruptive, though identifying them is difficult. (J. Miller interview)

Miller's initial assumption that most of the FTC staff was actively opposed to his administration's goals led to his decision to introduce himself and his political aides to the career employees in a manner designed to "get their attention." He gathered his senior political staff in his office, which is adjacent to the main commission meeting room where the career staff had gathered for their first introduction to the new chairman. Miller put a trumpet fanfare on the record player, stuck two devil horns to his forehead, and marched himself and his senior staff out to meet the FTC. Claiming he was not, in fact, the devil intent on shutting the agency down, he asked for the staff's help in rebuilding the FTC, so that its activities would be governed by sound economic analysis. Yet Miller's fervent entreaty, concluding with a resounding, "Are you with me?" was met with a deafening silence. This awkward and disappointing first meeting was emblematic of the distance between Miller and the career staff that was to plague his early days at the commission (Rock, 1987: 246; interview with FTC staff attorney, Aug. 12, 1987).

The view of the Reagan administration that regulatory politics was sustained by a well-entrenched and ideologically zealous bureaucracy led to an immediate focus on executive action to "clean house" that may have deflected attention from undertaking a broad-based attack on enabling statutes. Even at the FTC, where political appointees had a carefully reasoned understanding about the need to reduce the discretion of the commission, a considerable amount of political capital was expended on personnel matters. In view of Miller's admission that his view of the staff was wrong, the emphasis on imposing administrative controls on the career people at the FTC was a serious error that might have forfeited the opportunity to bring about permanent reforms.

In Miller's case, however, the perception of mistrust was reassessed in time to avoid the sort of agency paralysis and political backlash that characterized developments at several other agencies during Reagan's first term, including the EPA. Such a reassessment at the FTC was facilitated because Miller had an alternative vision of the agency's activities rather than simply an ideological commitment to get government off the back of business. As this became clear to the career people and Miller's suspicion of the staff declined, the tension at the agency subsided. As a result, there were no wholesale attempts to purge agency staff and generally there was an effort to retain, and in some cases even promote, capable personnel. In fact, compared to what happened with previous changes of administration at the FTC, only a small number of people were removed from their jobs, particularly given the major policy changes that were undertaken.

The development of a more positive atmosphere at the commission was most evident at the regional offices. Miller expended a great deal of political capital in a failed effort to get rid of these offices, but after losing this battle he was determined to leave this issue behind him. After many months of interchange with Congress, Miller struck a deal in February 1983, affirming ten regional offices, though with lower staffing levels. A reorganization of the regional offices was then carried out that entailed severe reductions, particularly in the New York and Chicago offices, but this job was accomplished so that the integrity of the regional offices was maintained. Even Michael Pertschuk, who was a bitter critic of the FTC under Miller's leadership, granted that Miller accepted the congressional refusal to eliminate any regional offices with "good grace" (Pertschuk, 1984: 8).

Yet even though morale at the FTC was on the rise by 1983, contributing to a successful reorientation of agency activities, Miller granted that some troublesome pockets of staff resistance continued because of his commitment to a more modest vision of the agency's mission:

> I simply feel that there is only so much this agency can do. When I spoke
> to the International Franchise Association recently, we stopped at Burger

King, where the manager had not even heard of the FTC. We have to be realistic about what we can really do. We need to look at horizontal mergers,[11] pursue cases of ordinary fraud and deception, and try to do a lot of education. Some members of the staff still do not accept this more realistic approach, but we're still working on it. (J. Miller interview)

But this "realistic" approach was in fact based on an unrestrained faith in economic analysis. It is interesting to note that Miller was the first economist to serve on the FTC; in fact, he was the first nonlawyer to be a member of the commission in over three decades. Miller's assault on past policies of the commission may in part have been reflective of a commitment to classical liberal principles at the basis of constitutional government. More fundamental, however, was his critique of social regulation that derived from a faith in economic analysis rather than constitutional principles and institutions. When this analysis dictated that government action was justified, Miller, as noted below, was willing to eschew political restraint, preempting laws in many states and localities if necessary. Nevertheless, when it came to the activities of the public lobby regime, which were animated by principles that posed a serious challenge to a market economy and the value of economic efficiency, an economic approach to the commission's activities was biased toward inaction.

Miller's faith in economic principles played a direct role in his administrative reorganization of the agency. For example, he greatly enhanced the role of the Bureau of Economics (BE) in the commission's decisionmaking process. When Miller assumed control of the commission each rulemaking proceeding pending within the bureau was assigned to an economist in the BE, whose responsibility and mandate was to report back to the Miller administration leadership on the economic viability of the remedies that had been proposed and the likely cost–benefit impact of the rule if promulgated (Latanich, 1984: 131–32). Thus, although the

---

[11] In proposing an antitrust policy that comported with the Reagan administration's commitment to reducing the government's intrusion in the marketplace, the FTC transition report supported, and the Miller administration pursued, a competition program that regulated "horizontal" mergers more rigorously than "vertical" mergers. As the transition report argued, horizontal mergers are those between competing firms, which have the greatest potential to "create monopoly power or facilitate industry collusion." Vertical mergers, on the other hand, take place among potential or actual producers and suppliers, which often result in increased efficiencies, thereby benefiting the consumer (*Transition Report*, S10163).

FTC as an independent regulatory commission was not subject to review by the OMB as a result of EO 12291 and EO 12498, the BE did set up an in-house evaluation of the agency's activities.

This increased role of economic analysis throughout the agency was a critical factor in the commission dropping or curtailing many pending rules, as well as preventing the initiation of ambitious programs in the area of consumer protection. Business interests recognized and appreciated the more pronounced economic orientation of the commission, which, on the whole, established a far less adversarial relationship with the private sector. As James P. Carty of the National Association of Manufacturers put it, "I think the country's much better off when you can have an economist rein in the attorneys over there" (*National Journal,* Dec. 5, 1981: 2151).

As noted in Chapter 4, the important administrative changes brought by the Miller chairmanship were reinforced by the budget austerity imposed on the FTC by the Reagan administration and Congress. After a decade of budgetary increases whereby appropriations rose from $20.9 million in 1970 to $70 million in FY 1980, the Reagan administration proposed slashing the 1981 budget to $67.7 million and the 1982 budget even further to $59.4 million. The budget as proposed would have eliminated the Bureau of Competition, as well as the regional offices. These draconian measures, however, were fought off by the combined efforts of the commissioners, the Congress, and the press. They were proposed prior to Miller assuming control over the agency, and reflected OMB Director David Stockman's view, expressed in an interview, that the FTC served no useful purpose. The *Washington Post,* whose parody of the children's advertising proceeding in 1978 had done so much to discredit the commission's work, was not willing to go this far in its criticism of the FTC. In a strongly worded editorial, the *Post* denied that past FTC indiscretions indicated that the commission did not have a useful role to play:

> One can quarrel with some of the initiatives the commission has taken—and still regard it as a worthwhile protector of business and consumers. The world might not know the difference if the FTC were eliminated, as Mr. Stockman asserted, but the marketplace would know the difference quickly in terms of advertising, pricing and collusion. (Feb. 25, 1981: A16)

When Miller became chairman he supported the administration's goal of cutting the budgetry outlays and staff of the commission, but not with the view, expressed by Stockman, of eventually dismantling the agency.[12] Miller's understanding that there was important work to be done by a leaner, yet still vital agency, ameliorated resistance to budget cuts. All of Miller's budgetary proposals were not accepted. In particular, his effort to eliminate the regional offices caused the appropriation committees in Congress to resist cutting the agency's funds as much as Miller suggested. Nevertheless, between 1981 and 1983, the budget of the FTC was reduced from $73 million to $63 million. Moreover, unlike the situation at the EPA, appropriations and staff were not markedly increased after 1983, restoring the agency to the point of surpassing FY 1981 levels. In 1985, the commission's budget authority stood at $69 million, while its staff had been reduced to 1075, a decline of 32 percent from the time the Reagan administration came into office. (OMB, *Budget Authority of the United States Government, FY 1987*).

One aspect of this budgetary austerity struck directly at the incipient, but ideologically significant, intervenor funding program. Consistent with the Reagan administration's campaign to "defund the left," no funds were requested for this controversial program during Miller's reign over the commission. We have noted that the assault on the public participation program began before Miller became chairman of the commission, and that no funds were requested for this program in President Carter's budget proposal for FY 1981. But Miller recommended that Congress take action to eliminate intervenor funding entirely by deleting the provision from the enabling statute of the FTC that authorized the program (U.S., House, 1982: 15). This recommendation was anticipated by the transition report, which claimed that affirmative programs to facilitate the participation of public lobby groups in rulemaking proceedings were unnecessary. The public lobby regime was inspired by the understanding that regulation in the public interest required citizen participation in regulatory proceedings so as to prevent agency capture and lassitude. The political appointees of the Reagan administration denied that an affirmative government effort was required to shield regulatory agencies from business dominance, especially at an agency like the FTC, and rejected the claim of consumer advocates to speak for the public. As the transition report read:

---

[12] Many of the FTC staff people felt Miller was behind Stockman's proposal to eliminate the Bureau of Competition, aggravating the tension that existed between the chairman and the career people when he first arrived at the commission. Miller, however, denies that he had anything to do with this proposal (J. Miller, interview).

Conceptually, intervenor funding would seem warranted whenever: (a) an agency's staff is captured by those who are regulated, or (b) such funding is the most efficient way of acquiring information. Because the FTC covers a broad spectrum of the economy rather than one industry, it is unlikely to be captured. Furthermore, while some information provided under this program is useful, there is no inherent reason why the staff cannot gather it at less cost. Put differently, the case has not been made that those groups have special insight into or nexus with the needs of consumers or the public interest, or that the Commission staff itself is unable to marshall evidence which such "public interest" intervenors now offer. (*Transition Report*, Introduction, S10168)

As the next section will show, the Miller administration failed in its effort to persuade Congress to alter the organic statute of the FTC, and the authority of the agency to disperse public participation funds was not eliminated. Yet the criticism of this program by the Miller administration and its administrative reorganization of the agency challenged a central tenet of social reform during the previous two decades: the participation of citizen action groups in administrative channels would lead to regulation in the public interest. The triumph of the Reagan philosophy at the FTC meant that the economist, armed with the analytic tools of cost–benefit analysis, was installed as the guardian of the public interest.

In effect, during his tenure at the FTC from 1981 to 1985, James Miller greatly modified the FTC through administrative changes. The agency became far more selective in establishing trade rules and reemphasized the case-by-case approach that prevailed prior to the Magnuson–Moss Act. Moreover, cases were selected only after economic analysis dictated that widespread consumer injury was involved that could not be ameliorated by the marketplace. In competition policy, the industrywide initiatives directed to restructuring American industry gave way to policies that emphasized competition and efficiency, especially as affected by horizontal mergers. Finally, a nonadversarial relationship was established with business that had not been evident since the revitalization of the FTC in 1969.

It is misleading to consider these changes as a consequence of the capture of the FTC by business, or special interests. Although the FTC has never been truly independent of political influence, its broad mission, covering virtually the entire economy, makes unlikely that it will become the captive of industry or other narrow commercial interests. In fact, strong efforts during the ninety-seventh Congress to eliminate FTC authority over the commercial activity of the professions failed (*Congres-*

sional Quarterly Weekly Report, Dec. 31, 1982: 3159–60). This movement, which was spearheaded by the AMA, was vigorously opposed by James Miller, who lined up support from the OMB and from Vice-President George Bush (*Business Week,* Dec. 6, 1982: 42). As noted, the transition report pointed out that the Miller people, committed to a free market, felt that the FTC should have an important role in checking restraints of trade that gave special advantage to certain groups or industries. This represents a prime example of how an active FTC can act to enhance rather than delimit the working of the marketplace. Providing an exemption to professional groups, such as doctors, lawyers, or business groups (e.g., the insurance industry), which also fought for an exemption from FTC oversight, Miller observed in 1982, "goes against the grain of everything I have stood for and my whole training" (*Business Week,* Dec. 6, 1982: 42).

The commitment to maintaining authority over the professions and policing price-fixing, fraud, and deception in those areas launched the FTC on an ambitious program of competition during the 1980s. This program involved the "conservative" Miller regime in an assault on the commercial practices of service industries that preempted the laws of many states and localities. For example, the Miller administration embraced the eyeglass rules, in which the FTC challenged as anticompetitive restrictive state laws on the advertising and the cost of ophthalmic services to consumers. A paper, done under the auspices of the conservative Washington Legal Foundation, warned that if the actions of executive agencies were unchecked in making such policy, "the delicate balance between federal and state governments may be destroyed." While admitting that agencies should sparingly be granted preemption power, the author, Julie Metzger Palmer, argued that "preemption without a congressional mandate should never be permitted" (Palmer, 1986).

Thus, rather than abandoning antitrust enforcement as many of its critics alleged, Miller's FTC in important respects radically transformed it, branching off in novel areas that were far removed from the traditional antitrust emphasis on monopolistic practices of big business (*Washington Post,* June 18, 1984: G1). Underlying this action was the view that antitrust activity should emphasize service industries, which constituted the increasingly dominant sector of the American economy. While not ignoring the older "smokestack industries" (the traditional target of antitrust policy), the Miller competition program stressed enforcement against anticompetitive activities by professionals, trade associations, organizations that set industry or trade standards, and other competitors in the service area of the economy (Muris, 1984: 52–55).

This emphasis on antitrust enforcement against the service sector was reinforced by the consideration that price-fixing and restraint of trade in these areas were usually established by regulations promulgated at the state and local level. In this sense, the competition efforts against the likes of doctors, dentists, lawyers, and real estate brokers fit neatly the Miller administration's "Chicago School" hostility to government interference with the market. Miller and his advisors did not take lightly the criticisms that their antitrust policy was undermining federalism, but denied that the vitality of state and local governments was harmed by fostering efficient competition. In the end, such a program was justified on the grounds that government action, at all levels of the political system, rather than private enterprise, posed the greatest threat to consumers' interests. As Timothy Muris, who, as director of the Bureau of Competition of the FTC during Miller's administration, played the leading role in developing this policy, put it:

> The fundamental antitrust problem of the 1970's was the power of big corporations. But I think, if you look back at the harm that has been done to consumers in society, it's not been from big corporations, unless it's the steel and auto industries that can get the government on their side. . . . The old "bigness is badness" view of antitrust law has failed in the courts and failed, intellectually. So what we're doing is applying old theories to new areas. (*Washington Post,* June 18, 1984: A9)

Even those sympathetic to these "old theories," however, questioned the political wisdom of applying them to so many novel areas. Many of the Miller administration's initiatives, though pursued under the banner of regulatory relief, were arguably as antithetical to the principles of constitutional government as were the more ambitious initiatives undertaken by the Pertschuk regime. Especially controversial were suits brought by the commission in May 1984 against New Orleans and Minneapolis, charging those cities with the violation of antitrust provisions of the Federal Trade Commission Act by agreeing with local taxi companies to fix fares and bar entrants. After reviewing these initiatives and other policies of the Miller competition program, a *Washington Post* article concluded:

> While striking a blow for rational economics, the FTC has also assaulted a far more cherished American tenet: federalism, or the constitutional principle that holds that the federal government should mind its own business when no overriding interest is at stake. (June 18, 1984: A9)

When the Miller competition program was applied to cities, constituting the federal government's first antitrust charges against local government, the commission provoked a strong congressional backlash. City officials and cabbies found legislators sympathetic to their view that such suits were unwarranted federal intrusion. A spokesman for the International Taxicab Association, complained, "How Jim Miller and Tim Muris can tell New Orleans they need more taxis is really beyond comprehension. That is big brother at its worst" (*National Journal,* Aug. 18, 1984: 1571). These complaints were echoed by local officials, who argued that regulation of price and entry for taxicabs was necessary to prevent price gouging and decreasing service to innercity residents. Consumer activists also denounced this policy claiming that it was absurd for the agency to approve large corporate mergers, such as the GM–Toyota agreement, while pursuing antitrust investigations of novel targets in the public sector (*National Journal,* Aug. 8, 1984, 1569–72). As Robert Reich argued, "When they go after taxi drivers and avert their eyes from General Motors, one has to worry that economic doctrine is being elevated above justice and common sense" (*Washington Post,* June 18, 1984: G9).

With the support of the Reagan administration and Strom Thurmond (R-South Carolina), who chaired the Senate Judiciary Committee, the commission was barely able to fend off Congress's effort to strip the FTC of authority to bring antitrust cases against cities. Michael Pertschuk, who voted against the taxicab proceeding, saw the backlash precipitated by such policies as evidence that the Miller administration was not only fundamentally misguided in its philosophy, but very clumsy politically. In the end, he felt, this would make a lot of friends for the revival of consumer activism at the agency (M. Pertschuk interview; Pertschuk, 1984: 195–203). Yet Miller's framework of regulatory change insulated him somewhat from charges that he went after the FTC with an ax; this framework provided a defense of his programs, which, particularly when it was supported by a campaign against special privilege, greatly diminished the prospect of the pendulum of consumer regulation swinging back to the public lobby era.

Moreover, the problems with the Miller program notwithstanding, it represented an alternative to traditional consumer activism. As such, the aggressive campaign against price-fixing, restraint of trade, and fraud reflected an understanding that reform required not the dismantling of the state, but putting it to new uses. The Miller people at the FTC believed that there was little prospect of reforming past regulatory practices by revitalizing a public commitment to limited government. Rather, the solution lay in promoting government programs that were subject to institutional restraint and consistent with the principles of a market economy. As Muris noted:

> [W]e do not believe that government is needed to solve all social and economic problems. The difficulty is we live in a world where people view government as a problem-solver for everything. Under these conditions, the thing to do is check government in its activities; there are no longer any cultural bounds to limit government. Conservatives, thus, must put checks on this commitment to government action—the courts represent such a check. Antitrust policy can also be useful, because it involves the use of government to advance a market-oriented philosophy. (personal interview, July 17, 1984)

Statutory Reform and the Future of the Federal Trade Commission

When James Miller and much of his staff left the FTC for the OMB in October 1985, they left behind an agency that had been remade largely in their own image. It is not certain, however, that the changes brought about after 1981 will survive over the long run. Most of the achievements of the Miller regime at the FTC were brought about by administrative practices and decisions that could be reversed by a new chairperson. Furthermore, although many career people committed to an activist role for the agency expressed despair about the Miller regime's modification of the FTC (in fact, many left the agency), some activist-oriented staffers did not lose hope and were determined to outlast the Reagan presidency. As one regional staff attorney remarked in 1982:

> Even though Miller can stop things, all of us civil servants are still here. If the bottleneck is removed, we won't have to build from scratch. When Pertschuk was chairman, hiring was done to bring aboard activists. That created a commitment in the agency which is still in place. (personal interview, March 30, 1982)

This commitment was weakened, but not abandoned by the end of Miller's tenure at the commission. Followup interviews with staff attorneys at regional offices and with those located in Washington in 1987 revealed that the "survivors" of the Miller administration who supported aggressive consumer protection felt somewhat isolated within a bureaucracy that had been significantly affected by the Reagan presidency. The same regional staff attorney who expressed determination to outlast the

Reagan revolution in 1982 was a bit less sanguine five years later. While observing that the situation at the regional offices was much better than it had been during the early days of Miller's regime, he felt that the overall impact of the Reagan presidency on the FTC, and most other government agencies, had been to "sap" the bureaucracy of its vitality:

> The situation [with the career staff] is very different than it was in 1979. A lot of people have left, and they have usually not been replaced. And even where hiring is going on, there does not seem to be very much interest in the FTC among the very best and brightest. When I came to the agency [in the early 1970s] only those who had been law review students at the best law schools were being hired. Those coming on board now have nothing noteworthy in terms of credentials. This is not really surprising— the gap between private and public salaries has grown from the time I began government service. And it is no longer true, as it was up until 1979, that you get a valuable apprenticeship at the FTC. There is just not very much to do here anymore. Finally, there is the matter of the declining prestige of public service—you can only be told so long that you are the enemy within and not have that affect the spirit of the civil service. (personal interview, July 9, 1987)

Thus, the Miller regime did not transform the bureaucracy at the FTC into a corps committed to the articulated economic principles that had governed policy change at the agency since 1981. But it did effect a significant change in the career staff that could not be easily altered by a new administration intent on revitalizing the commission's commitment to consumer activism. The present civil service would not be an obstacle to such a revitalization, but any chairman intent on making the agency more aggressive would certainly not find the same commitment to consumer activism among the staff that existed during the late 1970s.

Furthermore, the Reagan administration's ability to appoint all five members of the commission by 1988 ensured a more permanent impact on the FTC. Because FTC commissioners serve for fixed seven-year terms, this will slow any effort to start up an activist posture at the commission, just as Miller's efforts were constrained somewhat by holdovers from previous administrations. It was not, in fact, until the end of 1983 that Miller had a chance to build a majority on the commission. Michael Pertschuk and Republican Patricia Bailey, also a Carter appointee, were bitter critics of the commission's policies under Miller's leadership. Pertschuk, until he stepped down in September 1984, kept up a steady drumbeat of activist rhetoric and used every opportunity to join with allies in the Congress and the press to embarrass Miller, a task he likened to "being able to call in artillery on your own position" (*Washington Post,* Jan. 28, 1983: A18). With the occasional support of Republican David Clanton, a Ford appointee, Pertschuk and Bailey were able to defeat Miller on many important issues, evidenced by the commission's vote to promulgate the funeral practices rule and the decision against the elimination of the commission's regional offices.

After 1983, however, Miller, having built a solid majority on the commission, was able to bring about more substantial change in the commission's policy rulings and enforcement procedures. For example, in its reconsideration of the used-car rule, which was vetoed by Congress in 1982, the commission by a three-to-two vote rejected the original version, requiring dealers to post stickers on automobiles revealing any known defects. Instead, the Reagan appointees on the commission, over the dissents of Pertschuk and Bailey, chose to support a less stringent rule based primarily on disclosing warranty information (*Washington Post,* July 11, 1984: D4).

This decision and others taken by the commission after 1983 suggest that an FTC dominated by Reagan appointees would be unlikely to support readily the efforts of chairmen in the near future to restore aggressive consumer activism. Not only would rulemaking be affected by the political orientations of commissioners, but the standards governing law enforcement as well. For example, in October of 1983, the commission adopted the more restrictive definition of deception urged on it by the chairman, increasing the burden on the staff to prove that an advertisement was deceptive. The new ruling held that the commission would only find an act or practice deceptive "if there is a misrepresentation, omission or other practice that is likely to mislead the consumer acting reasonably in the circumstances." As a result, misleading information per se was still suspect, but the determination of whether an advertisement was "misleading" would no longer be based solely on the judgment of FTC commissioners. For an advertisement that the staff claimed was false, but was not obviously so, the new proposal required the staff to present corroborating evidence of deception, demonstrating that "reasonable" consumers would be caused injury if they believed the claims for the product. In effect this committed the commission and also bound the courts to a rule that, if adhered to rigidly, would for the most part restrict the agency's advertising initiatives to cases involving obviously false or grossly exaggerated product claims (*New York Times,* Oct. 27, 1983; Pertschuk, 1984: 80–84; Miller, 1984: 288–92).

Although this interpretation of the commission's standard on deception was not written into the organic statute of the FTC, the restoration of a broader standard will require the approval of three commissioners, a prospect that was not likely to materialize. When Patricia Bailey's term expired in 1987, the commission was made up entirely of Reagan appointees, ensuring that many of the changes brought by the Miller administration would prevail for some time to come. Contemplating the lingering effect of personnel changes on the commission, Nancy Drabble of Ralph Nader's Congress Watch noted in December of 1984, "Any new Administration that would come in would have to take a long time to dig out from the mess that was left by the Reagan Administration" (*National Journal,* Dec. 1, 1984: 2284).

Nevertheless, as noted above, Miller felt that long-term curtailment of activist regulatory policy would require changes in the organic statutes of regulatory agencies. This was particularly important for the FTC, given its broad legislative authority to prevent unfair and deceptive business practices. As noted, even Congress's misgivings about the activism of the commission during the 1970s, which culminated in the 1980 Federal Trade Commission Improvements Act, did not lead to a more careful specification of the agency's powers. The meaning of "unfair" was especially problematical for the Miller administration and certain business interests, as the lack of specificity of this term in Section 5 of the Federal Trade Commission Improvements Act authorized the commission virtually to get into anything. Congress's "negligence" in this regard was reinforced by the court's extraordinary generosity to the commission in interpreting its statute. For example, in a 1972 decision involving alleged illegal trade practices by the company issuing S&H trading stamps, the Supreme Court ruled that "unfairness" for all intents and purposes meant what the commission said it did (*Federal Trade Commission* v. *Sperry & Hutchinson Co.,* 405 U.S. 233).

According to the Miller administration, this discretion was a problem not only in allowing excessive regulation, but in "encouraging" the commission to undertake ambitious programs such as children's advertising that invariably brought the agency into disrepute. Timothy Muris noted in 1983:

> [T]he problem with the FTC has not been solved. Its mandate is still too broad, and this is a disaster for the agency. The S&H case was a disaster. . . . The view of some of the staff is that in the late 1970s they were out to do "God's Work," and the "malefactors of great wealth" stopped them.

> This is dead wrong. The consumer activists feel that all you need to do is get people and let them go. But this is a recipe for disaster. If the FTC's mandate is not limited, it will get itself in trouble repeatedly. (T. Muris interview)

As the transition report pointed out, Miller and his top advisors felt that the lack of institutional and legal restraints on the commission, rather than the people who had served in the agency, were most responsible for its unhappy history. The FTC had never quite fulfilled its promise of providing consistent and substantial protection to consumers, because Congress and the courts had failed to provide guidance on how the commission was supposed to proceed. Without such standards, the FTC vacillated from one regulatory strategy to another, never able to provide a settled, standing body of legal remedies for unfair business practices. This unsteadiness, of course, was aggravated by the exposure of the FTC to political influence from Congress and the courts, both of which at times chastised it for being impotent, at other times for running amok across the economy. As Muris put it in a March 1982 memo to Chairman Miller:

> With these broad standards, in one era the Commission did little, focusing largely on trivia. In the next, the Commission took upon itself the mantle of the second most powerful legislature in America, surely a task inappropriate for five unelected officials. . . .
>
> With a Congressional definition of deception—and of unfairness—the Commission can, and will, enter a new era. We will have a defined and obtainable mandate: protection of consumers from those serious deceptive and unfair acts and practices that still plague us today. And the public whom we serve, as well as regulate, will have a greater understanding of what the law is. (printed in U.S., House, 1982: 60)

Several measures were proposed by the Miller regime with a view to launching the FTC into a new regulatory era. Repeatedly, from 1982 until his departure in 1985, Miller proposed that Congress rewrite the organic statute of the FTC, clarifying the meaning of deception and unfairness. First, this entailed an effort to get written into law the deception standard that was adopted by the commission in 1982. Another proposal would have restricted the meaning of unfair business practices to those that caused substantial consumer injury that consumers could not have reasonably avoided. Such a change would force the FTC to focus on and prove widespread market abuse with systematic evidence rather than unfairness per se. In point of fact, this was the test of unfairness that the commission had applied since 1980, although it was not until 1982 that the commission agreed, with Michael Pertschuk dissenting, that this consensus definition of unfairness should be incorporated into law (U.S., House, 1982: 60). In addition to a more careful specification of standards, Miller proposed measures to "liberate" the FTC from the clutches of public interest groups. Thus, as noted, Miller asked Congress to delete the provision from the Magnuson–Moss Act that authorized intervenor funding. (For a discussion of Miller's legislative program, see U.S., House, 1982: 9–17.)

These efforts to curtail the legislative authority of the FTC notwithstanding, the commission did not receive a clearer mandate from Congress during James Miller's tenure as chairman. In fact, a deadlocked Congress failed to renew the authorization of the FTC in 1982, a situation that continued until Miller left the agency at the end of 1985. Congress continued to fund the agency through the appropriations process, but was unable to reach a consensus on how to streamline the FTC authorization. Consumer activists considered this a great victory. In their view, Miller's inability to modify the commission's statutory authority constituted an opportunity under a future administration to reverse the restrictive orders and budgetary policies imposed on the FTC by the "Reagan revolution." The personnel changes in the commission would surely retard such an effort, but as Miller himself admitted, without changes in the legislative base of the FTC, the prospects for regulatory realignment were very uncertain.

It was unlikely, however, that such changes in the FTC statute would be forthcoming. The momentum for fundamental legislative reform waned after the 1982 congressional elections, which strengthened Democratic control of the House and saw the defeat of several sharp FTC critics such as Representative Gary A. Lee (R-New York), who sponsored a 1982 proposal to suspend the agency's jurisdiction over doctors, lawyers, and practitioners of other so-called learned professions (*National Journal*, Jan. 29, 1983: 221). The outcome of this election encouraged supporters of the consumer movement to believe that they would outlast the deregulatory efforts of the Reagan administration. As Jay Angoff of the public interest group, Congress Watch, noted about Miller's achievements at the FTC, "our only goal is to keep the statutory authority intact so we can live to fight again" (National Journal, Jan. 29, 1983: 221). Without major statutory changes, Angoff argued, the administration has "done absolutely nothing to stop a future FTC chairman from suing the pants off business" (*National Journal*, Dec. 1, 1984: 2287).

Ironically, the Miller regime's effective administrative reform of the agency may have aided those who opposed changes in the organic statute. Because the agency became more moderate in its regulation of the economy after 1981, the FTC was no longer the agency everyone loved to hate, a situation that weakened the commitment to clarify the commission's organic statute. Miller, therefore, found himself in a "Catch 22" situation, whereby he reformed the agency in the short run, which detracted from the possibility of making this reform permanent (J. Miller interview). Contributing to the irony of this situation was the agency's wide discretion that abetted successful administrative changes in a conservative direction, because, unlike the case of the EPA, it is often difficult to make a solid case that such changes violated the legislative mandate of the agency.[13]

In the last analysis, however, the failure to achieve legislative reform at the FTC is attributable to Congress's disinterest in systematically reshaping the commission. Even though they were troubled by some of the activities of the FTC during the late 1970s, congressmen generally favored a strong law enforcement agency. Consequently, they supported mechanisms such as the legislative veto as a safety valve, yet refused to perform major surgery on the agency's legislative base. As Muris put it, "It is difficult . . . to get the Hill to address the problem of the FTC's organic statute. The people up there are problem-oriented, and their view is that the problem with the Commission was solved in 1980" (T. Muris interview).

This task-oriented approach was well suited to the decentralized structure of the legislature. The devolution of authority to committees, and often subcommittees, may make issue networks accessible to convulsive challenges from time to time; such was the case with the FTC and consumer activism during the late 1970s. This decentralization, however, also shields regulatory programs from broad-scale legislative changes required for a regulatory realignment. As Miller suggested about the problem in achieving legislative reform, "the authorizing committees tend by nature to be supportive of the agencies for which they are responsible" (J. Miller interview). Committee members may scold—and even punish—the agencies they oversee; they will be much less enthusiastic about *dismantling* the institutional foundations that increase their political and human capital. As he watched Congress's assault on the FTC subside during the 1980s, Michael Pertschuk described the uneasy but mutually

---

[13] This point was suggested by Michael Mullin, former staff member of the Senate Commerce committee (personal interview, July 15, 1983).

supportive relationship between the Congress and the FTC in succinct and irreverent terms: "Congress wants an active FTC as long as it does not bite anyone's ass too hard" (M. Pertschuk interview).

Miller and his senior staff apparently recognized from the start that Congress would not make major changes in the authorizing statue of the FTC, but considered it important nevertheless to offer reform proposals. In fact, the administration persisted in its calls for statutory reform, because it knew that it could not succeed in bringing about an enduring departure in regulatory policy. As Timothy Muris noted: "Because we understood that the time to reform the FTC had passed because the Commission was no longer regarded as a problem, we knew we faced an impossible task. Nevertheless, we were trying to make a record for what was inevitable given the political swings in our society—the time when the FTC again tries to extend its authority" (T. Muris, correspondence with the authors, Sept. 9, 1987). Inasmuch as they thought that it was not possible to change the commission's statute, Miller and his staff were "relegated," or so they believed, to gaining control of the commission through administrative actions. While falling short of the type of changes required to bring about a more substantial transformation of the agency, these actions have left a record that might circumscribe future efforts to renew consumer activism at the agency.

Nevertheless, the reliance on administrative changes as the primary tool of regulatory relief had its costs. Indeed, the emphasis on administrative changes, which was generally characteristic of the Reagan regulatory program, might have precluded, rather than served as a preface, to enduring institutional reform. As a result of this approach, the Reagan appointees at the OMB and various regulatory agencies found themselves in the awkward position of attempting to rein in government intrusion on the marketplace by embarking on a program of unprecedented administrative aggrandizement. Even at the FTC, where Reagan appointees clearly acted on principle and followed a carefully considered prescription for institutional reform, the attempt to redirect the agency was deflected by a gratuitous assault on the career staff and controversial administrative decisions. Although the disarray precipitated by Miller's administrative actions was of relatively brief duration, the controversy during the early days of his tenure was extremely costly. It led to the loss of valuable momentum at the only time a brief opening might have existed for a serious challenge to the legislative base of the commission.

It is not certain, however, that the FTC could have been transformed into an "economic agency" under the best of circumstances. While purporting to be a more dependable basis for substantial and consistent con-

sumer protection, the economic theories underlying Miller's reform proposals seemed as unrealistic and immoderate at times as the consumerism
he sought to dislodge. If the most ambitious initiatives of Pertschuk's
reign reflected an uncompromising commitment to ideology that abhorred
legal and institutional restraint, Miller's celebration of economic principles also threatened to undermine legal standards and respect for institutions. Even critics of an activist FTC, such as Allan Caskie, associate
general counsel for the American Council of Life Insurance, argued that
Miller's emphasis on economic analysis indicated a lack of understanding
of the law and from where it comes. Making agency law enforcement
dependent on calculations of widespread material harm to "reasonable"
consumers, Caskie argued, ignores the purpose of consumer law to protect the individual from injury (personal interview, July 29, 1983). In this
respect, the formulation of legal standards requires a focus on the venality
and deception of business practice rather than a case-by-case analysis of
the costs and benefits of those practices.

The emphasis on economic theory also created serious problems in
Miller's effort to obtain statutory reform. Members of Congress and industry were most concerned about the vagueness of the unfairness doctrine. Had there been an immediate emphasis on writing a strict definition
of unfairness into the organic statute of the FTC, the authority of the
commission might in fact have been effectively curtailed. But Miller, at
the urging of David Clanton, accepted the commission's consensus definition of unfairness, which required the commission to show substantial
consumer injury, but did not restrict the type of commercial activities
covered by Section 5. The only kinds of proceedings that would be cut
out as a result of this change would be the most severe of measures, such
as banning children's advertising.

The pursuit of even such a moderate change in the unfairness doctrine, however, was weakened and perhaps seriously harmed by Miller's
attempt to change the meaning of "deception." This is ironic because
there was little political support to revise the "deception" standard. To be
sure, there were many critics in the academy and the bar of the definition
and use of "deception" by the FTC. Even liberal friends of the commission such as Robert Pitofsky, who served as head of the Bureau of Consumer Protection under Pertschuk, were critical of the way the commission brought deception cases (Pitofsky, 1977). But no one in Congress
was interested in modifying the deception standard; in fact, Miller's proposal was never even introduced in the legislature. And although the
advertising industry went along with Miller on his deception proposal,
their support was lukewarm; business interests were far more concerned

about the unfairness standard. There was at least seventy years of legal clarification on the meaning of deception. The thrust of deception precedents left the commission very wide discretion in distinguishing misleading from acceptable advertising (Grady, 1981). Yet as William W. Royal, general counsel for the American Advertising Federation, testified before the House in 1982, advertisers' concern primarily centered on unfairness because "at least there were some court decisions on deception [so that advertisers] could prepare some sort of defense, relying upon past precedent" (U.S. House, 1982: 390).

The attempt to change the deception standard, then, was symptomatic of a commitment to economic theory that on occasion appeared to defy political prudence. As noted, this commitment was generally an asset; Miller's reform program was governed by a set of economic principles that prevented his efforts at the FTC from devolving into the sort of crude campaign to get government off the back of business that marred the Reagan deregulatory program at several other agencies. Accordingly, Miller strongly affirmed his "deception" proposal in the face of criticism from members of Congress that there was no "clamor" to modify the standard in the authorizing statute of the FTC:

> [L]et me say sometimes people do not recognize problems, and let me say also that just because no one is particularly supporting a position that I feel is right and maybe even some people opposing [sic] the position that I feel is right, is no reason that I am going to turn my back on it. I have been engaged in a number of analyses over the past several years, and my professional career has been marked by my analyzing and making findings that did not comport with conventional wisdom, starting with the Volunteer Army, with airline deregulation, and trucking deregulation, and so forth. . . . [T]he fact that there is no groundswell for something is no reason that it is not right. . . . (U.S. House, 1982: 176)

The limits of theory, however, were demonstrated in one especially awkward moment during the 1982 reauthorization hearings of the House subcommittee responsible for consumer affairs. In the course of his testimony, Miller seemed to abandon his commitment to attaching material harm to the deception standard. When asked by Democratic Congressman Scheur of New York if an orthodox Jew who ate a hot dog falsely labeled kosher would be protected by his deception standard, even though "damage could not be proven," Miller claimed this case would meet his injury test because "[t]here would be psychological injury" (U.S. House, 1982: 165). This may have indicated that Miller's economic doctrine was not morally bankrupt, yet at the same time it revealed how what presumed to be an exact standard was in fact fraught with uncertainty. Moreover, it suggested, as Congressman Scheur argued, that there was "something right and appropriate about advertisers telling the truth, even though damage cannot be proved."

This exchange no doubt gave a somewhat distorted view of Miller's deception proposal. Given the relative prices of kosher and nonkosher items, economic harm could be demonstrated in the case proposed by Congressman Scheur. Moreover, if one pays for something one does not get, there is a prima facie case of economic injury (T. Muris, personal correspondence, Sept. 9, 1987). Yet Miller's difficulty in responding to this line of inquiry was symptomatic, in part, of an inclination to exaggerate the degree to which clear standards could be established in consumer law by making economic analysis a legal obligation. The commission, even if its judgments were informed by economic analysis, would necessarily still be required to determine injury in many cases by using its own expertise, by determining the capacity or tendency of the claims to deceive.[14]

The attempt to achieve permanent change at the FTC, therefore, was short-circuited not only by strategic errors and Congress's recalcitrance, but also by serious doubts on the part of legislators about the governing philosophy of the Reagan administration. Even when considered carefully and implemented effectively, as was the case at the FTC, this intellectual framework raised serious legal and moral questions. We have suggested that the consumer movement stalled because it was animated by a commitment to reform consumer behavior, a commitment that in important respects led to a virtual rejection of, rather than an effort to reform, the marketplace. Yet the economic theory that governed the efforts to transform the FTC after 1980 seemed all too indifferent to the need to temper market forces with concern for morality. If the crusade to save the consumer was quixotic and inappropriate in a commercial republic, the effort to exalt economic theory and analysis as a substitute for political prudence seemed indifferent to the standards of community and decency that were necessary to hold a society together. Thus, the Miller administration's critics were able to point to certain parts of social reform that should be preserved in the wake of the Reagan revolution, because these reforms clearly comported with fundamental principles of American society. As Michael Pertschuk put it:

[14] On this point, see the testimony of Mark Silbergeld, director of the Washington office of the Consumers Union (U.S., House, 1982).

The marketplace creates incentives which produce innovation and efficiency and productivity, but those incentives are so strong that they often lead to pressures to undermine the standards of a civilized society, to lie, to coerce, to cheat, to overreach. . . . That has been the experience of the human beings in the market system, and what the agency's authority is are the very words that Congress used in those acts, to preserve basic standards of fair dealing in truth, and the imagination and innovation of the economy in developing new methods of undermining those standards knows no narrow and specific bounds, and that is why Congress has never really attempted the task. (U.S., House, 1982: 174)

A half century of reform had raised serious questions about the value of a market economy. That these doubts were not sufficiently addressed by the intellectual framework of the Miller administration was, in the end, a critical factor in defining the limits of regulatory relief at the FTC.

Conclusion

In this chapter we have chronicled the controversial history of the FTC focusing especially on the dramatic changes in the agency over the past two decades. This history clearly demonstrates that the FTC cannot stay free of *major* shifts in regulatory politics. The changes in the FTC from 1969 onward suggest that public agencies—even independent regulatory commissions—are not always independent. During strong political movements to change regulatory politics, the constitutional and bureaucratic "inertia" we discussed in Chapter 2 can dramatically give way to fundamental shifts in the ideas, institutions, and policies that govern agency action. Although the New Deal regulatory regime (for the reasons we have detailed) virtually passed the FTC by, the commission became a principal focus of attention during the public lobby regime, undergoing an extraordinary transformation. It was unclear at that point that a new regulatory era had emerged, that the Reagan revolution had brought about still another regulatory regime. But in the short run the commission had been reshaped on the basis of an intellectual framework that posed fundamental challenges to FTC practices during the public lobby era. It was this sort of challenge, rather than the ad hoc approach adopted by Congress in 1979 and 1980, that was most likely to bring about an enduring shift at the commission.

Nevertheless, because this intellectual framework was not effectively incorporated into the authorizing statute of the FTC, the most recent transformation of the FTC may be short-lived. While the Miller administration successfully employed administrative practices to bring about major policy departures, these departures were not rooted in significant institutional reform. In fact, Miller's main accomplishment in reshaping the institutions of the FTC, according to one close observer, "consisted of revamping internal FTC rules, traditions and practices to make it much easier for an activist chairman to shove through an activist program in the future" (Arthur L. Amolsch, editor, *FTC: Watch,* personal correspondence, Nov. 10, 1987).

Thus, the FTC serves as a useful example of the powerful, but limited, influence of the Reagan presidency on regulatory politics. James Miller's ability to redirect the agency stands as one of the most notable administrative success stories of the Reagan era. Yet when Miller left the agency in October 1985, he left intact the institutional basis that was developed during the public lobby era. Miller's principal goal—to oversee the reauthorization of the agency—was therefore not achieved. As a result, the fate of the agency literally hung in the balance in 1986, while Congress continued to be deadlocked about whether or not to change the agency's authorization—and, if so, how to do so.

In a sense, the commission had come full circle. In 1914, despairing after three years of deliberations about how to define specifically unlawful business practices, Congress settled on delegating this responsibility to a trade commission. More than a half century later, Congress, after a six-year struggle, was still apparently unable to specify the obligations of the FTC. For all the changes in the political economy over the past century, the inability of the legislature to provide a clear mandate for the commission remains the most telling part of the agency's historical tradition. Given that tradition, the agency will remain a powerful regulatory institution, responsive to the influence of broad principles and political movements, yet constantly vulnerable to ad hoc and shortsighted manipulation by Congress, the courts, and interest groups.

This complex historical pattern of regulation at the FTC was unlikely to change significantly in the near future. In April 1986, Daniel Oliver became the new chairman of the commission. He was a former executive editor of *National Review,* and brought to the agency the same commitment to free enterprise that distinguished James Miller's leadership. Yet Oliver seemed to lack his predecessor's deft administrative hand, as well as Miller's ability to work closely with other commissioners and Congress. His heavy-handed leadership prompted Mark Silbergeld of Consumers Union to observe that Oliver's views "were a caricature of Miller's ideological positions" (M. Silbergeld interview).

In an attempt to start putting these views to work, Oliver made an effort to assert administrative control over the agency, alienating his four colleagues on the commission in the process. For example, he sought to exert sole control over the Office of General Counsel, a unit that organizationally and traditionally reports to the commission as a whole and routinely responds to requests from each of the commissioners. Especially controversial was Oliver's announcement, in August 1986, of a brand new commission policy office (the old one having been dismantled by the Miller regime) to be located within his own office. This incident, which was described by the trade journal *FTC: Watch* as "the internal equivalent of a *coup d'etat,*" led to a bitter split between Oliver and the other commissioners, who eventually forced the new chairman to establish the new planning office under the auspices of the entire commission. These actions, which violated the spirit and tradition of a collegial body like the FTC, combined with Oliver's less effective advocacy of free and unfettered competition, compared to Miller's approach, may have, as *FTC: Watch* put it, "essentially finish[ed] the Oliver chairmanship before it [had] hardly begun" (Sept. 12, 1986: 3–8).

The split between Oliver and the commission apparently went deeper than internal management. As Oliver militantly defended the legacy of Miller's chairmanship, the other commissioners showed signs of moving in another direction. Most intriguing in this regard was the commission's decision in June 1986 to take action against the R. J. Reynolds Tobacco Company's advertisement, "Of Cigarettes and Science." By a four-to-one vote, with Oliver dissenting, the commission claimed this advertisement, which was an attempt to convince readers that the link between disease and cigarette smoking was not yet scientifically established, misrepresented the facts. The advertisement failed to disclose, for example, that individuals who quit smoking during a National Institute of Health study discussed in the text showed a substantial decrease in death from heart disease. The crux of this ruling was that R. J. Reynolds' purportedly scientific report was really commercial speech and therefore not protected by the First Amendment right of free speech. It was interesting that the R. J. Reynolds Tobacco Company decision, supported by three Reagan appointees, involved the commission in the sort of controversial and complex deception case that was eschewed during Miller's reign over the FTC (*FTC: Watch,* June 20, 1986: 12–13). Moreover, the commissioners, once again with Oliver dissenting, threatened to disqualify the sitting director of the Bureau of Consumer Protection, William C. MacLeod, when he showed some reluctance to proceed with prosecution of the deceptive advertising charges against R. J. Reynolds Tobacco Company. This unprecedented development resulted in an FTC order that said, "The Commission finds that the director has continued to demonstrate either a lack of comprehension of his responsibilities . . . or unwillingness to carry out that responsibility" (Arthur Amolsch, personal correspondence, Nov. 10, 1987; *National Journal,* Feb. 7, 1987: 299).

This single proceeding did not necessarily mean a revival of con- sumer activism at the FTC. Yet the decision to sue R. J. Reynolds To- bacco Company did suggest that the intellectual framework so effectively employed by the Miller administration no longer held dominant sway over the commission. The loss of Miller's leadership and Congress's in- creasing interest in seeing a more active commission in areas such as the advertisement of alcohol and tobacco suggested that the consumer move- ment was still alive at the FTC. Thus, consumer advocates were much more optimistic in 1986 than they had been four years earlier. This opti- mism was further encouraged by the 1986 congressional elections, which restored Democratic control over the Senate. Consumer activists did not expect a revival of the sort of initiatives that characterized the Pertschuk era. In fact, many public lobbyists and FTC career staff felt that such a revival of uncompromising consumerism would be unwise. Yet, they are unwilling to concede that a new regulatory regime has emerged as a result of the Reagan regulatory program. As Mark Silbergeld of Consumers Union put it:

> The near future will not bring in all likelihood a revival of aggressive rulemaking by the FTC. But there will be a returned commitment to prob- lem solving, and seeing Washington as part of the solution as opposed to the Reagan view that Washington is the problem. . . . I expect that the position of moderate Democrats and Republicans—the government is part of the solution to our problems—will prevail in the long run. The Reagan phenomenon will prove to be ephemeral. (M. Silbergeld interview)

It remained to be seen whether or not the influence of the Reagan administration on the FTC would prove to be so transient. But, as the next chapter shows, the administration's efforts to curtail environmental regulation were decidedly less effective.

6

Regulation and Deregulation at the Environmental Protection Agency

> There is no more forlorn spectacle in the administrative world than an agency and a program possessed of statutory life, armed with executive orders, sustained in the courts, yet stricken with paralysis and deprived of power. An object of contempt to its enemies and of despair to its friends.
>
> NORTON LONG, "Power and Administration"

In the early 1980s the EPA, like the FTC, was a primary target in the Reagan administration's attack on the new social regulation. During the preceding decade Congress had passed environmental legislation at a furious pace (refer to Table 3.2), and had given the EPA responsibility for administering most of the laws enacted. In practice, this responsibility meant that the EPA developed the myriad of specific rules and regulations governing such matters as the environmental performance standards, design criteria for factories and toxic waste dumps, selection of pollution control technologies, enforcement procedures, the formal permitting procedures of new public and private construction, and the granting of waivers or variances to individual firms. The EPA, moreover, enjoyed wide discretion in writing and implementing these regulations, thus prompting the observation that it was exercising a quasi-legislative authority (Bardach and Kagan, 1982). Finally, the agency became not only the critical contact point with the federal government for the states, municipalities, and business firms affected by environmental policies, but also a lightning rod for their criticisms of those policies.

Of all the new social regulation, that dealing with environmental quality imposed the highest compliance costs on business firms (Business Roundtable Study, 1979) and created the greatest controversies about relations between Washington and the states. Given President Reagan's strong philosophical commitment to minimizing federal interference in the private sector and to resuscitating federalism, it was only natural that his administration was as responsive as possible to complaints about the EPA. Moreover, the president maintained that the election of 1980 had given him a mandate to reduce the cost and intrusiveness of the federal government. Clearly then, criticisms of the EPA and of the microeconomic or firm-level burdens of environmental policy evoked for philosophical and political reasons a sympathetic response from the Reagan administration. The president's advisors, however, were equally concerned about compliance costs from a macroeconomic standpoint. In their view, the tremendous expenditures on pollution control and permitting procedures were diverting significant amounts of capital from productive investment, thereby retarding the nation's economic growth in exchange for minimal gains in environmental quality.

In addition, the EPA attracted the attention of deregulators, because it drew the largest share of federal monies spent on regulatory policy. Within the agency's budget, the largest single item (the program for constructing sewage treatment facilities) was widely acknowledged, even by environmentalists, as a public works pork barrel for senators and representatives (personal interviews, July 21 and 22, 1980). This too made the agency an inviting target for deregulators and budget cutters in the administration. Finally, the EPA was involved in far more citizen lawsuits, rulemakings, and enforcement actions than any other social regulatory agency. Environmentalists' emphasis on these activities reflected both their belief that a cleaner environment was a matter of citizens' rights ultimately to be guaranteed by the legal system and their conviction that successful policy reforms depended on active participation in the implementation process. The extent of these activities surely did not go unnoticed by deregulators in the Reagan administration.

It was this involvement of public lobbyists in the courts and the bureaucracy that many in the Reagan administration found especially obnoxious. In their view, it seemed the height of hypocrisy for public lobbyists to proclaim themselves tribunes of the people and champions of participation, while fighting their greatest battles in the courts, the least democratic branch. Indeed, in an interview Carol Crawford, director of the Bureau of Consumer Protection of the FTC, insisted that the adjective "public" should not be accorded to environmental and consumer groups. She deemed them no more or less representative of the public than any special-interest group (personal interview, July 23, 1985). While not all interviewees from the Reagan administration were so blunt, it was obvious that a wide political and ideological chasm separated environmentalists from deregulators, and impelled the latter to pursue vigorously the goal of regulatory relief.

The magnitude and the pervasiveness of the influence of the EPA on both the specific political economic actors and the economy as a whole made it an inviting target for deregulation. That it dealt exclusively with social regulation only served to heighten this interest. Moreover, the EPA of course was the first and most prominent of the federal agencies created in the 1970s to administer the new social regulation. In contrast to the FTC, which had responsibilities not only for consumer protection, but also for economic competition, the mission of the EPA was unambiguously one of social regulation. Under these circumstances, it was hardly surprising that deregulators took aim at the EPA. Before examining the attempt to deregulate the EPA, however, it will be useful to review the creation of the agency. In that way we can develop a clear picture of the regulatory ideas, institutions, and policies as well as the inertial forces the Reagan administration confronted at the EPA.

Origins of the EPA

The EPA came into existence in 1970 at approximately the same time that the FTC was reinvigorated pursuant to the Nader report. To some extent it seems ironic, even anomalous, that the conservative Republican administration of Richard Nixon, an administration publicly committed to scaling down the domestic activities of the federal government, should preside over two developments so crucial to the emergence of the public lobby regime. The case of the EPA appears especially puzzling because the recommendation for a new regulatory body came from the Ash Council, a commission appointed by President Nixon to streamline the federal bureaucracy. The council did give the president considerable control over the new agency by structuring the EPA as an executive agency instead of an independent regulatory commission like the FTC. This meant obviously that the administrator of the EPA would serve at the pleasure of the president rather than for a fixed term. Nevertheless, the idea of a regulatory agency, even an executive agency, contradicted a major premise of the Ash Council's reorganization effort, namely to reduce the number of bureaucracies reporting to the White House because the council felt that there were too many agencies already reporting to the president. As Douglas Costle, a staff member of the Ash Council and later administrator of the EPA under Jimmy Carter, explained: "Initially [the Ash

Council] opposed it [creating the EPA] because it did not fit their conception of cabinet government and their bias to force trade-off decisions on cabinet secretaries" (personal interview, April 8, 1985).

The last thing the Ash Council, a body composed primarily of business executives, wanted was another agency reporting directly to the president and occupying him with bureaucratic conflicts that in principle could be resolved at a lower level. In fact, the Ash Council at first rejected its staff's recommendation to establish the EPA.

The creation of the EPA seems doubly puzzling, because public lobbyists played such a minimal role in establishing the regulatory body that played such a critical role in implementing environmental policy. The primary impetus came from Congress and in particular through the legislative staffs of Senators Henry Jackson (D-Washington) and Edmund Muskie (D-Maine). Jackson and Muskie were key sponsors of environmental legislation, but the initiative for the EPA came from the Ash Council. Environmentalists put their imprimatur on the agency only after the Nixon administration proposed establishing it.

Even with the influence of Jackson and Muskie, environmentalists did not strongly support the idea of an executive agency to oversee environmental policy. Their roots in the New Left made them naturally distrustful of the central government, especially the presidency. This reflexive wariness was accentuated by the political atmosphere of the late 1960s and early 1970s. In addition, it seemed clear that President Nixon's concern with the environment was purely reactive, a response to the emergence of the issue on the national agenda and that Jackson and Muskie, two potential rivals, were capitalizing on it (Caldwell, 1976). Despite these circumstances, environmentalists not only failed to oppose strongly the Ash Council's initiative, but eventually came to support the idea of an executive agency to coordinate environmental policy. How was it that the Ash Council came to recommend and environmentalists came to support the creation of the EPA?

As Douglas Costle noted, despite its initial bias against creating yet another federal bureaucracy that would report to the White House, the Ash Council eventually adopted the position set forth by its staff that such a measure was warranted by the unique character of environmental policy. Staff arguments eventually persuaded the council that the government's antipollution efforts ought to be consolidated in one agency, because there are interactions and trade-offs inherent in controlling the different types of pollution. Creating an EPA was presented as a means of "rationalizing the organization of environmental efforts, and giving focus and coordination to them" (Costle interview, April 17, 1986). In addition, the staff report emphasized that longer range ecological problems such as toxic waste management and acid rain, which cut across the various environmental media (i.e., air, soil, and water), required an integrated and holistic approach that could be achieved only by housing all environmental programs in one agency (Costle interview, April 8, 1985).

These staff arguments alone were not sufficient to convince the council that another agency was needed. The council's predictable response was to suggest placing responsibility for all environmental policy in one existing bureau, preferably a cabinet department. What ultimately swayed the council members to the staff's position was the response of the various cabinet secretaries to a call for recommendations on where to house environmental regulation. In the best tradition of bureaucratic competition for new resources (Downs, 1967), the Department of Commerce, Department of Health, Education and Welfare (HEW), Department of Housing and Urban Development (HUD), Department of the Interior (DOI), and Department of Transportation (DOT) each presented a case that it was the logical body to control environmental policy. The Department of Commerce argued that it should have responsibility for environmental policy because of the pervasive impact on business and the connection between environmental regulation and economic growth; HEW maintained that the public health aspects of antipollution efforts made it the logical choice; HUD suggested that because many of the worst ecological problems were in urban environments, it should control the new programs; DOT staked its claim on the tremendous importance of automobile pollution and the need for mass-transit alternatives. Perhaps the most incredible claim came from the Army Corps of Engineers, which made its pitch for the new agency by arguing that its extensive experience with river management and construction projects made it the appropriate organization, at least for water pollution control programs.

It became obvious that the logic of bureaucracy was reductionistic rather than holistic; each agency conceptualized environmental regulation as composed of distinct, more-or-less unconnected elements. Thus, the Ash Council eventually became convinced that a new agency was needed. Placing environmental policy in an existing cabinet department would likely result in environmental questions being buried or, at best, so skewed by the dominant concerns of any given department that interdependency, the central idea of ecology, would be lost.

Once the Ash Council members accepted the necessity of a new regulatory body, they readily opted for creating an executive agency, rather than an independent regulatory commission. Creating a commission would have required legislative action, and would open up the council's program to the vagaries of congressional politics. Putting an executive agency in place, on the other hand, allowed them to continue operating under their broad reorganizational authority and thereby ensure both expeditious action and maximum control. In addition, the members favored the executive-agency model because of their bias against collegial decisionmaking characteristics of the commission form. Such a decision process, in their view, minimized accountability and presidential control. Finally, the Ash Council believed that environmental policy demanded a strong scientific and technical component that could be best incorporated in an executive agency, because the commission form (in part because of its collegial decisionmaking) is dominated by legal and adjudicative expertise. Thus, the council came to support not only the consolidation of responsibility for environmental policy, but also the creation of the EPA.

Environmentalists, for their part, had little taste for executive agencies, but neither were they enamored of independent regulatory commissions. As we have noted in Chapter 3, this latter form of bureaucratic organization had long been considered inadequate by reformers. Supporters of the New Deal had criticized independent commissions as a "headless fourth branch of government." The Brownlow Committee concluded in 1937 that even if honest and competent, such regulatory bodies had "no place in a government based on the theory of democratic control" (President's Committee on Administrative Management, 1937: 40). Although Congress ultimately denied Franklin Roosevelt the extensive administrative control he sought, the New Deal emphasis on presidential government did raise questions about the efficacy of independent commissions (Emmerich, 1950: 88–89).

The New Deal challenge to independent regulatory commissions was given further impetus by a wealth of evidence adduced by scholarly research in the postwar period. This work indicated that the commission form almost invariably led to domination of regulatory politics by business interests (Bernstein, 1955; McConnell, 1965; Lowi, 1969; Stigler, 1971). In addition, everyday experience with the performance of such agencies as the Federal Communications Commission (FCC), the Civil Aeronautics Board (CAB), and the Federal Maritime Commission seemed to confirm the conclusions of scholarly analyses. It also seemed to corroborate the allegations of the New Left critics that independent regulatory agencies amounted to impotent and symbolic institutions (Gitlin, 1966). Business firms and their lobbyists appeared to enjoy a preponderant influence in regulation administered by independent commissions. Consequently, the environmentalist community shared the Ash Council's lack of enthusiasm for the commission form.

Yet the idea of a regulatory agency at the federal level did appeal to environmentalist groups. On the one hand, the character of environmental problems dictated a national approach. Because environmental problems cut across state boundaries, it is impossible to deal with them effectively below the federal level. On the other hand, an important legacy of the New Deal was a general consensus among liberal reformers that policy problems should be addressed not simply through national programs, but that those programs should be administered by federal agencies (Milkis, 1985; Milkis and Harris, 1986). New Deal-style solutions to policy problems had become so deeply ingrained in the public philosophy that environmentalists and their supporters in Congress never seriously questioned the need for a federal regulatory body. Environmentalists' belief in the need for a federal bureaucracy, combined with their antipathy toward independent regulatory commissions, might have mitigated somewhat their suspicion of an executive agency.

In addition, the political climate of the late 1960s and early 1970s was not very hospitable to the creation of new reform institutions at the state level. State governments had long seemed far more vulnerable to business influence than Washington, D.C. And, more important, given the live memories of the civil rights struggle, state governments had an aura of conservatism, even reaction, in the public mind. Therefore, activists were predisposed to seek reform at the federal level.

Once the EPA was established, public lobbyists' doubts were allayed somewhat by the agency's performance. Perhaps most important, the EPA in its formative years attracted what Anthony Downs has called "zealots," individuals who are committed to a relatively narrow set of *sacred policies* (1967: 88, emphasis in text). In other words, many environmentalists staffed the EPA at the outset. Joseph Krevac, a former director of Water Criteria and Standards at the EPA who had served at the agency since its inception, characterized the first people to staff the EPA as "shock troops committed to stringent environmental regulation" (personal interview, July 22, 1980). With personnel like that in charge of environmental policy, the agency gained credibility among public lobby groups concerned with ecological problems.

In addition, some public lobbyists recognized that under a hostile president, congressional mistrust of the White House ironically might bring legislators to the defense of an executive agency like the EPA more readily than an independent regulatory commission. Senators and representatives presumably would be more sensitive to the possibility of presidential encroachments on the legislative function through executive agencies than through commissions that technically are independent (personal interview, Douglas Costle, June 5, 1985). Gradually the environmentalist community, like the Ash Council, accepted the idea of a separate environmental regulatory body at the federal level, and that it should be structured as an executive agency. The active role of environmentalists in the formative years of the agency and in the enactment of enabling legislation ensured a significant impact for their ideas about institutions and policies.

New Ideas

Environmentalism, like any other "ism," is predicated on a set of ideas. Yet often in this age of television, the controversy and events of a political movement can eclipse its intellectual coherence, because image and immediacy tend to overshadow content and consideration. Indeed, the concept of an EPA emerged amid a rising tide of concern that simply overwhelmed many objections and second thoughts. Legislators, the Nixon administration, and even environmentalists were, to some extent, swept along by the social and political currents of the late 1960s. Like successful reform movements in the past, the environmentalist movement generated a tremendous national sense of urgency, almost a crisis atmosphere. Media coverage of oil spills and other ecological disasters brought this "crisis" into our living rooms and placed tremendous pressure on policymakers to do something. Television also focused attention on the first Earth Day event, a march on Washington of about a half million people, rather than the ideas that motivated those people. Nevertheless, ideas do count because they forge discontent into policy demands and programs.

In this case, the formative ideas combined elements of the New Left critique with the fundamentals of ecology consciousness. These two aspects of environmentalism are complementary in that they both reflect a very basic dissatisfaction with the operation and outcomes of "the establishment." For activist reformers, therefore, the transition from the issues of civil rights and the war in Vietnam to issues of environmental quality was facilitated by a common orientation. Whereas the New Left critics of the 1960s felt that corporate liberalism destroyed the individual psychologically, environmentalists in the 1970s felt that it destroyed the individual physiologically. Both, however, felt that American society was destroying the individual culturally.

In the spring of 1970 the first Earth Day was heralded by a "Declaration of Interdependence." This document, which we quote at some length, served as a manifesto, proclaiming the crucial ideas of environmentalism. It illustrates the linkages between the New Left and ecology consciousness, and also suggests their influence on the EPA and environmental laws. In a pastiche of the Declaration of Independence, this new document asserted that

> nature has instituted certain principles for the sustenance of all species, deriving these principles from the planet's life support system . . . *whenever any behavior by the members of any one species becomes destructive of these principles, it is the function of the other members of that species to alter or abolish such behaviors and to reestablish the theme of interdependence with all life.* . . . Prudence, indeed, will dictate that cultural values long established should not be altered for light and transient causes, that man is more disposed to suffer from its asserting a vain notion of independence than to right themselves *by abolishing that culture to which they are now accustomed.* (cited in Caldwell, 1975: 3, emphasis added)

This excerpt shows the "revolutionary" character of the ideas underlying environmentalism. Environmentalists demanded nothing less than a radical reorientation of American values. In their view, many of our "cultural values long established" set us at odds with the "planet's life support system." If we are to survive, they reasoned, our values would have to be brought into harmony with nature, because holism was to replace reductionism as a model of humanity's relationship with the environment; collectivism was to replace individualism as a model of human behavior; and regulation was to replace (or at least to compete with) the market as a model of resource allocation.

The ideas behind environmentalism were especially attractive to reformers who sympathized with the radicalism of the 1960s, because these ideas offered a powerful indictment of the capitalistic foundation of American society. Capitalism's claims of legitimacy and superiority rest on the argument that it ensures long-term improvements in material welfare, because the market allocates society's scarce resources *rationally,* that is, in the most efficient way. For environmentalists, though, this single-minded emphasis on efficiency and growth is a recipe for disaster. Capitalism, because it places humankind outside of nature, simply provides an efficient path to ecological ruin: nature is considered to be a warehouse of resources that should be exploited. Environmentalists, on the other hand, see nature holistically and humankind as part of a seamless ecological web. From that perspective, a capitalistic society myopically pursues an illusory goal of unlimited growth. Thus capitalism fails by its own criterion, because it is an *irrational* system of resource allocation. Moreover, this conclusion apparently confirms the New Left contention that American society is, in a profound sense, "absurd." Like

New Left critics, environmentalists expressed deep dissatisfaction with the culture and values of the establishment. That being the case, they were inclined to demand radical rather than incremental change.

Just as important, then, the Declaration of Interdependence carried a political message. The imperatives of nature required that members of the human species (environmentalists presumably) who perceived the disjunction between corporate liberalism and ecological principles act to "reestablish the theme of interdependence." Thus, there was civic duty to pursue actively environmentalist goals in the arenas of public policy. Again, the New Left seemed to provide a blueprint. The concepts of participatory democracy, direct action, and parallel institutions all can be seen in the environmental movement.

Over the course of the 1970s, though, the environmentalist ideas behind the creation of the EPA became adulterated. It was impossible to maintain the purity of these ideas in part because environmentalists mirrored the ambivalence of the New Left; they attacked the market, but called for regulation rather than planning, and they advocated collectivism, but often pursued it individualistically. In the heady days of the late 1960s many environmentalists openly expressed disdain for a capitalistic economy. However, they never advocated a truly radical solution; certainly none of their proposals ever approximated a call for centralized economic planning. Just as Sontag noted in regard to the New Left activists, environmentalists in a way were prisoners of their own political romanticism. The problems they addressed and their rhetoric seemed to point to a genuinely collectivist response. Yet, they advocated individualistic action that at its most basic level called on each American to begin developing a simpler, less materialistic life-style—in other words, exactly the kind of moralism that surfaced in the consumer movement, as noted in Chapter 5. On another level, because environmentalists, like other public lobbyists, proceeded from the perspective of programmatic rights, they "naturally" focused on the individual. A rights-based environmentalism is inclined toward protecting the individual citizen from the behavior of overbearing political and economic institutions, rather than promoting a collective response to those institutions. The more radical political ideas also were enervated by adherence to the New Deal formula of addressing policy problems programmatically through the federal government. Indeed, environmentalists ironically found themselves acting more like lobbyists and lawyers than political activists.

Part of their success was in remaking the policymaking establishment, and opening up issue networks to alternative points of view. However, in doing so environmentalists themselves became a fixture in this reconstituted establishment. While it would be erroneous to portray them as merely another special interest, environmentalists did become Washington insiders. As such they found it necessary to operate incrementally rather than holistically at times, to moderate their antiestablishment rhetoric, to take seriously economic arguments about market efficiency, and to spend much more time in the corridors of the Capitol than in the streets of the capital.

Although the ideas set forth in the Declaration of Interdependence could not be maintained in a pristine form, they remain central to a full appreciation of environmentalist institutions and policies that emerged in the 1970s. Those ideas accurately reflect the intellectual and ideological underpinnings of the environmentalist vision, and that vision in turn shaped their demands. To see this, it is instructive to examine their early congressional testimony; these early pronouncements best reflected the new regulatory ideas. In particular, their demands before Henry Reuss's (D-Wisconsin) Subcommittee on Conservation and Natural Resources illustrate very well their attempt to translate environmentalism into government action. In addition, the strident tone of these demands indicates the sense of outrage and urgency that surrounded the creation of the EPA. In such a political atmosphere, an executive agency for environmental regulation might have been the best conservatives in the Nixon administration could have hoped for.

As part of the House Committee on Governmental Operations, Reuss's subcommittee solicited recommendations on what the federal government should do in the area of environmental policy. In responding, environmentalist groups ranging from the Audubon Society to Zero Population Growth enunciated the ideas set forth in the Declaration of Interdependence. Their testimony, published in a volume entitled *The Environmental Decade: Action Proposals for the 1970's,* exemplifies the effort to carry over the new regulatory ideas to formal policymaking arenas.

Undoubtedly, the basic premise of environmentalism is ecological interdependence. All environmental lobbyists testifying before the Reuss subcommittee predicated their demands on a holistic view of the environment. Indeed, it was their conviction that our culture's reductionistic foundations explained the deepening environmental crisis. Not only did the individualistic pursuit of self-interest set us in opposition to basic ecological principles, but we failed also to address environmental problems from a holistic perspective. Remarking on the American celebration of self-interest, Michael McCloskey, executive director of the Sierra Club, maintained that:

> We have a society composed of a host of forces that are conducting piece-
> meal warfare on the environment. Each does as it pleases and acts as if its
> small contribution were not cumulative. (U.S., House, 1970: 165)

Regarding efforts to deal with the environment, Denis Hayes, national
coordinator of Environmental Action, complained to the Reuss subcommittee:

> But so far the environmental crisis has inspired only *piecemeal programs*
> and insipid rhetoric. Most of the politicians and businessmen who are
> jumping on the environmental bandwagon don't have the slightest idea of
> what they are getting into. . . . But a movement is building that will not
> stand for more of the *step-by-step, reckless decisions* that dump sewage in
> our air and water. (U.S., House, 1970: 239, emphasis added.)

Perhaps the clearest statement of the reasons for adopting a holistic
perspective came from the cochairman of a student environmentalist
group at the University of Michigan. Douglas Scott argued:

> [O]ne way we might go on this matter of [environmental performance]
> standards is to call for a major review and overhaul of all environmental
> standards as general standards instead of looking at just the air pollution
> regulations to see how they look, or just the water pollution regulations.
> . . . If in fact the air pollution created by the internal-combustion engine
> and other sources puts a great many nitrates in the air and eventually cause
> water pollution, how is that ecological interconnectedness reflected in the
> way we set standards? (U.S., House, 1970: 290)

Scott's testimony illustrates clearly the way that holism shaped policy
critiques and demands.

No less than holism, environmentalists stressed the importance of
collectivism in presenting their case for governmental action. For environmentalists, the legitimacy of policy derived not from natural law or
natural rights that sheltered the individual from collective expressions of
political will, but from the "principles of the planet's life support systems," which subordinated the individual to the preexisting ecological
order. Thus, individual interests were to give way to collective interests
as defined by ecological principles. Michael McCloskey eleborated on
this point:

> [T]he parameters of ecological health are not negotiable. Nature has its law
> of limits. Absolute results ensue when certain thresholds are crossed,

whether our political and economic institutions care to recognize them or not. (U.S., House, 1970: 165)

Environmentalist testimony before the Reuss subcommittee also demonstrated a strong hostility to the market as a mechanism of resource allocation in society. This hostility, rooted in New Left critiques of capitalist culture and values, led David Brower, the head of Friends of the Earth, to suggest that the 1970s be a "Decade of Renunciation." He went on to assert at the 1970 hearings, "We have now advanced to the 'cowboy economy.' . . . We still think there are no limits to our resources. . . . And that is the cowboy attitude in a fixed, closed ecosphere, spaceship earth, which will not stand that kind of economy." In a more strident attack, Garrett De Bell of Zero Population Growth concluded that:

> To get at the root of our problem [the environmental crisis], the goal of production and consumption for its own sake must be changed. . . . We can put the highway people and the detergent industry out of business if we just don't buy their products. We can adopt simpler life-styles that require less material goods and leave us more time for enjoyment. (U.S., House, 1970: 185)

Identical views about the self-defeating character of American capitalism and the market economy were expressed by Charles Callison of the National Audubon Society, Ted Pankowski of the Izaak Walton League, Michael McCloskey, and Denis Hayes.

Finally, even more directly than the Declaration of Interdependence, environmentalist testimony expressed the need for participatory democracy. Like other public lobby groups, environmentalist organizations had little faith that the public interest would be adequately represented throughout the policy process. For that reason, they insisted on playing a permanent participatory role in decisionmaking. In this regard, Mr. McCloskey of the Sierra Club warned the Reuss subcommittee:

> Many fine programs are established by Congress, but they are often not implemented to achieve their aims. Administrative indifference or hostility frustrates their purpose. Mechanisms, therefore, should be provided to ensure that this is not the fate of environmental legislation. (U.S., House, 1970: 168)

McCloskey and his fellow environmentalists recommended a number of specific measures to ensure the success of environmental policy.

Perhaps the most ambitious idea was a constitutional amendment specifying a "bill of environmental rights." On a more practical level, though, environmentalists insisted on a variety of specific institutional reforms, including federal assistance for public lobbies in their lawsuits, legislative grants of standing to sue polluters and federal agencies to ensure enforcement of federal statutes, central coordination of environmental policy, federal scientific and technical assistance to state and local organizations, and amendment of federal tax law to facilitate the formation of public lobby groups.

New Institutions

As in the case of consumer protection, the ideas underlying environmental policy were translated into specific institutional forms. The EPA and public lobby groups undoubtedly were the most visible institutional manifestation of the new social regulatory ideals in the area of environmental policy. The new ideas, however, were reflected not only in the EPA and environmentalists, but just as important in its relationships with other actors in the environmental issue network. When we speak of institutional forms, therefore, we refer to these relationships as well as organizations such as the EPA or public lobby groups. It is in these subgovernmental relationships that we can see the application of the principle of participatory democracy and the extent to which public lobbyists have succeeded in overcoming inertial forces to alter the policy process. To get a picture of the precise nature of the institutional changes, it is useful to examine the enabling legislation for the EPA. These statutes established new institutional forms.

The first major law that helped to shape the EPA and its role in the policy process was the National Environmental Policy Act of 1969 (NEPA). Although the NEPA was enacted prior to the formation of the EPA, the law was instrumental in establishing the modus operandi of the agency as well as in structuring its relationships with other participants in environmental politics. The NEPA not only empowered the EPA to act as a sort of national gendarme for environmental policy, but did so in a way that implemented the ideas underlying the environmental movement. The concept of interdependence is expressed clearly in Section 101(a), the Declaration of National Environmental Policy:

> The Congress, recognizing the profound impact of man's activity on the interrelations of all components of the natural environment . . . and recognizing further the critical importance of restoring and maintaining environ-

mental quality to the overall welfare and development of man, declares
that it is the continuing policy of the Federal Government . . . to create
and maintain conditions under which man and nature can exist in productive harmony. (PL 91–190)

The NEPA, moreover, acknowledged the importance of mechanisms
for public involvement in environmental policy. In particular, the NEPA
mandated environmental impact statements (EIS) in its Section 102(2)C.
This provision required that the agency oversee the submission and evaluation of EIS for any projects receiving federal funding. Such a provision
assured that the EPA would assume a paramount role both in the public's
eye and in practice. The crucial point about Section 102(2)C is that it
was not originally part of the NEPA. Rather, it was added in a self-
conscious attempt by environmental advocates to ensure a mechanism of
participatory democracy. In fact, the EPA itself balked at the prospect of
applying Section 102(2)C to its own activities (personal interview, Douglas Costle, April 22, 1986).

The 102(2)C clause was proposed after consultation with Lynton
Caldwell, an Indiana University political scientist. Following discussions
with Caldwell, Senator Henry Jackson, the key legislative player in the
development of the NEPA, and his staff became convinced that it would
be advisable to include "an action-forcing element" in the legislation beyond a statement of broad policy goals (Henning, 1977). The EIS, the
product of this determination, mandated a consideration of the interdependence of human beings with their environment; it embedded a holistic
view in the policy process. In addition, the authority to review EIS, subsequently lodged in the EPA, provided an invaluable access point to the
regulatory process for public lobbyists. It proved especially important in
establishing a documentary basis for lawsuits brought by environmentalist
attorneys against individual corporations for noncompliance or even
against the EPA itself for lax enforcement. This litigation approach
stemmed at least in part from reformists' animosity toward business and
their suspicion of government–business relations.

It is essential to keep in mind that political and legal access to subgovernmental decisionmaking was a conscious demand of the environmentalist movement. A common complaint in early citizen "how-to"
books on environmental policy was that without money or legal standing
public lobbyists were often too late to control deleterious business practices. EIS offered a remedy by providing public lobbyists with entree to
federal policymaking procedures. In a variety of ways, subsequent environmental laws reinforced the idea of participatory democracy institution-

alized through the EIS. For example, statutes specified the EPA and industry responsibility about publicizing permit hearings or EIS reviews. Initially, such "public" proceedings were held without sufficient notice, in small, remote communities (Henning, 1977). Later, Congress required public notice in such details as to where publicity should appear and how far in advance of the hearings. Under the 1977 Surface Mining Control and Reclamation Act, for example, citizens—and this clearly meant public lobbyists or their allies—could initiate enforcement actions at the Office of Surface Mining on the basis of their own observations of mining operations. In effect, this bureau in the Department of the Interior augmented its force of mining inspectors with environmentalists. Congress was a willing partner in developing these participatory mechanisms, in part because legislators were unable to play a strong oversight role themselves, and in part because they were allied with environmentalists who felt it imperative that interested citizen groups be involved in every phase of the policy process. In particular, the EPA's status as an executive agency prompted suspicion and jealousy in Congress.

The publication provisions in various statutes sought to maximize the prospects for participatory democracy in the administrative as well as the legislative phase of the policy process. This aim was consistent with the view (characteristic of the new social regulators) that the weakness of Progressive Era and New Deal regulation was their neglect of the prospects for special interests undermining the public interest in the implementation of policy. Therefore, public lobby organizations paid particular attention to participation in the administrative phase of regulatory policy.

Beyond statutory assistance in finding out about administrative proceedings such as permit hearings, in some cases environmentalists acquired the right to initiate agency actions, especially with respect to enforcement (Harris, 1985). In addition, activists received funding from a variety of government agencies. For example, under the Toxic Substances Control Act, they succeeded in establishing a program similar to intervenor funding at the FTC. Daniel Becker, director of legislative affairs for Environmental Action noted that his and other environmentalist groups had received financial support through grants from the Department of Energy (personal interview, June 11, 1986). Such monies often were used for educational purposes at the grass roots level to facilitate public participation in permitting. In this way they attempted to offset the considerable resource advantages business enjoys in administrative activity. Peter Schuck notes: "the most striking thing about public interest group participation in agency proceedings is how little of it there is at a *formal* level. The reasons are not difficult to perceive, and most of them revolve around limited resources, and limited information" (1975: 208, emphasis in text). Statutory provisions on publication, initiation, and subsidies for participation in administrative proceedings were clear attempts to overcome these deficiencies, and to the extent they succeeded, regulatory institutions were altered to reflect the ideal of participatory democracy.

Taking advantage of these institutional changes required that environmentalist groups develop their own organizational resources, particularly at the national level; this was a natural result of the centralization of authority in the EPA. For example Maureen Hinckle, as lobbyist and legal affairs expert at the Audubon Society, noted an important distinction between her organization's early mission of localized conservation and wildlife preservation efforts and its current mission of fighting economic exploitation of the environment. This latter mission requires substantial political and organizational resources as well as a national perspective on environmental problems (personal interview, July 30, 1982). In order to utilize these resources effectively the Audubon Society saw a need to establish a permanent presence in the issue networks of environmental policy; it had to continue its participation beyond the enactment of laws protecting the environment. Maureen Hinckle was emphatic, in this regard, about her organization's determination to augment its inhouse legal staff in order to participate more effectively in the regular proceedings of administrative law, watchdog activities established under environmental statutes, and hearings on proposed regulations. Formerly, effective participation in these implementation activities had been the province of business lobbies.

Douglas Costle maintained that by the time he became head of the EPA in the late 1970s, public lobby groups were permanent players in the regulatory game. Even if limited resources prevented their extensive participation at the formal level, Costle noted that "they interacted at all levels of the EPA, particularly below the office of administrator where they were involved on a regular basis" (personal interview, April 8, 1985). Of course, environmentalists' success in gaining entree to the policymaking process was a double-edged sword. It surely guaranteed an alternative voice in the politics of issue networks, because business lobbyists would have to accommodate a new and influential set of actors: public lobby groups. Nonetheless, in becoming, as it were, part of the establishment, environmental groups exposed themselves to the threats of cooptation, declining zeal, and most important, a certain distance from the grass roots on which they depended for money.

The ideal of participatory democracy also provided the basis for revamping legal institutions. Undoubtedly, a major success was the establishment via case law and legislation of standing to sue for "interested parties" in environmental controversies. In order to have one's case heard, an individual or organization must be granted "standing" by the court in which suit is brought. In new areas of law, such as environmental suits in the 1970s, establishing standing is a major concern. However, once it is established and affirmed by the courts, it becomes more or less a legal formality in bringing suit. An interested party is an individual or group adversely affected by some public or private operation. Significantly, though, in the realm of environmental policy an interest need not be defined in economic terms. In a series of Supreme Court decisions, *Sierra Club* v. *Morton* (405 U.S. 727, 1972), *United States* v. *Students Challenging Regulatory Agency Procedures* (412 U.S. 669, 1973), and *Duke Power Company* v. *Carolina Environmental Study Group* (438 U.S. 59, 1978), environmentalists succeeded in establishing that an interest may be based on aesthetic as well as economic criteria. In the Sierra Club case, the Court asserted:

> Aesthetic and environmental well-being, like economic well-being, are important ingredients in the quality of life in our society, and the fact that particular environmental interests are shared by the many rather than the few does not make them less deserving of legal protection through the judicial process. (*Sierra Club* v. *Morton,* 405 U.S. 727, 1972)

Although in this case standing was denied to the environmental plaintiffs, the Court made it clear that the grounds for denial were simply that the Sierra Club did not allege that any of its members were injured. Thus, the justices established a broader basis for standing to sue. This new criterion of aesthetics became a part of subsequent federal legislation on the environment, and these later laws provided for so-called citizen suits.

Specifically, the court decisions were reinforced by statutory grants of automatic standing for "interested parties" to bring civil suits. In this way, national environmentalist organizations gained an important legal toehold in the enforcement of federal statutes. They acquired leverage against not only recalcitrant business firms, but also potentially hostile chief executives and weak administrators. This is another example of public lobbyists carving out for themselves a permanent niche in the policy process by restructuring institutional relationships.

Environmentalists, like other public lobbyists, attempted to advance their aims and protect their achievements through judicial mechanisms, thus thrusting the federal courts into a new and more positive role in the policy process. In their analysis of the judicial role in an increasingly administrative political system, Greanias and Windsor show:

> [A]s long as government power is permitted to expand, the role of the courts will persist and loom even larger. Because the courts are passing on the activities of an expanding government, they will perform a steadily expanding policymaking function—regardless of whether they claim such policymaking power or not. (1981: 407)

A broader role for the courts also ermerged, according to William Ruckleshaus, because mistrust of the government in the environmentalist community, coupled with their legal expertise, made litigation a natural outlet for citizen oversight activities. As a result, he suggested, half facetiously, that "80 percent of EPA decisions wind up in court" (personal interview, June 5, 1985). In a similar vein, Richard Ayers of the Natural Resources Defense Council (NRDC) asserted that the crucial development enabling public participation to be meaningful was the establishment of standing:

> The basic formula for public interest activities is for the public to form a balance against industry. In the past, business had the advantage in administrative settings, but now the courts are a lever against the agencies . . . I live in terror of the present [Supreme] Court shutting down the avenue of litigation as a means of asserting balance in the administrative process. (personal interview, July 21, 1986)

This new role for the courts must be counted as an extremely important institutional change advancing the new regulatory idea of participatory democracy. On the one hand, the courts have come to play a new institutional role in the policy process. More important, though, they now provide an invaluable access point to regulatory decisionmaking for public lobbyists and their allies in litigation, public interest law firms (Schuck, 1982).

There were, however, other equally important ways in which advocates of environmental regulation promoted greater involvement in federal policy. Sympathetic congressional staff played a key part in providing environmentalist lobbies with access to the legislative process. Mark Griffiths, director of Natural Resources and Environmental Quality for the National Association of Manufacturers (NAM), saw this "talented and energetic group" as pursuing "ideological objectives wholeheartedly" since their arrival in the early 1970s. Especially in the Senate, Griffiths argued, staffers were able to shape legislation, because senators hold several committee assignments and, consequently depend more on staff than representatives (personal interview, July 29, 1983). Even if Griffith's suggestion of an unambiguously proenvironmental ideology among newer staffers was exaggerated owing to the opposition of NAM to much environmental legislation, it seems clear that these people were intelligent and creative. In the political climate of the 1970s, writing and passing environmental legislation was a natural outlet for their energies and abilities. Also, social regulatory policy in general was attractive to legislators from a reelection standpoint during the 1970s. If staffers could satisfy their own ideological proclivities as well as achieve a sense of accomplishment while serving the interests of their legislators, thereby advancing their own careers, so much the better. The important point is that staffers, for whatever reasons, provided an important legislative conduit for environmental ideas. As a result, the role of public lobbies within environmental issue networks was further enhanced.

The institutional character of these issue networks, of course, was also shaped by the EPA itself as well as the redirected Department of the Interior and, to a lesser extent, the Council on Environmental Quality. In many ways the EPA was a reflection of its personnel. In the agency's formative years they were both extremely talented and strongly committed to environmentalism. A program analyst in the Region III office of the EPA noted that when he joined the agency in its early years "EPA was a freewheeling and booming agency" (personal interview, Feb. 18, 1982). Such an organization naturally attracted talented and energetic people who, regardless of their political leanings, were interested in working in an exhilarating atmosphere. The strong leadership of William Ruckleshaus and Russell Train as the first administrators of the EPA reinforced the incentives for creative people to join the agency. Those who did join included not only lawyers and professional bureaucrats, but also, as the Ash Council foresaw, scientists and engineers. Moreover, the lawyers who did join early reflected the same strong public advocacy stance of the lawyers who joined the FTC in the 1970s. As one official at the headquarters of the EPA put it, "Many of the lawyers that came on board in the early seventies were infused with a certain zeal for the environmental cause" (personal interview, March 26, 1982).

Many nonlawyers at the new agency were scientific and technical personnel whose job it was to develop performance standards and data on pollution. This accent on scientific and technical analysis tended to endow the EPA with a certain credibility not available to other agencies cast in the adversarial culture of the legal profession alone. Unlike the FTC, for example, the EPA reflected a problem-solving rather than an adjudicatory approach. The agency also reflected the concepts of holism and interdependence advanced by environmentalists. In this respect, the scientific and technical image of the EPA bolstered the environmentalist notion that there existed an ecological order to which private interests must be subordinated. This being the case, there could be no justification for bargaining and compromise or balancing one interest against another, the traditional mode of operation at federal regulatory agencies.

An additional and unintended consequence of the accent of the EPA on the scientific and technical was that the agency and its environmentalist supporters developed lines of communication with their business opponents. Especially larger firms and trade associations had their own in-house engineering or environmental science staffs, and those personnel approached environmental policy from the same problem-solving perspective as their environmentalist counterparts, because both were trained in the same intellectual tradition. This common grounding emerges clearly in congressional hearings at which the staffs of large firms, national environmental lobbies, and the EPA often engage in a colloquy on the technical aspects of environmental legislation. This communication tends to exclude smaller firms. More important, it tends to legitimize environmental policy. The questions are framed in terms of how best to craft a federal program for rectifying an environmental problem, rather than should the central government be involved in environmental regulation or whether comand–control type regulation is the most efficacious.

Ultimately, the impact of the new institutions and relations has been to promote the legitimacy of federal regulatory programs, and to facilitate regular access for environmentalists to the implementation phase of the regulatory process. In a testimonial to public lobbyists' success in achieving and maintaining an important role in regulatory subgovernments, William Ruckleshaus observed after his second term as the EPA administrator that "ten years later the same people are there, only they're smarter, more knowledgeable and more sophisticated than in 1970. . . . Public interest groups are in control in the present regulatory proess; they represent the *status quo*" (W. Ruckleshaus interview). Such groups as the Sierra Club, the Izaak Walton League, the Environmental Defense Fund, and the national Audubon Society as well as businesses and their trade associations have entree to environmental issue networks.

In the final analysis, the institutional changes brought about by environmentalism meant that the EPA would function in a new way compared to older regulatory bodies. Because it was required by statute to pay heed to public lobbyists, the influence of public interest groups was assured, even after a decline in the zeal of agency personnel or the emergence of a conservative administration. The ideal of participatory democracy, though adulterated by the realities of regulatory politics and the administrative process, remained alive and was legitimized in the operation of the EPA. It should be emphasized that this legitimation was the product of a shift in power relations: not that business interests were by any means disenfranchised, but that their *relative* influence surely was reduced.

New Policies

In particular, the new regulatory policies embodied the tension with the free market inherent in the new social regulation. Environmental laws changed regulatory politics in two ways. On the one hand, they contained a procedural aspect that was aimed at altering issue networks and the institutional bases of regulatory politics by promoting the ideal of participatory democracy. On the other hand, these laws had a substantive focus that was directed at achieving environmental objectives. This subtantive aspect not surprisingly reflected the ambivalence toward capitalism that characterized the environmental movement. One of the important ideas underlying environmentalism was that the relatively unconstrained pursuit of private economic interest (the philosophical foundation of capitalist society) was responsible in large measure for ecological problems.

The development of new regulatory policies under the EPA covers roughly the decade of the 1970s. This period may be divided into two phases. The first phase, lasting until approximately 1977, entailed the passage of many pieces of environmental legislation, the most important of which were the Water Pollution Control Amendments Act and the Clean Air Amendments Act. These laws attempted to impose on industry stringent performance standards and timetables for environmental cleanup. The second phase, which extended until the election of Ronald Reagan in 1980, revolved around efforts to bring efficiency criteria into environmental regulation and to begin grappling with the more technical and complex ecological problems of toxic-waste management and acid rain.

In the latter phase, Congress had to deal with what a former deputy director at the EPA termed "technology-oriented issues" (personal interview, March 30, 1982). These issues took shape in the 1978 Water Pollution Control Amendments Act, the second Clean Air Amendments Act, the Toxic Substances Control Act (TOSCA), the Resource Conservation and Recovery Act (RCRA), and the Comprehensive Environmental Response, Liability and Control Act (Superfund). These laws, according to a former director of toxic substances at the agency, "enhanced the prominence of engineers and other scientific types at EPA" (personal interview, July 30, 1982).

In this second phase, the Office of Policy, Planning and Evaluation (OPPE) at the EPA also gained new prominence. In the late 1970s, under William Drayton, the OPPE began to introduce a stronger component of economic analysis into EPA decisionmaking. Although this second phase saw the moderation of some tough environmental standards in response to harsher economic times and the emergence of more complex environmental problems, environmental policy throughout the 1970s continued to reflect the fundamental ideas of environmentalism and the public lobby regime in general. The persistence of these ideas testifies to the success public lobbyists enjoyed in restructuring the institutional bases of regulatory politics and in protecting their policies against the traditional forces of bureaucratic and political inertia. While environmental policy was not immune to these forces, it did prove remarkably resistant.

In order to understand the nature of environmental policy in the first half of the 1970s, it is useful to recall the historical circumstances of that time. It was the height of the environmentalist movement, at least in terms of public attention to ecological problems. The Congress, particularly Senators Henry Jackson and Edmund Muskie, had made environmental protection a top priority, reflecting the environmentalists' success in setting the national agenda. The EPA had just been created. In sum, environmentalists and their political allies were in the ascendancy and there was a national sense of crisis about the impacts of pollution looming ahead.

As Douglas Costle explained, "At the outset, EPA had an overly ambitious agenda . . . Congress felt that to get business to move on environmental protection you had to 'hit the mule between the eyes with a two-by-four' . . . Ruckelhaus, as the first Administrator had to 'play capture the flag' " (personal interview, April 8, 1985). In other words, the political environment led both Congress and the EPA to advocate strong environmental laws.

Under these circumstances, it was relatively easy for public lobby groups to get essentially what they wanted in terms of environmental policy. Consequently, the legislation and administrative actions of that period clearly reflected environmentalist ideas. In particular, the laws revealed the tension between environmentalism and capitalism. Commenting on this situation, William Ruckleshaus argued that "the early formulation of environmental laws was flawed. The concepts of *no-effect level* and *ample margin of safety* posed impossible tasks for the EPA" (W. Ruckleshaus interview, emphasis added). These two concepts, along with the mandate in early laws that the "best available control technology"

(BACT) be employed by industry in cleaning up the environment. By requiring a particular antipollution technology, Congress severely restricted the prospects for developing new technologies by eliminating the economic rationale for doing so. If a steel firm knows that it must install scrubbers to control air pollution in its plants, it has no incentive either to develop better technology itself or to seek it out from other firms specializing in pollution control technology. All three concepts are linked by their omission of regulatory cost and efficiency as criteria in environmental policy.

On the administrative side of early environmental policy, the EPA was also guided by the political pressure that environmentalists generated. Once the EPA was established, legislators had every incentive to escalate demands for environmental action. Reorganizations like the Ash Council's recommendation for creating the EPA always come in the midst of a crisis atmosphere. In a crisis environment legislators are under a great deal of pressure to act, and the public demand for action enhances the influence of individuals or groups who have a clear set of ideas and proposals. In the late 1960s and early 1970s, the public perceived a need for drastic action in the realm of environmental policy, and public lobbyists had a program that gave voice to the public concerns. Consequently, environmentalists were able to transfer their ideas from legislation to administration relatively easily. The ease of transferral, of course, was enhanced by the strong congressional commitment to environmental protection and to the new institutional mechanisms for public participation in administrative procedures. William Ruckleshaus explained that in its formative years it was absolutely critical for the EPA to "reassure the American public that government was serious about attacking pollution" (W. Ruckleshaus interview). In writing the companion regulations for the early laws and in pursuing enforcement, therefore, the EPA adopted an activist posture. The agency wrote detailed rules and vigorously enforced them, consistent with the environmentalist rejection of cost and efficiency criteria.

In retrospect, the single-mindedness of environmentalists in pursuit of their policy goals and the strict subordination of economic values to the environmentalist ethic appear myopic and irrational. However, as Aaron Wildavsky has explained, environmentalists were perfectly rational given the intellectual underpinnings of their policies:

> [I]t is precisely this mode of thinking in terms of opportunity costs to which environmentalists object. . . . Environmentalists are trying to move the boundaries by which men distinguish between the profane—money, the

economic calculus—and the sacred—man's relationship to nature. (1978: 190–91)

The rationality of early environmental policy existed in its consistency with the values of holism, ecological interdependence, and collective responsibility. The policies seem irrational only if the standards of rationality are the neoclassic economic formulas of utility maximization and the efficient allocation of society's resources.

The second phase of new policy in the area of environmental protection focused on a new and different set of ecological issues. These issues were more technical and complex in nature. Douglas Costle, who headed the EPA in this second phase, pointed out that beginning in the late 1970s:

> There has been a shift from trying to decrease pollution by gross measures to dealing subtly with more complex issues . . . a shift from dealing with bulk pollutants to such problems as acid rain and groundwater contamination. We had to rethink the basic approaches underlying our laws, especially as our knowledge and sophistication increased. We ought to be thinking about policy effectiveness rather than strict performance standards. (personal interview, June 5, 1985)

Costle's comments indicate that the mission and policy of the EPA changed not only because of the emergence of new issues associated with more complex ecological problems, but also because there were some second thoughts, at least at the agency, about the efficacy of policies initiated in the early 1970s. Indeed, there was a significant reform component to environmental policy in the second half of that decade, and many environmentalists complained bitterly about it, prompting one of the program directors at the EPA to suggest that they had "compromised the Agency by laying a 'critical trip' on the EPA" (personal interview, July 22, 1982).

The impulse for reform derived also from traditional forces. Business opposition began to coalesce by the middle of the decade, and economists' criticisms of command–control regulation as a solution to environmental externalities began to have an effect. Moreover, as Costle noted, this opposition and criticism accompanied a regulatory backlash that was energized by the economic downturn of the mid-1970s. Even officials at the EPA began to wonder, in the words of a director of the agency's toxic-substances program, "How can we justify spending millions of dollars for such minimal results?" (personal interview, July 30,

1982). The public pressure for strong programs began to wane as the trade-off between environmental protection and economic productivity became clear. Strict performance standards and criteria such as BACT and no-effect level were called into question. Remarking on this slackening of public support, William Ruckleshaus opined that on environmental issues, in contrast to the economic policy areas, "Americans are ideological liberals and operational conservatives" (W. Ruckleshaus interview).

In this atmosphere of reassessment that was brought on by stronger business opposition, economic criticism of environmentalist policy, and the sobering effect of a deep recession, a number of reforms were instituted at the EPA. The EPA took a leading role in reform because, as Costle explained, the agency "wanted to be out in front in this situation in order to control its own destiny" (personal interview, April 8, 1985). Specifically, the EPA encouraged business participation in an emissions trading program, instituted interagency reviews of proposed regulations, and attempted to relax strict performance standards in cases in which the supporting data were clearly inadequate. Each of these reforms entailed a prominent role for the OPPE and its staff economists and policy analysts.

The general thrust was to introduce economic and cost criteria into environmental policymaking. For example, emissions trading, popularly known as the "bubble concept," placed an imaginary bubble over a particular plant and, rather than requiring the plant to comply with every legislative performance standard on air pollution, accepted a net reduction in all pollutants. This encouraged the firm to reduce pollution in a cost-effective manner, because any "rational" business manager would allocate pollution control resources to the least costly cleanups, while ignoring the most costly, and still satisfying the EPA with an overall reduction in emissions. The other reforms, in contrast to earlier policies, were also intended to bring costs explicitly into consideration. Interagency reviews of proposed regulations allowed additional opportunities for amending stringent policies. Requiring stronger data to justify strict performance standards was an attempt to promote policy effectiveness instead of simple adherence to environmentalist ideas.

The policy reforms at the EPA notwithstanding, it must be pointed out that the second half of the 1970s did not witness an undoing of environmental policy. These reform measures were adjustments, often instituted on a limited and experimental basis; the bubble concept clearly fit this approach to reform. Moreover, all of these reforms were administrative. None of the environmental statutes was altered despite the bureaucratic attempts to relax BACT and other "questionable" environmental standards. Consequently, the reforms eliminated neither institutional nor policy changes effected by the environmentalists. Also, it must be noted that Congress continued to enact major pieces of environmental legislation into the late 1970s. Although these new laws dealt with complex "second-generation" ecological issues, they reflected the legislators' commitment to environmental policy. Beyond that, however, they also reflected the strength acquired by environmentalists within issue networks.

Despite support for reform within the EPA, many at the agency "saw EPA as the vested interest of the people," and this perception helped to define the relations between bureaucrats and Congress, and to maintain environmentalist influence (W. Ruckleshaus interview). The reforms of the late 1970s began to make inroads into the ways in which the EPA implemented the laws, but did not supplant the ideas behind environmentalism with the values of efficiency and cost effectiveness. By the end of the 1970s, though, even strong supporters of the EPA like Douglas Costle felt a need to reassess the agency's modus operandi as well as the environmental protection laws themselves:

> Environmental policy has been developed improvisationally: as problems arise we improvise first in legislation, then in rulemaking, then in administrative law, and finally in the courts. Legislative reform might bring more coherence and a planning perspective to environmental policy. (personal interview, June 5, 1985)

William Ruckleshaus echoed Costle's frustrations, asserting; "The way we decide these environmental policy questions is just nuts! Three to five years after the initial decision, there is a negotiated decision among industry, environmentalists, and [EPA] with a federal judge acting as referee" (W. Ruckleshaus interview). Their disenchantment with the process of reforming environmental policy reflects the success of environmentalists and their allies in changing regulatory politics to promote their aims and protect their gains. On the whole, the emergence of the public lobby regime meant that inertial forces now favored advocates of the new social regulation.

The EPA and Deregulation

If environmentalists and other architects of the public lobby regime sought to ensconce their ideas and policies in institutions that would resist political attacks, the election of Ronald Reagan clearly offered a test of the effectiveness of these prophylactic measures. Participation in rule-making, use of the courts as a means of oversight, assiduous cultivation of congressional staff, and the promoting of public hearings on the permitting of private economic activities, were all institutional means intended to shelter environmental regulation from attempts originating with either business or the government to weaken either the laws or their enforcement. Environmental lobbyists employed all of these means in combatting regulatory reforms initiated under President Carter and Administrator Costle. However, compared to the Reagan policy of regulatory relief, these reforms evoked skirmishes on the perimeter of environmental policy. Deregulation under President Reagan, in contrast, mounted a frontal assault on the ideas and institutional bases underlying the new social regulation generally, and environmental regulation specifically.

The emphasis on regulatory relief emerged at the outset of the Reagan presidency (refer to Chapter 1). The Bush Task Force on Regulatory Relief, EO 12291 mandating cost–benefit analyses on new regulations, and the centralization of regulatory authority in the Office of Information and Regulatory Affairs (OIRA) at the OMB all unmistakably signaled the importance the new administration attached to regulatory relief, and in particular to reducing the burdens of the new social regulation. The policy of deregulation under the Reagan administration amounted to an effort to change the regulatory regime that had emerged in the 1970s. It is important, therefore, to inquire into the effectiveness of the deregulation at the EPA.

Even before taking office, President-elect Reagan appointed a study group on his transition team to come up with specific recommendations for changing environmental regulation. That group, which included former EPA chiefs Russell Train and William Ruckleshaus, made a number of suggestions. However, by the time of Ronald Reagan's inauguration in 1981, conservative forces led by James Watt had gained control of this group (Kraft and Vig, 1984). This contrasts markedly with the situation at the FTC, where James Miller not only wrote the section of the Reagan transition team's report dealing with the FTC, but also was eventually appointed to head that agency to carry out his own recommendations.

Representing the views of the extremely conservative Heritage Foundation, and articulating ideas of the "sagebrush rebellion," Watt and his supporters succeeded in putting together an aggressive program of regulatory relief in the realm of environmental policy. The Heritage Foundation had issued a report on federal regulation that not only laid out a philosophical position opposed to extensive federal regulation, but also came to serve as a blueprint for regulatory relief in the Reagan administration.

One of the main arguments advanced by the Heritage Foundation report was that federal bureaucrats seemed to operate from an a priori presumption that businesspeople were not to be trusted. The report thereby focused the attention of deregulators on the bureaucracy as a problem. The report also attacked the role of public lobby groups in the regulatory process, suggesting that governmental support such as the intervenor funding program ought to be terminated. While this report proved extremely important in shaping the general thrust of deregulation in the 1980s, the regulatory relief effort at the EPA also was heavily influenced by the so-called sagebrush rebellion, a general public outcry emanating from the western and mountain states and directed against the intervention of Washington bureaucracies in private economic affairs. Many of the objections stemmed from environmental and land management policies that had the effect of sharply curtailing economic development plans in such states as Wyoming, Colorado, Idaho, and Montana. In a sense, what fueled this rebellion was the very success of the public lobby movement; in the past, the federal government had in effect subsidized mining and forestry industries through its policies, but public lobbyists had succeeded in changing federal natural resource policy from a development orientation to a regulatory orientation. James Watt represented the western interests that chafed under the new regime and sought to "get government off their backs."

Their success was attributable, in no small way, to the influence of Joseph Coors, the Colorado beer magnate who had contributed heavily to the Reagan campaign. In fact, it is widely believed that Coors specifically recommended James Watt to the president-elect in order to ensure a strong antienvironmentalist posture as advocated by himself and other leaders of the sagebrush rebellion. They wanted not only to reverse the trend of increasing command–control type regulation, but also to eliminate what they perceived to be the unwarranted influence of "ultraliberal" environmental lobbyists and their bureaucratic allies at the EPA.

Any analysis of deregulation at the EPA must begin with President Reagan's initial appointee as administrator, Ann Burford (formerly Gorsuch). A lawyer and former state legislator from Colorado, Burford was recognized as an ally of James Watt. Her conservative credentials were impeccable with respect to environmental policy. In fact, one environmental lobbyist remarked derisively, "She operates under a Joseph Coors view of the world," suggesting the close political and ideological connections among the architects of regulatory relief (personal interview, July 29, 1982). Undoubtely she took with her to the EPA the views of the Reagan transition team report on regulatory relief, and James Watt was the dominant actor in the team's assessment of environmental policy. Her appointment was another indication of the administration's deep commitment to relief in the area of social regulation.

According to a highly placed official at the EPA, himself a Reagan appointee, Ann Burford arrived at the agency with three immediate goals: delegate authority and responsibility for environmental protection to the states, in keeping with Reagan's commitment to a "new federalism"; introduce "reliable scientific criteria," because past regulatory decisions were often "based on wrong conclusions"; and decrease management costs (personal interview, March 30, 1982). Each of these goals was geared to reduce regulatory burdens on business, in other words to advance the cause of regulatory relief as opposed to reform. Burford appeared interested in deregulation for its own sake, ignoring such obvious problems as the inconsistency between ceding responsibility for environmental regulation to the states and the lack of resources at the state level to meet this new responsibility. In a less charitable assessment, an environmental lobbyist characterized the EPA under Burford as following what he termed "Reagan's environmental federalism, that is, more pollution for fewer tax dollars." As for Ann Burford herself, he saw her as "a good lieutenant heady with victory and venom" (personal interview, July 29, 1982). Even the above-mentioned Reagan appointee noted that the striking feature of Burford's goals was "the absence of any environmental aim, any concept of what EPA's mission was" (personal interview, March 30, 1982). Indeed, it was this realization that led this official and the Burford administration to a mutually agreeable parting of the ways. From the outset Ann Burford unwaveringly pursued her goals for the agency. She did so through a series of measures that we may conveniently divide into categories of personnel policies, budget cuts, and regulatory review.

The personnel policies initiated by Burford had as much to do with style as with substance. Her approach to leadership clearly affected the people who worked at the EPA. Her conscious or unconscious hostility to the agency translated into a detached, aloof relationship with the professional bureaucrats who staffed the EPA. More important, communication linkages between her office and the staff were attenuated, thereby exacerbating the anxieties of the staff that naturally developed after her appointment. In the words of one EPA official from the agency's Region III office:

> The primary impact of the Gorsuch [Burford] administration has been uncertainty. The entire organization is suffering from a paralysis from the top

down . . . and this owes to her personal traits and penchant for wanting to review all decisions in private without consultation. (personal interview, Feb. 8, 1982)

By late 1981, the *Wall Street Journal* reported that even Ann Burford acknowledged the pervasive moral problem at the EPA (Jan. 17, 1981). The cumulative effect of this managerial style was that any public administrator with significant responsibility in program development or enforcement would think at least twice before initiating an action. Indeed, a regional director suggested that this might have been a "conscious effort at uncertainty" (personal interview, Feb. 18, 1982). Even if it were not, just that a relatively high-ranking EPA official could conceive of such a strategy indicates the potency of the effect. As a former program director put it, "When Gorsuch [Burford] first arrived, nothing happened. Everything flowed to the twelfth floor [i.e., the administrator's office] and disappeared into a black box" (personal interview, July 30, 1982).

A more concrete personnel policy was the merger of the enforcement division of the EPA with the general counsel's office. This move served two functions. Under the pretext of streamlining the agency, it gave Burford the opportunity to eliminate some "unwanted lawyers." More important perhaps, it helped to centralize control over enforcement actions, a generic approach of the Reagan administration's deregulatory effort. Despite its formal pyramidal structure, the EPA had operated as a relatively decentralized agency with divisional and program heads acting in a semiautonomous manner. The enforcement merger was clearly designed to end this situation by facilitating central control over what conservative advocates of regulatory relief perceived to be the most burdensome and intrusive aspect of the regulatory apparatus of the EPA.

The second approach to regulatory relief taken at the EPA was the sharp reduction in budgetary allocations. What was most striking about this strategy was that Ann Burford herself called for deep cuts in the budget of the EPA. The unprecedented combination of the president and the EPA administrator advocating reductions proved sufficient to effect major budgetary cuts, and these cuts were the most visible manifestation of deregulation at the EPA. When President Reagan assumed office in 1981, the EPA had an overeall operating budget of $1.347 million. By 1983, primarily through the efforts of Ann Burford, James Watt, and OMB Director David Stockman, that figure had declined to $1.039 million. In fact, were it not for the institutional strength and media support of environmentalists, the Reagan administration might have come closer to its original objective of achieving a 50 percent reduction in the agency's budget. Besides fueling uncertainty among agency personnel, the reductions in funding resulted in severe qualitative and quantitative declines in staff. The immediate impact of the cuts was to reduce employment levels drastically. According to one study, the EPA nationwide lost over 1500 full-time employees between 1981 and 1983. That same study showed that the Washington staff of the EPA (full-time as well as part-time) dropped from 4700 at the beginning of 1981 to just over 2500 by the fall of 1982 (Kraft and Vig, 1984).

Just as devastating to the overall effectiveness of the EPA as the total decline in staff was the severe cutback in the area of research and development, which was cut roughly in half. These particular cuts were especially significant given the increasing complexity and technical demands of environmental policy in the late 1970s. Except for the pesticides and toxic-subtances programs, all regulation at the EPA depended on the general scientific and technical staff to develop rules and performance standards to meet these new demands. Thus, the timing of the cuts in research and development staff proved particularly onerous in light of the agency's shifting responsibilities. Moreover, the high-ranking Reagan appointee who left the EPA maintained that this entire situation, prompted by the budget cuts and Ann Burford's personnel policies, induced many talented and highly experienced scientific staff to leave the agency out of sheer frustration (personal interview, July 30, 1982). Again, it was almost irrelevant whether these results were intentional or not, because the effect undermined the regulatory mission of the EPA.

The third element in the program to relieve the private sector of what Ann Burford and other Reagan appointees to environmental posts deemed overburdensome regulations was the review of not only all new, but also many existing regulations. This process began in earnest with the development of Vice-President Bush's Task Force on Regulatory Relief. That organization actively solicited business leaders recommendations on which environmental regulations to relax.

In a 1982 speech before the U.S. Chamber of Commerce, the chief counsel for the Bush task force, C. Boyden Gray, bluntly stated:

> If you go to the agency [EPA] first, don't be too pessimistic if they can't solve your problem there. If they don't, that's what the Task Force is for. . . . You can act as a double check on the agency you encounter problems with.

The obvious implication of Mr. Gray's remarks was that the task force was intended not only to promote regulatory relief as a general policy, but also to act as an ombudsman and troubleshooter on behalf of businesses that did not receive satisfaction operating through the regular institutional channels. This is not surprising, because the architects of regulatory relief were well aware that the institutions of the new social regulation were specifically designed to thwart business in its attempts to influence regulatory policy. As far as the EPA itself was concerned, Mr. Gray might well have suggested that businesses could act as a triple check on the agency, because Ann Burford cooperated fully with business and the task force; if there was an institutional sticking point at the EPA with respect to the emerging regulatory relief program, it was the permanent staff who were committed to the programs they had developed in the 1970s.

A second important aspect of the regulatory review program was the new role played by the OMB. As we have seen already, that agency empowered the OIRA to oversee new regulations and the execution of EO 12291 on mandatory cost–benefit analysis. The ostensible reason for the OIRA and EO 12291 was to introduce an economic perspective, thereby ensuring a more "balanced approach," to use the Reagan administration's term, in the writing of social regulations (DeMuth, 1984). However, considering the relatively primitive state of cost–benefit analysis (Dunn, 1981; Nagel, 1984; *Government Operations Committee Report,* 1981), especially with respect to the measurement of benefits, the OMB essentially emphasized the costs of environmental policy while soft-pedaling the benefits.

Within the EPA, the one bureau that received a significant increase in funding amid the budget cuts was the Office of Policy, Planning and Evaluation (OPPE). According to one environmental lobbyist, the OPPE functioned as a "mini-OMB," carrying out White House policy directives on regulatory relief. That the OMB and the EPA made such a controversial policy-analytic technique a pivotal element of regulation only exacerbated the fears and resentment of environmentalists and their allies in government. Their impression was that intervention in environmental policy by the OMB was intended solely to weaken potentially costly regulations rather than to ensure reasonable ones. Mark Green, a prominent public lobbyist, noted that the form developed by the OMB for bureaucrats to fill out in compliance with EO 12291 contained four different categories of regulatory costs, but no category for potential benefits, thus minimizing the prospects for benefits outweighing costs. Even more damning of the cost–benefit reviews of the OMB is the evidence adduced by Susan and Martin Tolchin, which shows that even the staff at the OMB saw their economic analyses performed pursuant to EO 12291 as simply a rationalization for regulatory relief (1983). Not only did OMB, OIRA, and OPPE activities violate a sense of fairness in their conscious effort to exclude public lobbyists from policymaking, but as Kraft and Vig point out in their assessment of environmental policy under Reagan, "It is doubtful that [the regulatory review process] can be reconciled with the basic premises of the Administrative Procedures Act, which applies to all executive agencies" (1984: 438–39).

As for regulatory review within the EPA, it is clear that Ann Burford set about altering or abolishing regulations perceived as overburdensome by some vocal elements of the private sector. In the words of one EPA official, "In a de facto way EPA's agenda became what business wants. Gorsuch [Burford] would back off a law if a firm objected" (personal interview, March 30, 1982). He added that, "Gorsuch perceived a mandate to cut government regulation and, among the various regulatory agencies, viewed the EPA as the worst of the lot . . . the career bureaucracy was the enemy." This animus toward the professional staff at the agency helps to explain her personnel policies. It is also consistent with her efforts to cooperate so readily with budget-cutting measures and the efforts of the OMB to intervene in environmental policy. Just as important was her belief that the EPA staff was undermining the health of the economy by enforcing regulations too stringently, which led her to curtail enforcement actions as much as she could. She pursued this policy by reductions in enforcement personnel and centralizing control of these activities under the general counsel's office. In this way aggrieved businesses would know exactly where to go to get results if a field inspector or regional office refused to offer them regulatory relief.

Although identifying personnel, budgetary, and review strategies is useful analytically, all three kinds of measures were elements of a program directed toward the single goal of regulatory relief. Moreover, all were linked in that each was geared toward reducing the regulatory capabilities of the EPA generally, but especially in the critical areas of research and enforcement. There is little doubt that the policies pursued by Ann Burford had immediate and significant impacts on the agency: fewer rules were written, enforcement actions declined, workforce decreased dramatically, morale and initiative among staff plummeted, institutional memory was destroyed, and implementation of newer, more complex statutes was delayed.

Nevertheless, the impacts, particularly the long-term impacts of Burford's tenure at the EPA, are not so easily portrayed. There are strong reasons, not the least of which is the institutional safeguards of the public lobby regime, to doubt that her policies achieved lasting deregulatory objectives. Assessing the EPA one year after Ann Burford's appointment, the *Wall Street Journal* reported:

> With her determination to make government less of an adversary to business, Mrs. Gorsuch [Burford] has indeed shaken up the EPA. . . . In the process, though, Mrs. Gorsuch has alienated not only environmental groups, but also many lawmakers and business leaders who otherwise support the Administration's goals. (July 2, 1982)

Maureen Hinckle of the Audubon Society indicated curiously that in her estimation, "The Reagan Administration has institutionalized the environmental movement" (M. Hinckle interview). By sharpening the issues, she felt, deregulation had offset the increasing issue complexity and decreasing "trendiness" that had beset environmental activism in the late 1970s. Daniel Becker of Environmental Action also suggested that the Burford approach to deregulation had not succeeded:

> Reagan failed fundamentally, especially in the environmental area. He totally mishandled the toxics issue, for example. Instead of a $1.5 billion bill, we have an $8.5 billion one. The basic mistake they made was their venality and appointment of [shut-eye] sentries. This bought the Reagan administration exactly the opposite of what they wanted. The antideregulatory excesses led to regulation by Congress. Congressmen resented the administration ignoring and undermining their intent, so they not only told regulators what to do, but how to do it. The Superfund law is a 400-page document that manages to restrict discretion for administrators in certain key areas. (D. Becker interview)

The regulatory relief effort also fostered closer cooperation among opponents of Reagan's policies. All environmental lobby organizations at which we conducted interviews noted improved relations between environmental and consumer advocates. The two groups, for example, had been at odds over some key policy issues such as natural gas deregulation, with environmentalists favoring it because higher prices might limit its use thereby reducing the potential for environmental problems, and consumer advocates opposing it because the same price increases would be burdensome to public utility customers. In the face of the common threat from the Reagan administration, these policy disputes were set aside. This was exactly the kind of backlash that sophisticated business leaders had hoped to avoid in their efforts at deregulation. As Mr. McCormick of the Environmental Policy Center (EPC) noted, the policies of Ann Burford and James Watt were "stripping away business's fig leaf," in that a weakened agency was less likely to be perceived as effectively controlling polluters (J. McCormick interview). In this regard, William Ruckleshaus termed the Watt and Burford tenures a "bonanza" for environmental groups, noting that they increased their membership three-fold between 1980 and 1983 (W. Ruckleshaus interview).

Ann Burford's reduction of the resources of the EPA and her support for easing regulatory laws, especially those dealing with toxic substances and air pollution, drew a firestorm of protest from environmentalists. This outrage, of course, was to be expected. However, businesses that had spent the better part of the 1970s working out a modus vivendi with the EPA and public lobby organizations were also unwilling to change drastically the rule of the regulatory game. Larger firms were primarily interested in predictability in the regulatory environment. Under Ann Burford, the EPA was offering uncertainty. As a water quality director at the EPA noted, "Business, especially big business, was 90 percent in compliance. They have sunk billions of dollars in cleanup operations, and sudden shifts in the wind make them nervous" (personal interview, July 15, 1982). Also, many business leaders are wary of reinvigorating the environmentalist movement, exactly what Maureen Hinckle claimed the Reagan deregulation had accomplished.

Indeed, businesses and trade associations were often highly critical of the administration's approach to deregulation. Specifically, many business interests favored changes in the organic statutes of environmental law, but the advocates of regulatory relief followed an administrative strategy of deregulation. Among business leaders, legislative changes were seen as the only way to ensure lasting deregulation. In the estimation of Mark Griffiths of the National Association of Manufacturers (NAM), there existed a "window of opportunity for major regulatory [i.e., legislative] change from 1980 to 1982" (M. Griffiths interview). That window closed with the approach of the 1982 elections, because as Griffiths succinctly put it, "Nobody was ever defeated for voting environmental in Congress." More to the point, though, the NAM and its membership expected a strong effort from the Reagan administration at revamping environmental statutes, most of which were coming up for reauthorization in the early 1980s. In a position paper on the Clean Air Act, the NAM laid out its objectives, the most important of which was limiting the EPA to research and the setting of federal guidelines, while turning program development and enforcement over to the states. The ostensible reason for the decentralization was to promote flexibility in adapting performance standards to local conditions (NAM, 1983). According to Griffiths:

After the 1980 election, business acquired a sense of well-being, but Reagan and his people didn't come up with legislation; they misled the business community. . . . In 1981, Gorsuch [Burford] apparently changed her mind about seeking amendments to the Clean Air Act and she got testy when we brought up the idea of an administration bill. (M. Griffiths, interview)

This, in the view of the NAM, was not simply a betrayal of campaign promises, but also a critical political error.

To be sure, NAM members appreciated Ann Burford's efforts at deregulation, in particular her expediting the approval of state plans for implementing the Clean Air Act and bringing cost considerations and strong scientific criteria to bear on the activities of the EPA (personal interview, James Carty, July 28, 1983). Such measures, however, were limited in nature, and no substitute for legislative action. NAM officials recognized the extent to which the new social regulation was embedded in the enabling statutes of environmental policy. They saw as misguided and myopic the view of Watt and Burford that the real problem was an entrenched ultraliberal bureaucracy. Mark Griffiths suggested that the Reagan appointees at the top two environmental posts "misread a mandate to sweep away all regulatory roadblocks to economic recovery" (M. Griffiths interview). The other NAM officials interviewed essentially concurred, hypothesizing that such an error in judgment was to be expected only from ones who operated outside the Washington environmental policy community (personal interviews, July 27 and 29, 1983).

Among those interviewed, both inside the EPA and out, the consensus was that Burford paralyzed the agency with a draconian personnel policy, massive budget cuts, and a "general ratcheting down of regulation across the board," as the Reagan appointee who left the EPA put it (personal interview, March 30, 1982). The most serious impact of deregulation, suggested by Mr. McCormick of the EPC, was the "willful breaking of the agency's scientific infrastructure . . . Gorsuch [Burford] wrecked the laboratory's professionalism, integrity and institutional memory. This undermines the primary task of writing credible regulations" (J. McCormick interview).

Nevertheless, as the above-mentioned Reagan appointee noted, environmental regulation easily "could be ratcheted up later." In this fundamental sense deregulation did not succeed. Because Ann Burford followed an administrative rather than a legislative strategy, the institutional bases of the new social regulation were left intact. Moreover, the administrative approach to relief did not gain strong adherents even within the business community. The question is, why did deregulation at the EPA proceed as it did?

Undoubtedly there is something to the argument that, as NAM officials pointed out, "Reagan's people spent their political capital on the defense budget and tax relief, and were forced to follow a second-best strategy of nonenforcement" (M. Griffiths interview). Yet, there also is a deeper reason why environmental deregulation under Ronald Reagan fell short. The low morale and disarray at the EPA between 1981 and 1983 reflected the lack of any coherent view about what the agency *should* do. Burford's approach to deregulation was characterized by one EPA official as "shallow in an intellectual sense . . . the idea of deregulation per se is not a powerful one" (personal interview, March 30, 1982). An environmental lobbyist similarly concluded, "It is difficult to figure out any coherent administration policy at the EPA; their strategy includes a sort of enemies list and their ideology is superficial, cliches and labels" (M. Hinckle interview). In the realm of environmental policy the Reagan administration never offered any ideas to challenge those underlying the new social regulation. It never redefined the national agenda, only tried to delete items from it. As far as the NAM was concerned, the lack of any clear intellectual framework for deregulation or sense of mission at the EPA cast Reagan, Watt, and Burford as despoilers of the environment catering to the whims of businesses at the expense of public health and environmental quality. This displeased business interests as much if not more than it displeased the Sierra Club.

Environmentalists, EPA bureaucrats, and business leaders all remained suspicious of deregulation under Ann Burford. Under these circumstances it is hardly surprising that her efforts to reduce permanently federal intervention in the area of environmental policy floundered. Douglas Costle perhaps summed up Burford's difficulties best:

> American politics operates within a broadly defined consensus. That consensus [on environmental policy] may be difficult to identify precisely, but the American people can see if you go clearly beyond that boundary. And if you do, they will hand you your head on a platter. That is what happened to Ann Burford. . . . The early years of the Reagan Administration amounted to a plebiscite on environmental protection. (personal interview, June 5, 1985)

It was the insensitivity to popular support for environmental protection along with the lack of any coherent argument for deregulation that cost the Reagan administration a real chance for regulatory change in the environmental area and cost Ann Burford her job.

While the response of environmentalists to the Reagan challenge was facilitated by the heavy-handedness of Watt and Burford, it was the institutional safeguards built into the public lobby regime that actually helped to thwart a number of deregulatory initiatives. For example, in March 1982, the EPA reversed its suspension of a ban on dumping liquid toxics in landfills. The suspension has been announced only three weeks earlier, but was not preceded by public hearings or requests for comment from public lobby groups, a violation of both law and precedent. In addition, the EPA was forced by public pressure to withdraw a proposal for relaxing regulations that limited the amount of lead permitted in gasoline. Neither environmentalists nor their congressional allies who had fought for strong auto emissions regulation would brook such a willful effort to deregulate. The EPA never could muster a credible scientific case in this instance; the main argument was that less government interference was in the public interest. Moreover, this case is illustrative of a general problem faced by Ann Burford. When she assumed office, one of her primary goals was to impose stronger scientific criteria on writing regulations. Yet the same level of stringency apparently was not required to eliminate regulations. This approach put the EPA in a very weak position when it attempted to justify its policy recommendations to a suspicious Congress.

Both of these examples illustrate Costle's point about clearly overstepping the bounds of consensus on environmental protection. The EPA acted unilaterally, with what can only be described as disdain for the ideas underlying environmental regulation and established administrative procedures, and as a consequence discredited itself with the press, the public, Congress, and even the business community.

Environmentalists also were successful in combatting deregulation in some instances by using their considerable legal resources and taking advantage of the new role played by the courts in protecting the public lobby regime. The use of the courts to protect environmental policy from a hostile White House or federal bureaucracy, of course, was clearly envisioned by the architects of the public lobby regime. From the time that the Reagan administration came into office, environmentalist groups initiated thirty-five lawsuits involving federal agencies overseeing environmental policy. All of these cases were pursued to the appeals court level. While many of these suits were against the Department of Energy and the Nuclear Regulatory Commission, fifteen were against the EPA. Of those fifteen, four were cases in which the environmentalists filed amicus curiae briefs on behalf of the EPA; and of those four, three were cases that had originated during the Carter administration. Still, that meant that environmentalists sued the EPA for nonenforcement eleven times between 1981 and 1985 (Lexis search, 1980–1985).

Between 1981 and 1982 alone, environmentalists were successful in three important cases brought against the EPA. In one, the EPA had decided to delay indefinitely, again without public comment or hearings, the implementation of four regulations dealing with the discharge of toxic waste into municipal treatment facilities. The Natural Resources Defense Council (NRDC) sued the agency and won. The U.S. Appeals Court in the Fourth Circuit decided that the action of the EPA clearly violated not simply the spirit of the laws, but also the Administrative Procedures Act (APA):

> There could be no reason for failing to comply with the APA under the circumstances of this case other than the approach of the March 30 effective date of amendments and a desire by the EPA to write an RIA [Regulatory Impact Assessment] pursuant to EO 12291. However, the imminence of a deadline . . . is not sufficient to constitute "good cause" within the meaning of the APA . . . EPA in this case could have complied with both the APA and EO 12291. (683 F.2d 752, 1982: 765)

In a second case, the NRDC won a judgment against the EPA that prevented the suspension of regulations pursuant to the Clean Air Act (683 F.2d 1034, 1982).

In a third important case, the Sierra Club had agreed to federal compensation for legal expenses it had incurred in a case it lost against the agency during the Carter administration, *Sierra Club* v. *Costle* (657 F.2d 298, 1981). The Reagan administration appointees in charge of deregulation were opposed to the idea of federal support for public lobbies to begin with, and in this instance they were outraged by the prospect of paying environmentalists for a suit they had lost. As a result, Ann Burford tried, not simply to contest, but (consistent with the broad effort to "defund the left") to abrogate ulilaterally the settlement. Again the federal courts decided for the environmentalists, thus maintaining the concept of federal support for public lobby suits, a cardinal principle of the new social regulation (684 F.2d 972, 1982).

In the wake of disappointments within the business community, outrage among environmentalists, a drumbeat of criticism from the media about politicizing the EPA, and a contempt citation from Congress for refusing to turn over agency documents for legislative hearings, Ann Burford stepped down as administrator. Even though the House Judiciary Committee and Burford eventually worked out a compromise that expunged the contempt citation, by 1983 the EPA was at its nadir in terms of effectiveness and credibility.

Reviving Regulatory Reform

When President Reagan appointed William Ruckleshaus to succeed Burford, a measure of credibility was immediately recaptured. The return of Ruckleshaus was also a tonic for staff morale both at headquarters and in the regional offices. This in itself was significant. However, the new administrator also brought concrete policy changes to the EPA; he attempted to recapture some of the reform momentum generated in the late 1970s that was undermined in the early years of the Reagan administration. As Mr. Ruckleshaus lamented to the *National Journal,* in the early years of the Reagan administration "the public got the message by every kind of language—body language, everything else—that we were going to abandon the ends of clean air, clean water. That had the unfortunate result of discrediting the argument over means [of environmental protection], which is where the debate ought to be" (Jan. 12, 1985: 113–14). The argument over means was the focus of regulatory reform.

Before any step could be taken to get back on the road to reform, Ruckleshaus had to convince Congress and the public that the EPA was once again serious about environmental protection. Ironically, then, his initial problem in 1984 was the same as his initial problem as administrator in 1972, to assure the American people that the laws would be vigorously and scrupulously enforced. Both the NAM (M. Griffiths interview) and environmentalists (*National Journal,* July 6, 1983: 8) were certain that under William Ruckleshaus the agency's budget would receive major transfusions of funds, especially in the research and development area critical to the more complex tasks of the 1980s. Indeed, this turned out to be the case as the budget of the EPA was restored to its 1981 dollar level (Kraft and Vig, 1984).

As the image and credibility of the EPA were gradually restored, attention turned to reviving the idea of regulatory reform, that is, the development of cost-effective means of protecting the environment. To that end, William Ruckleshaus sought more reliable scientific criteria for writing regulations and enforcing statutes. He also promised to bring cost estimates to bear in running the EPA. These, of course, were the same objectives stated by Ann Burford at the beginning of her tenure as administrator. The difference was that under Ruckleshaus, these policy goals were presented in the context of a framework for regulatory reform rather than simply regulatory relief, which amounted to little more than getting the Washington bureaucracy off the back of business. He clearly understood that reform required the administrator to play an educational role with respect to the public as well as the Congress. As he explained:

> Newer, more complex issues at EPA demand public education. Where the agency gets in early enough we can explain things to the public. The public has to decide what costs it will bear . . . up to now we have been giving them only half the equation [i.e., benefits and not costs]. Cost-free public involvement is a recipe for public agitation. . . . The agency must educate the people to think in terms of efficient risk management rather than the elimination of risk. (W. Ruckleshaus interview)

This educational approach not only accepted a legitimate role for EPA and the environmental lobbies, but more important, presented a coherent set of ideas with which to confront those underlying environmentalism. In a 1985 article he laid out this challenge:

> [B]ecause the early goals of environmentalism were so obviously good, the requirement to ask, "Is it worth it?" was not firmly built into all our environmental laws. Who would dare to question the worth of saving Lake Erie? Environmentalism at its inception was a grand vision, one that nearly all Americans willingly shared. Somehow that vision of the essential unity of nature and of the need for bringing industrial society into harmony with it has been lost among the parts per billion, and with it we have lost the capacity to reach social consensus on environmental policy. (Ruckleshaus, 1985: 30)

Ruckleshaus countered the environmental position with an intellectual framework, namely, risk management that was gaining credibility both in and out of the EPA prior to the 1980 election. In this sense, William Ruckleshaus revived the idea of regulatory reform (Ruckleshaus, 1985: 19–25).

By the time William Ruckleshaus left the EPA, the agency had recouped much of its reputation as well as its budgetary base. Once again it was poised to embark on regulatory reform as opposed to regulatory relief. Mr. Ruckleshaus's successor, Lee Thomas, was determined to pursue reform from the foundation laid between 1983 and 1985. The concept of risk management remained a central feature of this effort. Thomas's head of the OPPE, Milton Russell, went so far as to assert that "EPA's mission is to reduce risk to public health as fast as we can." He went on to suggest that a critical component of risk management is cost assessment: "EPA wants to achieve the healthiest and cleanest environment *that the American people are willing to pay for*" (personal interview, April 28, 1985, emphasis added). Risk management, then, challenged the bases of environmental policy such as "no-effect level" and "ample margin of safety" by imposing economic criteria. If the relevant regulatory issue is controlling risk rather than eliminating pollution, cost logically becomes a primary consideration.

Even though Ruckleshaus and Thomas resuscitated the idea of regulatory reform, there is good reason to question the prospects for success. Reform is likely to move at a glacial pace as it did under President Carter, because just as in the late 1970s there are no strong political proponents. Outside of the OPPE at the EPA there is little strong commitment to reform. Ruckleshaus suggested there were two good chances for regulatory reform, the second Nixon administration and the first Reagan administration. The first opportunity was lost in the Watergate fiasco, and the second was squandered by appointing ideologues to the top environmental posts. While the Reagan administration still supports the concept of regulatory change, the issue is clearly no longer a top priority. Perhaps Milton Russell summed up the prospects for regulatory reform best: "There is the power of good ideas [e.g., risk management and cost-effectiveness]. I am not sanguine about regulatory reform flying on many peoples' banners, but I have not given up hope either" (M. Russell interview). If there is any chance for reform, it must be predicated on a coherent set of ideas with which to challenge environmentalism. Nevertheless lasting reform, as Costle, Ruckleshaus, and Russell all agreed, requires a legislative strategy at least as a complement to administrative measures, and changing the environmental statutes requires the investment of tremendous amounts of political capital that no one seems willing to expend.

During this current political situation, environmentalists and their allies in Congress, the EPA, and the courts appear to have staved off the attempt to change the regulatory regime constructed in the decade of the 1970s. Indeed there were indications that after the 1984 election in which the Democrats held their own in the Senate and maintained their control of the House, environmentalists had gone on the policy offensive. For example, in November 1984 Congress significantly increased the lands protected by the National Scenic Rivers Program (*Congressional Quarterly*, Nov. 24, 1984: 2985). This was the first expansion since the election of 1980. By January 1985 the *Congressional Quarterly* also reported:

"The environmentalists are likely to shape the legislative agenda during the 99th Congress. It is they, not industry or the administration, who are defining the issues right now" (Jan. 12, 1985: 81).

The election of 1986 reinforced the environmentalists' advantage as the Democrats retook control of the Senate. In fact, preceding the election, President Reagan had to back down from his threatened veto of the Superfund legislation when it became apparent that bipartisan support was strong enough to override his veto, and that Congress was determined to stay in session as long as necessary to prevent a pocket veto. President Reagan vetoed the 1986 Clean Water Act, but did so after the election. Moreover, he left intact all of the performance standards and enforcement procedures that Watt and Burford had sought to eliminate in his first term; his objections to the bill focused on the "budget-busting" allocations budgeted for the sewage treatment program.

Perhaps even more significant than the environmental lobbyists' success in recapturing the legislative initiative were indications that they had reasserted themselves in the administrative process. In February 1985, employing a special procedural provision of the Toxic Sustances Control Act, the EPA abandoned plans to regulate the manufacture of products containing asbestos, a known carcinogen, and referred the matter to the OSHA. In the judgment of Lee Thomas and his advisors, the agency had all it could handle in regulating the 60,000 chemicals sold in the United States annually. In addition, that asbestos problems occurred in the work environment seemed to indicate that the OSHA was the logical regulatory body. These arguments notwithstanding, the EPA reversed itself one month later under sustained pressure from environmentalists, EPA staff, and Representative John Dingell's (D-Michigan) Energy and Commerce Subcommittee on Oversight and Investigations (*National Journal,* March 16, 1985: 597). All of these parties were concerned that the withdrawal of the asbestos regulations reflected industry's attempt to influence the EPA through the OMB, a strategy that smacked of the discredited regulatory relief policies.

The final two years of the Reagan presidency were characterized by environmentalists both taking to the offensive in legislative affairs and their struggling against determined efforts on the part of the administration to curtail their hard-won access to federal courts and regulatory agencies. Beginning in 1987, legislators began to take seriously the idea of acid rain legislation and by 1988 seemed poised finally to reauthorize both the Pesticide Act and the Clean Air Act after years of delay and frustration. In the realm of policy implementation and enforcement, however, the climate was decidedly less hospitable. The administration—in particular the Department of Justice headed by Edwin Meese, and the OMB, by then under James Miller—challenged public lobbyists' standing to sue under environmental statutes and contested their participation in agency decisionmaking. The Department of Justice and the OMB also sought to limit the enforcement activities of the EPA. In a sense, Meese and Miller were fighting an administrative rearguard action on behalf of regulatory relief, while the Congress, public lobby groups, and in some cases the EPA once again were forging ahead with an aggressive environmental policy agenda.

In the first year of the Reagan term (1981–1982), environmentalists, as we have already seen, fended off an effort to weaken substantially the Clean Air Act. This triumph was not only a major political achievement, but also a good test of the public lobby regime's institutional staying power, for environmentalists confronted and defeated the imposing coalition of an enormously popular president, automobile manufacturers along with their affiliated industries and unions, and John Dingell (D-Michigan) who, as chairman of the House Energy and Commerce Committee, exercised extraordinary authority over the proposed legislation. The ability to thwart the efforts of this powerful coalition reaffirmed the popularity of environmental issues and the place of public lobbyists in the Washington establishment. However, it is far easier to say "no" to a policy initiative in American politics than to score a positive victory. The adamant opposition of the Reagan administration and Dingell continued to undermine efforts at reauthorizing this important law, arguably one of the centerpieces of environmental policy.

Dingell proved to be an especially formidable obstacle. Representing the Detroit area, he naturally vigorously opposed stronger clean air legislation, particularly those portions pertaining to tailpipe emissions. As head of the Energy and Commerce Committee, he successfully prevented legislation from getting onto the House floor for a vote. Through control of the committee's schedule as well as political pressure on committee members, he kept the legislation bottled up. Indeed, the primary sponsor of the bill and chairman of the Energy and Commerce Subcommittee on Health and Environment, Henry Waxman (D-California), only once got his reauthorization bill to Dingell's full committee for consideration. On the Senate side, George Mitchell's (D-Maine) Environment and Public Works Committee continued to churn out strong reauthorization legislation that not only tightened existing performance standards on tailpipe and smokestack emissions, but greatly extended the mandate of the EPA to deal with acid rain, toxic air pollutants, and ozone depletion. Invariably though, the Senate bills ran into the roadblocks of Dingell and the administration.

By early 1988 prospects began to brighten. Waxman noted that the election year atmosphere would provide an incentive for many fence sitters to support a popular environmental measure despite pressure from Dingell and Reagan (*National Journal*, March 5, 1988: 600–601). Also, Reagan's opposition was muted by two sets of circumstances. First, the effects of a lame-duck status, revelations of the Iran–Contra affair, and the special-prosecutor investigations of Edwin Meese and former aide Michael Deaver combined to devalue substantially the president's political capital with Congress. Second, Reagan's efforts to pursue a free-trade agreement with Canadian Prime Minister Brain Mulroney played into the hands of Waxman and his environmentalist supporters. Because Mulroney was under tremendous domestic pressure to wring concessions from the Reagan administration on the question of a bilateral acid rain policy, the president could not strongly oppose the clean air bill, which contained acid rain measures. Finally, in 1987, medical evidence began to emerge showing that toxic air pollutants posed significant public health risks. By casting the clean air legislation as a public health issue, especially to children and the elderly, environmentalists were able to take the political high ground and put great pressure on undecided legislators.

This more favorable environment was confirmed in December 1987 when the House overwhelmingly defeated (162 to 257) a Dingell amendment to an omnibus appropriations bill. This amendment would have delayed until 1989 any action on ozone regulation; instead, the deadline was fixed at August 31, 1988 (*National Journal*, March 5, 1988: 600–601). Because ozone regulation is part of the Senate version, which undoubtedly will be approved again, the House was under additional pressure to act on a clean air bill in 1988.

Optimism developed not only about the Clean Air Act, but also about reauthorizing the Pesticide Act, which had languished in Congress for years, and about the control of lead additives in gasoline. Largely a victim of domestic budget cutting and the early vigor of regulatory relief, pesticide legislation too faces brighter prospects for reauthorization. Environmentalists are getting closer to a long-sought goal of banning lead in gasoline as well. In late 1987 only the strenuous opposition of the American Farm Bureau prevented the ban. Farm machinery is the last major outlet for leaded gasoline, and American farmers were facing such severe economic hardship that it was practically unthinkable to add to their woes by legislating higher-priced gasoline. Still, public lobbyists had put together a nearly unanimous coalition within the environmental issue network, because they were joined by key legislators, the petroleum industry, the auto industry, and the EPA in pressing for a ban. It appears to be only a matter of time before they succeed.

While public lobbyists beat back the challenge of regulatory relief on the legislative front and in fact have retaken the initiative, the Reagan administration still exercised substantial authority over implementation and enforcement. Indeed, the transfer of James Miller from the FTC to the OMB ensured that that office would continue to play a strong deregulatory role. Moreover, the move of Edwin Meese from the White House counsel to attorney general meant that the federal law enforcement machinery would be headed by a vigorous and implacable foe of extensive public interest litigation. A number of examples illustrate the efforts of these two individuals to forestall the revitalization of environmental activism in the federal government. They also show how the Reagan administration was put in the awkward position of opposing state initiatives in environmental policy, surely an irony given the president's often-stated commitment to reviving federalism.

Both Miller and Meese recognized that the federal courts were a key to public lobbyists' participation in regulatory decisionmaking and enforcement. In particular, the standing to sue the EPA for nonenforcement had proved to be a powerful lever for environmentalists, as much for insinuating themselves into agency decisions as for winning judgments against the agency of businesses. As one EPA official noted in regard to cases brought against the EPA by environmental groups, "A significant number of these challenges are in order to get a kind of regulatory elite [public lobbyists] involved in the suit so it can be negotiated" (*National Journal*, Feb. 13, 1988: 390). Indeed certain provisions of the reauthorized Clean Water Act were negotiated exactly in this manner; court action allowed public lobbyists to interpose themselves on negotiations, and to do so from a strong position, because they had judicial imprimatur. The other significant advantage of standing in the federal courts was that it aided social regulatory agencies, especially the EPA, in enforcement as public lobbyists could bring legal actions against firms for noncompliance. Francis Blake, the general counsel for the EPA, frankly asserted that standing for environmentalists in effect provided the agency with "an off-budget enforcement technique" (*National Journal*, Feb. 13, 1988: 389).

As many of our previous interview citations make clear, the acquisition of standing in federal court was undoubtedly a major achievement of environmentalists. Miller and Meese attempted to circumscribe sharply that achievement. For years conservative critics of the public interest movement had complained bitterly about the use of the courts to press vigorous enforcement actions when environmentalists did not have the political muscle to win in "more democratic" arenas. President Reagan, moreover, had appointed some leading exponents of this viewpoint to the federal bench, most notably Robert Bork and Antonin Scalia to the Washington, D.C., Court of Appeals, which enjoyed jurisdiction in many such cases. When he became attorney general, Edwin Meese lent his considerable energy and influence to the crusade to limit standing. It is widely believed that Meese was the driving force behind a bold initiative to challenge environmentalists' standing. In late 1987, the White House issued a presidential directive to the Department of Justice stating that any staff attorney litigating a case involving the EPA and public interest groups and *not* challenging the groups standing to sue would have to get his or her section chief to prepare a memorandum to the appropriate deputy attorney general explaining why no challenge was filed (*National Journal,* Feb. 13, 1988: 762–71). Clearly, in the long run, this was an effort to curtail public lobbyists' use of the courts. However, its more immediate effects were to delay court action and impose great resource demands on the public interest lawyers. Because challenges to standing may be filed at any point in the legal process, this strategy gave a tremendous tactical advantage to lawyers opposing the environmentalists' suits. In addition, it required environmentalists to spend a great deal more time and money to establish standing; most public interest lawyers thought that this issue had been settled in the 1970s and no longer required extensive work on standing in each case. More to the point, the Department of Justice and business lawyers also thought the question was settled and rarely bothered to challenge standing in public interest suits, because they knew they would lose. This entire situation changed as the more conservative appointees to the Washington, D.C. Court of Appeals and the Meese administration in the Department of Justice in effect gave the green light to begin challenging standing indiscriminately. In fairness to the administration, the argument for more stringent standing criteria was not entirely without merit, and many environmental lawyers were quick to point out that they could meet the criteria. However, the political reality of this policy shift at the Department of Justice was that smaller and local environmental organizations were effectively precluded from playing as prominent a role as they had in the courts. In turn, this depleted the EPA off-budget enforcement corps. Another important impact is that it can delay substantially public interest lawyers collecting attorneys' fees due to them under environmental statutes. Congress had provided for attorney's fees in environmental suits to encourage public interest lawyers and equalize the confrontation with corporations that could keep their staff attorneys in court indefinitely. Under the Meese regime, lawyers representing environmental groups could win a case, and then have to fight a standing battle with a corporate attorney or the Department of Justice before seeing a dime of the fees due to them.

One case in particular nicely illustrates the impact of challenging standing: *National Wildlife Federation* v. *Hodel*. This case involved a suit against the Office of Surface Mining for nonenforcement of the 1977 surface mining law. Secretary Hodel, as head of the Department of Interior (DOI), ultimately was in charge of enforcing the act and therefore was named as the defendant in the case. The important point for our purposes is that the case was initiated in 1979, and after a lengthy battle, the U.S. District Court of Washington, D.C., decided against the DOI. By that time, President Reagan had been elected and James Watt was secretary of interior: naturally the verdict was appealed to the Court of Appeals. In the course of the litigation, Hodel took over at the DOI and Meese at the Department of Justice. In 1985, the Department of Justice raised the question of standing regarding the plaintiffs and the case was remanded to the district court to resolve the issue—this after more than five years of litigation. Eventually the Department of Justice lost its challenge, but not before forcing the plaintiffs to acquire over 1300 affidavits from private citizens and log many hours of additional legal work, and forego attorneys' fees in the interim (*National Journal,* Feb. 13, 1988: 388–91).

If challenges to standing were a major irritant for public lobbyists, other actions by the Department of Justice and the OMB were an affront to them, and to Congress as well. A question that arose early in the development of environmental policy was the extent to which the federal government would be held accountable to the performance standards developed by Congress and the EPA. In the 1980s, Congress began to express its intent on this issue, most notably in the area of hazardous-waste disposal. In reauthorizing the Resource Conservation and Recovery Act (RCRA), and the Superfund law, the legislature made its intention known that the EPA would enforce standards on other federal agencies. Moreover, the testimony at the reauthorization hearings left little doubt that the EPA was to use administrative orders as its primary enforcement device in this area. Section 3008 of the new RCRA statute empowered the EPA to issue administrative orders to other federal agencies as a means of requiring compliance with hazardous-waste standards. The Superfund was a little more ambiguous. It also established, in its Section 106, administrative orders as the appropriate tool for imposing standards on federal agencies, but it delegated that authority to the president rather than the EPA. Still congressional intent seemed clear enough: the federal government must comply with the RCRA and Superfund standards.

Yet Meese and Miller took actions that appeared to border on ignoring the will of Congress. In one instance, under the RCRA statute, the EPA, Washington state, and the Department of Energy (DOE) drafted an administrative order to clean up the DOE disposal site in Hanford, Washington. However, in the eleventh hour and despite Section 3008, the DOE, with the blessing of the Department of Justice, challenged EPA authority to impose such an order. In the end that order came unraveled as the EPA was pressured into backing out. In fact, the Department of Justice intervened on behalf of the DOE in another RCRA order and oversaw a negotiation with the EPA on the matter. Still, the law seemed clear that the EPA had the authority to issue such an order without the interference of the Department of Justice.

As noted above, the new Superfund law delegated the authority to issue administrative orders to the White House. As it turns out, the executive order implementing this measure did originally delegate the full authority to the EPA. However, the OMB intervened in this case, and the executive order was rewritten at the OMB to ensure that any administrative order issued by the EPA to implement the Superfund would have "the concurrence of the Attorney General" (*National Journal*, March 28, 1987: 762–71). Again, the Department of Justice, this time with the collusion of the OMB, would be able to oversee the administration of a major environmental statute, thereby assuring their conservative input and curtailing the influence of public lobbyists.

One cannot help noting the impressive irony of these administrative actions in a presidency so fully dedicated to reducing the role of the central government. The heavy-handed intervention of the Department of Justice in the RCRA negotiations over the Hanford site of the DOE seems to abandon a strong commitment to federalism. At a minimum it shows that the concerns of a state received relatively short shrift when they conflict with conservative principles. It is difficult to see how, in the abstract, this situation differed from Democratic administrations intervening in state affairs to impose some liberal principle such as affirmative action. In addition, the actions of Miller and Meese were consistent with the pattern of the entire Reagan administration pattern of employing the full power of the federal government and centralizing control over that government in the defense of a policy agenda: it would seem that Franklin Roosevelt and the New Deal cast a long shadow indeed. There is no reason, moreover, why a future administration could not use the same bureaucratic levers to grease the skids for environmental policy instead of hamstringing it. As it was, Meese and Miller antagonized Congress as well as the environmental community, but did not score a major victory.

Conclusions

The portrait we have drawn of deregulation of the EPA suggests that, while the Reagan administration achieved significant successes in its first three years in terms of budgetary cutbacks, reductions in enforcement actions, and the near-elimination of new regulations, the institutions and policies of the public lobby regime held firm. The successes appear to be a series of pyrrhic victories that provided temporary regulatory relief rather than lasting regulatory change, and resulted in serious political losses for the administration. In this sense deregulation failed. There was no regulatory regime change.

The reasons for the failure revolve around our finding that those in charge of environmental deregulation approached their task without any set of alternative ideas with which to challenge environmentalism. Rather, they perceived their mission simply in terms of reining in the professional bureaucrats whom they saw as undermining the political economic well-being of the United States. Despite their initial claims about introducing scientific criteria and cost–benefit analysis, their actions bespoke an attempt merely to "ratchet down" regulation. As Kraft and Vig concluded:

> The administration's early assertions that policy would be based on better scientific evidence and that more efficient management would allow the environmental agencies to "do more with less" are belied by the record. . . . Treating the career civil service as the enemy is not the way to achieve either political accountability or lasting regulatory reform. (1984: 439)

Douglas Costle expressed essentially the same criticism, arguing that "Reform is a long-term institutional process; you have to structure incentives for the staff. The point is to get the job [reform] done defensibly and effectively, not to turn off programs administered by committed bureaucrats with legislative mandates backing them up" (personal interview, April 8, 1985).

That Watt and Burford invested the overwhelming majority of their political resources in an administrative strategy rather than a legislative strategy of deregulation revealed both their lack of any conception of legitimate regulatory activity and their misperception of the real sources of influence developed by the new social regulation. Public lobbyists' strength lay in the broad acceptance of their ideas about environmental protection and in the institutional safeguards embedded in the statutes. The deregulators could not have conceived of a worse strategy given these circumstances. On the one hand, disregard for the public support of environmental protection and ideas reinvigorated a flagging environmental movement. On the other hand, the decision to focus on controlling the career bureaucrats infuriated not only many in the EPA, but also their patrons in Congress who resented what they saw as a blatant attempt to circumvent legislative intent by administrative action. The conclusion seems inescapable that the Reagan administration, in its quest for regulatory relief, squandered the best opportunity for regulatory change likely to occur for a long time.

Although the public lobby regime apparently weathered the attempt at deregulating the EPA, environmentalists did not regain the degree of influence they enjoyed in the halcyon days of the early 1970s. According to Richard Ayers:

> In terms of the public interest [movement], I think it is frailer in a way. Institutional charity, grass roots support, and the new legal framework sustain it, but a Rehnquist Supreme Court could make a difference. Nixon tried to kill us, but didn't succeed. Things are different now. We are an institution . . . even big business no longer questions our legitimacy, our right to speak for the public. The question is whether we can survive a long period of conservative rule. (R. Ayers interview)

Obviously, as long as Ronald Reagan remained in office, environmentalists would not play as strong a role in policymaking as they once did. More important, though, the issue of cost effectiveness, which arose in the second half of the 1970s, occupied environmentalists, because for the first time they were presented with an intellectual challenge, a challenge that went to the heart of the social consensus underlying environmental policy. While public support for the principle of environmental protection remained strong, the citizenry, federal bureaucrats, and even some environmentalists began to have doubts about the price being paid. It was this element of doubt that spawned attempts at regulatory reform in the late 1970s and that William Ruckleshaus sought to rekindle in 1983. In this sense, the drive for regulatory relief at the EPA may be seen as an interregnum between two periods of regulatory reform, although neither relief nor reform predicated on the ideas of risk management and cost effectiveness is likely to bring about a shift in regulatory regimes. Reformers never tried to overturn the public lobby regime, but simply to modulate its regulatory excesses. Without strong political support from the White House or Congress, though, even this limited objective was bound to fail. The regulatory situation by the late 1980s appeared to be one of policy stalemate; the new social regulation remained the status quo, but portions of the intellectual framework underlying its institutions and policies were being called into question by competing ideas. Economists, policy analysts, and others advocating those competing ideas had not succeeded in reshaping the national agenda.

7

Regulatory Relief: To Be or Not to Be?

He who walks in the middle of the road gets hit by both sides.
GEORGE SCHULTZ, quoted in *RN: The Memoirs of Richard Nixon*

The past two decades have brought remarkable change in regulatory politics. The emergence of the public lobby regime was associated with the prominence of ideas that raised fundamental questions about the market economy and altered dramatically the institutions and policies that govern the American political economy. The far-reaching effect of this regulatory regime on the political system precipitated a strong reaction, which has led to a contending set of ideas supportive of building market-oriented regulatory policy. Whenever the Reagan administration's efforts at regulatory relief were grounded in these contending ideas, they stood a reasonable chance of challenging the institutions and policies of the public lobby regime. Those efforts, however, too frequently predicated on ideological antipathy toward consumer and environmental advocates instead of on market-based regulatory reforms, consigned the broad policy of regulatory relief to the ministrations of White House staffers and bureaucrats at the OMB, whose actions were legitimated by executive orders. In the end, the sweeping institutional and policy changes ushered in by the public lobby regime remained largely intact.

What is especially notable about these jarring changes in regulatory politics is that they occurred amid broad developments in the American political system that many scholars and politicians have viewed as inimical to change. During the 1970s, it has been said, a "new American political system" was born, characterized by a pathological fragmentation, making it virtually impossible to build broad coalitions and subjecting government policy to immobilism (see especially King, 1990). What is misunderstood in such analyses is that the reforms of the 1970s, of which the new pattern of regulatory politics we have described was a critical element, fostered a decentralization of institutions that made the political system responsive to broad ideas and social movements, resulting in dramatic change. Indeed, the social reforms that transformed American government sought to displace the pluralistic character of American politics, dominated by the give-and-take of particular interests. In the place of a politics of interest, reformers sought to establish a policy process founded on principles and citizen action. This policy process was embedded in a decentralized institutional framework, one, to be sure, that often resulted in stalemate. At the same time, though, this more disparate political system was responsive to the clash of ideas and convulsive institutional developments that, in an unprecedented fashion, overcame rather than reinforced the "inertial forces" traditionally associated with constitutional government in the United States (Wilson, 1970; Derthick and Quirk, 1985: 252–58). The American constitutional framework established conditions whereby "ambition [would] counteract ambition," as Madison wrote in the *Federalist Papers* (No. 51), fostering a system of mutual restraints among a diversity of interests. The regulatory system that emerged during the 1970s established an institutional framework that frequently subordinated these particularistic political ambitions to the programmatic ambitions of social reformers, although their programs were usual constructed within discrete issue areas.

As a result, regulatory politics, hitherto dominated by economic policies and "special" interests that focused on agency action, were restructured to address "quality of life" issues and provide more avenues for public participation. The decentralized institutions of the public lobby regime, in many respects, made regulation a far more politicized and public matter; the regulatory activities of the 1970s, therefore, were not simply the consequence of a few citizen activists and zealous bureaucrats running amok through the economy. That some members of the Reagan administration viewed social regulation as such both weakened and misplaced their efforts to achieve regulatory relief.

In fact, after the 1980 election, Reagan's grand plan to rescue the American economy from what he deemed excessive, costly, and overly intrusive regulation confronted a far-flung, yet coherent, policy process that was remarkably resilient. Indeed, deregulation may have been so difficult to accomplish not because regulatory policy was so fragmented but because it was so coherent. Or perhaps it was doubly difficult because the public lobby regime combined institutional fragmentation with intellectual and political coherence. An effective challenge to social regulation, therefore, requires the formulation of an alternative philosophical framework and wide-ranging institutional reform. Yet a fundamental difficulty for those who advocate deregulation is that, the political changes in recent years notwithstanding, there is still a belief among the American people that government is needed to solve social and economic problems (Peterson, 1985: 386–89). Such a belief is unlikely to be changed; indeed it may be reinforced by a poorly conceived effort to "get government off our backs." Perhaps it was a realization of this public sentiment as much as the tenacity of public lobbyists and their supporters that led George Bush, Reagan's point man on regulatory relief, to adopt a less confrontational approach to regulatory policy after the 1988 election. For at least the first year and a half of his presidency, Bush appeared to veer away from his predecessor's regulatory policy rather than stay the course of regulatory relief.

The Regulatory Program of the Bush Administration

In an important sense, we can take the true measure of the "Reagan revolution" by examining the regulatory program of the Bush administration. While not necessarily a guru of free-market philosophy, Bush, as head of the Task Force on Regulatory Relief, vigorously championed the program of freeing business from its regulatory burdens. Moreover, he helped to coordinate the centralization of regulatory controls implemented under EO 12291 and EO 12498. One, therefore, might have expected him, upon his election in 1988, to sustain the program of regulatory relief as best he could. This was not to be. While the executive orders remained in place, as did the centralized regulatory review process they mandated, President Bush clearly signaled early on that his regulatory program would be less stridently antigovernment in its orientation than that of Ronald Reagan. Whereas the ringing phrase "Government is not the solution to our problems; government is the problem!" provided a mantra for regulatory relief under Reagan, Bush's vision of a "kinder, gentler America" avowed a positive role for government in developing solutions. In his campaign rhetoric he almost seemed to be articulating a traditional Progressive Republican agenda of bringing big business and big government together with concerned citizens to address societal problems. In fact, this approach harked back to the rhetoric and style Bush exhibited in the 1970s, when he exemplified the notion that a government career was an honorable endeavor, if not a civic obligation. His public life through 1980 seemed to stand as a testimonial to the ideal of government service. Indeed, when he campaigned for the presidency against Ronald Reagan, he took pride in contrasting his record of government experience with his opponent's transparent disdain for government as a drag on the economy and a threat to individual liberty. After acceding to the White House, George Bush apparently wanted to do what was right for the environment and the consumer without undermining business. He sought, it appeared, to resuscitate the notion of regulatory reform initiated under Jimmy Carter and quietly revived at the EPA by William Ruckleshaus in the mid-80s. The shift to a more favorable view of regulation made political sense too, in light of the backlash against regulatory relief during Reagan's second term and the heavy use the Democrats made of that backlash in the 1988 presidential campaign, particularly with respect to environmental policy.[1]

Whether the apparent shift from uncompromising opposition toward federal regulation to a serious-minded, if critical, approach can be attributed primarily to the authentic George Bush reemerging from the shadow of Reaganism or more to a presidential candidate reading the political signs of the late 1980s, is difficult to discern. Indeed, even as Bush evoked certain social goals as part of his commitment to a kinder, gentler version of domestic policy, he expressed strong reservations about imposing additional regulatory burdens on industries in order to serve these goals (Quirk, 1991). This ambivalence, one suspects, influenced the wayward path of the Bush regulatory program: initially, Bush's policy marked a significant departure from regulatory relief; by the end of his term, however, that departure proved difficult to sustain, and President Bush reverted to an openly antiregulatory policy. Ironically, this reversion highlights the fact that neither regulatory relief nor free market ideology ever really supplanted the public lobby regime at the level of institutions and policies, though economists' ideas on market-based regulatory reforms remain part of the policy process, to be drawn upon sporadically as challenges to social regulation.[2] The Bush administration's regulatory

---

[1] A *Los Angeles Times*/Cable News Network exit poll revealed that 10 percent of the electorate considered "protecting the environment" the most important issue to their vote in the 1988 campaign. Of these voters, 70 percent reported voting for the Democratic nominee, Massachusetts governor Michael Dukakis, and 28 percent for Bush. (*National Journal,* November 12, 1988: 2854.)

[2] Our view contrasts with an argument proposed by Marc Eisner in *Regulatory Politics in Transition* (Johns Hopkins University Press, 1993). Eisner, relying on our conceptual framework, suggests that indeed a new regulatory regime has emerged. He dubs it the "efficiency regime," suggesting the triumph of market-based regulation. While we agree that economists' ideas have gained currency in policy debates over the last decade, we cannot find the institutional and policy transformations that would thoroughly legitimize those ideas as a public philosophy and clearly signal the emergence of a new regulatory regime.

program represents an effort to come to terms with, if not supersede, the public lobby regime. That effort ultimately foundered, not simply because it underestimated the political resiliency of that regime and because it never effectively engaged public lobbyists seriously at the level of ideas, but perhaps just as importantly because the deep suspicion of big government and federal control held by advocates of regulatory relief prevented them from turning energetically to the task of remaking America's regulatory institutions.

Executive Oversight, Personnel, and Budgets under Bush

Unable to effect a legislative overhaul of American regulatory policy, the Reagan administration, as we have documented, pursued its policy of regulatory relief by means of a three-pronged administrative strategy of: (1) a strong centralized oversight of the federal agencies charged with implementing and enforcing regulatory laws; (2) a personnel policy of punishing or purging agency "zealots" and appointing individuals who were deeply skeptical of federal regulation to run the agencies; and (3) a budgetary policy of repeated sharp reductions in the annual outlays for regulatory agencies. It is instructive to compare the Bush program to Reagan's on these three parameters. What we find is an attempt to preserve executive oversight, while at the same time putting individuals who took the government's regulatory role seriously in charge of federal agencies and augmenting substantially the budgets of those agencies.

Executive oversight under the Bush administration continued to be a top priority, and in this regard it constituted an important legacy of the Reagan presidency. Even if executive oversight had its precursors in the Ford and Carter administrations, Ronald Reagan more fully developed this federal capacity through the implementation of his Executive Orders 12291 and 12498. More important than Reagan's commitment to centralized regulatory review, though, is the fact that everyone in the policy process, including the staff at regulatory agencies, came to accept this kind of review as a legitimate, even a necessary, exercise. That is not to say that everyone thought that OMB and OIRA under Reagan acted impartially and professionally in applying the executive orders. Indeed, many members of Congress and the public refused to acknowledge the broad regulatory powers claimed by the Reagan executive orders, since they were never written into law. Nevertheless, there was widespread agreement on the need for some kind of oversight to manage federal regulatory policy. As journalist Margaret Kriz observed in an assessment of regulatory oversight, "by the dawning of the Bush Administration,

OMB's review practices had become institutionalized, an established cog in the federal government machinery" (*National Journal*, Mar. 31, 1990: 785). Even individuals who were critical of Reagan on policy questions acknowledged the need for oversight. Luana Wilcher, the EPA's director of Water Programs under Bush, for example, criticized Reagan's environmental record. She insisted, nevertheless, that in regard to the Reagan administration's regulatory review process, "the key role given to the OMB and OIRA was necessary. There was a need to have some coordination of federal agency policy across agencies. Also, OMB assured that agencies had a cost–benefit capability and would employ it. You couldn't develop regulations without cost–benefit analysis" (personal interview, Dec. 2, 1992). This sentiment generally reflected President Bush's point of view on regulatory review; it is just good government to impose a level of oversight and management on regulatory agencies, not only to avoid duplication of effort or conflicting policies, but also to assure a serious measure of cost control. To be sure, under David Stockman and James Miller, OMB and OIRA employed regulatory review and claims of executive privilege to delay agency initiatives and frustrate congressional intervention, whereas Richard Darman, Bush's OMB director, was more inclined to seek consensus. Still, executive oversight was central to the regulatory programs of both Bush and Reagan.

There was an obvious difference, however, in regulatory personnel policies between the early 1980s and the early 1990s. Generally, Bush's appointments suggested that political savvy, professionalism, and administrative skill, rather than ideology or commitment to philosophical principles, served as the litmus test in selecting people to head key agencies. This contrast between Bush and Reagan appointees is drawn sharply in a comparison of their initial nominations to chair the FTC and run the EPA. Janet Steiger, Bush's chairman of the FTC, and William Reilly, his EPA administrator, exemplified a personnel policy very different from that of James Miller and Ann Burford, Reagan's chiefs at those respective agencies.[3] As we have seen, Miller was a man determined to impose a framework of economic analysis at the FTC and bring to heel the activist lawyers he believed had dominated that regulatory body. To his credit, he demonstrated enough political insight and managerial ability to reassess his view of the FTC personnel and, in the end, develop a working relationship with them. Nevertheless, he doggedly insisted on remaking the outlook and culture of the Federal Trade Commission to reflect market-

---

[3] Janet Steiger referred to herself as "chairman."

based principles. Janet Steiger, on the other hand, exemplified tremendous political and managerial expertise without any ideological or theoretical agenda. Steiger emphasized vigorous enforcement of the law rather than a specific regulatory philosophy. Consequently, she both exhibited a greater confidence in the Congress and enjoyed warmer relations with that body than did Miller, who frequently found himself at odds with legislators when his economic principles conflicted with their view of consumer protection law. In addition, Steiger's experience at the Postal Commission sensitized her to the environment of an independent regulatory commission. She drew on that experience to identify and revive relations with key stakeholders, such as the state attorneys general, who had practically become *personae non grata* with the Miller FTC. In fact, as we shall see below, her principal objective as chairman was to restore good working relationships with the Commission's major constituencies. Similarly, William Reilly brought a purpose and vision to the EPA vastly different from that of Ann Burford. A former executive with the National Wildlife Federation, Reilly carried with him bona fide environmentalist credentials, as opposed to Burford, who, by all accounts, arrived at the EPA a product of the Sagebrush Rebellion and displaying a deep antipathy for the personnel at the EPA as well as the environmentalist movement. Much like Steiger, Reilly sought to invigorate his agency in a purposeful and pragmatic way, to restore damaged relations with Congress, to conscientiously enforce the laws, and to reach out to a variety of constituencies. Even public lobbyists described these two appointees with a sense of respect and, at times, even a grudging admiration they could never imagine themselves bestowing on Reagan's first appointees.

Finally, we can see the mark of Bush's personnel policy in terms of his selection to direct OMB. As conservative as he was, Richard Darman was much more a consensus builder than either David Stockman or James Miller, both of whom adopted a highly combative style in challenging agencies' proposed regulations as well as Congress's support for strong social regulation. For example, shortly after assuming the directorship of OMB, Darman negotiated a "gentleman's agreement" with John Conyers (D-Michigan), the chairman of the House Committee on Government Operations, under which OIRA would cease using regulatory review as a means of delaying or obstructing the development of new rules. Such an agreement would have been unthinkable under Reagan appointees. Even accounting for the institutionalization and general acceptance of OMB's regulatory review process, Darman operated in a much more open and conciliatory manner than either of Reagan's OMB directors. Again, his appointment was indicative of Bush's approach to personnel decisions of seeking out highly professional individuals with administrative and political skill. Unlike the Reagan appointees, Bush's were intent on making their agencies professional administrative bodies that had good relations with Congress and a breadth of constituency groups. Bush's key people in charge of regulatory bodies did not adopt regulatory relief as their number one agenda item. Rather, they sought to write regulations and enforce regulatory laws effectively, but with due attention to cost and governmental intrusiveness. In short, the distinction drawn earlier between regulatory reform and regulatory relief aptly distinguishes Bush's personnel policy from Reagan's. If Reagan's regulators were determined to "get government off business's back," Bush's seemed intent upon prudently easing business's regulatory burden while professionally implementing the law.

The third dimension along which we can compare Reagan's regulatory program with Bush's is the budgetary allocation to regulatory activities. Both the FTC and the EPA received significant budgetary increases under Bush. In part, this reflected a redemption of campaign promises. However, the increases at the FTC and the EPA were more than what was needed for mere political symbolism; their budgets were augmented in real rather than nominal dollars. Across the board, President Bush's 1991 budget for regulatory matters exceeded Jimmy Carter's by over 20 percent after adjustment for inflation, and the EPA was the major beneficiary of this infusion (*National Journal,* Nov. 30, 1990). Although not entirely satisfied with this level of increase, congressional staff and federal regulators acknowledged the budgetary benefits of the Bush program (personal interviews: Seth Mones July 22, 1992; Victor Kimm Jan. 13, 1993; and Dick Morganstern, Sept. 23, 1992). Both the FTC and the EPA were more than restored to their pre-Reagan budgets, though it is clear that the long-term negative impacts of budget cuts on bureaucratic and technical expertise could not be mitigated by one-year budget infusions. The in-house scientific capacity at the EPA was not fully restored during the Bush years; the addition of competent new scientists helped, but it would take time for them to learn how to navigate the regulatory environment. Similarly, the FTC newcomers could not easily replace the experienced lawyers lost during the Reagan years. Moreover, the FTC staff of 964 people in 1992 was still half what it was in the 1970s. Nonetheless, when compared with the sharp budgetary reductions these agencies experienced under President Reagan, the EPA and the FTC were treated quite generously by the Bush administration. As was the case with George Bush's personnel policy, there was little in his budgetary policy that reflected the Reagan initiative on regulatory relief. In fact, it was not without a considerable degree of irony that in 1991, a decade after Bush settled in as the chief of Reagan's Task Force on Regulatory Relief, the *National Journal* labeled him "The Regulatory President."[4]

In a carefully documented article, Jonathan Rauch demonstrated that Bush presided over "the broadest expansions of government's regulatory reach since the early 1970s" (*National Journal,* Nov. 30, 1991: 2902). According to Rauch, staffing of regulatory agencies increased from approximately 102,000 in 1985 to over 122,000 in Bush's 1992 budget. Similarly, the number of pages in the Federal Register, a benchmark for regulatory activity, jumped from a three-year plateau of around 52,000 for the last three years of the Reagan administration to over 65,000 at the end of 1991. This assessment was echoed in a stinging *Wall Street Journal* editorial that suggested that, in signing the Clean Air Act, the Civil Rights Act, the Nutrition Labeling Act, and the Americans with Disabilities Act, Bush oversaw a tremendous expansion of federal regulatory authority that inevitably would have a markedly deleterious effect on American business (April 22, 1991: A12:1). Arguably, not since an earlier Republican president, Richard Nixon, had the country witnessed such a flurry of major regulatory initiatives. Perhaps this was to be expected, given Bush's pragmatic Republican conservatism, his Nixonian concern with foreign rather than domestic policy, and his record of government service. By the middle of his term, however, the negative reaction of the Reaganites who had always suspected that Bush was never a "true believer," combined with the infinitesimally small political payoff for being an "environmental president" and behaving reasonably on other major social regulatory issues, induced George Bush to make a nearly 180° shift in his regulatory program.

Bush Turns Hard Right on Regulation

President Bush set out in 1989 to bring a new pragmatism to social regulation. He intended, by all accounts, to take seriously government's mission of protecting the consumer as well as the environment while maintaining a watchful eye on the costs and intrusiveness of the social

---

[4] Significantly, James Miller coined this term: "Bush became, not just the Education President, but the Environmental President," Miller complained, "and this translated into his being the Regulatory President." (*National Journal,* November 30, 1991: 2903)

regulation necessary to pursue those ends. Although this program embodied a genuine effort to make regulation work well, it also was based on a political calculus through which Bush intended to reposition the Republican party on issues of social regulation, thereby inoculating himself, if not future Republican presidential candidates, against the rather effective attacks from public lobbyists and their supporters in Congress or the press (personal interview, David McIntosh, Dec. 3, 1992). This approach, reminiscent of Nixon's assent to the creation of the EPA, the CPSC, and a host of social regulatory laws in the early 1970s, turned into a political nightmare for the president. On the one hand, Bush aroused the ire of the strong regulatory relief advocates who refused to compromise with public lobbyists whose appetite for federal intervention in the economy was, they believed, insatiable. On the other hand, environmentalists and consumer advocates were hardly generous in giving Bush credit for the regulatory laws enacted on his watch, thereby denying him the possibility of answering those critics who scoffed at his regulatory program. This no-win situation was best illustrated by two post mortems offered on the 1990 Clean Air Amendments Act, one by an environmental advocate and the other by Bush's director of Policy and Planning at the EPA.

According to a key aide to Senator Lautenberg (D-New Jersey) and a strong promoter of environmental policy:

> The evolution of the Clean Air Act actually contains an interesting story that is not widely reported. Bush is given a great deal of credit for the enactment, and he does deserve more credit than Reagan. However, at the outset the Senate had a very aggressive bill. The White House sent out word that it would block movement to the floor through filibusters by its surrogates in the Senate. At this point protracted negotiations were undertaken in which a heavy cost in forgone environmental protection was extracted. (personal interview, July 22, 1992)

Dick Morganstern, Bush's acting director of Policy and Planning at the EPA, had a very different take on the politics of the Clean Air Act. In his view:

> The last election sent a strong pro-environment signal which brought [William] Reilly and [Assistant Administrator for Air and Radiation, Bill] Rosenberg on board. Progressively the conservatives became entrenched at the White House and gridlock set in. The entrenchment came about because Bush became disillusioned with the environmental policy process. . . . When the administration's bills on the 1990 CAA came up to Con-

gress, they were treated as the opening ante, and things moved to the left from there. Environmental policy seemed like a runaway train, and Bush wondered, "How do we stop this thing?" (D. Morganstern interview)

These two starkly contrasting appraisals both typified the political gulf that separated environmentalists from even the well-intentioned, if comparatively modest, Bush program and indicated the impossible situation facing the president.

In the final analysis, Bush's efforts to restore the badly frayed consensus on social policy were undermined by fundamental disagreements among liberals, moderates, and conservatives about the appropriate role of government in regulating the economy. Although Bush's promise to provide a kinder, gentler version of Reaganism might have resonated with the electorate and some regulatory professionals, it had little appeal to the activists who shaped the politics of regulatory policy. No matter how forthcoming he thought he was, he would never satisfy the environmentalist community enough to undercut the support it regularly provided for Democratic candidates. The same held true for consumer advocates with respect to issues such as food labeling.

This general problem was doubly exasperating since Bush necessarily angered members of his own party who were philosophically opposed to government regulation. "The article in the National Journal describing this administration as the 'regulatory presidency' is true," complained Timothy Muris, one of the principal architects of Miller's program at the FTC. "Like Nixon, [Bush has] governed as a Democrat on [social] issues—increasing spending and regulation and showing little patience or confidence in market forces" (personal interview, July 24, 1992). Especially galling for staunch Reaganites was the fact that Bush's brand of pragmatism surrendered the political high ground and the field of ideas to advocates of increased federal regulation. Bush's accommodation to social regulation compounded his sin in abandoning his celebrated "no new taxes" campaign pledge, thus confirming the widespread perception that the president had no use for the ideas and foot soldiers of the Reagan revolution. "In a sense," Muris observed, "the Bush people reject a presidency informed by ideas. Many hated the Reagan people" (T. Muris interview, July 24, 1992). Another leading conservative, Clifford White, complained bitterly that Bush's personnel staff, in complicity with the president's appointees to head regulatory agencies, had purged all the Reaganites from the second and third levels of the administration and from positions of public policy. "It is not unreasonable that Bush would want to rebuild the administration in his own image and to put his own people into positions of authority," he fumed, "but it was an act of treason to betray the *ideas* that had built the modern Republican Party and the great coalition of 1980" (White, 1993: 73).

Bush's own displeasure with what he perceived to be the intransigence and ingratitude of public lobbyists and their congressional patrons began to dissuade him from pursuing his original regulatory program; the growing chorus of disenchantment from his staunch conservative allies made it all but certain he would abandon that course. To be sure, the complaints of those allies were somewhat disingenuous, since regulatory activity and costs were already escalating in the final term of the Reagan presidency. Indeed, in terms of rulemaking and enforcement the first two years under Bush were very similar to the last two years under Reagan (*National Journal,* November 30, 1991: 2904). What set Bush apart, however, was his willingness to approve major new regulatory laws that conservatives feared would drastically impinge on the market: he signed the Clean Air Amendments Act, the Civil Rights Act, and the Nutrition and Labeling Act, all of which Reagan had vetoed. Bush also strongly supported the 1991 Americans with Disabilities Act, which was dedicated to guaranteeing the civil rights of the disabled in access to buildings and finding employment. However laudable or even popular these laws and their objectives might have been, signing them clearly veered off the path blazed by the Reagan revolution.

In truth, Bush was not a "stealth liberal." Even as the president accepted these new social objectives, he hoped to use the regulatory review process to inoculate business against excessive costs. "The president would say that if we keep our hand on the tiller in the implementation phase, we won't add to the burdens of the economy," reported a member of the Competitiveness Council, the successor to the Task Force on Regulatory Relief, chaired by Bush (*National Journal,* November 30, 1991: 2904). As Bush soured on these regulatory policies, the burden of reversing course fell to the Competitiveness Council and the Office of Management and Budget.

Bush's faith in the regulatory review process proved illusory. Indeed, conservatives accused the Bush administration of allowing Congress "to neuter" the Office of Information and Regulatory Affairs (Brookes, 1991: 32). They claimed that Darman's gentleman's agreement with Representative Conyers reflected the OMB director's indifference to regulatory policy, as well as his preference to focus on the budgetary process. "With some issues, such as acid rain, Darman made an effort to affect regulatory policy," Muris noted. "But he was not willing to go to the trenches over most regulatory . . . matters" (T. Muris interview, July

24, 1992). Darman, in fact, acknowledged as much, claiming that the Reagan administration's regulatory review efforts resulted in a costly and unsuccessful war of attrition. Responding to his critics in an interview for *National Review,* Darman was defeatist about "how easily the regulatory agencies can beat the process. Again and again they will get court orders generated by third parties—advocacy groups—to which they already have leaked their proposed regulation. By the time we can get a regulatory proposal we already have a court order demanding review and clearance within 24 hours!" (Brookes, 1991: 32).

Such opposition did not faze David Stockman and James Miller, who were willing to engage Congress in bitter struggles over OIRA's regulatory review powers. The Reagan administration's assault on regulation, however, aroused deep resentment among legislators who had been circumscribing OIRA's powers since the mid-1980s. At first, as we have noted, Congress, led by John Dingell (D-Michigan), sought unsuccessfully to cut off funding for OIRA's regulatory reviews. Eventually, a modus vivendi was worked out that took effect in the 1987 omnibus fiscal spending bill. In particular, Congress made future directors of OIRA subject to Senate confirmation and restricted use of the agency's funds to the task originally assigned to it by the Paperwork Reduction Act—reviewing the information collection requests contained in another agency's rule or regulation.

Thus, Congress began to circumscribe OIRA's powers during Reagan's second term. Ultimately, by the early 1990s, Darman's indifference to regulatory policy (at least in comparison to his predecessors in the Reagan administration) and ongoing congressional hostility to centralized regulatory review left OIRA enervated. Moreover, on Bush's watch two important events called into question the entire framework of OMB and OIRA imposing centralized control on the costs of regulation. First, in February 1990, the Supreme Court issued a seven-to-two ruling that curtailed OIRA's oversight authority. In a case revolving around OSHA regulations requiring companies to inform workers about the use of hazardous chemicals in the workplace, OMB, through OIRA, had rejected three rules, including one that required that "employees who work at multiemployer sites (such as construction sites) be provided with data sheets describing the hazardous substances to which they are likely to be exposed, through the activities of any of the companies working at the same site." OIRA determined that these three rules were not justifiable; with respect to transient construction workers, it concluded that "workers on multiemployer sites would be adequately protected if each employer kept chemical manufacturers' labels intact, supplied data sheets to other employers at the site on request, and taught its own employees about chemicals with which they worked directly, and explained how to recognize hazards likely to be introduced by other employers" (*Federal Register,* vol. 43, 1987: 46077).

In its first interpretation of OMB's legal authority, the Court ruled that, regardless of the merits of OIRA's argument, it lacked discretion under the Paperwork Reduction Act to disapprove the regulations drafted by OSHA. Speaking for the majority, Justice William Brennan offered a strict interpretation of the statute, claiming that the act empowered OIRA only to review paperwork burdens imposed as a result of requirements for business reporting *to federal agencies*. It did not apply, thereby, to rules mandating that firms provide information to third parties but not delivered to a federal agency. "There is no indication in the Paperwork Reduction Act," Brennan claimed, "that OMB is authorized to determine the usefulness of agency-adopted warning requirements to those being warned," in this case the workers (*Dole* v. *United States Steelworkers of America,* 495 U.S. 37–39, 1990).

The *Dole* decision applied to a broad category of regulations over which the budget office had asserted control, affecting such areas as food ingredients, housing inspections, and pensions (*New York Times,* February 22, 1990: A1). More significantly, it was the first clear instance in which OMB's ability to impose its will on the regulatory process was delimited. To be sure, the Court's ruling did not eradicate OMB's authority to review regulations, nor did it raise questions about the constitutionality of Executive Orders 12291 and 12498. It did, however, erode the confidence of the Bush administration in its regulatory strategy of using oversight to ensure what it viewed as a measure of prudence in the development of new regulations. It also aroused fears among conservatives who viewed oversight as their deregulatory trump card.

Of even greater concern to advocates of regulatory relief was Congress's failure, in the late 1980s, to appropriate monies for implementing the Paperwork Reduction Act. A number of appropriation proposals were offered in both houses, all of which aimed at limiting cost–benefit reviews and imposing stringent timetables on such reviews to preclude what legislators and public lobbyists perceived to be OMB's abuse of the law to delay and harass federal regulators. These proposals, however, were opposed both by liberals who resented any form of centralized oversight and by conservatives who rejected efforts to restrict OIRA's authority. John Glenn (D-Ohio), chairman of the Senate Committee on Governmental Affairs, sought to break the impasse by working out a last-minute compromise with Darman to reauthorize OIRA for four years with new executive orders that would commit the agency to disclose information on its rulemaking activities. Glenn's counterpart in the House, John Conyers (D-Michigan), did not, however, assent to this eleventh-hour agreement. In the Senate, a small group of Republicans led by conservative Phil Gramm (R-Texas) killed the Glenn–Darman deal when they refused to allow the measure to come up for action under unanimous consent procedures invoked during Congress's final session (*Government Computer News,* January 21, 1991: 1). In the end, Congress merely enacted a continuing appropriation that left the legal status of OIRA, and particularly its regulatory review role, unsettled.

Bush's nominee for OIRA administrator, James Blumenstein, a Vanderbilt University professor of law, was a casualty of this spat over reauthorization. Glenn linked Blumenstein's confirmation to the OIRA appropriation question. When this legislation died, the White House's nominee was doomed as well. In the absence of another nomination from the president, James B. MacRae Jr., a career OMB executive, first appointed by Lyndon Johnson, assumed the office of acting OIRA administrator. Without a permanent chief, OIRA's power and prestige sank even lower. "At OIRA, you have a civil servant who is a very capable guy," James Miller observed toward the end of 1991. "But that civil servant is talking to a political appointee who is confirmed by the Senate . . . and does not take kindly to being told what to do by a civil servant" (*National Journal,* November 30, 1991: 2906).

Thus, by 1991, conservatives considered Bush's promise to control regulatory costs in the trenches of administrative politics seriously compromised. As David McIntosh noted, political appointees [to regulatory agencies] who were making policy decisions did not comply with the requirement in EO 12291 that there be a cost–benefit test applied to regulations" (personal interview, Sept. 21, 1992). In the eyes of conservatives, at least, the administration's pragmatic regulatory program was badly discredited, inasmuch as OIRA, its primary institutional mechanism for asserting control through Executive Orders 12291 and 12498, was so weakened.

As the 1992 presidential campaign appeared on the political horizon, President Bush began to think about shoring up his base support rather than pursuing an apparently feckless strategy of wooing the environmental and consumer vote. That decision was all but rendered a fait accompli not only by the drumbeat of criticism from conservatives but also by the portrayals of Bush in the *Wall Street Journal* and the *National Journal* as a new godfather of federal regulation. Bush's shift to the right was heralded by the increasing prominence, during the spring of 1990, of the

President's Council on Competitiveness. Bush had formed the Council in March 1989 as a successor to the Reagan administration's Task Force on Regulatory Relief. Like the Reagan task force, the "Quayle Council," as it was soon dubbed by its critics, also derived its authority from Executive Orders 12291 and 12498. For the first year of its existence, though, the Council was little utilized, a natural consequence of the Bush administration's policy of regulatory pragmatism.

In the aftermath of the notorious *Wall Street Journal* and *National Journal* articles and Congress's assault on OIRA, the Council's activities expanded and intensified. Alan Hubbard, a Harvard-trained lawyer and a successful businessman who was considered to have a good feel for the political realities of interest group politics, was appointed as the Council's executive director. David McIntosh, a young lawyer and economist from the University of Chicago, with experience in the Reagan administration's Justice Department, was selected to be deputy director. His knowledge of Washington policymaking and legal issues was intended to complement Hubbard's strengths (McIntosh interview). Hubbard's role was somewhat compromised by the end of 1991, however, by charges that he had a conflict of interest because of his personal holdings in a chemical company, and he eventually left the position to become Quayle's campaign manager. In 1992, McIntosh succeeded Hubbard as executive director of the Council.

The principal task of the Competitiveness Council was to revitalize OIRA and lend political support to its beleaguered acting director, James MacRae. "Jim MacRae has done a great job at OIRA," McIntosh noted in 1992, "but there is only so much you can do in the civil service capacity. The council represents the elected head of the executive branch—this makes our defense of OIRA, our participation in the regulatory review process, essential for it [OIRA] to have a meaningful effect" (D. McIntosh interview). In practice, however, the Council, rather than OMB, was in charge of coordinating regulatory review, a responsibility it readily assumed, given OIRA's forlorn state. Yet with only six full-time staff members, the Competitiveness Council could not take the place of OMB. As Timothy Muris, who served in both the FTC and OMB during the 1980s, put it, "OMB (and OIRA), itself, can only deal with the tip of the iceberg. . . . It is unable, really, to control regulatory policy without some significant commitment in the agencies. But the Competitiveness Council is not even on the tip of the iceberg. . . . It was spread way too thin" (T. Muris interview, July 24, 1992).

Limited resources, however, were only part of the problem. Just as significantly, critics of the Competitiveness Council alleged that it was a forum for special interests, a back door through which business gained undue influence on the regulatory process. In almost every place he visited, Vice-President Quayle held closed-door roundtables with business people, many of them large contributors to the Republican party, as well as state and local officials. Hubbard, and later McIntosh, would travel with the vice-president and sit in on these meetings, in which opponents of regulation were invited to lodge specific complaints. McIntosh revealed that many of Quayle's campaign stops were devoted to such gripe sessions:

> I have had the opportunity to talk with a lot of people who are interested in the council's work. We have held roundtables in Illinois (on OSHA regulations such as material data sheets) and California (on complaints of growers in the Imperial Valley about the prohibitive costs of regulations affecting pesticides). I have also spoken with organized constituencies, usually at the request of their representatives on the Hill. If people on the Hill request it, we will make an effort to listen, as we have recently in the case of cattlemen and lumber people. (D. McIntosh interview)

Certainly, there was nothing irregular about the vice-president meeting with important political interests, nor with his office acting as a sounding board for those who were bearing the costs of regulation. In fact, as Quayle's chief of staff, William Kristol, put it, the Competitiveness Council was less intent on responding to political interests, narrowly understood, than in "carving out a niche for philosophical conservatives" (cited in Langston, 1992: 186–87). Yet the council's melding of interest-group and regulatory politics created a perception that it was an appeals court for special interests (Portnoy and Berry, 1993). Had Richard Darman displayed a strong interest in regulatory review, visibly allying OMB's economic expertise to the Council's deregulatory mission, this perception might have been avoided. As it was, the director of OMB occupied himself with other matters; he did not oppose the Council's activities, nor did he object to its use of OIRA staff in carrying out its review and screening of specific regulations. As Kristol pointed out, however, Darman's forbearance "left the Quayle Council alone in its quest to ameliorate the burdens of regulation" (personal interview, July 22, 1994).

The staff of OIRA was generally not unsympathetic to the council's objectives and did not feel their professionalism compromised by its deregulatory fervor; however, the absence of strong support for this enterprise within OMB tended to cast OIRA's economists as tools of the Quayle Council. Indeed, staff in the agencies and on the Hill complained that it was virtually impossible to determine who was responsible for the regulatory review process. As Luana Wilcher, the EPA director of Water Programs, observed, "There is a blending and blurring among the OMB, the Competitiveness Council, and the Office of the Vice-President. . . . If you put them all in a bag and shook them up you never knew who would come out" (L. Wilcher interview). Seth Mones, a legislative aide to Senator Frank Lautenberg (D-New Jersey), echoed this sentiment, pointing out that:

> The Competitiveness Council operates pretty mysteriously. [Domestic and Economic Policy Advisor Roger] Porter and [Associate Director Robert] Grady of OMB seem to be informally involved in checking out regulations. It may well be that the same cast of characters is involved in the second half as in the first half of the Bush administration's outreach to business; it's just that there is an identifiable body called the Competitiveness Council under the direction of Vice-President Quayle. (S. Mones interview)

Although the same cast of characters might have been involved during the last two years of Bush's term, the Competitiveness Council clearly enhanced the roles of those who were most sympathetic to business interests. William Rosenberg, the EPA's assistant administrator for Air Programs, accused the council of serving as "basically a kangaroo court of appeals" for businesses dissatisfied with legislation or regulations. Unlike Mr. Mones, though, Rosenberg saw a definite shift in the review process. Prior to the Quayle Council's assuming the burden of regulatory review, he claimed, the Bush administration handled the Clean Air Act through Porter and Grady as well as White House counsel C. Boyden Gray, and while they raised serious objections, "Bush's commitment to the legislation meant that disputes were handled substantively and professionally" (personal interview, Dec. 1, 1992). After the Council began operations, professionalism was supplanted by ideological crusading, according to Rosenberg.

The perception that the Competitiveness Council held OIRA hostage to its ex parte contacts with business was strengthened by the secrecy of its activities. The council did not operate with a formal docket. Nor did it open up its operations as OIRA had done since Jim Miller and his director of OIRA, Wendy Lee Gramm, negotiated a deal with Congress in 1987 that gave the public greater access to the regulatory review process (see Chapter 4). Not surprisingly, the council's secretive modus operandi proved extremely vexing for public lobbyists, who strongly supported Congress's efforts for public disclosure of OIRA's interventions

in the regulatory process. Vice-President Quayle and his lieutenants violated the cardinal principle of the public lobby regime: the regulatory
process must be open to all on an equal basis. As Christine Triano, a
senior staff member of the public lobby group OMB Watch, complained:

> Actually, OIRA is a bastion of accountability, compared to the Competi-
> tiveness Council. OIRA [under Wendy Gramm] negotiated a deal with
> Congress that brought more openness to the process. But now the manage-
> ment of executive orders affecting regulations is tucked into the vice-
> president's office. . . . Claiming executive privilege, the council has not
> been willing to accept sunshine regulations. In fact, its people have argued
> that the purpose of moving regulatory oversight to the vice-president's of-
> fice is to, as Quayle puts it, "leave no fingerprints." Putting matters on
> OIRA's docket was good for people but bad for business. . . . Awareness
> was increased because of sunshine rules. The Competitiveness Council
> means to help business. (personal interview, July 21, 1992)

For their part, many legislators and congressional staff were equally per-
turbed by the in camera regulatory review process. Although the council's receptivity to behind-the-scenes pleas for relief from particular business interests rankled Congress as much as it did environmentalists, a
deeper problem legislators had with the council was its ability to weigh
into the review process and frustrate congressional intent. As Henry Waxman (D-California), the powerful chairman of the House Subcommittee
on Health and the Environment, explained: "It's unacceptable to me as a
member of Congress to have the law flouted by an agency that is not
spelled out in any law or in the Constitution as having the kind of centralization of power to operate behind the scenes and to respond solely to
the pressures of big business" (*National Journal,* July 6, 1991: 1676).
The Congress, obviously, was just as concerned with its own legal and
constitutional prerogatives as it was with protecting the public through
regulation. Indeed, the "stealth politics" of the Competitiveness Council
revived legislators' fears of a White House-directed review process that
existed beyond the reach of congressional oversight. This situation was
particularly disconcerting because it developed less than a year after legislators had worked out a more or less acceptable modus operandi with
OMB director Darman. Many legislators, not surprisingly, viewed the
Council as usurping the role of OMB and OIRA in a well-established
regulatory review process. In particular, congressional Democrats and
their staff condemned Bush's born-again zeal for regulatory relief, embodied in the Quayle Council, as a less principled, more insidious brand

of Reaganism.[5] Even Republicans in Congress who expressed support for the Council's objectives expressed serious reservations about its methods. As one Republican House staffer lamented:

> The [Competitiveness Council's] hard look at regulation can be valuable. But the Council's activities sometimes have been . . . arbitrary and heavy-handed. In truth, its regulatory review has been more a matter of public relations than of substance. First the White House gives away the store [in the form of major regulatory initiatives], then they make the passing out of exemptions a big deal. The Council did mediate the Disabilities Act. But in regulation overseen by the EPA, the DOT, and Justice, they have mainly been beating up on discretionary rulemakings [that follow from legislation that President Bush signed]. (personal interview, September 21, 1992)

Federal bureaucrats, of course, did not take kindly to these "beatings," to the Council's interference in delicate rulemakings, derailing, in some instances, years of work. The Council's influence on social policy was especially irksome to regulators at the EPA who felt that they were just emerging from beneath the pall of the Burford years and beginning to use strong scientific criteria and risk analysis to make policy. EPA director Reilly played the good soldier, insisting that his agency and not the Competitiveness Council made the final calls on regulations (*National Journal,* July 6, 1991: 1676). Yet he and his staff privately fretted over what they saw as an overt attempt to interject ideological considerations into essentially technical analyses (personal interviews, EPA staff, Dec. 2, 1993; Jan. 13, 1993. Even some of those lobbyists who benefited from the Council's decisions were a bit uneasy about how it got the job done. As Barbara Paley, an associate legislative director for the National Association of Counties, confessed after the Council helped her organization and business lobbies kill an EPA recycling regulation, "It's nice that we got [relief from the EPA's ruling], but I guess that there may be times when we will be concerned about an organization like the Competitiveness Council, which nobody knows a whole lot about. . . . We don't think that you should have to go around the back door to groups that are not out there in the open and who do not function in a substantive area to achieve this kind of objective" (*National Journal,* July 6, 1991: 1679).

In a sense, the Council was following the formula James Miller established at the FTC, namely, introducing new ideas and a new frame-

[5] For an example of this view, see Tiefer (1994: 27–30).

work of analysis to contest pro-regulation advocates. Hubbard and McIntosh, however, differed from Miller in that their claim of advancing the cause of consumer welfare was not supported by reliance on a regular group of staff economists who participated in policy decisions. Although they employed OIRA economists to do initial screenings of regulatory measures that were of special concern to business interests, the small staff of the Quayle Council charted its own course. According to McIntosh, the Council's task was to ensure that cost–benefit analysis played some role in the political struggles that invariably followed the publication of environmental, consumer, and health and safety measures. He argued, in fact, that the Competitiveness Council was a "neutral group" rather than an advocate for business or other special interests. "The Council's work," he claimed, "emphasized cost–benefit analysis, in an effort to minimize the number and cost of regulations." In providing political support and policy guidance for OIRA, "it could be fairly argued that we represent the general public interests in weighing competing arguments made by special interests" (D. McIntosh interview).

This interpretation of the Council's role in the policy process, however, underplayed its commitment to conservative principles that were avowedly hostile to regulation. Indeed, the Council's activities were animated by an extreme and novel (at least by modern standards) interpretation of property rights. Quayle and his staff favored, for example, legislation that would require regulatory agencies to reimburse the Treasury if a court decided that, as a result of federal regulations affecting property values, "just compensation" would be required by the Fifth Amendment's "takings clause." In 1987, the Supreme Court began to issue rulings asserting that regulation often serves as a substitute for the power of eminent domain and, consequently, that such indirect government control of property, as much as outright confiscation, can be subject to the constitutional requirement of just compensation. The Competitiveness Council's legislative proposal would greatly enhance the political and economic consequences of such rulings, which, in effect, threatened to resurrect the late-nineteenth-century doctrine of substantive due process, which permitted regulation without compensation only if there were a "harmful and noxious use of land" (*Connecticut Law Tribune,* May 23, 1994: 24). This bill, for which Quayle lobbied personally, would also prevent the issuance of any regulation unless the Attorney General certified that it complied with EO 12630, issued by Reagan in 1988 and requiring agencies to review their actions to minimize the taking of private property (*National Journal,* July 6, 1991: 1679). Even Charles Fried, the Reagan administration's conservative Solicitor General, viewed the Council's proposed use of the takings clause as mischievous and as "a radical project [that would give the Justice Department and the courts a virtual carte blanche authority] . . . to use the Fifth Amendment as a severe brake upon federal and state regulation of business and property" (Fried, 1991: 183–86).

Director McIntosh did not flinch in the face of such criticism, alleging that the Council's support of property rights, if successful, "would change the dynamic of how much regulation the society will have." Under the property rights framework, not only would regulatory advocates and their congressional allies have to demonstrate a universal benefit significant enough to outweigh the rights of individual property owners—a very daunting legal exercise—but they also would have to factor into their deliberations the cost of compensating them for the losses that a proposed regulation would cause. According to McIntosh, "the future of individual freedom" itself was at stake in this effort to impose constitutional restraints on regulatory activity. "If the government can control private property with regulation," he argued, then "what prevents the complete elimination of the line between the public and the private spheres?" (D. McIntosh interview).

Thus, the Competitiveness Council was hardly a neutral forum, where diverse and competing interests sought to resolve conflict over social regulation. Rather, it was dedicated to renewing the project of regulatory relief introduced by the Reagan revolution; the Council's interventions were informed by a commitment to property rights and a conviction that government regulation was much more likely to be a problem than a solution.

Although, by providing business interests an avenue of appeal that was insulated from the open processes of the public lobby regime, Vice-President Quayle incensed many who were committed to the cause of social regulation, it is important to emphasize that this enterprise signaled the deep frustration felt by the Bush administration over its effort to fashion a pragmatic regulatory program. The strengthening of the Competitiveness Council's influence in regulatory politics signified an acknowledgment that Reagan and his conservative political advisors might have been correct in their assessment that getting a handle on regulatory cost and intrusiveness required engaging public lobbyists and legislators at the level of ideas. Sacrificing the philosophical high ground and simply skirmishing over the scope and methods of social regulation apparently bore little fruit in the struggle to limit the economic and financial burdens of command–control regulation. While Dan Quayle spearheaded the resuscitation of a centralized White House coordination of regulatory review, heavily informed by ideological considerations, it was George Bush who ordered a counterattack on the regulatory front. In his 1992 State of the Union message, with which he sought to set the tone of his reelection campaign, Bush declared a ninety-day moratorium on new federal regulations. Although this measure was significant in putting a hold on new regulatory programs, it threatened to go much further, by also calling for a review of all existing regulations. "The impact of the President's proposal sends a chilling message to agencies that the President is waging a war on his agencies," OMB Watch lamented (*OMB Watch Alert,* January 24, 1992).

As the case studies that follow reveal, Bush's war did not succeed— he was no more successful than Reagan in displacing the public lobby regime with one dedicated to regulatory relief. As in the case of Reagan's regulatory program, Bush's belated assault on social policy relied principally on administrative action, yet there was little prospect that a philosophical battle over the costs and benefits of social regulation could be won behind the doors of the vice-president's chambers. In the end, the Competitiveness Council could provide little more than piecemeal intervention on regulatory issues of concern to specific businesses or local governments. It was not, by any measure, a systematic executive oversight body. Perhaps more important, the Council's agenda of bureaucratic infighting over the details of regulatory rules precluded a clarion call for rethinking social regulation. It might have been an ideological triumph of sorts to have raised the challenge of just compensation for regulatory takings, but the Council's flare-ups with regulators over relatively narrow questions tended to obfuscate the larger principles and issues at stake.

In truth, neither a strategy of administrative confrontation over ideas promoted by the Council nor a strategy of political engagement initiated by President Bush can, by itself, threaten an established regulatory regime. What is necessary is both the articulation of an alternative philosophical framework and persistent political engagement; but that requires a tremendous investment of time, energy, and political capital that neither Reagan nor Bush felt they could afford. Although Hubbard, McIntosh, and others in the Office of the Vice-President cared deeply about challenging the ideas and impact of social regulation, they were essentially fighting a rear-guard action that proved more a major annoyance than a serious threat to the ideas, institutions, and policies of the public lobby regime. To be sure, important regulations were delayed or amended, but no laws were changed, nor was there any guarantee that the Council's role would outlive the Bush administration. As the end of Bush's term approached, McIntosh acknowledged the limits of the Council's influence, recognizing that meaningful change required "a strong regulatory office in OMB, a greater commitment within the agencies to reduce regulatory burdens, and statutory changes that would constrain regulation and codify the regulatory review process" (D. McIntosh interview). Our case studies of the Bush regulatory program in the Federal Trade Commission and the Environmental Protection Agency confirm this observation, revealing that aggressive regulatory oversight and talented White House staff were no substitute for a comprehensive plan of action.

8

Janet Steiger's Federal Trade Commission: The Limited Possibilities of Consensus Politics

> All new laws, though penned with the greatest technical skill and passed on the fullest and most mature deliberations, are considered as more or less obscure and equivocal, until their meaning be liquidated and ascertained by a series of particular discussions and adjudications.
>
> *Federalist* 37

"Janet Steiger came to work, and the sun came out." This is the way one long-time observer of the Federal Trade Commission described the tenure of Janet Steiger, George Bush's choice to chair the Federal Trade Commission (personal interview, Arthur Amolsch, September 23, 1992). No less fulsome praise for Steiger was offered by an extraordinary array of participants in consumer protection and antitrust policy, including business lobbyists, consumer advocates, congressional staff, and legislators. To be sure, Steiger's reign did not escape criticism and controversy; yet after fifteen years, during which the FTC had gone through what the *National Journal* described as "regulatory mood swings" that altered its identity from militant regulator of business to ardent champion of the free market, the Steiger-led Commission seemed to have achieved a remarkable stability (*National Journal*, May 19, 1990: 1217).

Still, for all her achievements, Steiger could not overcome fundamental disagreements among commissioners and members of the FTC's oversight committees on the Hill about the appropriate role of the federal government in protecting consumers and economic competition. In truth, Steiger represented the promises and disappointments of the Bush presidency—just as she provided competent and pragmatic management of the Commission's affairs, so did she studiously avoid offering an intellectual framework and political strategy that could ameliorate the philosophical and institutional estrangement of the Reagan years. Her style of consensus building required a political strategy that would keep to the minimum time devoted to philosophical debate.

The Mission of the FTC in the Bush Years

When appointed as chair of the FTC by President Bush in 1989, Janet Steiger defined her mission as "rigorous, but rational law enforcement." The legal standards of "deception" and "unfairness" had undergone important change in the Reagan years. These changes did not occur without considerable struggle, both within the Commission and among its major constituents, that centered on James Miller's quest to hitch consumer protection and antitrust policy to careful, indeed painstaking, economic analysis. These battles had thwarted Miller's efforts to see the administrative changes he brought to the FTC codified in law; in fact, the Congress, bitterly divided over the meaning of *unfairness* and *deception,* had refused to reauthorize the commission since 1980. Steiger sought to move the agency beyond the fundamental conflicts of the 1980s, defining her task as one of "clarification [of the new legal standards] through enforcement" (personal interview, December 18, 1992).

At first glance, Steiger seemed a good candidate to refine, or institutionalize, the changes in the FTC brought by the Reagan administration. Her career was one distinguished by competent administration rather than philosophical commitment. The first woman to head the Commission, Steiger was neither a lawyer nor an economist; she served both the Carter and Reagan administrations at the Postal Rate Commission, where, in a relatively obscure forum, she honed her managerial skills in heading a commission that dealt with issues that were not dissimilar to those of the FTC—economic analysis, antitrust issues, and advertising. Sufficiently adroit and competent to hold a political appointment under two administrations representing fundamentally different views of social regulation, Steiger came to the FTC promising not only to refine the changes of the Reagan era but also to restore good relations with the agency's erstwhile allies in Congress, the states, and public interest groups who were estranged from, if not avowedly hostile to, those changes.

The widow of a prominent Republican congressman from Wisconsin, William A. Steiger, Janet Steiger was no stranger to politics or government. A Fulbright scholar, Steiger became legendary at the FTC as a "preparation freak," who always required—and consumed—enormous quantities of briefing and background materials. During the process of adjustment, Steiger began to rely on a coalition of career and noncareer senior staff, who worked well as a team and whose collective historical experience and outlook buttressed Steiger's natural tendency to lead from the center.

By promising, so to speak, a "kinder, gentler" FTC even as she remained true to the spirit of free-market principles that governed the Commission under her two predecessors, Steiger faced a difficult, if not impossible balancing act. But she was abetted in this pragmatic mission by the unhappy legacy of Chairman Dan Oliver. "If Steiger could have invented a chair to succeed, it would have been Oliver," a staff attorney observed. "On the Hill, in the states, in the Commission itself, she was viewed as a breath of fresh air" (personal interview, July 20, 1992). Miller had difficult relations with the FTC's constituencies, but these relationships became openly hostile on Oliver's watch. Whereas Miller sought to reform the FTC, to dedicate it to a regimen that fostered competition, Oliver appeared eager to preside over the Commission's demise. As part of his efforts to master the art of inactivity, Oliver tended, as one of his staff acknowledged, to make "outrageous statements," on the numerous tours he took about the country, that alienated the Commission's staff, goaded consumer activists, and infuriated members of Congress.[1] "Oliver was more comfortable with ideology and bomb-throwing

---

[1] One episode, in particular, revealed how nasty things had become by the end of Oliver's reign, marking virtually a complete break between the chairman and the commission's oversight committee in the House. Oliver gave a speech, quoted in the *Washington Times,* describing Congress as "Candyland USA to the special interests." It came to the attention of the powerful chairman of the House Commerce Committee, John Dingell, who told a member of his staff to "get that son of bitch in his [Dingell's] office by 5 o'clock." At the appointed hour, Oliver arrived at the office of his oversight committee's chair, where he was sternly admonished for "demeaning Congress" and reminded that the FTC was "a creature of Congress." When Oliver refused to apologize, claiming that his criticism of Congress was both legitimate and clever, Dingell exploded, shouting, "You have gone over the line! I am the one here with the election certificate. You are nothing but a pipsqueak who got a job through your Republican friends." Oliver defiantly banged his first on Dingell's desk, saying he would not take that, whereupon the congressman held up the clipping from the *Washington Times,* assuring the FTC chair that he would take "quite a bit," that the Commerce Committee would watch his every move. "In seven years on the Hill," a member of Dingell's staff observed, "I had never seen a meeting like that." Within two weeks, Dingell's committee initiated an examination of all of Oliver's extensive travel. "Nothing awful came out of this," an Oliver staffer related, "but it was unpleasant and wasted limited resources." (Telephone interview Dingell staff member, July 16, 1992; Oliver staff attorney, July 21, 1992.)

than complex economic analysis," an attorney in the General Counsel's office observed; "even as chairman of a government agency, he viewed himself as an outsider, believing that there was something wrong with being an insider" (personal interview, July 20, 1992).

Even business, which appreciated Oliver's ardent commitment to free enterprise, became uneasy in the face of the FTC's wholesale retreat from aggressive consumer protection. States responded to this perceived void in policing unfair and deceptive business practices with heightened activities. The National Association of Attorneys General (NAAG), in fact, established guidelines on car and rental advertising practices that threatened to short-circuit national advertising campaigns (American Bar Association, 1989: S13). The prospect of confronting such a balkanized system of regulation made business look more favorably on uniform national standards. As one FTC observer observed, business came to view Miller and, especially, Oliver as "sorcerer's apprentices—who chopped up one broom, only to give life to fifty." By the time Oliver left the agency in 1989, businesses had begun to plead, "Give us back one broom!" (personal interview, Barry Cutler, April 8, 1993).

Steiger's principal objective was to restore the morale and reputation of the Commission. "When I arrived, there was the perception, which may or may not have been based on reality, that the Commission had lost communication with Congress and the state attorneys general," she explained. "I wanted to put an end to that perception," to the view that "there was a vacuum with respect to national responsibility to prevent unfair and deceptive business practices," and "that somebody else [the state attorneys general] had to fill that vacuum" (J. Steiger interview). According to one staff attorney, Steiger's task was not unlike the situation Ann Burford's successors faced at the EPA. "Just as William Ruckleshaus wanted to repair the EPA after Ann Burford's administration," he observed, "so Steiger saw her task as restoring the FTC after Miller and Oliver" (personal interview, July 20, 1992).

A key part of this "restoration" project entailed increasing the resources of the agency. Between 1980 and 1989, the commission's staff was cut by more than 50 percent, from 1,719 to 894 work years (*Budget of the United States Government*, 1990: I-Z41–I-Z42). Unless the budgetary situation of the agency was improved, Steiger recognized, there would be no capacity to conduct new investigations or undertake new initiatives.

The seeds for Chairman Steiger's actions were in the 1989 report of the American Bar Association, which was chaired by Miles Kirkpatrick. Kirkpatrick had also convened the 1969 ABA committee, which issued the report that informed his and subsequent chairs' efforts to remake the

FTC during the public lobby era. The 1989 Committee, which included both attorneys who had participated in the ginning-up of the agency during the 1970s and those who attempted to tame it in the 1980s, sought to propose in broad strokes a program for the FTC on which consumer activists and more conservative regulators could agree. They proposed: an increase in the FTC's resources, albeit not one that would restore it to the growth years of the 1970s; a clearer articulation of the agency's advertising-law enforcement agenda, with a view to reducing the States' regulation of *national* campaigns; an enhancement of the Commission's nonmerger antitrust activity that would, consistent with sound economic principles, identify cases not subject to easy application of the per se rule; and a greater emphasis on "guides and policy statements in the enforcement program" as an alternative to the Hobson's choice between the controversial rulemaking that dominated the public lobby era and the cautious case-by-case enforcement that was stressed during the Reagan years (American Bar Association, 1989: 4).

In responding to the ABA report's recommendations, Steiger had to find common ground in a forum that had been fundamentally divided over the FTC's mission for two decades. Her most impressive accomplishment in this fractious environment was to achieve stability in the Commission's resources. After only a little more than a month as chairman, Steiger successfully defended the Commission's budget to the OMB and Congress, calling for a slight increase in funds and staff. These gradual increases in the Commission's resources would continue throughout Bush's term in office; between 1989 and 1992, the FTC's budget grew by 11 percent (from $66.5 million to $82.5 million), while the staff increased from 894 to 964 (*Budget of the United States Government,* FY 1990 to FY 1993). Although these increases were modest in absolute terms, they were significant in that other small agencies had not fared as well (interviews, House and Senate staff, July–Sept., 1992).

Steiger had well prepared herself for her confirmation hearings and was well read in the contemporary literature on the FTC. She possessed a keen political understanding of the Commission's historical reputation for going too far or not far enough in defining its role. As a pragmatist, Steiger strove to achieve general recognition that the Commission could operate from "centrist" rather than "extreme positions" (personal interview, FTC staff attorney, June 19, 1995).

Steiger attributed her success as a consensus leader to her studious pragmatism, a position she championed as the proper "mission of the agency." The effort of her predecessors to "push the envelope"—to interpret the statute so as to conform with their view of regulatory policy—

led to a "jarring conflict between the Commission and Congress." But Steiger sought to show Congress that she would not seek to impose her personal stamp on the Commission but would encourage the staff to carry out the law as members of Congress understood it. "When Congress found that the agency was serious about its mission," she observed, "we won support on all sides—OMB and Congress—for a slight increase in our budget" (J. Steiger interview). Members of Congress and their staff tended to support Steiger's view of the FTC's return to grace. As a Republican member of the Senate staff put it:

> [Under Steiger, the FTC] is a conscientious regulatory agency—one that listens to all sides, including consumer and business interests. The Commission is now run by gentlemen and ladies who regard their job as enforcing the law. There are no longer efforts to torture the statute; rather, there is a concern to carefully respect its history and mission. This collection of commissioners are centrist; they do what the law requires them to do. (personal interview, July 23, 1992)[2]

In short, Steiger practiced the pragmatic approach to regulatory policy that informed the early days of the Bush presidency. Unlike her counterpart at the EPA, William Reilly, however, she was not subjected to the antagonisms of the Competitiveness Council when the White House moved toward a more conservative regulatory position. As an independent regulatory commission, the FTC was not subject to the administration's regulatory review process; moreover, consumer protection and antitrust matters did not exercise devotees of regulatory relief to the degree that environmental policy did. Still, Steiger did not have her own way. She was hampered by a badly divided Commission, which in some respects reflected the divisions of the Bush presidency. By 1992, Bush had an opportunity to appoint all five commissioners—two of these, Steiger and the Democratic appointee, Dennis Yao, were willing to pursue a

---

[2] Democrats on the Hill endorsed Steiger's leadership in very similar terms. As a member of Congressman Dingell's staff observed, "In general, Steiger has made a good faith effort to carry out the will of Congress. Congressman Dingell's general philosophy on oversight is that, if industry is not getting away with murder but acting within the law, the solution is not to beat up on industry. Instead, our responsibility is to close loopholes in the laws and ensure an honest effort to enforce them. It is not appropriate for the Commission to flout the will of Congress—this was the situation with Miller and Oliver; it has not been with Steiger. She has made a visible and definitive effort to enforce the law . . . (personal interview, staff attorney, House Energy and Commerce Committee, July 16, 1992).

more active program than was the Reagan era Commission. Two others, Roscoe Starek and Deborah Owen, both conservative Republicans, held the sort of circumspect view of regulatory activity that informed James Miller, and the fifth commissioner, Mary Azcuenaga, an independent, tended to be the swing vote.

The history of the Bush appointments to the FTC suggests that pro- and anti-Steiger influences were engaged in a backroom tug-of-war to tip the balance of policy decision making. This commission was especially divided on the controversial matter of national advertising; indeed, the ABA Committee's unanimous pronouncement that the FTC "can and should do more to articulate its advertising law enforcement" deflected attention from the differences its members had about what kind of policy was appropriate (American Bar Association: S-12). In the antitrust field, while there was a majority consensus on mergers, generally there was little agreement among commissioners on what the nonmerger antitrust program should be, particularly in the field of vertical restraints and monopolization. These differences limited Steiger's ability to push the Commission to embrace a more pragmatic program.

In the face of these serious disagreements, Steiger's leadership by consensus, as one of the FTC's regional directors put it, sometimes seemed to be "an oxymoron." "It is not clear how much change can really be accomplished with that sort of inclusive style," the regional official complained. "The Commission is badly fractured; and this has limited how much Steiger can do." Yet, she added, there was also a positive aspect of Steiger's style; her pragmatic approach, "dominated neither by conservative economic philosophy nor Nader-like consumer activism," allowed the agency to restore good relations with Congress and the state attorneys general, thus giving it a degree of freedom to pursue policies that it lacked under the more divisive leadership of Pertschuk and Miller (personal interview, November 20, 1992). Steiger's consensus style also made it difficult for any group or individual to level direct criticism of her leadership. This strengthened her hand as the Commission's spokesperson and allowed her to avoid the distraction of self-defense that had occupied so much of Pertschuk and Oliver's time. The danger was that, absent a clear sense of direction, without an agenda of its own, the Commission might become the servant of its congressional oversight committees and a faint echo to NAAG. A pursuit of law enforcement that was purely pragmatic, that is, might deprive the Commission of a meaningful place in the main drama of regulatory policy itself.

Consumer Protection and Antitrust Policy in the "Steiger FTC"—The Pursuit of Moderate Activism

When asked to describe Steiger's approach to regulation, Commissioner Dennis Yao, an economist from the Wharton School of the University of Pennsylvania, remarked a little cryptically that she "had blended the better aspects of the Miller approach to a more activist agenda" (personal interview, July 24, 1992). Like Miller, Steiger eschewed Magnuson–Moss rulemaking, pursuing instead a case-by-case approach in protecting the consumer and fostering competition. Moreover, economic analysis continued to play an important role in the selection of cases; Steiger, like her predecessors of the Reagan era, favored initiatives in which consumer injury, that is, economic harm, could be demonstrated. But whereas the fashion during the Miller and, even more so, the Oliver years was to highlight what the Commission would not do, Steiger encouraged the FTC staff to do more, to look earnestly for cases that could be pursued in the face of the more restrictive parameters that were established for the Commission during the 1980s. In truth, Steiger's objectives of more aggressive law enforcement and better relations with Congress and the state attorneys general were based on the premise that her two predecessors had too circumspect an understanding of consumer injury. Indeed, Steiger's programs of consumer protection and competition revealed that she had more faith in government than did Miller and Oliver.

Steiger relied heavily on her bureau directors to define and carry out a moderately activist program. Because the commissioners cannot systematically reject the staff's proposals for cases, the chairman and bureau directors play the principal part in determining the FTC's agenda (T. Muris interview). Steiger's bureau directors were not only capable but willing to give the staff considerable discretion in pursuing cases. If they believed that the basic business practice at issue was a problem, unlike bureau directors in the Reagan administration, they would allow the staff to proceed with little scrutiny of the staff's theory and allegations. As we will see later, this created tension between Steiger and her bureau directors, on the one hand, and the commissioners, on the other, in a few important cases. For the most part, however, the routine activities that dominated the Commission's docket were not affected by the disagreements among the commissioners about consumer protection and competition policy.

Steiger's choice to head the Bureau of Consumer Protection, Barry

Cutler, who had a previous stint at the commission as assistant general counsel, skillfully developed a program of cautious activism. Cutler inherited his agenda in part from the Reagan era; he emphasized a case-by-case approach that targeted fraud. But Cutler crafted a more ambitious assault on fraud than had his predecessors. For example, he developed a strategy against deceptive uses of telemarketing—his so-called Dandelion Approach—that not only challenged the perpetuation of telephone scams (the "boiler rooms") but also the major businesses that provided the support services that made deceptive schemes possible. One such case, *FTC* vs. *Passport Internationale,* led to the issuance of an order in April 1992, against a Maryland operation (Passport) that provided turnkey operations for fifty jet-set travel agencies throughout the country. In this way, Cutler claimed, the FTC's case selection had the greatest impact, getting at "the root of the problem" rather than merely "picking off dandelions" (B. Cutler interview). Similarly, to get at the source of fraudulent practices, Cutler took especially harsh measures against recidivism. Some individuals who had a history of flouting the law were banned from telemarketing; others were required to post a performance bond prior to engaging in any future telemarketing activities. These restrictions were written into the consent orders approved by the courts; when these orders were violated, the Commission attempted to have violators charged with criminal contempt.[3] In sum, the FTC's approach to fraud in the Bush years can be viewed as a creative application of Miller's regulatory philosophy, as an effort to strike a balance between vigorous law enforcement and tolerance of legitimate business activities.

In the area of national advertising, however, the Steiger commission departed somewhat from Miller's consumer protection agenda. The Miller and Oliver administrations had been reluctant to infringe on advertising campaigns unless there was clear demonstration of consumer injury. During the 1980s, advertisements considered deceptive were few, and the use of the broader "unfairness" doctrine was virtually nonexistent. When the FTC took action against the New York advertising firm Towne, Silverstein, Rotter, Inc. in 1990, it marked the first prosecution of an advertising agency since 1985. The commission charged that the ad agency made false claims in television commercials about the operation

---

[3] For example, Dean S. Flahos, a defendant in a Federal Trade Commission telemarketing fraud case, was charged in U.S. district court with criminal contempt for allegedly advertising automobile auction information without posting a performance bond—a violation of a court order issued at the request of the FTC in February (*FTC News,* September 30, 1992).

of certain Lewis Galoob Toys—the misrepresentation included a doll that could twirl on its own and a military toy that would fire a high-speed missile over long distances (*Legal Times,* March 11, 1991, 1, 17).

The Galoob Toys case signified Steiger's promise to respond to the 1989 ABA report's "mandate" to the commission that it do more to articulate its advertising-law enforcement agenda. But a tougher law enforcement program, signaled by high-profile cases against large advertising agencies, would not in itself restore the FTC's leadership role in national advertising. As Steiger acknowledged, "the FTC also had the very challenging responsibility" to articulate "a national advertising policy that can form the basis for a consistent and harmonious regulatory approach among the various state and federal agencies involved in the regulation of advertising" (Steiger, address to the Association of National Advertisers, October 12, 1992).

With the emergence of environmental advertising as a critical issue by the late 1980s, the Steiger FTC was pressed to achieve some resolution of these seemingly intractable obstacles. Just as George Bush believed that it was advantageous to position himself as the "environmental president," so corporations had come to the conclusion that "green" advertising could help the sale of their products. As a result, the FTC was faced with an explosion of advertising claims—many of them vague and some clearly deceptive—that products were environmentally sound. The complex problems posed by deceptive green advertising required all of Steiger's aptitude for consensus building. The FTC would have to fashion a policy statement, clarifying terms such as "biodegradable," "recycled," and "ozone friendly," on which at least three of its commissioners could agree. Moreover, in developing this policy the commission would have to obtain the cooperation of the EPA and environmental activists, as well as state attorneys general, who had their own ideas about regulating green ads.[4] Not surprisingly, Steiger and Cutler pursued a cautious approach—as Lee Peeler, associate director of Advertising Practices and the FTC's point man on environmental advertising, observed, they wanted a program to "ensure that environmental claims were properly substantiated, and not to establish environmental standards" (personal interview, Sept. 23, 1992).

This cautious approach informed the FTC's deliberations that began in 1989 and culminated in the publication of national guidelines for envi-

---

[4] For an account of the different regulatory approaches of the FTC and the states, see J. Howard Beales and Timothy Muris, *State and Federal Regulation of National Advertising* (Washington, D.C.: American Enterprise Institute, 1993).

ronmental advertising in late July 1992. The "Green Guides" required careful substantiation of environmental advertising claims but stopped short of setting standards for environmental policy. For example, marketers who sought the cachet of "recyclable" for their products were required to indicate, where appropriate, the limited availability of recycling programs. But the guides did not restrict the use of "recyclable," as some environmentalists and state attorneys general would have liked, to products that were readily recyclable, that is, where there were local recycling programs available to consumers.[5]

As the Bush administration found out in its pragmatic pursuit of common ground in the reauthorization of the Clean Air Act, moderation was not always—indeed was rarely—rewarded in the fractious area of environmental policy. But, although the Green Guides aroused some concerns among both industry representatives and public interest groups, they were generally well received. Industry found them fair, while most environmental groups acknowledged that they went about as far as the FTC's legal authority and political vulnerability allowed. Steiger took particular delight in the praise accorded the guides by the environmental newsletter *Green Market Alert*. "While specific passages of the moderate and well-crafted document are bound to cause grousing from one set of stakeholders or another, that's inevitable with any middle-of-the-road document," it editorialized. "Lawyers have a saying about negotiated settlements: 'If they're both unhappy, we know it's a fair deal.' And that's what the FTC guidelines are—a fair deal" (August 1992).

The Green Guides marked a triumph of Steiger's approach to regulatory policy, proving to her staff as well as a plethora of skeptics outside the agency that, at least on this important issue, leadership by consensus was not an oxymoron. The success of the guides stemmed largely from the inclusive process that led to their formulation. These procedures started from the premise that the Commission's role was essentially limited to protecting the consumer from deceptive advertising; but prodigious efforts were made to forge a consensus for this limited objective. The

---

[5] Thus, as the Environmental Defense Fund complained, "A product that is recycled at a national rate of only 1% would be allowed to carry a claim that it is 'recyclable,' as long as the recycling rate is disclosed. While such a claim may strictly be true, its environmental benefit is trivial and the majority of consumers reading such a claim will have no access to, or have no means of readily identifying, facilities that accept the product for recycling, and are therefore deceived." (Environmental Defense Fund, news release, "EDF Applauds Issuance of Guides on Environmental Claims by FTC but Says Regulatory Standards Must Follow from Congress and EPA," July 28, 1992.)

Commission heard testimony and received written comments that encouraged participation from a broad cross section of industry, the states, and environmental groups; in addition, the FTC participated in a joint federal task force with the EPA and the Office of Consumer Affairs, drawing both of her sister agencies into the deliberations over green guides. Steiger's inclusive style of leadership was well received; most parties, even the state attorneys general, who had been very critical of the FTC's record in national advertising, acknowledged that the Green Guides were sound, a realistic statement of what the commission could accomplish.[6] "Steiger improved relations with the states because to do so was consistent with her view of how government works," allowed one staff attorney. "Her view of the way you get the results you want [with state regulators] is to be nice to them" (personal interview, July 20, 1992).

With the favorable response to the Green Guides, Steiger took a first critical step toward meeting the most important challenge posed by the 1989 ABA report—to restore the FTC's leadership role in articulating a national advertising policy that could form the basis of a consistent and harmonious regulatory approach among the various state and federal agencies involved in the regulation of advertising. To be sure, the jury was still out. The Green Guides did not really have the force of law. Unlike the rules that were prescribed by Magnuson–Moss, guides were administrative interpretations by the Commission of the laws it enforced and, as such, not self-enforcing. As Commissioner Deborah Owen put it, they were formulated merely as "an educational mechanism for businesses and the bar." It would still be necessary for the FTC to follow a case-by-case approach, determining that individual environmental advertisements were deceptive (personal interview, December 1, 1992). Consequently, states such as New York, which had standards tougher than the FTC's Green Guides, could still prosecute environmental labeling and advertising claims that, while acceptable under FTC guidelines, violated its own more demanding standards. Indeed, Andrea Levine, an assistant attorney general for New York, indicated that her office would consider doing just that (*Green Market Alert,* August 1992).

---

[6] Minnesota State Attorney General Hubert Humphrey III, the head of the states' task force for truth in "green" advertising, offered enthusiastic, if not unqualified, support for the FTC's guidelines. "While the Attorneys General advocated tougher standards in some areas, overall the FTC's guidelines are a major victory," he proclaimed. "The FTC guidelines will help keep the green marketing revolution on track." (Press release, State of Minnesota, Office of the Attorney General, "Attorney General Supports FTC Action," July 28, 1992.)

Still, the carefully crafted consensus developed in the generation of the guides ensured general harmony among the FTC, other federal agencies, and the state attorneys general. Indeed, the very fact that guidelines, unlike Magnuson–Moss rules, did not have the force of law, recommended them to Steiger as a method to nurture this harmony. The ABA report, in fact, had called for the Commission to make use of "guidelines," which allowed more flexibility than formal rules, in tackling such controversial matters as national advertising policy. As Cutler acknowledged, the hopes for rulemaking ignited by the Magnuson–Moss Act in 1975, which potentially authorized the FTC to shape the economy with broad policy statements that had the force of law, proved illusory. The processes and procedures required by Magnuson–Moss, especially the celebrated opportunities for public comment, were extraordinarily cumbersome; and the costs of regulating entire industries, fraught with peril. Guides offered a safer, more pragmatic method for setting the boundaries of national policy (Cutler, 1993).

During the Reagan era, the FTC issued important policy statements on consumer unfairness and deception. As with guides, policy statements are broad declarations of the Commission's approach to recurring, important issues that do not have the force of law but inform the public of the standards that are employed in policing business practices. The ABA report recognized the Commission's recent use of policy statements as a "positive development" and urged that this trend be advanced further by the use of guides to put industries on notice of possible enforcement action (American Bar Association, 1989: S-19–S-20). Given Steiger's desire to find a middle way between the activism of Pertschuk and the forbearance of Miller, she viewed guidelines as the best solution to the delicate problems posed by environmental advertising (Steiger interview).

The FTC's cautious activism in consumer protection during the Bush years restored its relationship with Congress and the states without arousing a firestorm in the business community, clearing the way for an increased willingness to restore FTC resources for enforcement work. Indeed, for the most part, even trade association representatives, who still feared a recrudescence of the 1970s activism that earned the Commission the title of "National Nanny," appreciated Steiger's efforts to clarify national advertising policy. With the FTC, the Congress, and the states working cooperatively, trade associations enjoyed a respite from the volatility and "balkanization" that plagued them during the 1980s. "Business is horrified when collegiality breaks down at the Commission—a situation that weakens the FTC's authority," former commissioner Patricia Bailey observed in 1992. "In the final analysis, industry groups prefer a stable, predictable regulatory climate. Steiger has provided such a climate" (personal interview, September 24, 1992).[7]

The Commission's promulgation of strict rules regulating the "900-number" industry in 1993 was a mark of the more stable environment that Steiger had achieved. The 900-number market reached sales of nearly $1 billion in 1992, before going into a tailspin, in no small measure due to the bad reputation marketers had acquired as peddlers of smut and as unfair exploiters of children. At the behest of legitimate representatives of the industry and consumer activists, Congress enacted the Telephone Disclosure and Dispute Resolution Act in 1992, which enabled the FTC to bypass the tortuous rulemaking process and develop rules within 270 days. Among these rules was a "ban on pay-per-call services to children under the age of twelve, unless the service is a bona fide educational service" (FTC, "900 Telephone Numbers, Pay-per-call services, Trade practices, Section 308.3, part (e), July 27, 1993). Thus, as one staff attorney who had experienced the devastating controversy of children's advertising proceedings during the Pertschuk era observed, the Commission "revisited the same issues that aroused the so-called kid-vid debacle, with hardly a hint of controversy" (personal interview, July 29, 1993). Indeed, many legislators, including some who had attacked the Commission for its previous efforts to regulate children's advertising, praised the 900-number rules. "Ironically," the staff attorney added, "here, you have Senator [Ernest] Hollings [D-South Carolina], who nearly shut us down for kid-vid, now taking pride in what he formerly condemned."[8]

The imprimatur of Congress certainly helped shield the FTC from controversy in the "pay-per-call" procedure; just as significant was the fact that children were the targets of fraudulent practices that encouraged them to run up costly phone bills in calling the Easter Bunny, Santa Claus, or cartoon characters. In reviewing his record as director of Con-

---

[7] Timothy Muris dismissed Bailey's comment as "silly," arguing that business was not all that worried about disarray at the FTC—surely, he insisted, it was not "horrified when the Commission broke down in the late 1970s. It all depends on whose ox is gored" (letter to the authors, June 19, 1995). Arguably, trade groups preferred a fractious agency to a militantly aggressive one. Nevertheless, by the time Steiger arrived, many business interests looked to the FTC to preempt the regulatory efforts of state attorneys general, who responded to the perceived slackening of FTC enforcement with vigorous advertising and antitrust programs of their own.

[8] For the response to the 900-number rules, see Cindy Skrzycki, "FTC Issues Final Regulations For 900-Number Industry," *Washington Post,* July 28, 1993: D1, D5; and Edmund L. Andrews, "FTC Sets New Rules on '900' Services," *New York Times,* July 28, 1993: D1.

sumer Protection before leaving the Commission in 1993 for private practice, Cutler characterized the ban on directing 900-number advertisements
at children as reflecting "the Commission's concern with the needs of
real, vulnerable consumers with real-life everyday consumer problems"
(Cutler, 1993). Like the Green Guides, the 900-number rules emphasized
"hammering away at consumer fraud," and as such did not depart dramatically from the program initiated by Miller. Indeed, as Peeler noted:

> The cases we are pursuing are built on the policy statements formulated
> during Miller's tenure. Essentially, those statements [of unfairness and de-
> ception] call for the commission to proceed in a more judicious way. There
> is good factual research that is part of our casework presently that reflects
> a more careful consideration of what our limits are—we make an effort to
> develop more carefully our arguments in support of regulatory action. (L.
> Peeler interview)

Nevertheless, there was a change in the analysis of cases during the
Steiger years that gave the staff more flexibility in selecting them. Most
important, there was a slight, but significant decline in the status of economic analysis at the Commission. Miller not only brought the Bureau of
Economics (BE) into the FTC building for the first time, but also matched
this symbolic gesture by involving economists in every aspect of the
agency's work. Moreover, Miller appointed to the two policy bureaus
directors who were either economists or lawyers who championed economic analysis. With Oliver, economic analysis was subordinated somewhat to philosophical considerations that were avowedly hostile to the
FTC's mission; under Steiger, however, economic analysis was allied
uneasily to pragmatism, to a more prudent, if not activist, approach to
the selection of cases. The tension between the solidly "Chicago School"
economists and the enforcement-minded lawyers was preserved under
Steiger, albeit with a not-so-subtle shift toward enforcement-related outcomes. As the director of the BE, John Peterman, observed, "The economists are still involved—the Commissioners are interested in our work.
They have not cut us out, but there is not the same depth of interest in
our work presently as there was under Miller and Oliver" (personal interview, July 23, 1992).

The more flexible application of economic theory that characterized
the Steiger Commission was especially evident in the FTC's competition
program. First, at the request of Representative Jack Brooks (D-Texas)
and Senator Howard Metzenbaum (D-Ohio)—the chairs of the antitrust
subcommittees of the House and Senate Judiciary committees, respec-

tively—the Commission revisited its policy on corporate mergers during the 1980s. After doing a number of merger retrospectives, some of which suggested that the FTC had been too optimistic about the time for entry and the effect on prices, the Bureau of Competition began to scrutinize industry consolidation more strictly (personal interview with Kevin Arguit, July 21, 1992; Schuman, Rogers, and Reitzes, 1992). Consequently, the FTC conducted three times as many investigations and brought twice as many cases in 1990, the first full year under Steiger's leadership, as in a typical year during the Reagan administration (Mark Potts, "Toothless FTC Gets Its Bite Back," *Washington Post,* July 9, 1991).

This more pragmatic approach to competition policy was also evident in the area of nonmerger antitrust policy, especially in the renewed interest displayed by the Commission in pursuing vertical price-fixing cases. For the first time since 1982, the Bureau of Competition brought a resale-price maintenance case in 1990, settling charges with Nintendo that it dictated to retailers what to charge for its products. In the Reagan era FTC, these vertical cases were de-emphasized—indeed, all but deliberately ignored—on philosophical grounds. As James Langenfeld, director of Antitrust in the Bureau of Economics, observed, the Nintendo case and a similar resale-price initiative pursued against Kreepy Krawly, a manufacturer of mechanized swimming-pool cleaners, testified to the diminished interest in economic theory under Chairman Steiger. "Most economic thinking suggests that resale-price maintenance is not harmful to competition; nor does it raise the price consumers have to pay," he noted. During the 1980s, concerns for economic efficiency took precedence, "even though there were per se violations of the law" (personal interview July 23, 1992). The Commission's forbearance with respect to vertical constraints was supported by the courts, which issued rulings that made the burden of proof in such cases much more difficult.[9]

As soon as Steiger took over, however, the staff was encouraged to pursue such cases once again. As an attorney in one regional office put it, the clear message from "headquarters" was that vertical price-fixing "is still the law and ought to be enforced" (personal interview, November 20, 1992).

In departing from the competition program of her predecessors, Steiger was not content to renew past enforcement practices. The 1989

---

[9] The key cases are *Monsanto Co.* v. *Spray Rite Corporation,* 465 U.S. 752 (1984) and *Business Electronics Corporation* v. *Sharp Electronics Corporation,* 485 U.S. 717 (1988). For a discussion of Reagan's ability to transform the courts and the effect of this transformation on antitrust policy, see Kovacic, 1991.

ABA report had called for the Commission to bring innovative nonmerger cases that tested new legal theories of competition. In 1992, the Commission brought such a test case, charging three manufacturers of infant formula with "facilitating practices" that restrained competitive pricing, an initiative that set a potentially important precedent in the use of its statutory power. In analyzing market conduct under its Section 5 power to prevent "unfair methods of competition," the Commission has traditionally embraced the Sherman and Clayton acts. This has allowed certain types of anticompetitive behavior that did not involve an agreement or the danger of monopolization to slip through the cracks. The Commission has broader authority under Section 5 than allowed by either the Sherman or Clayton acts to arrest incipient trade restraints or practices that facilitated anticompetitive behavior; it was this so-called penumbra of Section 5 that encouraged the FTC to pursue controversial initiatives such as the "shared monopolization" cases during the heady days of the 1970s.

Under Miller and Oliver, the FTC was reluctant to make use of this discretionary power. In the so-called infant-formula case, however, the Commission relied purely on a Section 5 theory. Three companies selling infant formula to government-sponsored programs in Puerto Rico all followed the same pattern in raising prices. The Commission alleged that this was more than a coincidence, that the companies conspired to fix the cost of their products, even though there was no formal agreement that constituted a Sherman or Clayton violation. Two of the manufacturers, Mead and American Home Products, settled commission charges that they had engaged in "unilateral facilitating practices," such as providing information about preferred prices and marketing practices, to eliminate competitive sealed bidding in the federal government's Women, Infants, and Children program (WIC). The manufacturers agreed not only to refrain from such actions in the future but also to provide restitution in the form of 3.6 million pounds of free infant formula to the United States Department of Agriculture, which administers the WIC program. The settlement marked the first time that the Commission had used Section 13(b) of the FTC Act to obtain restitution in an antitrust case.[10]

Still, characteristic of the Steiger FTC, the infant-formula case was, as a staff attorney in a regional office put it, "cautious and safe innova-

---

[10] *FTC* v. *Mead Johnson and Co.*, No. 92-1366 (D.D.C., June 11, 1992) (consent order); *FTC* v. *American Home Products Corp.*, No. 92-1365 (D.D.C., June 11, 1992) (consent order). Litigation against the third manufacturer, Abbott Laboratories, which refused to sign the original consent order, continued in federal court. FTC lost in the district court, but Abbott settled a separate advertising complaint that was going through the FTC administrative procedure (press release, February 28, 1994, Office of Public Affairs, Federal Trade Commission).

tion." The architect of Steiger's competition program was Kevin Arquit, a former advisor to Oliver, who had no intention of returning to the activism of the Pertschuk era. Although acknowledging the innovative theory of the infant-formula case, Arquit averred that it rested on a strong factual record, one that determined, for example, that price increases oc- curred at twice the rate of inflation (Arquit interview). A respected anti- trust attorney in one of the regional offices agreed:

> This is not a revival of the Star Trek style of antitrust (an attempt to "go where man has never gone before") pursued during the 1970s—for exam- ple, the assault [alleging a "shared monopoly"] on the cereal industry. Al- though difficult to detect, this [infant formula] case involved price-fixing, which should be condemned. Also the Commission issued a sound theory of competitive harm and proved it with a lot of evidence. [The infant- formula case exemplifies] a pragmatic, problem-solving approach that is refreshing. Law enforcement rather than strict ideology is directing our efforts, as it should be. (personal interview, November 11, 1992)

In consumer protection as well as competition, then, the Steiger FTC had not institutionalized the changes brought by the Reagan revolution. Instead, during the Bush years, the Commission had fashioned a rough consensus that sought a middle ground between the Pertschuk and Miller regimes. Commissioner Owen, the most conservative member of the Bush FTC, observed, "This effort to work out a consensus matches pen- dulum swings throughout the country. There is a feeling that a polarized form of politics is not effective, that there are a number of goals about which those who call themselves conservatives and liberals are not at variance. At the FTC, we have tried to focus on areas of agreement" (D. Owen interview). Many consumer advocates agreed, praising Steiger for restoring the integrity of the Commission. Even Pertschuk gave Steiger credit for bringing an approach to consumer protection and antitrust pol- icy that was reminiscent of "the Nixon-Ford era, when the Commission was really an exemplary agency" (*National Journal*, May 19, 1990).

The Limits of Consensus

For all her success in fashioning a program that restored the reputation and morale of the FTC, there was only so much order that Steiger could make from the contentious regulatory politics of the Bush presidency, and she seemed reluctant on her own to proclaim policy positions that she had no basis to believe reflected the administration. In consumer pro- tection, the consensus on national advertising policy that made Green

Guides possible was sorely tested when the Commission was faced with issues such as the advertising of alcoholic beverages and tobacco, as well as health and nutrition claims in food advertising. As a new area of regulatory politics, "green" advertising was not yet the subject of fierce disputes; consequently, the FTC had an unusual degree of elbow room to develop standards (J. Steiger interview; T. Muris interview, July 24, 1992). The same luxury did not apply to health and nutrition claims in food advertisements, which were forced on the Commission's agenda in 1991 as a result of pressure from Congress, the Food and Drug Administration (FDA), and consumer groups. Moreover, the FTC's approach to environmental advertising centered on the "deception" standard, rather than the more controversial "unfairness" doctrine. As the FTC began to deliberate about applying "unfairness" in cases against the advertisement of alcohol and tobacco, the limited possibilities for extending the carefully crafted consensus that Steiger and her staff assembled in formulating Green Guides were exposed.

The controversy over food advertising stemmed from the enactment of the Nutrition Labeling and Education Act in 1990 (NLEA). This legislation authorized the Food and Drug Administration to establish standards that would prevent false and misleading nutrition and health claims on product labels. The FDA, headed by Dr. David Kessler, a much more aggressive regulator than Steiger, proposed regulations in 1991 that established strict standards for nutrition claims, such as "low-fat" and "fresh," as well as tough requirements for health claims, such as a link between dietary fiber and cancer.

Although the NLEA applied only to labels and not to advertisements, over which the FTC had jurisdiction, consumer groups and key personnel on the Hill demanded that there be a consistent and coordinated approach between the two federal agencies that shared principal responsibility for the regulation of food advertising and labeling. Legislation was brought before Congress in 1991 that would require the FTC to adhere to FDA standards. Further pressure for the FTC to harmonize its policy with the FDA's came from the state attorneys general, who were very active in this area of advertising. Indeed, the support of food industry groups that were deeply concerned about growing state regulation of national marketing gave impetus to passage of the NLEA.[11]

---

[11] For an informative and critical account of the National Labeling and Education Act and the FDA's proposals to implement it, see Beales and Muris, 1993, Chapter 5. The constellation of forces that came together to force harmonization in the area of health claims is evident in the hearings held by the House Subcommittee on Transportation and Hazardous Materials, November 21, 1991: 102–92 (1992).

The FTC defected from the institutional coalition for a coordinated policy on health and nutrition claims and fought against having to apply FDA standards to food advertising.[12] The Commission's hesitancy was due not only to Steiger's cautious approach to consumer protection but also to the different missions of the FTC and the FDA. Put simply, whereas the FDA embraced the dedication of nutritionists to educate, and change the diet of, consumers, the FTC's objective in regulating food advertisements was restricted to preventing false and misleading claims. As the lone Democratic FTC Commissioner, Dennis Yao, characterized the different approaches of the two agencies:

> The FTC's general view is that it would be inappropriate to bind us to the FDA's standards. . . . We are good at analyzing [consumers'] perceptions and determining whether [they are deceived]. There are also some policy views differentiating the two agencies. For example, some at the FTC believe that it might be useful for a consumer to learn from an advertisement that one product has 33 percent less fat than another. Yet if, according to FDA standards, the product with the lower fat content is nevertheless not a "low-fat" product (as that is defined by the FDA), the claim could not be made. This product might not be healthy in an absolute sense, but to prevent advertising claims that make such comparisons would deprive the consumers of valuable information (after all, a 33 percent reduction is better than none at all). In fact, such an incremental reduction might be the most realistic way to improve one's diet. Of course, if the ad claimed, deceptively, that it was "low-fat," then we would act. We would also be concerned if consumers thought a product was low-fat, when in fact it was not. Our major concern is to protect the consumer from deceptive ads. . . . The important thing is that we not be required in an inflexible way to apply FDA standards to advertising. (D. Yao interview)[13]

---

[12] Not surprisingly, food manufacturers were not part of this coalition to force harmonization on health and nutrition claims. They did not want the FTC to follow FDA policy in policing food advertising.

[13] According to FDA standards, a product could be labeled "low-fat" only if it did not contain more than three grams of fat per serving. A settlement agreement between the FTC and the Campbell Soup Company illustrated the differing approaches of the commission and the FDA. This settlement permitted Campbell to claim that its soups were low in fat and cholesterol and helped reduce the risk of some forms of heart disease, even though the soups were high in sodium and excessive sodium consumption is associated with high blood pressure, a condition which can increase the risk of heart disease. Rather than prohibit the "low-fat" claim, the FTC order merely required Campbell to disclose the sodium content of its soups (*Federal Register,* vol. 56, Apr. 18, 1991: 15880). In contrast, the FDA, in enforcing the NLEA, completely prohibits health claims in such situations.

Some consumer activists and their allies on the Hill refuted the FTC's position. The Center for Science in the Public Interest (CSPI), a consumer advocacy group with considerable influence in Congress, rejected the Commission's distinction between labels and advertisements. In the view of Assistant Director for Legal Affairs Sharon Lindan, "nutrition education professionals at the FDA were more qualified than lawyers and economists at the FTC to decide what types of health claims food companies can make about their products." According to Lindan, the purpose of regulating food advertisements should not be limited to protecting the consumer from blatant fraud; beyond this narrow objective, the task was to encourage manufacturers to produce more nutritious products. "If advertisers are held to FDA standards," she insisted, "then manufacturers will have the economic incentive to modify their products—to meet meaningful health standards" (personal interview, December 2, 1992).

The conflict between the Commission and its critics turned on the fundamental issue of the value of advertisement. Seeing little social value in commercial advertisement, consumer advocates at the CSPI and FDA nutritionists saw no reason to compromise the promotion of a healthy diet for the sake of crass competition among food manufacturers. In contrast, FTC attorneys, still chastened by the "kid-vid" controversy, did not believe they had the legal or moral authority to transform the eating habits of Americans. Even some consumer advocates dissented from the CSPI position on nutrition and health claims, commenting plaintively in the privacy of their offices that it would be nice if Americans ate less cheese pizza with pepperoni but that such a change in eating habits was not the responsibility of the FTC. The Commission's charge, they believed, was to stop deceptive practices. Indeed, moderate consumer advocates shared the view of attorneys and economists at the FTC that rigid regulation of food advertising would impair rather than promote the dissemination of truthful information to consumers about the vast array and diversity of food products. Chairman Steiger warned Senator Slade Gorton (R-Washington), a key member of the Commission's Senate oversight committee, "A blanket statutory provision that limits all advertising to a set number of FDA-predefined descriptors" could limit food advertising to "puffery and useless associational messages" (correspondence, Steiger to Gorton, September 25, 1991).

The controversy over food advertising occurred just as the 1992 election brought a Democratic administration to Washington. With Bill Clinton's victory over George Bush, consumer groups anticipated that a more activist Commission would vindicate their position on the regulation of food advertisements. Yet no commissioner was due to step down until September 1994, leaving the FTC in a rather uncomfortable holding pattern. Nevertheless, Steiger was determined to continue the cautious activism that had restored the integrity of the agency. The Commission began the process of formulating guidelines to promote consistency in food advertising and labeling claims, even as it recognized the distinct purpose of each medium. But the issue, as well as the postelection environment, made unlikely the same degree of harmony that was achieved in developing a policy for environmental marketing. "We find ourselves in the equivalent of a land war in Asia," one of Steiger's aides observed about the food controversy. "All we can do is stake out a responsible position, and, if we are lucky, in the end, we will get something that is not too much worse than that" (personal interview, July 26, 1993).

The FTC finally issued its food advertising guidelines in May 1994. As expected, the food guides allowed more flexibility for advertisers than did the FDA's standards for labeling. But the Commission promised "close scrutiny" for advertising claims that deviated from FDA rules (Beales, 1994). Whether the Congress and consumer groups would accept this effort to reconcile the divergent regulatory approaches of the FDA and the FTC remained to be seen. Two key Democratic members of the House, Al Swift, chairman of the subcommittee with oversight responsibility for the FTC, and Joseph Moakley, chairman of the Rules Committee, acknowledged the Commission's nutrition advertising-enforcement policy statement as "a good faith effort to achieve harmonization" with the FDA's Nutrition Labeling and Education regulations. But they remained "uncertain as to whether further legislation may still be necessary in order to provide the FTC with both the scope and efficiencies of directed statutory authority commensurate to that provided to the FDA under the NLEA." The FTC's ability to maintain its independence from the FDA labeling regulations, leaving marketers more freedom to advertise their products, they implied, would depend on Congress's evaluation of the cases the commission brought to implement the policy statement (correspondence, Moakley and Swift to Steiger, September 23, 1994).

Whereas the food controversy caused the FTC some difficulty with consumer advocates and their allies on the Hill, the fight over the regulation of alcohol and tobacco cut to the heart of the Commission itself. In her 1989 confirmation testimony and in several speeches delivered early in her tenure, Steiger had pledged to use agency resources to address the problems of alcohol and tobacco advertising to those below the legal age for purchasing the product. After her first four years in office, however, the FTC had concluded only two cases of alcohol and tobacco advertising, neither of which marked a strong enforcement stand against appeals targeted at underage consumers.[14]

Steiger's reluctance to pursue this matter could be attributed to the formidable legal and political constraints involved. Policing alcohol and tobacco ads that appealed to minors stood on the controversial *unfairness* standard—ads that apparently targeted underage consumers were not deceptive but a violation of public policy holding that it was unfair for marketers to induce youth to take up habits that were not only illegal but also hazardous. In the wake of the "kid-vid" controversy, the FTC had adopted a more specific concept of unfairness that made it more difficult for commissioners to justify action on the basis of public policy. According to the new standard, the Commission's judgment that a commercial activity was immoral no longer provided sufficient grounds for a complaint to be issued; it also was necessary for the FTC to prove that the act in question led to tangible "consumer harm."

Congress had required the Commission to prohibit appeals to youth in enacting legislation against abuses of "900 numbers," but legislators had not been able to agree on a standard to regulate commercial speech. Since 1980, in fact, Congress had barred the FTC from using its rulemaking power to issue industry-wide advertising regulations based on its Section 5 authority to outlaw unfair practices. Individual cases alleging unfair conduct could still be pursued, albeit not without stirring up a furious battle between antismoking and antiregulation forces (*FTC: Watch,* May 3, 1993: 1–2).

The Commission's struggle to resolve what one staffer characterized as "this horrendous trouble" turned on establishing the appropriate balance between public policy and consumer injury in alcohol and tobacco proceedings. Whereas some commissioners and antismoking attorneys in the Bureau of Consumer Protection believed that a well-articulated public policy against harmful activities such as underage drinking and smoking could serve as "the bulwark of inquiry," others in the FTC, wishing to preserve the more circumspect standards that Miller championed, required evidence of substantial consumer injury to take action (personal interview with staff attorney, November 2, 1993). This battle over the appropriate definition of unfair commercial practices defied Steiger's

---

[14] One of the cases involved action against the Canandaigua Wine Company for marketing its "Cisco" fortified wine as a low-alcohol beverage. The other targeted the Pinkerton Tobacco Company for alleged violations of the ban on television advertising of smokeless tobacco products. (Federal Trade Commission, "Law Enforcement Achievements of Ongoing Projects," Consumer Protection Mission, Oct. 1, 1989–Sept. 30, 1994.)

consensus-style leadership. Admitting that the chairman's record on alcohol and tobacco advertising was the one blot on an otherwise fine record, a member of Steiger's staff lamented that there was "not sufficient common ground to address cigarette advertising or the advertising of alcoholic beverages." "For most people in Washington that is no reason not to take action," he continued; "in fact, some see such divisive issues as just the place to take action. But . . . the chairman is different. Her position is that 'I am going to make an effort to involve a lot of people in an initiative,' so that something can get done" (personal interview, December 18, 1992).

Steiger's enthusiasm for consensus diminished somewhat, however, as consumer groups and Congress strongly urged the FTC to take some initiative on cigarette and alcohol advertising. The election of Clinton, one suspects, also encouraged more aggressive leadership by the chairman.[15] The transition report on the FTC flattered Steiger's record in antitrust but was critical of the consumer program, especially of the lack of attention to food, tobacco, and cigarette advertising. By the beginning of 1993, the staff at headquarters and regional offices had the impression that it was now appropriate to pursue controversial cases in these areas (personal interviews with staff attorneys, December 18, 1992; July 26, 1993; April 15, 1994; June 29, 1994). In April, as four of the commissioners and many of the staff of the FTC were throwing a farewell party for Consumer Protection Bureau Director Barry Cutler, some of Cutler's staff forwarded to the commissioners a recommendation that the agency charge RJR Nabisco with unfair advertising of cigarettes to minors through the controversial "Joe Camel" campaign. The Joe Camel case began in 1991, when the Coalition on Smoking or Health filed a petition that asked the FTC to act against the advertising campaign for Camel brand cigarettes featuring Old Joe, a cartoon camel. After an exhaustive study, the Bureau prepared a recommendation that was based on substan-

---

[15] Some observers of the FTC suggested that Steiger's more aggressive leadership after Clinton's election represented her bid to retain the position of chair. Similar speculation followed Dennis Yao's support of Steiger's efforts to push the envelope a bit, that is, he was making a bid, as the only Democrat on the commission to be named chair. Certainly, personal ambition might have played a part in the more activist posture that Steiger and Yao displayed after the election, but we have no evidence to support such a claim. We can confirm, however, that Steiger and Yao expressed support for strong action against alcohol and tobacco ads that appealed to minors prior to the election; that their personal ambition might have led them to take advantage of the more "liberal" political atmosphere that followed the 1992 presidential election hardly marks them as rank opportunists.

tial consumer injury and not on well-developed public policy considerations. This left the staff with the difficult task of persuading a skeptical
Commission that the Joe Camel character not only appealed to minors
but also persuaded them to start smoking (*FTC Watch,* May 3, 1993: 1,
2; personal interview with staff attorney, July 25, 1995).

The Joe Camel case, which roused a national debate over cigarette
advertising in general and the alleged marketing of tobacco products to
minors in particular, was the first test of Steiger's more aggressive leadership, of her efforts, despite a recalcitrant Commission, to redeem her
pledge to address the problems of alcohol and tobacco advertising to minors. The case against RJR Nabisco would also be an important test for
Cutler's successor, Christian White, a veteran FTC lawyer and executive,
who Steiger named as acting director of the Bureau of Consumer Protection. White knew that his staff and the Chairman faced a difficult task in
persuading two other commissioners to support an unfairness case, that it
would be difficult to prove that Joe Camel increased smoking among
minors. But he believed that the principles involved in the case and the
evidence accumulated by the staff demanded that the Consumer Protection Bureau support Steiger's fight against the tobacco industry's use of
advertising that had obvious appeal to minors (personal interview with
staff attorneys, November 2, 1993; July 25, 1995).

In the end, Steiger's exertion of leadership in the Joe Camel case
was to no avail. Although Dennis Yao supported her determination to
prosecute the case, the other three commissioners, Owen, Starek, and
Azcuenaga, voted no, effectively closing the R. J. Reynolds investigation. The "Joe Camel" case relied on circumstantial evidence of consumer
injury: according to one study, after the introduction of the cartoon character, Joe Camel, in R. J. Reynolds' promotions in 1988, Camel's share
of the underage market jumped from under 1 percent to over 32 percent
in Massachusetts (DiFranza et al., 1991); more recent public estimates
based on national studies, including those performed by the Department
of Health and Human Services, put the increase at from 2 percent to 3
percent before the campaign to 13 percent in 1993 (Kessler, 1995). Another study showed that the decade-and-a-half decrease in smoking
among minors had slowed down in the time since the Joe Camel campaign began (interview with staff attorney, July 5, 1995). Although the
evidence developed by the Commission staff during the investigation did
not offer direct evidence that Joe Camel caused increased smoking among
minors, Yao and Steiger believed the use of a cartoon character with
obvious appeal to minors in cigarette ads called for action on the part of
the Commission. The absence of "direct evidence that Joe Camel was the

decisive factor in increasing underage smoking was not surprising," Yao argued in a strongly worded dissent. But given the compelling public policy objective in this case—to discourage smoking among those least able to understand its heavy costs—he insisted that the evidence presented, revealing the appeal of Joe Camel to those under eighteen years of age, "was central to the agency's consumer protection mission" (Dissenting Statement of Commissioner Dennis A. Yao in *R. J. Reynolds Tobacco Company—Camel Cigarettes,* File No. 932-3162: 106).

In light of the strong dissents by Steiger and Yao and the widespread public interest the Joe Camel proceeding had generated, the three commissioners who voted to close the investigation took the unusual step of publicly defending their reasons for their action. In a joint statement, Owen, Azcuenaga, and Starek gave what amounted to a defense of the Reagan years at the FTC. Without evidence of consumer injury, they insisted, the commissioners had no authority to pursue worthy policy objectives. "Although it may seem intuitive to some that the Joe Camel advertising campaign would lead more children to smoke or lead children to smoke more," they argued, "the evidence to support that intuition is not there. Our responsibility as commissioners is not to make decisions based on intuition but to evaluate the evidence and determine whether there is reason to believe that a proposed respondent violated the law" (Joint Statement of Commissioners Mary L. Azcuenaga, Deborah K. Owen, and Roscoe B. Starek III, in *R. J. Reynolds,* File No. 932-3162). In effect, the majority in this case were not persuaded that the Joe Camel ad created new smokers; the evidence could be interpreted in such a way that the cartoon character was merely a successful marketing device that encouraged brand-switching among those who already smoked. That Joe Camel was a commercial practice of questionable morals was possible; that cigarette smoking threatened the health of children was certain. But the FTC had no authority, Owen, Starek, and Azcuenaga claimed, to make moral judgments about ads or to inoculate children against unhealthy habits. The Commission's task was limited to preventing consumer injury—and there was no evidence that would provide reason to believe that Joe Camel increased smoking.

The FTC's deadlock over national advertising was symptomatic of the fundamental disagreement in the Bush administration over regulatory policy. Yet, as Clinton could not replace any of Bush's commissioners until Deborah Owen's term ended in September 1994, political time seemed to have passed the Commission by. We are not depressed," an attorney in Chairman Steiger's office noted in the summer of 1993. "We are still pursuing the cautious activism that has distinguished the chairman's tenure here. But clearly we are not part of the new regime; we are not on the new administration's radar screen; and nothing will change this year" (personal interview, July 26, 1993).[16]

The impression of the FTC's staff that the main drama of regulatory politics might not include the FTC was strengthened by the Commission's paralyzing split in its celebrated antitrust case against Microsoft. The Microsoft case marked the FTC's most ambitious attempt to revitalize enforcement action against vertical restraints of trade. After a three-and-a-half-year investigation, the staff recommended that the Commission issue complaints against the world's largest software company for holding computer manufacturers to agreements that allegedly stifled competition. Among these practices was "exclusive dealing," in which Microsoft licensed its popular operations software, DOS and Windows, on an all-or-nothing basis, requiring computer companies to pay royalties to Microsoft on every personal computer they shipped, even if another company's operating system was installed in the machine.[17] The Microsoft case received substantial attention by both the general and computer press. Not only did this case rely on vertical restraints, which conservatives tended to discount as irrelevant to consumer welfare, but it involved a company that had sales of nearly $4 billion during 1993. More significant, conservatives and certain business concerns celebrated Microsoft as a "national treasure" because it had helped the United States dominate the international computer software market. According to the FTC staff, however, Microsoft's ruthless control of operating systems for personal computers threatened U.S. dominance in the long run by retarding price and perfor-

[16] This is not to say that the problems at the Commission level left the agency in a condition of ennui. Indeed, by the summer of 1993, all the important staff positions at the FTC were filled by long-time activist professionals who encouraged the staff to pursue consumer and antitrust cases aggressively. Mary Lou Steptoe, who replaced Kevin Arquit as head of the Bureau of Competition, and Christian White, who replaced Barry Cutler at the Consumer Protection Bureau, continued the "enforcement-oriented" agenda of their predecessors. Their impressive records further confirm the importance of the Chair and the Bureau directors in controlling the day-to-day business of the Commission (for example, see Cindy Skrzycki, "Shaping an Anti-trust Agenda: Tinsletown Pales Next to the FTC's Crew of Acting Activists," *Washington Post*, November 30, 1993: D1).

[17] Another part of the complaint against Microsoft was direct tying of the licensing of Windows to the licensing of DOS. Computer vendors charged that Microsoft told them if they wanted to purchase Windows, they had to purchase DOS as well. Still another complaint charged Microsoft with "technological tying," the manipulation of code in its Windows system to create the appearance that other DOS systems, such as Novell's DR DOS, was not compatible with it.

mance competition (*FTC: Watch,* August 2, 1993: 1–2). Indeed, Microsoft's near-monopoly of the market for operating systems installed in personal computers differentiated it from the sort of vertical restraint cases that many economists oppose, that is, those where a company's market share is not an issue.

Just as she had in the Joe Camel case, Steiger exerted strong leadership in bringing the bitterly divisive Microsoft initiative before the Commission. But, again, her efforts went for naught. The Commission divided evenly, with the chairman and Yao supporting the case, while Owen and Azcuenaga opposed it.[18] A tie vote, in effect, ended the Commission's investigation of Microsoft. But the FTC's deadlock in this matter did not end the government's investigation of the software giant. In a startling and virtually unprecedented development, the Justice Department, whose Antitrust Division was now led by Clinton appointee Ann Bingaman, asked the FTC for a copy of the file that the Commission had compiled during its exhaustive investigation of Microsoft. The Bureau of Competition could not have handed over the file if the Microsoft case had been closed. But three votes were needed to end the investigation. With the approval of Steiger and Yao, but over the objections of Owen and Azcuenaga, Mary Lou Steptoe, who had recently replaced Kevin Arquit as Director of Competition, informed the commissioners that she intended to honor the Justice Department's request. This was a dramatic development in the annals of antitrust policy; as *FTC: Watch* reported soon after Bingaman's action, "Experts cannot recall another time in the 79-year history of the FTC that the Department of Justice picked up a case that the FTC had been unable to dispose of" (August 2, 1993: 2). Bingaman's bold stroke was due in part to congressional pressure: the request for the FTC's files followed letters from two members of the Senate Judiciary Committee, Howard W. Metzenbaum (D-Ohio) and Orrin G. Hatch (R-Utah), suggesting that Justice take over the investigation if the FTC could not decide what to do with it. No less important was Bingaman's ambition to address the problem of "monopolization," to focus Justice's gaze on the concentration of business power that was encouraged by the Reagan revolution. Microsoft, with its more than 80 percent share of the market for operating systems to run IBM-compatible desktop computers, represented just the sort of antitrust case that would signal a dramatic departure from the Reagan and Bush years (*New York Times,* July 25, 1993).

---

[18] Commissioner Roscoe Starek recused himself from the Microsoft case because of his inherited stock holdings in IBM.

Thus, notwithstanding Steiger's masterful efforts to forge a new consensus at the FTC, by 1993 the Commission was badly divided. Some of this might be attributable to the dissolution of discipline and loyalty to the defunct Bush regime and its holdover chairman. Moreover, as Commissioner Azcuenaga warned, the intrusion of the FDA and the Justice Department on the agency's prerogatives in consumer protection and antitrust policy might "create a public perception that the agency is irresolute and inept" (cited in *FTC: Watch,* August 2, 1993). That such a view was gaining currency both within and outside the FTC testified to the failure of the Bush administration's strategy to stake out a middle ground in regulatory policy that would transcend the bitter factionalism of the Reagan years.

Ultimately, Steiger's leadership by consensus was defied by fundamental disagreements between liberals and conservatives over the meaning of unfair and deceptive business practices. Pragmatism and good administration, in the absence of a conceptual framework, could not overcome these disagreements. The philosophical differences about the appropriate authority of the Commission, Steiger acknowledged in late 1992, had also thwarted her efforts to persuade Congress to reauthorize the FTC (J. Steiger interview). Whereas the Senate, fearing that the Commission might once again run amok, supported continuing the restriction on the Commission's authority to employ the controversial unfairness standard in advertising rules, the House, persuaded that this restriction on the Commission's authority crippled its ability to police the unethical marketing of alcohol and cigarettes, wanted it lifted.

This legislative impasse finally came to an end in 1994, when Congress gave the FTC its first legislative mandate in twelve years. But this statute is based on an uneasy compromise, one that codified the disagreements that had buffeted the Commission since the late 1970s. The reauthorization ended the ban on unfairness rulemaking but codified the FTC's own policy statement of 1980—its mea culpa for the kid-vid controversy—that established a three-part test to determine unfair acts: those that cause or are likely to cause substantial injury to consumers; are not reasonably avoidable by consumers themselves; and are not outweighed by countervailing benefits to consumers or competition. Advertising interests and conservatives were appeased by this more precise definition. But the statute did not include the sort of limitations that Miller had hoped to see codified. Miller and Muris wanted to codify a more restrictive definition of deception, one that the Commission adopted in the 1980s but was not put into the reauthorization statute. They also wanted "public policy" relegated, at most, to a minor, reenforcing role—but the reauthorization bill allowed public policy to be used in support of action, although it can no longer be the "primary basis" for the determination of unfairness.[19]

In effect, then, the 1994 FTC Improvements Act marked a compromise between business and public-interest advocates; they had agreed to disagree over the meaning of unfairness.[20] The law was "a cut-and-paste solution to the legislative impasse," a staff attorney observed, "but no real resolution of the policy disagreement itself" (personal interview, June 19, 1995). Necessarily, the polarizing debate among Commissioners and staff about the appropriate balance between public-policy considerations and direct evidence of consumer injury that characterized the Joe Camel case would continue to be a principal part of any initiative to regulate commercial speech. Thus, the objective that Miller and Muris saw as essential to institutionalizing the Reagan revolution at the FTC—precise statutory definitions of deception and unfairness—remained an elusive goal.

Attempting to steer between the Scylla of militant activism and the Charybdis of undue restraint, Steiger set an extremely cautious course as chairman, choosing to increase output, restore lost resources, and rebuild relationships with important constituencies. Known as a consensus leader, and being as argumentative as neither a lawyer nor an economist, Steiger may have lacked the background to enter the policy debate vigorously. But perhaps she also read the politics of a fourteen-year stalemate accurately, choosing instead to achieve the results she could with her acknowledged gift of building internal consensus—results that might never have emerged under a more confrontational style of leadership.

[19] Conference Report on H.R. 2243, Federal Trade Commission Act Amendments of 1994, *Congressional Record,* House, July 21, 1994, Section 9 (Definition of Unfair Acts or Practices), H6007. Muris argues that the reauthorization law represents a "complete victory," insofar as it does not allow public policy to constitute an independent basis of unfairness (correspondence with the authors, April 14, 1995). But many FTC staff members and consumer activists disagree, hoping that Congress and the courts will eventually accept public policy considerations as a significant, if not independent, basis for judging a business practice as unfair. "Tim [Muris] used to always say that when Congress comes to you guys with some crazy idea, you should be able to respond, 'Gee, we would like to do that, but our statute does not allow for it,' " an attorney in the Bureau of Consumer Protection recalled. "I don't think the reauthorization bill is quite that restrictive" (telephone conversation, November 11, 1994).

[20] See, for example, Wally Snyder (president of the American Advertising Federation) and Bruce Silverglade (legal director of the Center for Science in the Public Interest), "Does FTC Have an 'Unfair' Future?" *Advertising Age,* March 28, 1994.

9

The EPA under George Bush

> The devitalization of the governing power is the malady of
> democratic states. As the malady grows the executives . . .
> are pressed and harassed by the haggling of parties, by the
> agents of organized interests, and by the spokesmen of sectar-
> ians and ideologues.
>
> WALTER LIPPMANN, *The Public Philosophy*

The Environmental Protection Agency, along with environmental policy, provides a reliable barometer which we can use to gauge the shifts in the Bush administration's regulatory program. Perhaps more than any other policy area, protecting the environment illustrates the transition from an experiment with regulatory pragmatism to a reinvigorated commitment to regulatory relief. As we have noted, the hoped-for political benefits of a more moderate stance on regulatory policy never materialized for President Bush. Indeed, public lobbyists only grudgingly acknowledged the positive role played by the administration and continued to press for tight command–control-type regulations even after the president was forthcoming on issues of concern to them. Thus, the administration's initial experience with environmental policy served as a lightning rod for the conservative contention that a policy of pragmatism would lead to nothing but regulation run amok and costly, intrusive new programs that could never really be modulated by executive oversight. By late 1990, on the heels of President Bush's crowning environmental achievement, passage of the Clean Air Amendments Act, conservatives in the White House were already coalescing a strategy of regulatory confrontation that would employ the Competitiveness Council as their institutional base of operations.

To fully understand the Bush administration's retreat from regulatory pragmatism, one must appreciate the fact that the commitment to this approach, particularly with regard to environmental policy, was primarily a product of political expediency in the 1988 presidential campaign rather than the outgrowth of any high-minded evaluation of ecological principles. A turn to environmental policy, along with his public commitment to promote a more vigorous education policy, no doubt offered George Bush an opportunity to lend some substance into his vision of a kinder, gentler America and to put his distinctive stamp on policy, thereby emerging from the shadow of Ronald Reagan. However intuitively convincing these arguments may be, they are, in the end, merely speculative. If true, they probably facilitated the president's decision to embark on a more active environmental agenda, but, without any firm evidence about George Bush's deeper motives, the suggestion that embracing environmental protection was in some respects an oedipal exercise through which Bush could finally transcend Reagan in order to establish his own political identity amounts to little more than pop psychology. What we do know is that the packaging of Bush as an environmental president dedicated more broadly to a kinder, gentler vision of America was born out of an electoral calculation intended to assure Republican control of the White House. That calculation translated into specific campaign promises, including, most significantly, a reauthorization of the Clean Air Act, which, once asserted publicly, demanded a serious effort at redemption.

The Selling of an Environmental President

While the American public has witnessed many fascinating transformations through which politicians have reinvented themselves (our thoughts turn perhaps to "cold warrior" Richard Nixon's negotiations with the People's Republic of China or Dixiecrat/segregationist Strom Thurmond's hiring African Americans for his senate staff), surely one of the most remarkable was the emergence of George Bush as an environmentalist. Many environmentalists often chided Ronald Reagan for being a "cowboy capitalist," but that derisive moniker could perhaps more fairly be applied to George Bush, who after his service in World War II moved to Texas and started a successful oil business. Moreover, throughout his public career Bush drew his political support from a conservative corporate base. The improbability, indeed the irony, of George Bush as an environmental advocate registers most sharply when one reflects on the role he played as President Reagan's point man in the effort to rein in perceived regulatory excesses; Bush's position as chairman of the Task Force on Regulatory Relief clearly marked him as a leading protagonist in the morality play of the 1980s that pitted defenders of free enterprise against public lobbyists. How is it, then, that a millionaire Texas oilman, conservative friend of big business, and top administrator of a government body designed to ratchet down federal regulation became an apostle of environmental protection?

To answer this question we must begin by frankly admitting that, despite his protestation that he was always an environmentalist, George Bush never publicly embraced the cause prior to the 1988 presidential election campaign. We in fact can date precisely the emergence of environmental protection as a central issue for the Bush campaign. According to Vince Breglio, a polling analyst for the vice-president's campaign organization, those managing the election for Bush and his running mate, Dan Quayle, became concerned with their findings that by mid-summer of 1988 the economic issues that had propelled Ronald Reagan into the White House were not striking a strong, responsive chord with the electorate (*Congressional Quarterly Weekly Report,* Jan. 20, 1990: 139). This anxiety was compounded by their numbers indicating that the critical state of California, with its electoral votes, was looking like a toss-up race. It was in this context that the campaign managers began casting about for an issue that would "connect" for the vice-president. Through careful polling and focus-group study they hit upon a nearly perfect solution, namely environmental protection: not only would this issue play well across the country, but more important, it would find a very receptive audience among California voters, who had demonstrated a deep interest in the entire array of environmental issues, from conserving natural resources to controlling air pollution and nuclear energy. The only problem was how to accomplish the metamorphosis of George Bush from champion of regulatory relief and unbridled economic growth to a patron of the environment.

This task entailed a twofold strategy. In the first instance the Bush campaign devoted a great deal of energy and resources to chipping away at its opponent's credibility on environmental protection. Thus began a powerful and unremitting attack on Governor Michael Dukakis's environmental record; the most memorable element of this approach was the Bush campaign's effective highlighting of the severe pollution problems of Boston Harbor. In a campaign television commercial exceeded in effectiveness only by the notorious Willie Horton ad,[1] the vice-president,

---

[1] This television commercial showed prisoners going through the proverbial revolving door, with a voiceover describing the release of first-degree murderers under the Massachusetts furlough program. The effectiveness of this ad was abetted by one that the conservative National Security Political Action Committee ran, featuring a police mug shot of Willie Horton, a convicted rapist, and a voiceover explaining how he skipped out on the furlough program supported by Governor Dukakis, only to rape and murder a woman in Maryland. The PAC Horton ad dared to break the unspoken rule against advertising that Horton was black, a rule that even the Bush campaign obeyed (Abramson, 1990: 34).

with Boston Harbor as a backdrop, explained how under Dukakis this body of water, which had enormous symbolic meaning as the site of the Boston Tea Party and the home of the frigate *Old Ironsides,* had become one of the most polluted in the nation. Undercutting the Massachusetts governor's environmental record, however, would not be sufficient in and of itself to make the issue work for the Bush campaign; something would have to be offered in an affirmative way to establish Bush's environmental bona fides. In a move designed to appeal specifically to the California electorate, Bush lent his support to a delay in issuing permits for oil exploration off the California coast, an astonishing position for one of the petroleum industry's best friends in government. More broadly and significantly, though, George Bush began to signal that as president he would press for reauthorization of the Clean Air Act, which had last been extended in 1977 and remained mired in Congress throughout the 1980s by concerted opposition from the Republican White House as well as prominent Democratic legislators. Specifically, he issued election promises to address the problems of acid rain and emissions of so-called greenhouse gases, both of which had been key sticking points on the various clean-air bills reported in the House and Senate (*Congressional Quarterly Weekly Report,* Jan. 20, 1990: 139). These pledges amounted to a campaign promise by George Bush to work for passage of a clean air act if elected.

Understanding the emergence of environmental protection as an election-year gambit, albeit a very significant one, sheds considerable light on the Bush administration's environmental program. To be sure, the immediate result was the one intended by the campaign staff: Dukakis looked less and less "green" as the summer of 1988 wore on, while Bush, by his specific assurances that he would tackle some of the central problems of clean air legislation, was able both to give some bite to his claim of pursuing a kinder, gentler vision of America and to establish enough credibility on issues of ecological concern to help win the White House. Looking beyond the horizon of the presidential election, the conspicuous place accorded environmental policy in the campaign committed Bush and his administration to a course of earnest, if pragmatic, efforts to deliver on his promises once he took office. The fact that this commitment was ostensibly formulated out of desperation in a political contest explains the deep suspicion with which Bush's environmental policy was regarded by public lobbyists. They had always been wary of placing too much faith in a president, much less in a Republican one who for eight years had chaired the Reagan administration's Task Force on Regulatory Relief. The somewhat facile and opportunistic development of the "new environmental George Bush" in 1988 also helps us to make sense of

Bush's abrupt return to the notion of regulatory relief three years later. Since there never was a deep and principled concern with environmental protection, it was a relatively painless matter to veer away from a pro-regulatory stance when it became obvious that little political ground was to be gained with environmentalists, while much was to be lost with core conservative constituencies of the Republican party. At the outset of his presidency, however, George Bush's electoral embrace of environmental policy yielded demonstrable gains for public lobbyists who had, so to speak, been wandering in the wilderness for eight years.

The Three Rs of Bush's Environmental Program

As President Bush assumed office in 1989, his environmental program began to take shape. The components of that program with the most important practical implications were the appointment of William Reilly as EPA administrator, the appointment of William Rosenberg as assistant administrator for air and radiation programs within the agency, and a determination to reauthorize the Clean Air Act. These components, Reilly, Rosenberg, and reauthorization, comprise what we might call the *three Rs* of the Bush environmental program. With the placement of Reilly, a professional environmentalist, at the helm of the EPA, President Bush signaled not only that he intended to highlight environmental policy but also that he intended the agency to adopt a proactive regulatory stance. In turning over the management of the EPA's air-quality programs to William Rosenberg, Bush placed a talented and energetic executive in a position critical to developing the centerpiece of the administration's environmental program, reauthorization of the Clean Air Act. Taken together, these measures illustrate a determination to get Bush's presidency into the environmental mainstream. It must be noted, though, that they were not intended to surrender en masse to advocates of environmental regulation; both Reilly and Rosenberg reflected the pragmatism that Bush favored, while their unflinching insistence on strong science as the foundation for any policy decision demonstrated that they were not willing to pay any price for a reauthorized Clean Air Act. Bush's three Rs meant that there would be vigorous leadership at the EPA that could count on strong White House support for sensible clean-air legislation. This environmental pragmatism was clearly illustrated by one of the new president's statements on environmental policy: "Our administration has crafted a new commonsense approach to environmental issues, one that honors our love of the environment and our commitment to growth"

(EPA, 1992: 5). Recalling our early discussion of environmentalism (Chapters 3 and 6), this statement is especially significant in that it explicitly articulates an intent to transcend the inherent tension between environmental protection and capitalist development that public lobbyists and proponents of regulatory relief took as a given. In retrospect, this was an extremely daunting, if admirable, undertaking.

Perhaps more than any single action, the appointment of Bill Reilly as EPA administrator exemplified what a feature article in *The Economist* referred to as "the greening of George Bush" (June 17, 1989: 29–31). In marked contrast to Ann Burford, Ronald Reagan's initial appointee as EPA administrator, Reilly brought with him a far different pedigree as well as a wealth of experience in environmental advocacy. Whereas Ms. Burford, a product of the Sagebrush Rebellion, reflected not merely a conservative's concern but a deep, Rocky Mountain-region resentment over the federal government's intrusiveness on private enterprise, Mr. Reilly came to the EPA with an Ivy League education—he, like Bush, was a Yale graduate—and a high degree of comfort with what can best be termed the "Washington establishment" (Fiorina, 1977). It would be fair to say that, as much as Ann Burford viewed herself and was viewed by others as an outsider intent on reducing the impact and burden of environmental laws under the banner of regulatory relief, William Reilly presented the image of a consummate insider committed to the prudent implementation of effective environmental protection programs. Moreover, Mr. Reilly came to the EPA from the presidency of the Conservation Foundation. Though not one of the more radical or uncompromising public-lobby organizations devoted to preserving the environment, the Conservation Foundation was unquestionably a key player in the subgovernmental politics as well as in the national debates on environmental policy. Mr. Reilly, for his part, had taken advantage of his advocacy position to advance the cause of international conservation efforts. The basis of this activity, a belief that effective environmental policy ultimately had to recognize that environmental problems spilled over national boundaries and therefore required transnational policy approaches, became a hallmark of Mr. Reilly's administration at the EPA. Explaining this commitment in an EPA report, Reilly insisted that:

> EPA and other federal agencies today face a host of international environmental problems that demand new levels of cooperation among the nations of the earth. Stratospheric ozone depletion, ocean pollution, species extinction, habitat loss, climate change, rain forest destruction, and acid rain are just some of the daunting problems that cut across national boundaries.

The United States has a limited ability to solve any of these problems alone. (EPA, 1992: 40)

Along with the reauthorization of the Clean Air Act, the eventual signing in 1992 of the Pact on International Environmental Cooperation at the Rio summit and the negotiation of eighteen bilateral agreements with other nations on ecological issues stand as testimony to the personal commitment of William Reilly to a strong, positive regulatory role for the federal government.

Beyond his educational and professional background and his devotion to the cause of conservation, Mr. Reilly differed from Ann Burford in one other very important respect: unlike Ms. Burford, he brought with him to his position as EPA administrator a philosophical framework that allowed him to develop pragmatic positions on the responsibilities of the agency. This framework entailed an unflinching determination to protect the environment, provided strong science offered a convincing justification for government action. Indicative of this determination, one of Reilly's first important decisions was to commission a study by the EPA's independent Science Advisory Board (SAB) to guide the agency's policy. That report, entitled *Reducing Risk,* served as a blueprint for EPA policy from 1990 to 1992 and emphasized the need for strong science, both to determine risk and to identify the most effective means of addressing those risks discovered to be significant. Reilly subsequently empaneled a group of outside scientists to develop specific recommendations on what the EPA needed to do to enhance the role of science in policymaking. This second report, *Safeguarding the Future: Credible Science, Credible Decisions,* was released in 1992 and detailed specific areas of scientific research that would strengthen the EPA's capacity to make good policy and reevaluate regulations already in place. Built on the commitment of William Ruckleshaus and Lee Thomas to develop a sound scientific foundation for any EPA action, Reilly's philosophical framework differed dramatically from Burford's insistence on strong science, which, as we have seen, was more of a mantra intoned to halt federal action, much as the tobacco industry historically had argued against regulation by insisting that there was no scientific proof of a connection between smoking and lung cancer. Insofar as science is an inductive process, it, of course, can never produce "proof" but only a preponderance of evidence to create a compelling case. Even this standard, however, is sufficient to provide decisionmakers with a firm basis to reject policies that do not meet the criterion of strong science. It was in this sense that Reilly sought to rely on strong science to guide EPA policy. A good example of how the strong science standards could work as a brake on regulation may be seen in the EPA's lifting of a ban on a family of chemical fungicides known as EDBCs, which are applied to fruits and vegetables to minimize spoilage. EDBCs had been shown to be carcinogenic in laboratory studies on animals. However, after more definitive scientific information was developed, Reilly reversed EPA policy, asserting:

> Good science drove this policy. . . . We have better data on the actual residues on food, showing very low or undetectable residues in all cases. We have more information on farmers' application methods and how they can change them to reduce residues on food. And, importantly, we are able to base our decision on a more thorough assessment of animal laboratory studies, which caused us to lower our estimate of EDBC's potency in causing cancer. (cited in *New York Times,* Feb. 14, 1992: B6)

Clearly, science, as delineated by the reports Reilly commissioned, was a double-edged sword at the EPA, which at times could cut against federal regulation.

Borrowing from the comments of the EPA official we cited in Chapter 6 as complaining about Burford's lack of commitment to environmental protection, we can say that Bill Reilly had a clear vision of both what the agency should do and what it should not do. Ironically then, we see that in the Bush administration the EPA and the FTC in some measure reversed roles, as Reilly relied on a pragmatism grounded firmly in an analytic framework, while his counterpart, Janet Steiger, employed a pragmatism oriented more toward professional enforcement than a grand vision. Not surprisingly, the EPA under Bush therefore proved to be a far more proactive and aggressive regulatory agency, though one that definitely was attuned to the idea that there were limits to agency action.

Science was for Reilly at the EPA much like economics for James Miller at the FTC—a regulatory pole star, guiding him on when to move aggressively and when to resist intervention. This comparison is all the more significant since science as a criterion, unlike economics, is less likely to predispose a decisionmaker to focus on the opportunity costs of a policy and thus more likely to invoke regulatory power. Indeed, some saw this as a serious weakness in Reilly's administration. Dick Morganstern, an acting director of the Office of Policy, Planning and Evaluation (OPPE), the EPA's economic analysis arm, credited Bill Reilly with rebuilding the agency and bringing to it the outlook of a "reasonable environmentalist" but also complained that Reilly was "not prepared to make hardball decisions on an economic basis" (D. Morganstern personal interview). This unwillingness to bring economic analysis sharply to bear on environmental policy may have been a disappointment to those at OPPE who believed that an economic framework offered the best means of achieving a pragmatic and balanced environmental policy, but more importantly, according to Morganstern, it antagonized the conservatives entrenched in the White House domestic-policy staff and OIRA. In this sense, Reilly's commitment to strong science accomplished two things: it did impose a discipline on environmental policymaking, but it also joined a philosophical debate with those in the Bush administration who still favored regulatory relief. Thus, with a strong environmentalist who advanced a philosophical framework promoting aggressive, albeit principled, regulation in charge of the EPA, it is little wonder that the agency became a flash point of regulatory politics. Reilly was able to continue to operate effectively in an increasingly hostile environment largely because he relied on strong scientific argument and, perhaps even more importantly, as Dick Morganstern noted, "He is very adroit at knowing when to fight and when to give in. Reilly is also very generous with his time for the [Republican] Party and earns his chits" (D. Morganstern interview).

If William Reilly was a strong advocate of what we have labeled Bush's "regulatory pragmatism," he was equally an heir to the legacy of regulatory reform begun in the late 1970s under the Carter administration and resuscitated under the second stewardship of William Ruckleshaus at the EPA. The main thrust of this reform effort remained making environmental protection more efficient. Reilly's insistence upon strong science, risk assessment, pollution prevention, and flexibility fit into this bipartisan reform model. At the end of the day, however, this kind of reform could never seriously challenge the public lobby regime and at best could nudge the Washington establishment toward a more efficiency-conscious direction. (On the limitations of reform under Reilly, see Landy, Roberts, and Thomas, 1994.)

The key flaw in regulatory reform is that it focuses on but two dimensions of a regulatory regime, ideas and policy. Reilly never seemed to recognize, as did his more radical adversaries on the Competitiveness Council and in the White House, that environmental regulation was driven as much by its institutional as its intellectual and policy dimensions. Indeed, we believe that unless institutions are addressed directly reform is unlikely to influence the core problems of regulation under the public lobby regime, namely, the tendency to write highly specific and inflexible laws, the propensity to make policy within a narrow, albeit fairly permeable, issue network, and the incentive to shift ultimate decisions into the courts as issues of programmatic rights. The one truly hopeful sign in the Reilly administration was the effort to rely on regnegs and other cooperative decision-making models. This clear effort at institutional reform, though, was never a top priority with Administrator Reilly. That an institutional strategy is indispensable to successful reform is clearly illustrated by the Miller tenure at the FTC where not only were the public lobby regime's ideas challenged by an intellectual framework, but also its institutional bases were confronted in a purposeful way.

Along with Bill Reilly, the most notable appointment George Bush made to the EPA was William Rosenberg as assistant administrator for air and radiation. His background as an effective administrator and engineer, along with his considerable state-level experience with air pollution control in Ohio, made him a strong choice to lead the fight for a tough but commonsense new Clean Air Act. Rosenberg, moreover, brought with him a commitment to putting in place a more cooperative approach to writing and implementing environmental regulations, an approach that would avoid the drawn-out and debilitating court struggles that had always followed the issuing of major new EPA rules. What Rosenberg hoped to bring into being was an approach to environmental policy that shifted the emphasis from compliance with specific deadlines, mandates, and rules to achievement of environmental objectives. As he put it, his model for environmental policymaking was predicated on "strong performance standards with a flexible [regulatory] process and measurable results" (W. Rosenberg interview). The assistant administrator expostulated that "in business as well as the "enviro" community there is too much emphasis on compliance and not enough on meeting goals" (Rosenberg interview). This results-oriented view of environmental policy comported well with the regulatory pragmatism advanced by the Bush administration and nicely complemented Administrator Reilly's insistence on strong science as a basis for progress in environmental protection. Rosenberg's cooperative style of policymaking was tested with the 1990 Clean Air Act, both at the stage of writing the legislation and later in the crafting of regulations to implement the law.

Reauthorization of the Clean Air Act, the third of Bush's environmental three Rs, was to be the primary legislative objective of the EPA in the Bush presidency and to boldly establish its environmental bona fides. Although George Bush's devotion to environmental protection grew out of a political campaign strategy, not a commitment to the cause, it did bind him to a postelection good-faith effort to produce tangible results in that policy arena. The new Clean Air Act was to reflect the president's "commonsense approach" to environmental protection, and the new EPA leadership took advantage of the opportunity to apply its notions of strong science and cooperation in pursuit of that larger purpose. Reauthorization, then, served broadly as a highly visible experiment in regulatory pragmatism but more specifically in the principles of strong science and cooperative policymaking as a basis for pragmatism. The results of that experiment demonstrated not only the tremendous promise of such an approach but also its inherent political limitations. To a great extent, the reauthorization of the Clean Air Act illustrated how good ideas combined with presidential leadership can carry the day in environmental politics. With equal force, however, the fate of the 1990 Clean Air Act after President Bush affixed his signature to the legislation demonstrated once again that successful pursuit of regulatory change requires not only good ideas and policies but, more importantly, a large and long-term investment of political capital to overcome the institutional inertia generated by established interests and patterns of regulatory politics.

The 1990 Clean Air Amendments Act

From its last amendment in 1977 through 1990, federal clean-air legislation had served as a case study in Washington gridlock. Although public lobbyists and their congressional allies had widespread popular support for a Clean Air Act, specific elements of the sweeping new bill helped to forge a coalition of aggrieved minority interests powerful enough to block enactment. Through the 1980s, moreover, the Reagan administration had vigorously resisted all major environmental initiatives in Congress. That opposition, as we have seen, was not sufficient to prevent Superfund reauthorization and other environmental measures, but, in the case of the Clean Air Act, Congress itself was a house divided. Unlike TOSCA, Superfund, or RCRA, air-pollution control pitted environmentalists against a united front of business and labor interests from the auto industry as well as eastern and midwestern states whose high-sulfur coal-mining industries and public utilities that burned that coal would be severely burdened by stringent new regulations. More importantly, though, congressional representatives of these interests occupied critical legislative positions: Robert Byrd of West Virginia, a leading coal state, was Majority Leader of the Senate, and John Dingell, whose congressional district included the Detroit area, home to the big three car-makers, chaired the House Energy and Commerce Committee, through which any legislation had to move. Their implacable opposition in combination with President Reagan's created a political bottleneck that choked off the repeated efforts of congressional sponsors to bring clean-air legislation to a floor vote. Under such circumstances any bill was doomed. After the 1988 election, however, the contours of environmental politics changed dramatically, and the prospects for clean-air legislation brightened considerably. In addition to George Bush replacing Ronald Reagan and promising to work for a new Clean Air Act, George Mitchell replaced Byrd as Majority Leader in the Senate. Mitchell, in contrast to Byrd, represented Maine, a state which suffered the ill effects of acid rain caused by the emissions from utilities using high-sulfur coal. Mitchell, like Bush, was publicly committed to working for a Clean Air Act. The only remaining obstacle to passage was Dingell, who adamantly opposed tough new tailpipe emissions standards for the auto industry, which he contended had already borne the lion's share of air-pollution-control costs in the 1970s.

With Bush and Mitchell pushing hard for a bill, Dingell was under tremendous pressure to compromise. That compromise would have to be worked out with his arch rival, Henry Waxman (D-California), who chaired the House Energy and Commerce Committee's Subcommittee on Health and Environment. Ground-level ozone pollution and smog, both generated from automobiles, made Waxman's Los Angeles district one of the worst air-quality regions in the nation. Not surprisingly, Waxman was as strong a proponent of relatively inflexible, command–control regulation of auto emissions and strict timetables for compliance as Dingell was of wide discretion in enforcement and generous timetables. As Bill Rosenberg explained, both Dingell and Waxman were pressed very hard by Bush, who wanted to redeem his pledge to be an "environmental president," and by Mitchell, who was determined to get a clean air act. A compromise was finally struck under which Dingell was able to extend the compliance period for tailpipe emission standards and to insert language directing the EPA to assess the possibility of less stringent standards than those proposed for the second-round performance target in the year 2003, while Waxman achieved agreement to tougher standards than either those in President Bush's bill or those advocated by the auto industry and at least the possibility of tougher standards in 2003 (*Congressional Quarterly Weekly Report,* Oct. 7, 1989: 2621). Most observers recognized, as Assistant Administrator Rosenberg did, that "once Dingell and Waxman resolved their differences, the CAA was a done deal" (W. Rosenberg interview). More precisely, the Dingell–Waxman compromise broke the gridlock and paved the way to deal effectively with the two remaining issues of contention, acid-rain provisions and the emission of airborne toxics.

As we have suggested in Chapter 6, the issue of acid rain moved into the headlines in the 1980s, propelled by an accumulation of scientific evidence that sulfate (SO_2) and nitrous oxide (NO_x) emissions from public utility plants in the midwest were reacting in the upper atmosphere to lower the pH levels of rain, which in turn, owing to prevailing weather patterns, was beginning to have measurable deleterious effects on forests and lakes in the northeast. Despite its instinctive suspicion of legitimating new regulatory issues, even the Reagan administration was drawn into acid-rain activities when it was pressured to sign a bilateral agreement by Canada, whose southeastern provinces were also feeling the impacts of acid rain generated by coal-fired utilities. Under these circumstances, it was inevitable that President Bush would include a significant set of acid-rain provisions in his clean-air bill. Just as important, George Mitchell's home state of Maine was one of the most severely affected by the problem.

Although the support of the White House and the Senate Majority Leader seemed to augur well for a strong bipartisan acid-rain provision, Bush and Mitchell approached the problem from fundamentally different perspectives. Their differences created a gap that had to bridged if a new clean air act was to emerge. The differences between Bush and Mitchell revolved around the fact that the president was determined to promote a pragmatic and flexible bill, while the Majority Leader favored a more *dirigiste* strategy. Essentially, the battle lines were drawn by Mitchell's initial support for an expensive scrubber bill, that is, one that mandated the installation of costly machinery in utility-plant smokestacks to "scrub" out the SO_2 or NO_x before they could be emitted. "This sort of command–control regulation," as Bill Rosenberg noted, "has always been the 'enviro's' bread and butter, and from Mitchell's point of view such a bill had the added virtue of protecting jobs in the Midwest where dirty [i.e., high-sulfur] coal was mined and burned" (W. Rosenberg interview). Of course, Mitchell's approach would also help to appease Senator Byrd and other representatives of Appalachian coal states. Unfortunately, this position ran directly counter to the administration's commitment to greater flexibility. In particular, Bush, Reilly, and Rosenberg all favored a market-oriented approach to environmental policy, long advocated by economists, and saw the new acid-rain problem as a golden opportunity to experiment along these lines.[2] Although not a problem as high-profile as that of auto emissions, acid rain was important enough to demand action, and therefore this impasse between the White House and Congress required a resolution. The logjam was broken by a critical compromise: Mitchell gave up the scrubber bill and supported the EPA's "least cost/ freedom of choice" proposal, that is, a market in pollution permits (see fn. 2, below), in exchange for the administration's commitment to a cap of 6 million tons of SO_2 emissions. In the end, largely through the efforts of Sununu, Darman, and conservatives in the Conference Committee, the emissions cap was raised to 10 million tons (still below the administration's initial proposal) in the final legislation, but the compromise was sustained. Neither environmentalists nor conservative critics of social regulation were entirely pleased with the outcome, though it is fair to say that the long-sought political prize of a reauthorized Clean Air Act with serious acid-rain provisions considerably assuaged all but the most hidebound environmentalists. Perhaps most important, argued Richard Ayers, then chairman of the National Clean Air Council, from the environmentalist point of view, the real story of the acid-rain provisions is that a definite cap was placed on SO_2 and NO_x emissions. If the market in permits worked more efficiently than command–control regulation, so much the better, but there would still be an enforceable limit on emissions (personal interview, July 1992).

The final area of serious contention in the 1990 Clean Air Act was the question of airborne toxics. Under the 1977 Clean Air Amendments Act and under congressionally sponsored reauthorizations, the EPA was required to "prove" a particular airborne toxic chemical was "unsafe" and then either regulate or ban its use. This method of policymaking flew in the face of both the criterion of strong science—proving the toxicity of over 189 suspect chemicals was not only painstaking but in many in-

---

[2] The EPA had been experimenting with market approaches, most notably emissions trading, since the late 1970s. The acid-rain provisions offered by the administration in 1990, however, went considerably beyond these experiments and sought to establish a market in tradable pollution permits. Based on the works of economist Ronald Coase, this approach allocates, through an auction, permits or licenses to emit pollutants at some arbitratary level (the 1990 Clean Air Act equated a permit with one ton of sulfur emissions, for example). A set number of permits is distributed via the auction, and then firms are free to use their permits, sell them, or accumulate them. Once the market is established, environmental organizations or private citizens may also enter the trade, thereby bidding up the price of permits and, coincidentally, the price of emitting pollutants. Acid rain is a particularly favorable choice for such a system, since it originates from large, identifiable, and easily monitored point sources, namely, power plants in the Midwest.

stances a highly indeterminate enterprise—and the criterion of pragmatism—there was no flexibility in the law, and the imprecision of the science involved almost invariably landed the EPA in court. The
administration's bill sought to attack the problem of airborne toxics differently by identifying industries suspected of generating the offending
chemicals and requiring them to install control technology. With regard
to the control technology, moreover, the 1990 act shifted away from the
1970s concept of Best Available Control Technology (BACT) to a more
flexible standard of Reasonably Available Control Technology (RACT).
The RACT standard applied not only to the question of airborne-toxics
provisions but also to the issues of acid rain and auto emissions. In the
Clean Air Act, RACT is defined as: ". . . a technology or emission
reduction strategy that is available in the market (used in other states or
nations) that is 'reasonable' in terms of cost." Under this new standard,
firms dealing with airborne toxics, public utilities dealing with SO_2 or
NO_x emissions, or auto manufacturers dealing with tailpipe emissions
would not be restricted to a single, high-cost option. In addition, the new
standard clearly shifted the policy emphasis toward pollution reduction as
opposed to technical regulatory compliance. This more flexible strategy
did not go far enough for environmentalists and, in fact, induced some
of their strongest supporters, such as Senator Albert Gore (D-Tennessee)
and Senator Frank Lautenberg (D-New Jersey), to lead an insurgent opposition to the entire piece of legislation (S. Mones interview). On the
question of airborne toxics, however, the Gore–Lautenberg gambit ultimately failed and the Bush administration essentially got its way; public
lobbyists and their allies would have been sacrificing too much to have
scuttled the entire bill for the sake of that one controversy.

With the enactment and signing of the 1990 Clean Air Amendments
Act, President George Bush, at least to his mind, had redeemed his campaign promise to pursue a vigorous but pragmatic environmental policy.
Reliance on the new RACT standard was an excellent example of this
pragmatism. Nonetheless, the law itself, according to an EPA publication, still represented a vast and complex undertaking that would require
the agency to issue fifty-five new regulations and thirty guidance documents in an initial two-year period (EPA, April 1992: 10). It was in the
writing of these regulations and the implementation of the law that Reilly
and Rosenberg really sought to put the stamp of regulatory pragmatism
on environmental policy.

As responsibility for the Clean Air Act shifted from Congress and
the White House for enactment to the EPA for implementation of the

law, it became clear that both Reilly and Rosenberg were intent upon instituting a more cooperative style of administration in environmental policy. The hallmarks of this style were (1) the promotion of voluntary pollution prevention agreements with industry and (2) the use of regulatory negotiations ("regnegs," for short) to write the rules necessary to implement the law. Both prevention strategies and regnegs were intended to increase flexibility and provide avenues for the introduction of strong science into policymaking. Just as importantly, though, they were intended to engender a policy process founded more on consensus-building than on the adversarial relations that had come to typify environmental regulation. To be sure, by the late 1980s any endeavor to increase cooperation among interested parties was significantly enhanced by their experience over two decades of contentious wrangling that almost invariably led to protracted court struggles over environmental regulation. Looking back over the Bush years, Deputy EPA Administrator Victor Kimm observed that there had been a "growing atmosphere of reconciliation" in environmental policy that was brought about not only by a concern with economic realities that could not be blithely ignored by public lobbyists but also by "a mellowing, more pragmatic approach" by business. Business, according to Kimm, exemplified "a higher sense of social responsibility, which was driven by market forces and a falling public image" (V. Kimm interview). This atmosphere of reconciliation no doubt contributed to the passage of the 1990 Clean Air Act; the tougher test of a cooperative approach, however, would lie in the implementation of the law and, in particular, the writing of specific regulations.

Fortunately, the EPA had been working hard to foster a climate conducive to cooperation and to establish its own credentials as an honest broker among competing interests. William Reilly's commitment to pollution prevention as an alternative to remediation through command–control regulation was evident from the outset of his tenure at the EPA. Indeed, he worked extremely hard for passage of the 1990 Pollution Prevention Act, which was approved along with the Clean Air Act, and reoriented national policy to accentuate source reduction rather than cleanup. Under Administrator Reilly, the agency established a number of outreach programs designed to induce business to "voluntarily" institute prevention measures toward the reduction of the emission of greenhouse gases, that is, those pollutants linked to the forecast of global warming through the greenhouse effect. These efforts included seven separate initiatives, including programs to establish corporate-wide purchasing frameworks through which energy efficiency and environmental costs are integrated into purchase decisions; promote mass purchasing of energy-efficient technology; and identify and publicize energy-efficient products. The most successful initiatives were the so-called green lights program, through which the EPA persuaded a number of major corporations to invest in lighting that reduced energy costs up to 54 percent in some cases, and the golden carrot program, an EPA-sponsored effort through which utility companies pooled over $30 million in rebate incentives to be awarded to the winner of a competition to build the greatest number of CFC-free refrigerators the fastest and the least expensively.[3] The significance of these and other programs was twofold. First, they signaled that the EPA would resist, even under an environmental president, any temptation to punish businesses for their "free ride" under regulatory relief by ratcheting up command–control regulation. Instead, the agency would explore a variety of market-oriented strategies and work with business firms to find mutually beneficial alternatives. Second, these efforts sent a message to the environmentalist community that, even in areas such as global warming where science had not established sufficiently powerful evidence to convince the agency to pursue tough regulation, Reilly was willing to attack a potentially serious problem. These initiatives therefore fostered a climate conducive to cooperating on the more nettlesome problems that arose in the implementation of the Clean Air Act.

The major challenge confronting the EPA in administering the new act, of course, was to write the fifty-five regulations necessary to implement the law. In order to avoid the bitter and litigious conflicts that had arisen in rulemakings for the early iterations of the Clean Air Act, both Reilly and Rosenberg were committed to bringing all sides together ahead of time to work out effective, if not always amicable, solutions. This meant a reliance on regnegs as a model for dispute resolution in rulemaking. As explained by the EPA:

> The goal [of regnegs] is to invite comment and develop agreement among all affected parties on a new regulation before it is formally proposed. (In the traditional approach, the Agency develops a proposal first, takes public comment, then reconciles diverse points of view.) Regulatory negotiations build consensus, avoid litigation, and demonstrate EPA's commitment to achieving the greatest environmental benefits in the most cost-effective ways. (EPA, 1992: 12)

---

[3] CFCs refer to chlorofluorocarbons, gases emitted from refrigeration compressors and linked to the destruction of the ozone layer in the upper atmosphere.

Although the EPA had engaged in some prior experimentation with reg-negs, Bill Rosenberg felt that they offered one of the few promising approaches to environmental policymaking and was determined to use the Clean Air Act as, in his words, "a model for negotiation on rulemakings." Of course, not all rules would be negotiated; some would be non-controversial and others would involve parties unwilling to compromise. Nevertheless, for those not infrequent cases of opposing parties with room to maneuver, regnegs held out an opportunity to pragmatically resolve differences.

Perhaps the best example of this approach is the writing of a Clean Air Act regulation on reformulated fuels. The act set strict regulatory performance standards for the automobile emission of volatile organic compounds (VOCs), which easily react in the air to form ground-level ozone, or smog. Under Rosenberg's guidance, the EPA sought to develop a less rigid approach and advanced the idea of using reformulated fuels to help control VOC emissions. Environmental scientists and engineers had known for some time that oxygenating gasoline and other fuels would reduce not only VOC emissions but also the evaporation of gasoline, which itself led to ozone formation. As reported in the *New York Times,* Rosenberg was able to bring about "an agreement . . . involving the environmental agency [EPA], state air regulators, the Sierra Club, the Natural Resources Defense Council and representatives of gasoline producers. In reaching a final accord, those organizations agreed not to lobby against the plan *or challenge it in court* (August 21, 1991; emphasis added).[4] Because these kinds of negotiations take place behind closed doors, a full airing of views without posturing is more likely, and the merits of scientific as well as economic and environmental arguments are likely to receive a fairer hearing. Moreover, Rosenberg felt that regnegs were more likely to move the environmental debate toward performance and away from mere statutory compliance.

Ironically, just as the EPA was commencing its efforts to implement

---

[4] The actual politics of the case were a bit more involved than the *Times* article suggests. According to Deputy Administrator Rosenberg, the negotiations also included the Environmental Defense Fund, the Automobile Association of America, and the American Petroleum Institute. After this group reached an accord, Senator Robert Dole weighed into the process to advance the interests of midwestern farmers and grain processors who wanted the agreement to lean more heavily on the use of ethanol for reformulation. Eventually this intervention bumped the negotiation up to the White House, and President Bush sided with Senator Dole. In the end, oil interests wound up with a bit less and ethanol producers more, but the agreement was honored.

the new Clean Air Act, the political winds were beginning to shift and a climate less favorable to cooperation began to emerge. By the middle of 1991, the White House domestic-policy staff and the Office of the Vice-President began a steady drumbeat of criticism, which supplemented the growing chorus of conservative critics who decried the growth of regulation under President Bush. It was clear, moreover, that the EPA was the primary target of their ire. In hindsight, Reilly and Rosenberg may well have left themselves (and the president) open to such criticism by relying so heavily on strong science as a criterion for policymaking. While conservative proponents of regulatory relief also advocated strong scientific backing for EPA policy, they, for the most part, saw science as a means of thwarting excessive regulation by setting a higher threshold for action. Reilly and Rosenberg saw science as a double-edged sword: it could surely help to ease regulation, as in the case of repealing the ban on EDBCs, but it could just as surely provide a powerful basis for regulatory action. Important too was conservatives' devotion to the criterion of strong science untempered by an equally strong dedication to strong economic criteria. Reilly, according to some at the EPA, was not overly interested in economics and, as a result, did not rely heavily on the EPA's Office of Policy, Planning and Evaluation, the one bureau in the agency specifically equipped to do cost–benefit analysis. The perception of Reilly as less than totally committed to employing economic criteria caused concern not only within the OPPE but, more significantly, at the White House. In fact, as the passage of the Clean Air Act became a virtual certainty in late 1990, Michael Boskin, Bush's chairman of the Council of Economic Advisors, felt it necessary to get a specific commitment from Reilly to "consider costs in clean air rulemakings" (*Inside EPA*, Jan. 8, 1993: 9–10). Little more than six months later, quiet agreements between Reilly and the CEA had given way to much more open criticism of the EPA administrator from the White House staff.

The Competitiveness Council Revives Regulatory Relief

It was in this environment that James Miller sarcastically dubbed Bush the "regulation president." In fact, Bush had alienated a substantial core of his political support by signing the Clean Air Act and other major new regulatory initiatives. Sadly for him, the hoped-for political pay-off never materialized, as he received only grudging credit from public lobbyists, and that evaporated quickly once conservative opposition from White

House domestic-policy staff developed around the implementation of the act and the writing of its attendant regulations. As Boyden Gray, Dick Darman, and John Sununu began raising the specter of over-regulation and as the 1992 presidential election neared, the lack of any political reward from his environmentally friendly policy of regulatory pragmatism drove George Bush back toward a policy of regulatory relief. Ironically, even as one presidential campaign caused the "greening" of George Bush, the subsequent one impelled him to revive the rhetoric of regulatory relief. As for Reilly, both he and his views on using strong science in conjunction with regulatory flexibility to promote a sound environmental policy became, as Rosenberg put it, "progressively frozen out of the policymaking circle." Conversely, conservatives favoring regulatory relief increasingly dominated those circles, and the primary instrument through which they were able to translate their critique into action was the Competitiveness Council.

As we argued in Chapter 7, a key to understanding the Competitiveness Council is the realization that, beyond helping to enforce the Paperwork Reduction Act (the ostensible basis for its operation), its staff was intent upon engaging the public lobby regime at the level of ideas. In no area was that more readily apparent than in the realm of environmental policy. In particular, the determination of Hubbard, McIntosh, and others at the Council to cast environmental regulation in terms of a *takings* problem meant that there was much more at issue than cost–benefit analysis or the financial impact of proposed regulations; cost issues revolve around the question of how much regulation, but the focus on property rights goes to the question of the legitimacy of regulation. This kind of discourse held the potential of transforming environmental policymaking by reopening questions that most had long considered settled, questions about whether the federal government ought to exercise broad regulatory powers to protect the environment and whether such regulatory powers posed an unacceptable threat to core political economic values.

This was a debate about philosophy, and the top leadership at the EPA clearly recognized it as such. Deputy Administrator Victor Kimm, a twenty-one-year veteran of the EPA, noted that the conflicts that developed between the Agency and the Quayle Council had to do mainly with the philosophical questions of what role the market should play in society and the sanctity of property rights (V. Kimm interview). Similarly, Luana Wilcher, the director of water programs, insisted that in their words and deeds on environmental policy the Council, as well as conservatives on the domestic-policy staff, was driven basically by ideological considerations (L. Wilcher interview). This was especially troublesome to Ms. Wilcher, a biologist, lawyer, and lifelong Republican who accepted the legitimacy of environmental protection as long as it was held to the standard of overwhelming scientific support. In her view, scientific defenses of regulatory action were, for the Quayle Council, ultimately beside the point since they did not address the philosophical issues. Both Kimm and Wilcher could point to specific examples to illustrate their frustration with the Council.

Kimm recounted a controversy with the Council over the use of a reporting form, known as "Form-R," which was developed to implement the Toxic Substances Control Act (TOSCA). Form-R was the reporting document for Title IV of TOSCA, the right-to-know provision of that law. According to Kimm, "this was a really dynamite piece of legislation. It got a clear commitment from business for a reduction in toxics . . . corporate America was willing to put its money into a greener image" (V. Kimm interview). The 1990 revision of TOSCA provided for more specific regulation of emissions inside plants, and Form-R was to be the reporting device to track those emissions. After the form was developed in consultation with business firms, the Council intervened at the urging of the Chemical Manufacturers Association and held up the issuance of the new form. While the public explanation from the Council was the excessive paperwork burden of the new document, Kimm insisted that the real issue that surfaced in the encounters with the Council was a philosophical objection to government intrusiveness. The debate about Form-R was especially vexing because businesses were in on the development stages and the EPA thought it had negotiated a good-faith agreement, only to have it undone in the eleventh hour.

In an analogous account, Wilcher related how the Council had interjected its own philosophical concerns on the issue of wetlands protection. In one of its most complex rulemakings, the EPA was charged with defining, for the purposes of preservation, what constituted a wetlands. The issue was joined when the Agency sought to prepare an updated manual for field staff who had to apply a definition in order to designate the borders of wetlands across the nation. Director Wilcher explained that:

> The EPA's approach was to define the surface and groundwater conditions that delineate a wetlands area. The right wing in the Bush administration, however, was not interested in science. Instead they cast the issue as an ideological one predicated on the constitutional question of *takings*. They were interested in a "philosophy of land ownership" rather than wetlands

regulation. Clearly, for them, if you destroy all economically viable uses there is compensation due. . . . They [landowners supporting the right wing] want to be able to do with their land whatever they please, and don't want government or anyone else telling them what they can do with it. This is the position advanced by the Competitiveness Council and was the basis for their holding up the wetlands regulation. (L. Wilcher interview)

Perhaps most striking in Wilcher's words is not so much her dismay as her near incredulity at having to reconsider, in the early 1990s, philosophical issues that environmentalists thought were resolved in the early 1970s. That incredulity, however, indicates the difference between, on the one hand, reformers like Wilcher, who wanted to pursue cost-effective regulation backed by strong science, or Kimm, who favored cooperative development of regulations, and, on the other, individuals on the Quayle Council who sought to carry out a regulatory revolution.

Their revolution, importantly, was not restricted to the substantive questions of environmental policy but also encompassed procedural issues that were just as integral to the public lobby regime. In this sense, the Competitiveness Council remained true to the initial promise of the Reagan revolution and regulatory relief. Their resolve to challenge the processes as well as the substance of environmental regulation is amply demonstrated in their intervention on the writing of the EPA's air-permits rule, a regulation critical to the successful implementation of the 1990 Clean Air Act. In one of the best commentaries on what the public lobby regime is really all about, *Congressional Quarterly* reporter Philip A. Davis observed, "To many key players in the 1990 debate over acid rain, automobile tailpipe emissions and air toxins, the linchpin of efforts to renew the Clean Air Act was Title V—the permitting section under which every major polluter was to have a permit delineating how much of which pollutants it could legally emit into the air" (*Congressional Quarterly Weekly Report,* May 23, 1992: 1441). At issue was Section 502(b-6) of Title V, a provision which states that the EPA administrator shall promulgate public permitting regulations, which establishes procedures under which public notice is given on permit applications and under which there is an opportunity for public comment as well as judicial review of final permit decisions at the insistence of not only the permit applicant but also *"any person who participated in the public comment process"* (PL 101-549). In other words, this section assured that environmentalists would retain a substantial role in the award of permits for any new plants or operations that might increase air emissions in a particular area and, beyond that, have standing to challenge any permit decision in court simply by virtue of their having participated in the public comment process.

The EPA did indeed promulgate such a rule on public notice to satisfy Section 502. However, at the behest of some businesses, the Competitiveness Council interceded and ultimately persuaded President Bush to intervene in support of an alternative rule. The administration's rule essentially would allow a firm to increase its pollution levels without submitting to a public comment period. Specifically, under the president's proposal the EPA would have forty-five days to review a new permit application, and state regulators would have the discretion to permit a firm to begin its production process before the review was finalized. On the surface, the vice president's people on the council were pushing to shorten the time frame with which businesses would have to cope in order to initiate a new plant or equipment. At a deeper level, however, this intervention struck at a central principle of the public lobby regime: public permitting. Just how radical a departure this was for Bush is indicated by the facts that (1) the Congress had defeated more or less the same loosening of public permitting when it was introduced as an amendment to the Clean Air Act in 1990, and (2) the Bush administration took the extraordinary step of overruling its own EPA administrator as well as the EPA general counsel, who asserted in a memorandum, "It is highly unlikely that a reviewing court would uphold the [administration's] regulation" (cited in *Congressional Quarterly Weekly Review*, May 23, 1993: 1441). Public permitting was, as Bill Rosenberg put it, "apple pie for the enviros" (Rosenberg interview). By attempting to directly weaken Title V regulations on public participation, the Competitiveness Council was striking at the heart of the public lobby regime in much the same way that the early Reagan appointees to regulatory agencies single-mindedly attacked what they perceived to be the privileged position enjoyed by public lobbyists.

Clearly, Vice-President Quayle and the Competitiveness Council were the heirs to regulatory relief, and they were in the ascendancy during the second half of President Bush's term. However, like their predecessors in the struggle for regulatory relief, the Competitiveness Council and its supporters on the White House domestic-policy staff were relegated to fighting a rear-guard action to protect their conceptions of economic freedom rather than leading a frontal assault on the regulatory state. The Council succeeded in once again establishing a bottleneck in the regulatory process that slowed the flow of new rules and provided opportunities to respond to particular business complaints. This strategy hinged on the use of centralized administrative control, which, in a delicious irony, placed the Quayle Council in opposition to more flexible approaches to regulation endorsed by the EPA.[5] The vice-president was also able to employ the Council as a sort of bully pulpit from which he and his aides could raise the philosophical questions they felt would reopen a vigorous debate about the nature of the public lobby regime. All of these accomplishments, however, it must be frankly stated, did not pose an immediate challenge to the regulatory regime. Indeed, just as in the Reagan years, the regulatory skirmishes at a high level of administrative centralization could not possibly substitute for a broad, popularly based political assault on the regulatory status quo. The Council's activities also shared another unfortunate parallel with the earlier regulatory relief effort; by raising the prospects of gutting environmental laws and emasculating the EPA through administrative action, the Competitiveness Council undermined pragmatic reforms favored by the agency's top leadership. The possibility of resuscitating that reform program would be left to the Clinton administration and the new EPA administrator, Carol Browner.

---

[5] An especially interesting example of the council's opposition to more flexible regulatory decisionmaking revolved around a controversy over writing a "top-down BACT" rule for prevention of significant deterioration permits (PSDs) under the Clean Air Act. Responding to White House concerns about regulatory cost and a 1987 lawsuit filed by the National Forest Products Association, Administrator Reilly promised to rewrite the EPA's strict 1987 BACT rule. After developing a new rule, Reilly balked at issuing it when he considered the intensity of the conflict among interested parties. Instead, he proposed a regneg that would encompass not only PSDs but the entire New Source Performance section of the Clean Air Act. The Quayle Council vigorously opposed the idea of a regneg, insisting, as its associate director, David Rivkin, argued, that the EPA had committed to issuing a new PSD rule and should honor that commitment. At issue for the Competitiveness Council and its supporters, particularly at OMB and OIRA, was the fact that regnegs would keep them out of the decisionmaking loop; despite their disdain for big and intrusive government, council members apparently were willing to insist on a highly centralized, bureaucratic process if it suited their purpose. As a final point, we should note that their opposition to regnegs was doubly ironic, since David Rivkin complained about the problem of regnegs not being open to the public, exactly the accusation leveled against the Competitiveness Council.

10

Conclusion: Social Reform and Divided Democracy—The Future of Regulatory Politics

> The most doubtful and difficult question connected with the administrative organization of progressive democracy concerns its ability to obtain and to keep popular confidence. Democracies have almost uniformly distrusted administrative officials who tend to escape direct popular control. The American people have had their fair share of this distrust.
>
> HERBERT CROLY, *Progressive Democracy*

The election of Democrat Bill Clinton in 1992 aroused the hope of public lobbyists that they had survived the Reagan revolution. For the first time in twelve years, the public lobby regime would have political allies inside the gates of the White House and the Executive Office Building, as well as the headquarters of regulatory agencies. Indeed, Clinton's running mate, Senator Al Gore of Tennessee, was a strong advocate of environmental causes. Environmentalists greeted Clinton's election with an inaugural ball and bold promises to strengthen federal environmental policies. Consumer activists were no less optimistic—many celebrated the election by hoisting sparkling cider, looking forward expectantly to renewed assaults on "unfair" advertising and noncompetitive corporate practices. Yet their hopes would soon be disappointed.

Neither Clinton's rhetoric nor his appointments conveyed a clear message about what purposes a national regulatory policy should serve. Shorn of a commitment to clearly defined purposes, the president's regulatory program degenerated into a promise to "reinvent government," a search for more efficient and responsive administrative methods that failed to instruct executive agencies about what the White House expected of them. In this sense, the Clinton administration displayed the same flaws as its predecessor, seeking to substitute bureaucratic competence and accountability for serious attention to a debate over the first principles of regulatory policy. As Peri Arnold has written about the Clinton plan to reinvent government:

> If government were nothing but a service provider about which consumers were displeased, reinvention through executive reorganization might be the solution. However, if our underlying problem is the inability to agree upon government purposes, then it is a ruse for the president to promise that the problem can be fixed by redesigning government. (Arnold, 1994: 31).

The wayward paths of the FTC and the EPA are instructive of the problems that attend efforts to subordinate a dialogue over the role of government to administrative design. As the case studies of the FTC and the EPA suggest, attacks on consumer and environmental regulation protection were strongly resisted unless supported by an intellectual framework that offered an alternative to social regulation. By the same token, our examination of these agencies during the Bush years revealed that aggressive regulatory oversight and talented White House staff were no substitute for a comprehensive plan of action. Bush's kinder, gentler conservatism failed to moderate the excesses of the Reagan revolution; nor did Bush's efforts to reach a modus operandi with public lobbyists establish a solid middle ground that could ameliorate the virulent, enervating administrative combat between advocates of social regulation and proponents of regulatory relief.

In the aftermath of the Reagan and Bush years, Clinton promised to heal the wounds left by the bitter struggles over social regulation during the past two decades. Just as Bush sought to ameliorate the more militant tendencies of the conservative movement, so Clinton ran as a "new" Democrat, promising to correct the worst deficiencies of progressive politics. But, as we indicate below, developments in consumer and environmental protection reveal that Clinton's new version of progressivism did not correct the worst deficiencies of the public lobby regime. As America approached the twenty-first century, the framework for a new consensus on social policy that could transcend the bitter antagonisms of the past two decades remained an elusive goal. At the same time, the very fractiousness of contemporary regulatory politics reinforces the systemic inertia of American politics, thereby posing a menacing obstacle to the emergence of still another regulatory realignment.

The Prospects and Limitations of Regulatory Change

Both the FTC and the EPA reflected the advent during the 1970s of the public lobby regime. The FTC was "seized" and invigorated by consumer lobbyists and their allies, while the EPA was created in the halcyon days of the environmental movement. The seizure and creation represent two significant examples of the realignment in regulatory policy that took place in the early 1970s. The general election of 1980, however, presented the public lobby regime with its first serious challenge. An administration came to power ostensibly intent on affecting another regulatory realignment that would undo much of what was accomplished under the public lobby regime. The FTC and the EPA were two prime targets in this effort, both having been singled out in the Reagan transition report on regulatory policy.

The Differences Between the FTC and the EPA

Undoubtedly the most important differences in deregulation attempts at the FTC and the EPA stem from personal differences between James Miller and Ann Burford. While the most casual observer of the Washington scene could see that Burford's pugnacity with Congress and calculated aloofness within the EPA created problems for deregulation not encountered at other regulatory agencies, two more profound differences go much further in explaining why Miller apparently enjoyed success. First, Miller, as we have seen, brought to the FTC a well-considered intellectual framework. On arriving at the FTC, he put together a more concrete deregulatory agenda based on this framework. Burford, on the other hand, came to the EPA with an agenda to get the agency off the back of business. This agenda was grounded in an intellectual commitment rather than an intellectual framework. This difference accounts, in great part, for Burford's problems and Miller's successes. As one former EPA official noted, you can't fight something (environmentalism) with nothing (Burford's strategy of ratcheting down). In this sense, Miller had something and Burford had nothing. His intellectual framework provided a basis for both attacking past FTC policy and defending his administrative and budgetary measures. Within such a framework, Burford was accused of "politicizing" the EPA and colluding with business against the public interest.

The second fundamental distinction between Miller and Burford was that he acknowledged the legitimacy of the FTC and its mission. Burford, on the other hand, never conveyed to members of Congress and the public a sense that the EPA had a legitimate role to play. This created uncertainty in the business community, demoralized the agency's staff, and provided a rallying point for environmental lobbyists and their allies.

Miller, of course, was not without his critics, but he could not very easily be accused of catering to special interests or seeking to dismantle the FTC. His defense of the private sector was based on a commitment to economic principles, which provided an alternative understanding of the public interest—one that saw consumer well-being connected to a competitive marketplace and a systematic scrutiny of government action through economic analysis. Indeed, Miller's most serious difficulties with Congress stemmed from his desire to reshape fundamentally the agency according to his understanding of economic principles, while legislators and business interests preferred a more ad hoc, problem-solving approach. As a result, critics could accuse Miller in certain instances of seeking change where there was no "clamor" for such change from the public or business. This was the case, for example, with Miller's attempt to change the meaning of *deception* in Section 5 of the FTC statute (see Chapter 5). Yet, Miller's response to such criticism (that he was acting on the basis of what he felt was right and comported with professional economic analysis) shielded him from the sort of political backlash that formed against Ann Burford. This was especially so because Miller's commitment to competition impelled him to challenge restraints of trade affecting professional groups. The competition program that culminated in 1984 with ambitious initiatives against health care organizations, attorneys, accountants, trade associations, and municipalities clearly distinguished Miller as someone intent on reform, rather than dismantlement, of the FTC.

Miller and Burford would leave their own distinct stamp on the agencies they led. When Steiger arrived at the agency, she found a legacy on which she could build. Indeed, she defined her mission essentially as consolidating the changes in the legal standards that Miller brought to the agency. As the associate director of Advertising Practices under Steiger, Lee Peeler, observed, policy statements formulated during Miller's tenure required "greater attention to economic analysis—this affects the view the Commission has of advertising: the cases we bring, the way we carry out enforcement, the general orientation of the Commission" (L. Peeler interview). In contrast, Burford's successors were confronted with a badly polarized environment that resisted even the most sober efforts to bring economic reform to the agency. Environmental activists and their allies in Congress seemed determined to hem in the discretion of the EPA's leadership in ways that defied the efforts of William Ruckleshaus, Lee Thomas, and William Reilly to base the agency's rulemaking on more careful economic and scientific analysis.

Although the differences between the EPA and the FTC indicate the central importance of leadership in achieving regulatory change, there are some structural and political gaps between these agencies that even good administration at the EPA could not have bridged. It is also important to note in this regard how the style of administrative management at agencies like the FTC and the EPA mixed with different institutional organizations. The FTC, of course, is an independent commission, a product of the Progressive Era, whereas the EPA is an executive agency that more faithfully reflects the institutional goals of the public lobby regime. In a formal sense, independent commissions are more autonomous from the president than executive agencies. However, the "informal" constraints placed on deregulation by the inertial forces of the public lobby regime and the environmental issue network in particular may, ironically, make deregulation at an agency like the FTC somewhat easier. The status of the EPA as an executive agency and a product of the public lobby regime has kept it under close scrutiny by public lobbyists, members and staff of key congressional committees, the courts, and the press. And the enabling statutes of the EPA, clearly reflective of the public lobby regime, were quite specific about the agency's mission and responsibilities. Thus any dilatory tactics or laxness in enforcement are easy to detect. The enabling statute of the FTC, crafted a half century ago, is much more loose and discretionary, therefore making it more difficult to identify and combat concrete deregulatory policy at the latter. The very discretion attacked by the Reagan administration as the crux of the historical woes of the FTC, interestingly, made it susceptible to James Miller's efforts to bring about a fundamental reorientation in consumer and antitrust policy.

Thus, the arrival of William Ruckleshaus and, subsequently, the promotion of Lee Thomas at the EPA reduced but did not eliminate the differences between that agency and the FTC, even though their leadership, like that of James Miller, was directed at reforming regulation rather than simply relieving business of regulatory burdens. Indeed, the efforts by Ruckleshaus, Thomas, and Reilly to make greater use of risk assessment were in no small part an effort by leaders to regain control over the EPA's agenda (Melnick, 1994: 45).

It is also significant that the principles of environmentalism are somewhat more rabidly antithetical than are those of consumerism to the economic analysis that governed the reform efforts of James Miller, William Ruckleshaus, Lee Thomas, and, to a lesser extent, William Reilly. In Chapter 5, we suggested that certain consumer advocates had expressed an antipathy toward conspicuous consumption, thus perhaps drifting imperceptibly into an attack on consumer preferences. Moreover, as noted by Derthick and Quirk, consumer activists are "ideological close cousin[s] of environmental activists, sharing with them "sponsorship, leadership goals, and adversaries in industry" (1985: 215). Nevertheless, those close ties between the consumer and environmental movements should not obscure the important differences between them. Influential organizations such as the Consumers Union have a primary interest in testing products and informing the buyer, and are critical of more ardent reformers such as Ralph Nader, who feels that the role of government and advocates is to reform directly people's lives and values. And consumer activism in areas such as airline and trucking deregulation, while primarily motivated by outrage at the collusion between government and business that imposed burdens on the consumer, also has revealed a keen interest in lower prices, better services, and a general acceptance of the consumer ethic.

Yet environmental activists more consistently eschew an interest in economic considerations, tending to adopt instead a strategy of regulatory policies that emphasizes doomsday predictions, limits to growth, and the destructive consequences of a life-style and cult of progress that worships at the altar of commodious materialism. This difference between the consumer and environmental movements has resulted in more strident opposition to regulatory relief at the EPA than at the FTC, making it more difficult to deregulate in the environmental arena.

Underlying this difference between the consumer and environmental movements is an important difference between the issues involved in those two areas of social regulation. As has often been noted, clean air and water, not to mention problems of toxic waste, define issues that dramatically and significantly affect communities and families. Naturally, this situation lends itself to media coverage. Consumer problems, though, are usually less focused, because they are less hazardous and less dramatic. In addition, much regulation at the FTC deals specifically with economic issues: competition and antitrust. Indeed, those issues, not consumer affairs as defined in the Wheeler–Lea and Magnuson–Moss acts, gave birth to the FTC. The effort to subject regulatory activity at the FTC to "economic" criteria, therefore, was deemed more appropriate than similar attempts at the EPA. Miller, unlike his counterparts at the EPA, could claim with considerable justification that the Reagan administration's approach to regulation at the FTC constituted a return to the original purposes of the trade commission Congress created (see, for example, Miller, 1983). To be sure, the consumer movement had managed successfully to focus attention on the immorality of commercial transactions, but, in general, subjecting these economic exchanges to the moral imperatives of consumerism did not strike as responsive a chord with the press and the public as did the importunities of environmentalists.

Indeed, when the Pertschuk-led FTC went after business in, as one former member of the Senate Commerce Committee staff put it, "an aggressive and surly way," the Commission suffered a backlash that nearly gutted its organic statute (personal interview, Michael Mullin, July 13, 1983). That most of the FTC staff, as well as many consumer activists, supported Steiger's cautious activism testified in no small part to their fear that a more aggressive revival of consumerism might renew the political assault on the Commission. Assuredly, many staff attorneys and their allies among consumer activists wanted the Commission to do some more innovative and attention-getting things, especially in the area of national advertising. But consumer activists were divided among themselves about how far beyond Steiger's approach the Commission could reach without arousing the backlash it suffered in the late 1970s. This split surfaced publicly when the Center for Science in the Public Interest (CSPI) issued a press release on March 10, 1993, claiming to speak for 275 consumer advocacy groups, that made public some of the contents of a letter to Clinton. The letter urged the president to appoint a new FTC chair from the ranks of consumer groups. Yet many important public interest representatives, including the Consumers Union, the Consumer Federation of America, and the Center for Consumer Public Interest Research, dissented from those parts of the press release suggesting that Steiger should resign, allowing the new administration to bring new, more aggressively consumerist leadership to the Commission immediately. As Mark Silbergeld of the Consumers Union wrote, "Consumers Union understands the letter to call upon the President only to achieve a more consumerist balance on the FTC by use of the suggested criteria in making future appointments as FTC vacancies occur. It does not call for the resignation or appointment of any particular individuals to FTC commissionerships" (letter to editor, *FTC: Watch,* March 24, 1993). Bruce Silverglade, the legal director for CSPI, found this defection in the ranks puzzling. "After all," he claimed, "Steiger has used the same standards that Reagan chairs—Miller and Oliver—used in consumer enforcement. . . . Her record in consumer protection is weak" (phone conversation, October 4, 1994). Yet Silbergeld and his colleagues were more tolerant of Steiger's caution, viewing her circumspect activism as the best practical solution to the fractious regulatory environment in which the FTC was forced to operate. A Commission staffed entirely by aggressive consumer activists might move beyond the fragile consensus for renewed activism that Steiger had forged, reviving efforts to curtail severely the FTC's legal authority.

In contrast to the fragile consensus for consumer activism, the environmental movement enjoyed a level of support for its causes that encouraged, indeed forced, Congress to fend off the most ardent of the Reagan administration's deregulatory efforts. In many respects, in fact, the Reagan administration revitalized the environmental movement; the specter of Burford and Watt abetted activists' fundraising and lobbying efforts. Most significant, the resilience of this province of the public lobby regime in the face of an administrative assault encouraged George Bush to support the reauthorization of the Clean Air Act, even after Congress included many provisions that he had opposed during the Reagan years as director of the Task Force on Regulatory Relief. As we noted in Chapter 9, the White House did get the Congress to accept acid-rain provisions that contained an emission-trading proposal; but in exchange for this market-oriented approach, environmentalists gained provisions that placed a definite cap on emissions. In fact, the 1990 Clean Air legislation was a remarkable victory for public lobbyists. With respect to airborne toxins and auto emissions, for example, it contained complex enforcement standards that would leave the EPA, as well as states and localities, little discretion in enforcing the statute. As Representative Henry Waxman, the chairman of the House Energy and Commerce Committee's Subcommittee on Health and the Environment explained, the "unprecedented" specificity of the 1990 amendments reflected that "without detailed directives . . . [and] statutory deadlines, industry intervention might frustrate efforts to put pollution control steps in place. . . . History shows that even where EPA seeks to take strong action, the White House will often intervene at industry's behest to block regulatory action." To prevent this, Waxman, a close ally of environmentalists and a skilled legislative tactician, pushed for "very detailed mandatory directives . . . [and] statutory deadlines . . . to assure that the required actions are taken in a timely fashion" (Waxman, cited in Landy, Roberts, and Thomas, 1994: 290). In all, the Clean Air Act included more than two hundred rulemaking actions in the first several years of its implementation. To ensure that EPA met all the standards written into the law, Congress added hammers to the statute, specifying exactly what would happen if a deadline were unmet.[1]

In the wake of the Reagan revolution, then, environmental lobbyists and ardent congressional supporters such as Waxman were able to further insulate environmental rulemaking from hostile executive administration. Indeed, the 1990 Clean Air Amendments Act revealed that public lobbyists were determined to treat the Burford era as the rule rather than the exception (Landy, Roberts, and Thomas, 1994: 285–91). That they succeeded in this endeavor testifies to the strong consensus in support of environmental regulation.

Similarities in the FTC and the EPA

The significant differences between the FTC and the EPA notwithstanding, there are strong similarities evident in the attempts to bring about fundamental change in regulatory politics at these two agencies. In each case we found the same pattern, a functionally organized agency operating in a relatively open issue network in which public lobbies played an important ongoing role. The attempts to deregulate at both the FTC and the EPA demonstrate the resilience of the public lobby regime. The resilience, of course, owes to the inertial forces present in the American political system generally and the public lobby regime specifically. The philosophical principles of the public lobby regime provide a strong base from which to defend consumer and environmental regulation. However, it is just as important to note that the foot soldiers in this defense, public lobbyists and congressional staff, constitute new actors strategically placed in the policy process. They are permanent participants in the issue networks of consumer and environmental policy. The elimination of funds for programs, such as intervenor funding under the Reagan administration, has not affected the institutionalization of public interest groups. As Mark Silbergeld put it:

> Public interest groups have fundamentally changed the policy process. Even Miller had some outreach to public interest groups. . . . Steiger has ongoing meetings with advocates—[the director of the Bureau of Consumer

---

[1] For example, the act requires that after January 1, 1995, the gasoline sold in certain nonattainment regions must meet special EPA specifications. If EPA does not meet those specifications on time, the sale of all gasoline in the designated area must cease (Landy, Roberts, and Thomas, 1994: 290).

Protection] Barry Cutler is especially interested in these contacts, asking consumer advocates what else they think the FTC should be doing. I think [the public interest movement] is stronger than ever. Consumer and environmental organizations are focused on important issues, strongly staffed, in excellent financial shape, and far more sophisticated in the methods they use. The Reagan years tested public interest groups, and they have emerged from this test in very good shape. (personal interview, July 23, 1992)

The role of public interest advocates is reinforced by their allies in the press. Consumer and environmental activists are the source of good stories, and advocates have used the press skillfully as a good means of communication. Although the growing concern during the late 1970s about excessive government intrusion in the economy tarnished somewhat the luster of public lobbyists, that their efforts were directed to defining and defending the interests of the public against the encroachments of big business and the lethargy of bureaucracy ensured favorable treatment by the press. This assured broad, if diffuse, public support. The success of public interest activists in parlaying this support into substantial and enduring political influence has, on occasion, even won them the grudging respect of business interests. In explaining the continued importance of public interest groups during the Reagan administration, Howard Vine, director of corporate finance, management, and competition at the National Association of Manufacturers (NAM) noted:

They [public interest groups] are viewed as a pro bono *[publico]*, since they represent a constituency that cannot organize itself. Congressmen use consumer groups to insulate themselves. They protect themselves from a backlash by supporting groups which define their mission as the public interest. . . . On the whole, I think the public interest groups are constructive; they do force accountability to the public. I lobby hard for business, but I am also a consumer. Something like public interest groups has to represent interests that cannot effectively organize themselves. . . . The problem with such groups is that they distort business's point of view. A lot of what public interest groups do is hype, but it is very effective hype. (personal interview, July 28, 1983)

Given the foothold of the public lobby regime in the American political system, it cannot be dislodged by the sort of guerrilla tactics the Reagan administration employed at the EPA. Rather, the achievement of a realignment in regulatory politics is unlikely without a "frontal" assault on the legislative base, requiring a clear program and a tremendous investment of political capital. Without such a major change, the achievements of the Reagan administration in modifying regulatory politics were doomed to be ephemeral.

In general, however, the regulatory program of the Reagan administration emphasized administrative and budgetary action rather than a broad challenge to the institutional fabric of the public lobby regime. Burford did not pursue changes in the enabling statutes of the EPA early, when it was likely to succeed, that is, when deregulation had a "window of opportunity," to use the phrase from NAM. Even at the FTC, where there was a good deal of concern about the agency's enabling statute, the Miller regime expended considerable political capital in seizing the administrative levers of power. As a result, there was a sharp and perhaps largely unnecessary conflict between the Reagan appointees and the permanent staff. Although this situation was short-lived, compared to the situation in the EPA, it nevertheless distracted attention from more fundamental reforms during the critical early days of the Reagan presidency.

In part, this emphasis placed on executive action at the FTC and EPA reflected a view that apparently emerged from the transition report on regulatory reform, namely that there existed an entrenched group of bureaucrats at the FTC and EPA who were committed to antibusiness policies. There is a striking parallel between Miller's admission that he arrived at the FTC thinking that 80 percent of his staff would oppose him on ideological grounds and the feelings expressed by the EPA officials and environmentalists that Burford saw government bureaucrats as the enemy. As we suggested in the case studies of the Reagan years, this view may have led to an immediate focus on administrative and budgetary matters to clean house rather than a broad-based legislative attack on enabling statutes. But it took a sustained political effort to put the public lobby regime in place, and only a similar effort can dislodge it. An administrative and budgetary clampdown can be effective in the short run, but it cannot effect a regulatory realignment. The failure to achieve statutory reform was celebrated, accordingly, by advocates of social regulation and bitterly received by many of the Reagan administration's allies, who had hoped for a more farsighted approach to regulatory reform.

From such a long-term perspective, the Bush administration compounded the impropriety of Reagan's administrative aggrandizement. Bush not only failed to narrow the legislative base of the public lobby regime; he expanded it. In the aftermath of the president's support not only for the Clean Air Act but also for major social initiatives such as the Civil Rights Act and the Nutrition Labeling Act, conservatives in the administration had to resort to tactics that appeared arbitrary and heavy-handed. Even after 1990, with the emergence of the Competitiveness Council as an important player in regulatory politics, advocates of regulatory relief were relegated to a rear-guard action, to administrative politics that struck many Republican committee staff, as well as civil servants at OMB, as more a matter of public relations than of careful oversight. Bush's pursuit of a kinder, gentler version of regulatory politics ended in a self-defeating attempt to influence regulatory policy by "unilateral fiat" (Tiefer, 1994: 16).

In many respects, however, as we noted in Chapters 3 and 4, the emphasis that the Reagan and Bush administrations placed on executive action in the pursuit of regulatory relief was a logical continuation of long-term developments in American politics. Since the New Deal, the development of public policy has increasingly been centered in the executive department. This has led to a merging of politics and administration that allows for extensive policy change without statutory reform. The development of "the administrative presidency" means that there is now the potential for presidents to play a major role in bringing about such change. The significant expansion of executive administration as a tool of policy initially occurred in the Roosevelt and Johnson administrations as a means of overcoming the institutional restraints of constitutional government and the inadequacies of the party system. Ironically, however, the levers of administrative power developed in the pursuit of liberal reform were employed—and strengthened—by Nixon and Reagan, both of whom recognized that the modern presidency was a double-edged sword, which could cut in a conservative as well as a liberal direction. Indeed, Republican presidents, facing hostility not only in the bureaucracy but also in the Congress and the states, were, even more than Democrats, encouraged to pursue policy goals by seeking to concentrate executive power in the White House. Having seen the Clean Air Act written more on the terms of the environmentalists than his own (or, as the *Wall Street Journal* put it, after watching the "Green machine rout" his own "team"), it is not all that surprising that Bush turned to the Competitiveness Council for regulatory relief (Gigot, 1990). Only with the benefit of hindsight is it so clear that this was not a reasonable response to historical trends and historical necessity.

There is a real sense in which the public lobby regime was born of a concern to safeguard consumer and environmental protection from hostile presidential administration. We have noted that the legislative foundation of the public lobby regime was a response to what contemporary reformers viewed as the failure of the modern presidency to fulfill expectations that shaped the administrative reforms of the New Deal and the Great

Society. The regulatory politics of the EPA illustrate especially well a form of post–New Deal administrative politics, which are based on legal restraint rather than presidential and bureaucratic discretion. These statutes are supported by a beleaguered but still influential coalition of public interest groups, courts, bureaucratic agencies, and congressional subcommittees that continues to impose severe limits on presidential influence of regulatory policy.

Of course, Miller's success in modifying the FTC demonstrated dramatically how, with the expansion of executive capacities in American politics, energetic and carefully conceived administrative action can bring about substantial alterations in regulatory policy. And these changes remained largely intact, indeed were ratified in important respects, during Janet Steiger's reign over the Commission. We have suggested, however, that such change is largely confined to those areas of the regulatory apparatus that predate the public lobby regime. Furthermore, there was nothing to prevent ardent consumer activists from searching for more hospitable forums. As we noted in Chapter 8, the authors of the 1989 ABA report on the FTC urged the Commission to depart from Miller's national advertising policies, so as to preempt aggressive action by the states that was undermining national campaigns. The activism of state attorneys general in national advertising, in fact, often resulted in former opponents of regulation at any level of government favoring a revitalization of national standards, so as to fend off the possibility of business having to confront a multiheaded regulatory beast. Public interest groups both adapted to and encouraged this shift to the states. "Up until 1984 we were trying to get the Reagan administration to act on deceptive food advertising and labeling," noted the CSPI's Bruce Silverglade in 1988. "But after knocking our heads against the wall for years, we started working with state attorneys general in New York, Texas, and finally about fifteen other states." This alliance between consumer activists and the state attorneys general led states to resolve many complaints that had been filed with federal agencies, pressuring the FTC to reestablish a strong federal presence in the regulation of advertising (*New York Times*, February 8, 1988: A17). In the face of this pressure from the states and beleaguered marketers, the Steiger FTC did undertake some initiatives, such as the "green guides," that marked an important policy change from the Miller years.

We have seen that the FDA also pressured the FTC to take a more active posture in overseeing the advertising of food, alcohol, and tobacco. Significantly, in those instances when Steiger could not persuade the Commission to take a more aggressive position, the FTC's forbearance did not put the issue to rest. The decision of the Commission not to take action against "Joe Camel," for instance, set consumer activists off in search of government allies elsewhere. Public lobby organizations filed lawsuits in California and Washington state that made essentially the same claims against R. J. Reynolds. These suits not only sought to ban Joe Camel from the marketing of cigarettes but also to saddle R. J. Reynolds with the responsibility for corrective ads and financial penalties (*U.S. News and World Report,* June 20, 1994). Even more ominous for the tobacco industry was the firestorm ignited by David Kessler, whom the Clinton administration, in recognition of his aggressive regulatory politics during the Bush years, reappointed as FDA commissioner. In a well-publicized hearing before Henry Waxman's Subcommittee on Health and the Environment, Kessler charged that new evidence indicated that nicotine was addictive and that the tobacco industry had manipulated levels of the substance to keep smokers hooked.[2] Although Kessler's allegations were sometimes depicted as a campaign to treat nicotine as a drug, so that the FDA would have the power to ban cigarettes, his real objective was to gain regulatory control over the tobacco industry's marketing practices. Indeed, the hearings gave momentum to legislation that would shift regulatory authority over tobacco manufacturing, distribution, and advertising from the FTC to the FDA (*Advertising Age,* June 27, 1994). In the face of the FTC's controversial decision to close the Joe Camel case, Kessler hardly demurred in suggesting that Congress should carry out such a transfer of regulatory power. When asked by the host of National Public Radio's *All Things Considered,* Noah Adams, whether the government should ban Joe Camel, Kessler responded, "We normally yield to our sister agency, the Federal Trade Commission. But I certainly think that if one's looking at policy options, if I were sitting in the Congress, I would certainly look at the whole range of policy options. And I think that would include advertising . . ." (transcript, *All Things Considered,* June 22, 1994).

Thus, although the Reagan regulatory program was more successful at the FTC than at the EPA, this success, based on administrative changes, failed to define sharply the boundaries of policy disputes. At the end of the day, the emphasis placed on administrative action by the Reagan administration may have been the most "cost-effective" route to policy change; however, it did not nurture a fundamental transformation of the public values and institutions that sustain an elaborate regulatory

---

[2] Kessler's testimony before Waxman's committee was televised live on CNN. See CNN transcript, March 25, 1994.

apparatus. Most obviously, it put the advocates of regulatory relief in the uncomfortable position of carrying out a program to reduce the burden of government regulation through what amounted to unprecedented administrative aggrandizement. Regulatory relief, therefore, led not to institutional reform that imposes restraint on government action but to an important confirmation of a substantial government presence in overseeing social and economic activity. To be sure, the use of administrative power by the Reagan and Bush administrations was often directed to imposing a ratchet on government activity, thereby serving the commitment to restrain federal intervention in the society and economy. Yet, as in the case of the regulatory relief program at the EPA, such power was often rejected as illegitimate presidential intrusion on agency affairs. Or, as in the case of the FTC, administrative aggrandizement was accepted as confirmation of the importance of positive government. In neither case was the broad commitment of contemporary American politics to expansive government responsibility for an unlimited number of social and economic problems challenged fundamentally. The opposition to the public lobby regime did not result in a challenge to national administrative power, but in a battle for its services.

Clinton and the Trials of Reinvention

Clinton's victory in 1992, an EPA official observed, put an end to the question of whether environmental regulations were legitimate. In the wake of that campaign, in which Clinton and his running mate, Senator Al Gore of Tennessee, excoriated the Bush administration's regulatory goals and methods, he claimed, there were no more "Black or White Hats." With respect to environmental objectives, "everyone was now 'Green,' " he argued; the remaining fights would take place on the more narrow ground of how to regulate. These fights would be far from trivial, however; for just as everyone was now environmental, with respect to objectives, so there were growing concerns that the *methods* of regulation were badly flawed. There was a general frustration with the regulatory control system—its inflexibility, excessive cost, and indifference to the victims of regulatory burdens—so much so that even many ardent environmentalists acknowledged that administrative agencies could and must do better (Morganstern, 1995).

The need to reform the methods of regulatory policy seemed to be the central premise of the Clinton program. Although Clinton and Gore attacked the Bush administration's record on regulation, they hardly sought a mandate for a program of aggressive environmental and consumer protection. Indeed, during the 1980s, both the president and vice-president had been active in the Democratic Leadership Council, a moderate group in the Democratic party that developed many of the ideas that became central themes in the general election. One of these ideas, Clinton's proposal to "reinvent government," became the main principle of the administration's regulatory philosophy.[3] The task was not to reduce government; in fact, the Clinton administration presumed the presence and benefits of regulation and government management of the economy. Rather, the objective was to reduce the infirmities of centralized administration, so as to increase the efficiency and, more important, the accountability of regulatory politics. "The argument is no longer pro-regulation or anti-regulation," said Vice-President Gore in October of 1993. "The argument is about how we regulate" (*Washington Post,* October 1, 1993). The Clinton administration promised to develop a regulatory program that transcended the exhausted left–right debate of the past two decades, one that promised neither boundless expansion of government intervention in the economy nor militant protection of property rights. Clinton trumpeted this middle path as part of a "new social contract," a "new covenant," that would revitalize the progressive tradition in American political life.

When fleshed out, however, Clinton's regulatory philosophy did not sound very different from his predecessor's original formulation of regulatory philosophy, one that beheld a vision of an active state, albeit one that was sensitive to the costs that government intervention imposed on the economy:

> The American people deserve a regulatory system that works for them: a regulatory system that protects and improves their health, safety, environ-

---

[3] The "reinventing government" program was inspired by the work of David Osborne and Ted Gaebler (1992), who called for the public sector to confront "the need to reinvent itself for the information age," that is, to become less "centralized and bureaucratic" and more "entrepreneurial." As Osborne wrote in *Mandate for Change,* the Democratic Leadership Council's "action plan" for the Clinton presidency, "The model of government we inherited from the industrial age achieved great things in its day, but it is no longer effective. With its monopolies, its preoccupation with rules and regulations, and its hierarchical chains of command, it simply cannot keep up with the rapidly changing, highly competitive, information-rich society and economy within which we live" (Osborne, 1993: 263). Entrepreneurial government required the introduction of choice, competition, and market incentives into the public sector through such innovations as managed competition, public school choice, social service vouchers, and market-based ways to combat pollution. For a critique of the Clinton administration's application of these ideas, see Kettl (1994).

ment, and well-being and improves the performance of the economy without imposing unacceptable or unreasonable costs on society; regulatory policies that recognize that the private sector and private markets are the best engine for economic growth; regulatory approaches that respect the role of State, local, and tribal governments; and regulations that are effective, consistent, sensible, and understandable. We do not have such a regulatory system today (Executive Order 12866, *Federal Register,* vol. 58, no. 190, September 30, 1993).

In seeking to succeed where Bush failed, to establish a positive, albeit circumspect, regulatory program, the Clinton administration could not abide the Council on Competitiveness, which was abolished in one of the new president's first executive orders. It then fell to Gore, who gleefully announced the banishment of the Quayle Council in his first act as vice-president, to construct a new regulatory review process. In spite of their excoriation of the Competitiveness Council, there was no prospect that the administration would do away with centralized regulatory review or deprive the OMB's Office of Information and Regulatory Affairs (OIRA) of its responsibility to oversee regulatory activity. Even the most bitter opponents of the Reagan and Bush procedures acknowledged that the White House could not leave regulatory policy to departments and agencies. In fact, an ad hoc working group of public interest, environmental, and labor groups drafted a plan for regulatory review that accepted the concept of White House oversight of agency rulemaking. This plan, developed at the initiative of the public interest organization OMB Watch, urged the Clinton administration to embrace regulatory review in a manner that was more congenial to advocates of social regulation, one that was "open and accountable, and based on selective, well-coordinated assessments for effectiveness and fairness in achieving the agency's mission" ("Changes in the Federal Regulatory Review Process: Options for President-elect Bill Clinton," December 10, 1992). The administration's Executive Order 12866, issued on October 4, 1993, revealed that Vice-President Gore was sympathetic to many of the OMB Watch's concerns. Reflecting the Clinton administration's belief in social regulation and the active role of government in enhancing "national values," EO 12866 called for a centralized review that departed from the Reagan and Bush years in requiring greater "sunshine" during regulatory review, engaging agency and OIRA officials in consultation earlier in the process, limiting the number of regulations reviewed to those defined as "significant," imposing time constraints on reviews, and expanding assessments of regulations to consider more fully their impact on environmental quality, technological innovation, and low-income groups (*Federal Register,* vol. 58, no. 100: 51735–44).

In some respects, the Clinton order marked the emergence of a remarkable consensus on the need for the White House to enlist the support of economists, armed with the weapon of cost–benefit analysis, in ameliorating the intrusiveness of national intervention in society. Although the Clinton administration responded to the demands of public interest groups for more openness and attention to the benefits of social regulation, it upheld the authority of OIRA to oversee the activities of agencies. In turn, many conservatives had come to realize by the end of the Bush years that the sub rosa deliberations of the Competitiveness Council had stigmatized its work (D. McIntosh interview). Indeed, the conservative economist William Niskanen granted that in some ways the new order could be an improvement on those that shaped the review process during the Reagan and Bush years. "The activities of . . . OIRA may be better focused on "significant regulatory actions," he wrote in an editorial for *Regulation.* "[And] increased attention to openness and accountability in the regulatory review process is probably necessary to protect this process against charges of backdoor deals with special interests" (No. 3 [1993]: 9).

The widespread agreement on the need for centralized review, albeit in a more focused and open forum, one suspects, made it possible for the Clinton administration to win Senate confirmation for an administrator of OIRA for the first time in four years. Clinton's choice, Sally Katzen, a widely respected administrative lawyer with considerable experience in government, seemed perfectly suited to restoring the integrity of centralized review. Indeed, her swearing-in as head of OIRA, the *National Journal* gushed, "looked like some sidewalk caricaturist's conception of Inside the Beltway impossibility" (July 17, 1993: 1801). Joining Clinton administration officials at the ceremony in the Old Executive Office Building were such devotees of regulatory relief as C. Boyden Gray, James Miller, and Antonin Scalia. This bipartisan assembly embodied the Clinton administration's hope to transcend the bitter regulatory battles of the past twenty years. "Clinton ran as a New Democrat," Katzen noted about the administration's regulatory philosophy. Having been a governor who experienced firsthand the burdens of national controls, and a revisionist liberal who dismissed the traditional Democratic "sense of unlimited resources," she observed, there was no chance that the president would become a "rabid regulator" (personal interview, July 20, 1994). Sensing the Clinton administration's efforts to establish a moderate regulatory position, public lobbyists did not expect to get everything they wanted. Margaret Mellon, director of the National Wildlife Federation's biotechnology policy center, greeted Katzen's appointment and EO 12866 with a mixture of patience and skepticism. "This is a centrist administration," she said. "They want things that will make both sides happy or both sides equally unhappy" (cited in *National Journal*, July 17, 1993: 1802).

The lesson of the Bush administration was that pragmatism, lacking a reasoned defense, risked exposing the White House to political attacks from both public interest groups and free market activists. During the 1992 campaign, Clinton pledged to dedicate his party to a "New Covenant," one that would seek to constrain, in the name of responsibility and community, the demand for programmatic and regulatory rights first summoned by the Roosevelt revolution. Invoking Roosevelt's Commonwealth Club address of 1932, in which FDR first outlined the "economic constitutional order," Clinton declared that the modern liberal commitment to guaranteeing entitlement and regulatory programs had gone too far. The objective of the New Covenant was to correct the tendency of Americans to celebrate individual and programmatic rights without any sense of mutual obligation to each other and their country. In one sense, this was a challenge to the public lobbyists and their commitment to extending the "economic constitutional order" to "quality of life" issues; in another, it resonated with the public lobbyists' assault on New Deal principles and policies in the name of community and citizenship. Indeed, Clinton's commitment to educational opportunity embodied the public lobbyists' professed concern to balance rights and responsibilities; its central feature, a national service corps, was emblematic of the core New Covenant principle—national community. Similarly, the proposal to reinvent government was compatible with the public lobby regime's concern to make administrative politics more responsive to public concerns. In challenging the explosion of rights and hidebound bureaucracy that arose from the New Deal and the opposition it spawned, Clinton pledged to dedicate his party to a new concept of justice that might redress many of the troubling aspects of the progressive tradition—the decline of parties as civic associations, the rise of virulent administrative politics, and the deterioration of public trust in American political institutions.

Although Clinton promised during the campaign to dedicate his party to the new concept of justice he espoused, his words and actions during the early days of his presidency failed to connect this vision to a coherent program of action. In fact, the major themes of Clinton's campaign rapidly dissolved into vacillation between conventional and new Democratic positions, leaving liberals and conservatives alike profoundly uncertain about where the president stood on such issues as entitlements and regulatory policy. With respect to social regulations, the Clinton White House appeared to be at war with itself. On the one hand, the administration touted an activist posture, appointing environmentalists and consumer activists to key administrative posts. On the other hand, Vice-President Gore and Sally Katzen embraced the causes of reinventing government and regulatory review in a manner that emphasized "the need to ease the adverse effects of regulation on citizens, business, and the economy as a whole" (National Performance Review, 1993: 34). Deprived of a commitment to clearly defined purposes, reinventing government and regulatory review became exercises in procedure that left regulators at the EPA and the FTC twisting in the wind.

Of course, the Clinton administration had no opportunity to make an appointment to the FTC until September 1994, leaving the Commission in a rather uncomfortable holding pattern. This interregnum was made somewhat more uncomfortable by the inability or unwillingness of the new administration to convey any sense of the Commission's importance or future. "The staff can only guess," an attorney in the Bureau of Consumer Protection observed plaintively in the summer of 1994, when asked what a "Clinton" Commission would look like (personal interview, June 29, 1994). The only hint of the Clinton administration's program for consumer protection and competition came in the dramatic denouement of the Microsoft case, which deadlocked the FTC (see Chapter 8). But after taking the extraordinary step of asking the FTC for its file in this case, the Clinton Justice Department reached a settlement with the software company that the trade press and Microsoft's rivals received with deep disappointment. Under the terms of the agreement, Microsoft agreed to give up the practice of locking computer-makers into royalty agreements that charged fees for every computer sold by the PC-maker regardless of whether it used Microsoft's software. But the terms of the consent decree did little, in critics' eyes, to remedy Microsoft's alleged anticompetitive behavior in the application-software business; in controlling the technical information about its widely used operating systems, Windows and DOS, they charged, Microsoft hampered its rivals' ability to compete in the sale of application software such as that for word processing (*Boston Globe,* July 17, 1994: 8). In a story that was characteristic of the trade press's harsh response to the Justice Department's settlement, *Computer Reseller News* called the consent decree the most anticlimactic story in the history of the microcomputer industry, amounting to little more than political rhetoric and a way to justify the huge sum spent on a four-year investigation (cited in *FTC: Watch,* August 1, 1994). Ann Bingaman, head of the Justice Department's antitrust division, took exception to the press coverage of the Microsoft settlement; such a reaction was not surprising, however, given the fanfare with which the case was dislodged from the FTC. Rather than marking a significant departure from the Reagan and Bush years, as promised, the Justice Department's resolution of the Microsoft case did little to dispel the notion that the Clinton administration lacked a coherent regulatory program. Like his pragmatic predecessor, Clinton seemed to be muddling through.

Just as Bush's political pragmatism failed to settle disputes between public lobbyists and deregulators, so Clinton's centrism did little to ameliorate regulatory battles. The Clinton administration's limited influence on the regulatory arena was underscored by the court's refusal to accept the Microsoft settlement. District Judge Stanley Sporkin issued a judgment in February 1995, in which he overturned the Microsoft consent decree; in his understanding, it failed to furnish necessary supporting information, was too narrow in its scope, relied on an ineffective remedy for anticompetitive behavior, and depended on enforcement mechanisms of questionable vitality. In effect, Sporkin's decision signaled the continuing resilience of the public lobby regime—indeed, a new manifestation of it. Relying on a 1974 statute, the Tunney Act, a law that mandates judicial review of Justice Department settlements to determine if they are in the public interest, Sporkin ruled that the settlement did not force Microsoft to abandon enough of its anticompetitive practices so as to sufficiently protect consumers. The court's ruling represented the first time that a judge had rejected an antitrust settlement, thus setting the stage for a novel and contentious examination of how much leeway judges are permitted in examining consent decrees. If upheld, Clinton's attorney general, Janet Reno, warned, Sporkin's decision would undermine the independence of the executive—nothing less than the separation of powers was at stake (*Los Angeles Times,* February 17, 1995).[4]

---

[4] In June 1995, the U.S. Court of Appeals in Washington reinstated the antitrust settlement between Microsoft and the Justice Department. The court's opinion delivered a harsh rebuke to Judge Sporkin, insisting that "the Tunney Act cannot be interpreted as an authorization for a district judge to assume the role of Attorney General" (*Wall Street Journal,* June 19, 1995: A3). The decision set a precedent that appeared to bolster the Justice Department's discretion in negotiating settlements with companies it has investigated. Still, the widespread criticism of the consent decree and Judge Sporkin's stinging criticism of the Justice Department "embarrassed" everyone involved in the anticlimactic Microsoft settlement and seemed to have toughened the agency's resolve (personal interview with FTC staff attorney, July 25, 1995; *Wall Street Journal,* June 19, 1995: A3). In May, the Justice Department filed suit to block Microsoft's acquisition of Intuit, forcing the soft-

The Clinton administration was no more successful in establishing the boundaries for environmental policy. Unlike the situation it faced with the FTC, the administration did not have to wait several months to put its stamp on the EPA. Carol Browner, a protegé of Vice-President Gore, on whose Senate staff she had served, and for two years the head of Florida's department of environmental regulation, was named to head the EPA. But five months into her appointment, the agency did not look noticeably different from the Bush days (*Wall Street Journal*, July 8, 1993). In fact, the morale of the EPA had suffered considerably under her leadership. One of Browner's first acts was to testify before the House subcommittee chaired by Representative John Dingell (D-Michigan), whose relationship with the EPA had always been cool. To the surprise of the staff, Browner blasted them. "I am appalled by what I have learned about the EPA's total lack of management, accountability, and discipline," she said. The EPA director went on to indict her agency for "poor management practices, serious violations of rules and intolerable waste of taxpayers' money" (Committee on Energy and Commerce, 1993: 7). Although Browner's comments were not totally without substance, calling in artillery on her own troops was a questionable strategy—a glaring lack of political sensitivity that reflected her limited experience in the arena of environmental politics (Wilkinson, 1993). As our comparisons between James Miller and Ann Burford suggest, the only reform of lasting value in regulatory politics is what career people buy into. Yet Browner's relationship with the professionals of her agency was only slightly less hostile than Burford's, even though she professed a commitment to the agency's mission and was closely allied with environmental groups.

Browner's attack on her agency was especially damaging because she never projected a vision or imposed a clear sense of direction on the agency. In this sense, the EPA director's travails reflected those of the administration she served. Like the administration, she conveyed the need

---

ware giant to abandon a deal that would enable it to play a major role in electronic banking. As of this writing, the agency is conducting several other investigations into Microsoft's business practices, some of which look like new attempts to refight the battles seemingly settled by the original consent decree. Most significant, the Justice Department is examining Microsoft's plan to bundle its forthcoming Windows 95 operating system with software that helps personal computer users tap into its new on-line services (*Economist*, June 24, 1995: 59). Rather than securing a firm middle ground on competition issues, then, the Clinton administration's foray into the Microsoft case ended with the software giant and the Justice Department at war.

to remake the regulatory process, without making clear what purposes a revamped process should serve. Indeed, Browner had weak support from the White House, which was slow to nominate her key policy operatives and virtually absent in the legislative maneuvers to elevate the EPA to cabinet level. The cabinet bill stalled in the 103rd Congress when Senator J. Bennett Johnston (Dem–Louisiana), chairman of the Energy Committee, tacked an amendment on to the legislation that would require the EPA to carry out cost–benefit and risk analysis for each new regulation. As the White House maintained a sphynxlike silence on this amendment, it passed overwhelmingly, causing environmental advocates in the House to block the cabinet bill. In fact, the administration's unclear, sometimes indifferent, position on environmental matters allowed a number of important laws to stall in the 103rd Congress, including a bill to reauthorize Superfund. Two years after they celebrated President Clinton's election with an environmental inaugural ball and bold promises to strengthen federal environmental policies, environmental activists pushed only one major piece of legislation through Congress: the California Desert Protection Act. The April 1994 Earth Day celebration produced mutual recrimination between environmentalists and Clinton administration officials, each blaming the other for a disappointing legislative session, described by Congressman Phil Sharp as "the nadir of the political influence of the environmental movement in the Congress" (cited in *National Journal,* December 3, 1994: 2825; see also, *National Journal,* May 7, 1994: 1097).

The Clinton administration did depart from the Bush administration's environmental policy in one major respect—the absence of a White House Council on Competitiveness. As Browner insisted, this was "not an insignificant change" (*Wall Street Journal,* July 8, 1993: A14). For all their criticism of the administration, public lobbyists and their allies in the EPA granted that this kindlier oversight of regulatory activity favorably distinguished the Clinton administration from its two immediate predecessors. The regulatory review process set up by Vice-President Gore's office and administered by OIRA under the direction of Sally Katzen obviously lacked the contentiousness that attended White House oversight in the Reagan and Bush years. As OMB's first report on the implementation of EO 12866 claimed, "One of the major changes during the [first] six-month period is the improved relationships that have been developed between OIRA and the agencies." Remnants of the mistrust and hostility that often characterized relationships between OIRA and regulators at agencies like the EPA during the previous decade remained, the report admitted, but "for the most part this [had] been replaced by a spirit of cooperation" (Office of Management and Budget, Report on Executive Order 12866, May 10, 1994, *Federal Register,* vol. 59: 24276). This claim was confirmed not only by permanent staff in OIRA and the EPA, but also by public interest lobbyists who had attacked regulatory review in the previous two administrations. The Clinton administration's regulatory review process even received good marks from OMB Watch, hitherto a hostile monitor of OIRA, which praised the program administered by Katzen for its "openness" and "accountability" (*Washington Post,* May 20, 1994). Indeed, so cordial were relations between OIRA and regulatory agencies that Katzen's staff poked fun at its new boss by identifying her leadership style with that of "Barney," the loving dinosaur of children's television.

In truth, this gentle satire reflected the permanent staff's respect for Katzen, their view that her more inclusive style had restored the integrity of the regulatory review process. Katzen herself insisted there was a method to her madness. OIRA's adversarial relationship with agencies in previous administrations, she claimed, had backfired and was rejected out of hand by those in the regulatory agencies as "heavy-handed." By carrying out a discourse with the agencies, she insisted, OIRA could be more successful in getting regulators to adopt more cost-effective regulations. "We engage the agencies in a discourse about what they want to achieve," Katzen said, "and attempt to persuade them that they can get to the same place in a more sensible way" (S. Katzen interview). Slowly, the OIRA administrator insisted, she had seen "a difference" in the regulatory habits of the agencies; gradually, as mutual trust was established between OIRA and the agencies, regulators were becoming responsive to the importunities of the economists on her staff. Katzen claimed, then, that the Clinton administration had begun to succeed where the Bush administration had so conspicuously failed, that is, in developing a regulatory process that was forged on a consensus among regulators, public lobby groups, and business interests. In support of this claim, OMB reported that OIRA returned roughly 35 percent of the rules it reviewed during the first year that EO 12866 was in existence; the return of these rules, by most accounts, initiated a constructive, even-handed consideration of the questionable regulations' impact on the economy, as well as on state and local governments (OMB, Report on Executive Order 12866, *Federal Register,* vol. 59: 24285; BNA's Banking Report, January 2, 1995; *Washington Post,* May 20, 1994).

There was no prospect, however, that the Clinton administration's regulatory review program could significantly ameliorate the fractious environment of regulatory politics. Business representatives worried that

OIRA was giving too much discretion to agencies to decide what rules were "significant" and thus subject to review (*Washington Post,* May 20, 1994). OIRA, in fact, was concerned that the "triage" system, which limited the review process to regulations that had an annual effect on the economy of $100 million or more, was "not self-executing."[5] Even more problematic, however, was that OIRA found much of the regulatory process beyond its control; many agencies, most notably EPA, had to develop regulations "under severe time constraints set in statutes or arising from litigation resulting from missed statutory deadlines" (OMB, Report on Executive Order 12866: 24288). In effect, the Clinton administration found that environmental policy, shaped by the laws of the public lobby regime, defied the sort of gentle restraint it hoped to impose on the regulatory process.

The inability of the White House to modulate regulatory policy became dramatically clear with the administration of the 1990 Clean Air Amendments Act. Unlike with the original Clean Air Act, the states were given virtually no discretion in administering the 1990 statute. Given the strictness of the standards and timetables established by the reauthorization legislation, this posed a daunting challenge for governors and mayors. The first serious challenge of the amendments, the requirement that governments in areas with moderate carbon monoxide pollution had to impose vehicle inspection and maintenance programs and require cleaner fuels, ignited a firestorm around the country that saw several state capitols openly challenge the Clean Air Act (*New York Times,* February 14, 1995: A1, A16). Most controversial, this provision of the amendments would require states to create new, centralized inspection and maintenance programs, even though many states already had their own decentralized programs in place. In the face of this revolt, the Clinton administration was under relentless pressure to grant delays in the emissions program. Although granting delays in several states, including New York and New Jersey, the EPA's Browner threatened that she would cut off highway funds to states that adamantly refused compliance. Still, if states simply refused to cooperate, the Clinton administration might find itself in the awkward position of withholding huge chunks of highway transportation aid—at the end of 1996, around the time of the presidential elec-

---

[5] As the first report on the implementation of Executive Order 12866 revealed, "Some agencies have told OIRA that they are fulfilling their responsibilities [in ensuring that significant and nonsignificant rules follow the principles of the executive order]. OIRA has no independent basis for confirming or denying these reports" (OMB, Report on Executive Order 12866, *Federal Register,* vol. 59: 24288, May 10, 1994).

tion. But such political headaches were almost beyond the point, for the 1990 amendments limited the administrative discretion of the White House and the EPA only slightly less than that of the states. In the end, the threat of a Clean Air Act debacle was a glaring indictment of the Clinton administration's plan to reinvent government, without revisiting in any meaningful way the purposes or laws of regulatory politics.

The 1994 Elections and the Future of the Regulatory State—Reagan Redux?

The Republican party's surprising victory in the elections of 1994 brings us full circle. As in the late 1970s, the Republicans benefited from a growing public concern with "big government" and its cumbersome regulatory structures. In contrast to the late 1970s, however, which culminated in the election of a president promising to reduce the role of the federal government and bring regulatory relief to business, the 1994 elections led to dramatic changes in Congress and the states. The Republicans took control of both legislative chambers, gaining fifty-two seats in the House and eight in the Senate. Moreover, they won dramatic victories at the state and local levels: Republicans increased their share of governorships to thirty, their first majority since 1970; they also reached near parity in state legislatures, a status they had not enjoyed since 1968. Significantly, the Republicans achieved this sweeping victory after running a national, ideological campaign, which promised to fulfill the failed promise of the Reagan revolution—to get government off the backs of the American people. The national character of the campaign owed largely to House Minority Leader Newt Gingrich (R-Georgia). Gingrich, his party's choice to be the new Speaker of the 104th Congress, persuaded more than 300 House candidates to sign a "Republican Contract with America," a "covenant" with the nation, that promised to restore limited government by eliminating programs, cutting taxes, and revitalizing the Reagan program of regulatory relief. Clinton's attack on the Republican program during the campaign seemed to backfire, serving only to abet Republicans in their effort to highlight the president's failure to "reinvent government." Examining exit polls that suggested that a "massive anti-Clinton coalition came together" to produce the "revolution" of 1994, political analyst William Schneider wrote of the voters' desire for change, "If the Democrats can't make government work, maybe the Republicans can solve problems with less government" (Schneider, 1994).

In the aftermath of the 1994 elections, public lobbyists braced for what they feared would be a "radical reexamination" of regulatory policy. Retiring Senate Leader George Mitchell (D-Maine), who played a pivotal role in enacting the 1990 Clean Air Amendments Act, warned soon after the election that conservatives' desire to bring policies of "unrestrained economic growth and disregard for the natural environment," would bring Eastern European-style devastation to the United States (cited in Kriz, 1994). Consumer activists were no less fearful, viewing with great alarm, for example, the ascent of Representative Thomas Bliley (R-Virginia) to the chairmanship of the House Commerce Committee; Bliley, a militant protector of his state's tobacco industry, would surely stall, if not put a stop to, the momentum created during the 103rd Congress to impose more severe restrictions on the marketing and use of cigarettes. Scholars confirmed the fears of public lobbyists. "Given the importance of congressional entrepreneurship and oversight for sustaining environmental regulation and given the anti-government rhetoric of the now dominant Republicans," wrote political scientist R. Shep Melnick after the election, "it is hard to see how current patterns of governance can survive" (Melnick, 1994).

The "Republican Contract With America" promised that they would not, promoting a legislative program that threatened a direct assault on the public lobby regime. The Contract did not propose to change environmental or consumer protection laws but promised a major overhaul of the regulatory process. In effect, it committed the House Republicans to consider a bill in the first 100 days of the new Congress, the Job Creation and Wage Enhancement Act, that would codify the restrictive administrative actions of the Reagan and Bush years. Indeed, one provision of the proposed bill would supplant Clinton's Executive Order 12286 with Executive Order 12291, the cost–benefit requirements enforced by the previous two Republican administrations, thus ending Sally Katzen's brief experiment to engage regulatory agencies such as the EPA in enlightened discourse (Republican Contract With America, the Job Creation and Enhancement Act, Title VI: 45). Beyond this legal obligation of regulators to balance costs and benefits, the Republican program for regulatory relief included provisions that would require agencies to strengthen their scientific analysis in issuing rules—in particular, to assess as part of their cost–benefit analysis health, safety, or environmental risks. Added to these onerous cost–benefit requirements were two other proposals that would dramatically reshape the regulatory process: an initiative that would prevent the federal government from imposing unfunded mandates on state and local governments; and legal protection for property rights, compensating landowners whose property values decreased 10 percent or more as a result of a regulatory action. During the past two years, public lobbyists and their allies in Congress had fought tooth and nail to block all property rights, cost–benefit/risk analysis, and "unfunded mandates" proposals; they disparaged them as "the unholy trinity" of the extreme right wing, and no more. Now they confronted a majority in the House pledged to make these provision the law of the land.

Adding insult to this threatened injury, some key Republicans on Capitol Hill prepared to set up new committees on regulatory reform, dedicated to protecting property rights. In an ironic twist, the newly elected Republican congressman from Indiana, David McIntosh, none other than the former executive director of the Dan Quayle's Competitiveness Council, was charged with forming a Subcommittee for Economic Growth, Natural Resources and Regulatory Relief. Whereas the Competitiveness Council had met with opponents of social regulation in the secluded offices of the Old Executive Office Building, Congressman McIntosh planned to use his new congressional committee to publicly air the grievances of "ordinary citizens adversely affected by government regulation." More than most of his colleagues, the former chief of the Competitiveness Council understood that the public lobby regime was as much about *who* decides ("participatory democracy") as about *what* is decided (consumer and environmental protection). Thus, McIntosh proposed to take on the public lobbyists on their own terms, hoping to answer the alarm bells they were sounding against the GOP's Contract, to forestall the sort of tactics that had so effectively defied past regulatory relief efforts (*Wall Street Journal,* December 22, 1994: A16).

The manner in which public lobbyists and deregulators squared off suggested that the 1994 elections promised to continue in a new form, rather than resolve, the fundamental conflict that had characterized regulatory policy since 1980. For the past fourteen years, divided partisan realms had institutionalized this administrative combat. The nation would now experience a different form of divided government—a Republican Congress with a Democratic White House—that was likely to produce novel symptoms of this intractable conflict. It was possible, of course, that the new Congress and the Clinton administration would agree on methods for reforming the regulatory process. The Contract with America did not propose to weaken environmental and consumer protection laws per se but to revamp the process by which those laws were administered. Of course, the methods glimpsed by House Republicans would impose an administrative straitjacket on regulatory agencies that would indirectly weaken, if not gut, consumer and environmental laws. But the situation for public lobbyists was less bleak in the Senate, where Senator John

Chafee (R-Rhode Island), a strong environmentalist, would chair the Environment and Public Works Committee. Moderate Senate Republicans, such as Chafee and Mark Hatfield (R-Oregon), the new chair of the Appropriations Committee, will probably temper the more extreme demands of their Republican brethren in the House, allowing the new Congress to meet the Clinton administration halfway—to forge a consensus on reinventing the regulatory process. During the 103rd Congress, in fact, there was some movement in this direction, most notably in the formulation of a revamped Superfund program, in which Carol Browner was instrumental in getting environmental activists to sit down with representatives of the chemical and insurance industries to craft compromise legislation. In the weeks before the 1994 election, when polls began to register growing support for Republicans, environmental activists who had belittled their more moderate colleagues for working with industry lobbyists to rewrite the Superfund law began preaching the virtues of cooperation (*National Journal*, December 3, 1994: 2827).

Yet the 1994 election appeared to poison these incipient efforts of cooperation. Emboldened by the election, conservative Republicans in the House and Senate seemed determined to reduce the cost and reach of the federal government. Not content to overhaul the procedures of regulatory politics, the House also passed legislation that would drastically cut the EPA's budget and weaken the Clean Water and Endangered Species acts (*New York Times*, July 17, 1995: A11). The all-out attack on existing environmental, consumer, health, and safety measures stalled in the Senate in late July 1995, as Republicans repeatedly failed to cut off debate and force a vote for final passage of their bill to revamp regulatory procedures. But the united Republican front—all fifty-four Republican senators, including the moderate Chafee, voted to bring the regulatory relief bill to a vote—suggested that the assault on the public lobby regime would resume when the 104th Congress considered budgetary reductions and specific pieces of social regulatory legislation later in the year.

The congressional lurch to the right, in turn, nudged the ever-cautious Clinton administration to move in the other direction. The Bush administration was moved to abandon its short-lived modus operandi with environmentalists, once it was clear that little political capital could be gained from this uneasy alliance; so the Clinton administration, seeking to avoid the stigma of "Gingrich lite," will be tempted to cease efforts to reinvent government. As the House relentlessly enacted the regulatory provisions of the Contract with America, in fact, Vice-President Gore rediscovered his environmental roots, charging that the GOP covenant would lead to an "unprecedented assault" on environmental rules, "in the dark of night," without public debate (*Boston Globe*, March 6, 1995: 5). President Clinton also bestirred himself, suspending his search for "common ground" with the Republican majority on Capitol Hill and threatening to veto legislation that would roll back social regulation (*New York Times*, August 3, 1995, A12).[6]

In truth, given the irreconcilable differences between public lobbyists and deregulators, the prospects for a dialogue on the role of the regulatory state were very dim, indeed. As was the case in the Reagan and Bush years, the hope of forging a new regulatory consensus was all too likely to degenerate into contentious administrative politics. The Clinton administration would be tempted to resort to strengthening regulatory policy with a "stroke of a pen," through executive administration, thus attempting to undermine the newly installed majorities in Congress.[7] In

---

[6] At the time of this writing, it is not clear how the FTC will fare amid this regulatory turmoil. In April, Robert Pitofsky, law professor and former FTC commissioner, became the new chair of the agency. Public lobbyists and proponents of regulatory relief agreed that Clinton had made a good choice—a respected moderate who would attempt to steady the centrist course chartered by his Republican predecessor, Janet Steiger (*Washington Post*, April 13, 1995: D12). The new chairman was unlikely to antagonize the new Congress; indeed, during his first few months at the FTC, Pitosfsky moved the Commission, as one staff attorney put it, "a couple clicks to the right" (personal interview, July 25, 1995). In a rare move, the Commission rejected a consent decree worked out on Steiger's watch that would have required Nestlé Food Company to divest an Iowa cat food plant (*FTC News*, June 7, 1995). In another unusual development, the Commission issued an order staying an administrative proceeding raising allegations that New Balance athletic shoes made deceptive "made in USA" claims for its footwear. With the decision to suspend the New Balance case, Pitofsky announced that the FTC would conduct a comprehensive review of consumers' perceptions of "made in USA" claims and called for public hearings to reexamine antitrust policy in order to reevaluate the FTC's mission in an age dominated by global markets (*FTC News*, July 11, 1995). "Pitofsky has always been able to stick his finger in the air, and to tell which way the wind is blowing" a former FTC official observed dryly (personal interview, July 26, 1995). But Pitofsky was too principled and skilled an administrator to lead a full-scale retreat from the charge of the conservative 104th Congress. Many FTC observers suspected that eventually he would carefully but firmly put his own stamp on an enforcement-minded program for consumer protection and competition. Like his colleagues in the Justice Department, however, Pitofsky will not find it easy to stake out moderate positions as the White House and Congress head for an almost certain "train wreck" over budgetary and regulatory measures.

[7] On August 8, President Clinton, near the Patapsco River in Baltimore, Maryland—one of the East Coast's dirtiest and most toxic spots—announced an executive order directing companies doing business with the government to continue making public their toxic emissions, even if Congress passes a rider to the House version of the EPA budget that limits the federal agency's power to collect such information (*Boston Globe*, August 9, 1995: 10).

retaliation, Republicans in the House and Senate would be pushed to use the levers of administrative power available to Congress to torment the Clinton administration with investigations and "micromanagement" of social policy, just as a Democratic Congress assaulted the executive during the Reagan and Bush years.

In part, the chronic combat of regulatory politics reflects the striking ambivalence of the American people themselves about social regulation. As Melnick argues with respect to environmental protection, divided government councils give institutional effect to a "public schizophrenia" that has been induced by the public lobby regime:

> On the one hand, environmental protection is highly popular in the abstract. The public expects the federal government to protect it against a variety of health risks, particularly carcinogens. It also expects the government to prevent corporate America from despoiling the land in order to gain larger profits. On the other hand, few Americans trust the government "to do what is right most the time." They want less red tape, less interference with their daily lives, lower taxes, and fewer restrictions on business entrepreneurs. (Melnick, 1994: 47)

Ultimately, the public's uncertainty about the public lobby regime follows from the development in the United States of an "uneasy state," as the historian Barry Karl has put it (1983), one in which a national administrative apparatus and activist public philosophy were grafted onto a rights-based constitutional system and political culture. As we argue in Chapter 3, the new social regulation is an offspring of the New Deal and New Left; it combines federal programs with a freewheeling public interest advocacy to promote collective rights of citizens. Perhaps as well as anything the concept of a collective right reveals the internal tension with which the new social regulation is fraught. In American political culture rights are something that, by definition, shield individuals from the collective will rather than binding them to it. Strangely, however, public lobbyists have never really confronted this apparent contradiction. Indeed, the idea of a collective right seems to be an attempt to reconcile participatory democracy with extensive use of the courts, a decidedly undemocratic institution. A focus on rights impels public lobbyists to legal recourse, yet they see themselves as defending the broad masses rather than individuals. In the end this untidiness may simply reflect the realities of democracy in a modern society driven by huge political, economic, and social institutions. Just as surely, the public's contradictory expectations about the public lobby regime reveal the profound difficulty of combining a modern positive state with the American natural rights tradition.

In a deeper sense, however, the chronic conflict between advocates of social regulation and those of regulatory relief testifies to the severe challenge that the public lobby regime poses to the foundation of the American political economy. To be sure, the consumer and environmental movements are not anticapitalist; public lobbyists have never conveyed an urgency to eliminate private property or redistribute wealth. In fact, in defending policies dedicated to clean air and public safety, environmental and consumer activists champion values that cut across traditional class conflicts, explaining, in large part, their success in achieving broad, if not deeply rooted, support among the American people. Yet the emphasis on "quality of life" issues, the warning about resource limitations, and the criticism of consumer preferences that characterize much public interest advocacy implicitly reject the foundation of a society dedicated to the pursuit of material satisfaction. To the more aggressive consumer and environmental activists, the rhythms of advanced capitalist societies reduce the human condition to a joyless quest for things that could never truly bring joy. It is this rejection of what Lincoln referred to as the "race of life" that distinguishes the public lobby regime as radical. Whereas social regulation has now reached a stage of development in which complex technical questions and expertise have become as important as ardent ideological commitment, it is unlikely that this evolution has gone far enough to allow for an easy accommodation with business interests or the principles of a market economy.

The moral basis of the public interest movement requires it to maintain an uneasy, paradoxical relationship to the American public. Although advocating a participatory democracy, public lobby groups articulate an ethos that indirectly expresses grave reservations about core principles of American life. If the frenetic materialism and conspicuous consumption of commercial republics could be attributed merely to the machinations of corporate capitalism, then direct and widespread citizen action might be consistent with the radical criticism of public interest advocates. To the degree that relentless materialism is deeply embedded in the American way of life, however, consumer and environmental advocacy are in tension with a commitment to democratic politics. Widespread support can be readily obtained for many of the specific goals of social regulation, yet the principles underlying these specific programs are largely unacceptable in the context of American politics and, when unchecked, are capable of creating a strong backlash against the public interest movement. Thus, in seeking to depart from the New Deal's emphasis on economic security, contemporary social reformers were alienated from the values and institutions that earlier progressives accepted as an inherent part of American life. As Tocqueville noted, citizens in commercial republics would invariably be indifferent to "revolutionary" challenges to this way of life:

> Although Americans are constantly modifying or repealing some of their laws, they are far from showing any revolutionary passions. One can easily see, by the promptness with which they stop and calm themselves just when public agitation begins to be threatening and when passions seem most excited, that they fear a revolution as the greatest of evils and that each of them is inwardly resolved to make great sacrifices to avoid one. In no other country in the world is the love of property keener or more alert than in the United States, and nowhere else does the majority display less inclination toward doctrines which in any way threaten the way property is owned. (Tocqueville, 1969: 638–39)

Undoubtedly, public lobbyists, especially consumer activists, are not simply "antimaterialistic." Nor is American political culture simply materialistic; the concerns for democratic citizenship and the criticisms of big business that characterized the reform activists who first became influential in the late 1960s and 1970s have a long tradition in American politics. But the public plainly is simply not willing to reject the materialism that many citizen advocates find unacceptable. The public lobby regime, then, has not always been in harmony with the public it purports to represent. It is not surprising, then, that consumer and environmental advocacy have focused on administrative and legal channels that were somewhat insulated from the mass political institutions of American politics. Administrative tribunals and courts have been, frequently, more appropriate forums for efforts to remake so substantially the character of political life in the United States.

Nor is it surprising that the public interest movement has galvanized a strong opposition based on a zealous adherence to free enterprise. The "Free Market Radicalism" espoused by President Reagan, and presently championed by many members of the new Republican majority in the Congress, is as much anathema to political consensus as are the principles of the public lobby movement. Indeed, self-styled conservative public interest groups have sprung up, eagerly mimicking the tactics and organizational style of environmental and consumer activists. Many foot soldiers of the conservative movement identify with associations such as the Center for Individual Rights, the Washington Legal Foundation, and the

Pacific Legal Foundation, which, like their progressive forebears, "revel in their pose as Davids taking aim at liberal Goliaths" (*New York Times,* December 30, 1994: B6). As a result, industry-directed confrontation with environmental and consumer activists is being supplanted and perhaps replaced by a more ideological and less pluralistic phase of regulatory politics. Whereas doubters, among whom are included many advocates for business, speak of limitations and trade-offs, conservative public interest groups militantly pursue property rights in a manner that, as Hugh Heclo puts it, "proclaims an era of boundless private market growth with no worrisome, much less tragic, side effects" (Heclo, 1986: 46).

The conflict between these two worldviews touches on fundamental questions about the appropriate role of government, as well as the just ends of the American political system. The question that must be faced as America approaches the twenty-first century is whether this fundamental theoretical conflict can be conveyed to the public in a way that is meaningful and subject to resolution. In the final analysis, this will determine whether the ideological posturing and endemic contentiousness of current regulatory politics can evolve into a new regime that is consistent with the principles of republican government.

References

Abramson, J. "The New Media and the New Politics." *The Aspen Institute Quarterly* (Spring 1990): 18–49.

Ackerman, B. and W. Hassler. 1981. *Clean Coal/Dirty Air*. New Haven, CT: Yale University Press.

Allaby, M. 1971. *The Eco-Activists*. London: Charles Knight and Co. Ltd.

American Bar Association. 1969. *Report on the Federal Trade Commission*.

American Bar Association, Special Committee to Study the Role of the Federal Trade Commission. 1989. *Report of the American Bar Association Section of Antitrust Law*.

Argyris, C. 1978. "Ineffective Regulating Processes," in C. Argyris, et al. (eds.), *Regulating Business: The Search for an Optimum*. San Francisco: Institute for Contemporary Studies.

Armstrong, R. "The Passion that Rules Ralph Nader." *Fortune* (May 1971): 144–47.

Arnold, P. E. 1986. *Making the Managerial Presidency: Comprehensive Reorganization Planning, 1905–1980*. Princeton, NJ: Princeton University Press.

Arnold, P. 1994. "Reform's Changing Role: The National Performance Review in Historical Context." Woodrow Wilson International Center for Scholars.

Bagge, C. 1975. "The Changing Regulatory Scene," in D. P. Moynihan (ed.), *Business and Society in Change*. Washington, DC: American Telephone and Telegraph.

Barber, S. 1984. *On What the Constitution Means*. Baltimore: Johns Hopkins University Press.

Bardach, E. and C. Kagan. 1982. *Going by the Book: The Problem of Regulatory Unreasonableness*. Philadelphia: Temple University Press.

Beales, H. J. 1994. "In the Wake of the NLEA: Advertising Regulation in a Changed Environment." Mimeo copy obtained from the author.

Beales, H. J. and T. Muris. 1993. *State and Federal Regulation of National Advertising*. Washington, DC: American Enterprise Institute.

Beer, S. H. 1978. "In Search of a New Public Philosophy," in A. King (ed.), *The New American Political System*. Washington, DC: The American Enterprise Institute.

Bell, D. 1957. *The End of Ideology*. Glencoe, IL: The Free Press.

Bennett, W. J. "Why Johnny Can't Abstain." *National Review* 39 (July 1987): 36–39.

Berle, A. and G. Means. 1939. *The Modern Corporation and Private Property.* New York: McMillan.

Bernstein, M. 1955. *Regulation by Independent Commission.* Princeton, NJ: Princeton University Press.

Berry, J. 1977. *Lobbying for the People.* Princeton, NJ: Princeton University Press.

Boyer, B. "Funding Public Participation in Agency Proceedings: The Federal Trade Commission Experience." *Georgetown Law Review* 70 (1981): 51–172.

Brand, D. 1985. "Corporatism and the Rule of Law: *The End of Liberalism* Revisited." Prepared for delivery at the annual meeting of the American Political Science Association, New Orleans.

Brand, D. 1988. "Reformers of the Sixties and Seventies: Modern Anti-Federalists?" in R. Harris and S. Milkis (eds.), *Remaking American Politics.* Boulder, CO: Westview Press.

Breyer, S. 1982. *Regulation and its Reform.* Cambridge, MA: Harvard University Press.

Brookes, W. T. "Dead Wrong Again." *National Review* (October 7, 1991): 29–35.

Buchanan, J. and G. Tullock. "Polluters, Profits and Political Responses: Direct Control Versus Taxes." *American Economic Review* 65 (March 1975): 139–47.

Burns, J. M. 1963. *The Deadlock of Democracy.* Englewood Cliffs, NJ: Prentice-Hall.

Business Roundtable. 1979. *The Incremental Costs of Regulation.* Prepared by Arthur Anderson Co.

Caldwell, L. 1975. *Man and His Environment: Policy and Administration.* New York: Harper and Row.

Cameron, J. "Nader's Invaders are Inside the Gates." *Fortune* (October 1977): 252–65.

Campbell, A. K. 1985. " 'Comments' on E. N. Goldenberg, 'The Permanent Government in an Era of Retrenchment and Redirection,' " in L. M. Salamon and M. S. Lund (eds.), *The Reagan Presidency and the Governing of America.* Washington, DC: Urban Institute Press.

Chase, S. and F. J. Schlink. 1935. *You're Money's Worth: A Study in the Waste of the Consumer Dollar.* New York: The Macmillan Company.

Clarkson, K. W. 1981. "Legislative Constraints," in K. W. Clarkson and T. J. Muris (eds.), *The Federal Trade Commission Since 1970.* Cambridge: Cambridge University Press.

Cox, E. F., R. C. Fellmuth, and J. E. Schulz. 1969. *The Nader Report on the Federal Trade Commission.* New York: Richard W. Baron.

Creighton, L. B. 1976. *Pretenders to the Throne.* Lexington, MA: D. C. Heath.

Croly, H. 1909. *The Promise of American Life.* New York: Macmillan.

Croly, H. 1914. *Progressive Democracy.* New York: Macmillan.

Crozier, M. 1963. *The Bureaucratic Phenomenon.* Chicago: The University of Chicago Press.

Cushman, R. 1941. *The Independent Regulatory Commissions.* New York: Octagon Books.

Cutler, B. 1993. "History of the FTC—Part II." Address to the American Bar Association Antitrust Section, Washington, DC, March 31–April 1.

DeMuth, C. "Strategy for Regulatory Reform." *Regulation* (March/April 1984): 25–29.

DeMuth, C. and D. H. Ginsburg. "White House Review of Agency Rulemaking." *Harvard Law Review* 99 (March 1986): 1079–88.

Derthick, M. and P. J. Quirk. 1985. *The Politics of Deregulation.* Washington, DC: The Brookings Institution.

DiFranza, J., J. W. Richards, P. H. Paulman, N. Wolf-Gillespie, C. Fletcher, R. D. Jaffe, and D. Murray. "RJR Nabisco's Cartoon Camel Promotes Camel Cigarettes to Children." *Journal of the American Medical Association* 266 (December 11, 1991): 3149–53.

Djilas, M. 1957. *The New Class: An Analysis of the Communist System.* New York: Praeger Press.

Dodd, L. and R. Schott. 1979. *Congress and the Administrative State.* New York: John Wiley & Sons.

Downs, A. 1967. *Inside Bureaucracy.* Boston: Little, Brown & Co.

Dunn, W. 1981. *Public Policy Analysis.* Englewood Cliffs, NJ: Prentice-Hall.

Eads, G. and M. Fix. 1984. *The Reagan Regulatory Strategy.* Washington, DC: The Urban Institute.

Eads, G. and M. Fix. "The Prospects for Regulatory Reform: The Legacy of Reagan's First Term." *Yale Journal on Regulation* 1 (1985): 293–318.

Eisner, M. 1993. *Regulatory Politics in Transition.* Baltimore: Johns Hopkins University Press.

Elazar, D. J. 1972. *American Federalism: A View from the States.* New York: Crowell.

Ellis, D. D. 1981. "Legislative Powers: FTC Rule Making," in L. W. Clarkson and T. J. Muris (eds.), *The Federal Trade Commission Since 1970: Economic Regulation and Bureaucratic Behavior.* Cambridge: Cambridge University Press.

Elzinga, K. 1982. "The Robinson-Patman Act: A New Deal for Small Business," in G. Walton (ed.), *Regulatory Change in an Atmosphere of Crisis: Current Implications of the Roosevelt Years.* New York: Academic Press.

Emmerich, H. 1950. *Essays on Federal Reorganization.* Birmingham; University of Alabama Press.

Fiorina, M. 1977. *Congress: Keystone of the Washington Establishment.* New Haven, CT: Yale University Press.

Fisher, L. 1986. "The Administrative State: What's Next After *Chaddha* and *Bowsher?*" Paper prepared for delivery at the annual meeting of the American Political Science Association, Washington, DC.

Fix, M. 1984. "Transferring Regulatory Authority to the States," in G. Eads and M. Fix (eds.), *The Reagon Regulatory Strategy: An Assessment*. Washington, DC: Urban Institute Press.

Flacks, R. "Is the Great Society Just a Barbeque?" *The New Republic* (January 29, 1966): 18–22.

Foer, A. 1979. "Antitrust Policy at the Federal Trade Commission," Address to the Intensified Antitrust Course, Ohio Legal Center Institute, June 15.

Foote, S. B. "Beyond the Politics of Federalism: An Alternative Model." *Yale Journal on Regulation* 1 (1984): 217–225.

Fried, C. 1991. *Order and Law: Arguing the Reagan Revolution—A Firsthand Account*. New York: Simon and Schuster.

Fruchter, N. and R. Kramer. "An Approach to Community Organizing Projects." *Studies on the Left* (March/April 1966): 65.

Fuchs, E. 1988. *Presidents, Management and Regulation*. Englewood Cliffs, NJ: Prentice-Hall, Inc.

Fuchs, E. and J. E. Anderson. 1984. "Institutionalizing Cost–Benefit Analysis in Executive Branch Regulatory Agencies." Paper prepared for delivery at the annual meeting of the Midwest Political Science Association, Chicago.

Galbraith, J. K. 1978. *The New Industrial State*. Boston: Houghton Mifflin Co.

Galloway, L. and T. Fitzgerald. "The Surface Mining Control and Reclamation Act of 1977: The Citizen's Ace in the Hole." *Northern Kentucky Law Review* (1981): 259–76.

Gardner, J. 1972. *In Common Cause*. New York: W.W. Norton & Co.

Gigot, P. "Clean Air Game: Green Machine Routs Bush Team." *The Wall Street Journal* (April 6, 1990): A18.

Gitlin, T. "Power and the Myth of Progress." *The New Republic* (June 1966): 29.

Goodman, P. 1960. *Growing Up Absurd: Problems of Youth in the Organized System*. New York: Random House.

Goodnow, F. 1900. *Politics and Administration*. New York: Mcmillan.

Goodsell, C. 1983. *The Case for Bureaucracy: A Public Administration Polemic*. Chatham, N.J.: Chatham House.

Grady, M. F. 1981. "Regulating Information: Advertising Overview," in K. W. Clarkson and T. S. Muris (eds.), *The Federal Trade Commission Since 1970: Economic Regulation and Bureaucratic Behavior*. Cambridge: Cambridge University Press.

Gray, B. C. "Regulation and Federalism." *Yale Journal on Regulation* 1 (1983): 93–110.

Graymer, L. and F. Thompson (eds.) 1982. *Reforming Social Regulation: Alternative Strategies*. Beverly Hills, CA: Sage Publications.

Greanias, G. and D. Windsor. "Is Judicial Restraint Possible in an Administrative Society?" *Judicature* 64 (April 1981): 400–13.

Greider, W. 1982. *The Education of David Stockman and Other Americans*. New York: E. P. Dutton.

Greve, M. S. "Why 'Defunding the Left' Failed." *The Public Interest* (Fall 1987): 91–106.

Haefele, E. 1978. "Shifts in Business–Government Interactions." A paper presented to the National Chamber of Commerce, Washington, DC.

Harris, R. 1985. *Business Firms under the New Social Regulation,* Durham, NC: Duke University Press.

Harris, R. and S. Milkis. 1983. "Deregulating the Public Lobby Regime: A Tale of Two Agencies." Prepared for the annual meeting of the American Political Science Association, Chicago.

Harrison, D. and P. Portnoy. 1982. "Regulatory Reform in the Large and Small," in L. Graymer and F. Thompson (eds.), *Reforming Social Regulation: Alternative Strategies.* Beverly Hills, CA: Sage Publications.

Hawley, E. 1966. *The New Deal and the Problem of Monopoly.* Princeton: Princeton University Press.

Hawley, E. 1981. "Three Facets of Hooverian Associationalism: Lumber, Aviation and Movies, 1921–1930," in T. McCraw (ed.), *Regulation in Perspective.* Cambridge, MA: Harvard University Press.

Heclo, H. 1978. "Issue Networks and the Executive Establishment," in A. King (ed.), *The New American Political System.* Washington, DC: The American Enterprise Institute.

Heclo, H. 1986. "Reaganism and the Search for a Public Philosophy," in John L. Palmer (ed.), *Perspectives on the Reagan Years.* Washington, DC: Urban Institute Press.

Heclo, H. 1987. "The In and Outer System: A Critical Assessment," in G. Calvin Mackenzie (ed.), *The In and Outers* Baltimore: Johns Hopkins University Press.

Heclo, H. 1988. "Conclusion: American Politics Remade," R. Harris and S. Milkis (eds.), *Remaking American Politics.* Boulder, CO: Westview Press.

Henderson, G. C. 1924. *The Federal Trade Commission: A Study in Administrative Law and Practice.* New Haven, CT: Yale University Press.

Henning, D. 1978. *Environmental Policy and Administration.* American Elsevier Publishing Co.

Herman, W. 1976. "Deregulation: Now or Never! (Or Maybe Someday)." *Public Administration Review* 36 (March/April 1976: 131–37.

Hofstadter, R. 1955. *The Age of Reform: From Bryan to FDR.* New York: Alfred Knopf.

Hoge, D. and T. Ankey. "Occupation and Attitudes of Student Activists Ten Years Later." *Journal of Youth and Adolescence* 11 (1982): 355– 71.

Hunt, G. (ed.) 1906. *The Writings of James Madison.* New York: Putnam.

Huntington, S. 1976. "The Democratic Distemper," in N. Glazer and I. Kristol (eds.), *The American Commonwealth.* New York: Basic Books.

Jaenicke, D. W. "Herbert Croly, Progressive Ideology, and the FTC Act." *Political Science Quarterly* 93 (Fall 1978): 471–94.

Jennings, M. K. "Residues of a Movement: The Aging Protest Generation." *American Political Science Review* vol. 81 (1987): 367–82.

Kahn, A. 1982. "Political Feasibility of Regulatory Reform: How Did We Do

It?", in L. Graymer and F. Thompson (eds.), *Reforming Social Regulation: Alternative Strategies*. Beverly Hills, CA: Sage Publications.

Karl, B. 1983. *The Uneasy State: The United States from 1915 to 1945*. Chicago: The University of Chicago Press.

Katzmann, R. 1980. "The Federal Trade Commission," in J. Q. Wilson (ed.), *The Politics of Regulation*. New York: Basic Books.

Kaufman, H. 1977. *Red Tape, Its Origins, Uses and Abuses*. Washington, D.C.: The Brookings Institution.

Kessler, D. 1995. Remarks before the Samuel Rubin Program, Columbia University School of Law, New York City, March 8.

Kettle, D. 1994. *Reinventing Government? Appraising the National Performance Review*. Washington, DC: The Brookings Institution.

Keynes, J. 1927. *The End of Laissez Faire*. London: Hogarth Press.

King, A. 1978. "The American Polity in the Late 1970's: Building Coalitions in the Sand," in A. King (ed.), *The New American Political System*. Washington, DC: American Enterprise Institute.

King, A. 1990. "The American Polity in the 1990s," in A. King (ed.), *The New American Political System*, 2nd ed. Washington, DC: American Enterprise Institute.

Kohlmeir, L. 1969. *The Regulators*. New York: Harper & Row Publishers.

Kolko, G. 1965. *Railroads and Regulation: 1877–1916*. New York: W. W. Norton & Co.

Kovacic, W. 1980. "Competition Programs." Federal Trade Commission, January.

Kovacic, W. E. "Reagan's Judicial Appointments and Antitrust in the 1990s." *Fordham Law Review* 60 (October 1991): 49–124.

Kraft, M. and N. Vig. "Environmental Policy in the Reagan Presidency." *Political Science Quarterly*. 99 (Fall 1984): 415–40.

Kristol, I. 1973. *Two Cheers for Capitalism*. New York: Basic Books.

Kristol, W. "Can-Do Government: Three Reagan Appointees Who Made a Difference." *Policy Review* 1 (Winter 1985): 62–66.

Kriz, M. "The Conquered Coalition." *National Journal* (December 3, 1994): 2824–28.

Kriz, M. E. "Policing the Paperwork." *National Journal* (March 31, 1990): 785–87.

Landy, M. K., M. Roberts, and S. R. Thomas. 1994. *The Environmental Protection Agency: Asking the Wrong Questions, From Nixon to Clinton*, expanded ed. New York: Oxford University Press.

Langston, T. S. 1992. *Ideologues and Presidents: From the New Deal to the Reagan Revolution*. Baltimore: Johns Hopkins University Press.

Latanich, T. 1984. "FTC Testimony." Mimeographed copy provided by the author.

Lave, L. 1981. *The Strategy of Social Regulation: Decision Frameworks for Policy*. Washington, DC: The Brookings Institution.

Leuchtenburg, W. E. 1963. "The Case of the Contentious Commissioner: Humphrey's Executor v. U.S.," in H. M. Hyman and L. W. Levy (eds.), *Freedom and Reform*. New York: Harper & Row.

Lexis Search of Cases in Federal Courts, 1981–1985.

Lilley, W. and Miller, J. "The New Social Regulation." *The Public Interest* 47 (1977): 49–61.

Lippman, W. 1955. *The Public Philosophy*. Boston: Little, Brown & Co.

Litan, R. and W. Nordhaus. 1983. *Reforming Federal Regulation*. New Haven, CT: Yale University Press.

Lowi, T. J. 1969. *The End of Liberalism: The Second Republic of the United States*. New York: W. W. Norton & Co.

Lowi, T. J. 1979. *The End of Liberalism*, 2nd edition. New York: W. W. Norton & Co.

Lowi, T. J. 1985. *The Personal President: Power Invested, Promise Unfulfilled*. Ithaca, NY: Cornell University Press.

Lynd, R., with A. C. Hanson. 1933. "The People as Consumers," in *Recent Social Trends in the United States: Report of the President's Research Committee on Social Trends*. New York: McGraw-Hill.

Lynd, R. "Democracy's Third Estate: The Consumer." *Political Science Quarterly* 51 (December 1936): 481–537.

Lynd, R. 1957. "Power in American Society," in A. Kornhauser (ed.), *Problems of Power in American Democracy*. Detroit: Wayne State University.

Maas, A. 1951. *Muddy Waters: The Army Engineers and the Nation's Rivers*. Cambridge, MA: Harvard University Press.

McCann, M. 1986. *Taking Reform Seriously: Perspectives on Public Interest Liberalism*. Ithaca, N.Y.: Cornell University Press.

McConnell, G. 1966. *Private Power and American Democracy*. New York: Vintage Books.

McCraw, K. 1984. *Prophets of Regulation* Cambridge, MA: Harvard University Press.

McCraw, T. (ed.). 1981. *Regulation In Perspective*. Cambridge, MA: Harvard University Press.

McFarland, A. 1976. *Public Interest Lobbies*. Washington, DC: The American Enterprise Institutue.

Mailer, N. 1959. *Advertisements for Myself*. New York: Putnam's.

Malbin, M. 1980. *Unelected Representatives: Congressional Staff and the Future of Representative Government*. New York: Basic Books.

Mansfield, H. "The 1984 Presidential Election: Entitlements Versus Opportunity." *Government and Opposition* 20 (Winter 1985): 1–17.

March, J. and H. Simon. 1958. *Organizations*. New York: John Wiley & Co.

Marcus, A. 1980. *Promise and Performance: Choosing and Implementing an Environmental Policy*. Westport, CT: Greenwood Press.

Mayhew, D. 1974. *Congress: The Electoral Connection*. New Haven, CT: Yale University Press.

Melnick, R. S. 1983. *Regulation and the Courts: The Case of the Clean Air Act.* Washington, DC: The Brookings Institution.

Melnick, R. S. 1985. "The Politics of Partnership: Institutional Coalitions and Statutory Rights." Occasional Paper No. 84-3, Center for American Political Studies, Harvard University.

Melnick, R. S. 1986. "The Politics of Statutory Interpretation: Congress, Courts, and Welfare Rights." Prepared for delivery at the annual meeting of the American Political Science Association, Washington, DC.

Melnick, R. S. 1989. "The Courts, Congress, and Programmatic Rights," in R. Harris and S. Milkis (eds.), *Remaking American Politics.* Boulder, CO: Westview Press.

Melnick, R. S. 1994. "The Political Environment—Why Regulation Is Such Risky Business Today." Paper presented at the Conference on Governing, Woodrow Wilson Center, Washington, DC, December.

Merriam, D. and J. Lyman. "Testing the Constitutionality of Land Use Extractions." *Connecticut Law Tribune* (May 23, 1994): 24.

Merton, R. 1957. *Social Theory and Social Structure.* Glencoe, IL: The Free Press.

Michels, R. S. 1959. *Political Parties: A Sociological Study of the Oligarchic Tendencies of Modern Democracy.* New York: Dover Publishers.

Milkis, S. "Franklin Roosevelt and the Transcendence of Partisan Politics." *Political Science Quarterly* 100 (Fall 1985): 479–504.

Milkis, S. "The New Deal, Administrative Reform, and the Transcendence of Partisan Politics." *Administration and Society* (February 1987a): 433–72.

Milkis, S. 1987b. "The Presidency and Political Parties," in Michael Nelson (ed.), *The Presidency and the Political System,* 2nd edition. Washington, DC: Congressional Quarterly Press.

Milkis, S. and R. Harris. 1986. "Programmatic Liberalism, and the Administrative State and the Constitution." Prepared for the annual meeting of the American Political Science Association, Washington, DC.

Miller, J. C. 1983. "The Reagan Philosophy at the FTC." Remarks before the Independent Insurance Agents of America, San Francisco, September 26.

Miller, J. C. 1985. "Real Economics." Address before a conference jointly sponsored by the Center for Education and Research in Free Enterprise of Texas A&M University and the Heritage Foundation, Dallas, April 2.

Miller, J. C. 1986. "Executive Regulatory Oversight." Prepared written statement before the Subcommittee on Intergovernmental Relations, Committee on Governmental Affairs, U.S. Senate, mimeographed copy provided by author.

Mitnick, B. 1981. *The Political Economy of Regulation.* New York: Columbia University Press.

Moe, T. M. 1985. "The Politicized Presidency," in John E. Chubb and Paul E. Peterson (eds.), *The New Direction in American Politics.* Washington, DC: The Brookings Institution.

Morganstern, R. 1995. "The Future of Environmental Regulation." Lecture, Brandeis University, Waltham, MA, January 18.

Morrison, A. B. "OMB Interference with Agency Rulemaking: The Wrong Way to Write a Regulation." *Harvard Law Review* 89 (March 1986): 1059– 74.

Mosher, F. C. 1985. " 'Comments' on E. N. Goldenberg, 'The Permanent Government in An Era of Retrenchment and Redirection,' " in L. S. Salamon and M. S. Lund (eds.), *The Reagan Presidency and the Governing of America*. Washington, DC: Urban Institute Press.

Muris, T. 1981a. "Statutory Powers," in K. W. Clarkson and T. Muris (eds.), *The Federal Trade Commission Since 1970: Economic Regulation and Bureaucratic Behavior*. Cambridge: Cambridge University Press.

Muris, T. 1981b. "Judicial Constraints," in K. W. Clarkson and T. Muris (eds.), *The Federal Trade Commission Since 1970: Economic Regulation and Bureaucratic Behavior*. Cambridge: Cambridge University Press.

Muris, T. "Rule without Reason at the FTC." *Regulation* (September/October 1982): 20–26.

Muris, T. 1984. "The Competition (Antitrust) Mission." Washington, DC: Federal Trade Commission. Mimeographed copy provided by author.

Muris, T. and K. W. Clarkson. 1981. "Introduction," in K. W. Clarkson and T. S. Muris (eds.), *The Federal Trade Commission Since 1970: Economic Regulation and Bureaucratic Behavior*. Cambridge: Cambridge University Press.

Nader, R. 1973a. "A Citizen's Guide to the American Economy," in R. Nader (ed.), *The Consumer and Corporate Accountability*. New York: Harcourt Brace Jovanovich.

Nader, R. 1973b. "Action for a Change," in R. Nader (ed.), *The Consumer and Corporate Accountability*. New York: Harcourt Brace Jovanovich.

Nader, R. 1973c. "The Case for Federal Chartering," in R. Nader (ed.), *The Consumer and Corporate Accountability*. New York: Harcourt Brace Jovanovich.

Nader, R., et al. 1976. *Taming the Giant Corporation*. New York. W. W. Norton.

Nagel, S. 1984. *Public Policy: Goals, Means and Methods*. New York: St. Martin's Press.

Nathan, R. 1983. *The Administrative Presidency*. New York: John Wiley & Sons.

Nathan, R. and F. C. Doolittle. "The Untold Story of Reagan's 'New Federalism.' " *The Public Interest* 77 (Fall 1984): 96–105.

National Association of Manufacturers. 1983. Position paper on the Clean Air Act Amendments.

Newfield, J. 1966. *A Prophetic Minority*. New York: The New American Library.

Newland, C. A. 1985. "Executive Office Policy Apparatus: Enforcing the Reagan Agenda," in L. M. Salamon and M. S. Lund (eds.), *The Reagan Presi-*

dency and the Governing of America. Washington, DC: Urban Institute Press.

Niskanen, W. 1971. *Bureaucracy and Representative Government.* Chicago: Aldine, Atherton Press.

Niskanan, W. A. "The New Regulatory Order." *Regulation* 3 (1993): 7–9.

Noll, R. and B. Owen. 1983. *The Political Economy of Deregulation: Interest Groups in the Regulatory Process.* Washington, DC: The American Enterprise Institute.

Oi, W. Y. "The Economics of Product Safety." *Bell Journal of Economics and Management Science* 4 (Spring 1973): 3–28.

Osborne, D. 1993. "Reinventing Government: Creating an Entrepreneurial Federal Establishment," in W. Marshall and M. Schramm (eds.), *Mandate for Change.* New York: Berkeley Books.

Osborne, D. and T. Gaebler. 1992. *Reinventing Government.* Reading, MA: Addison-Wesley.

Owen, B. and R. Brautigam. 1978. *The Regulation Game: Strategic Use of the Administrative Process.* Cambridge, MA: Ballinger Publishing Co.

Office Files of Bill Moyers, Lyndon Baines Johnson Library, Austin, Texas.

Office Files of Horace Busby, Lyndon Baines Johnson Library, Austin, Texas.

Palmer, J. M. 1986. "Proposed FTC Preemption of State Health Care Laws: An Impermissible Infringement on Federalism?" *Legal Backgrounder,* Washington Legal Foundation (October 3).

Papers of the Presidential Committee on Administrative Management. 1935–1936. Hyde Park, New York.

Peltzman, S. "The Effects of Automobile Safety Regulation." *Journal of Political Economy* 83 (August 1975): 677–726.

Peltzman, S. "Toward a More General Theory of Regulation." *Journal of Law and Economics* (August 1976) 211–40.

Perkins, F. 1946. *The Roosevelt I Knew.* New York: Viking Press.

Perlman, J. E. 1978. "Grass Roots Participation from Neighborhood to Nation," in S. Langton (ed.), *Citizen Participation in America.* Lexington, MA: Lexington Books.

Pertschuk, M. 1982. *Revolt Against Regulation: The Rise and Pause of the Consumer Movement.* Berkeley, CA: University of California Press.

Pertschuk, M. 1984. *FTC Review (1977–1984).* Washington, D.C.: U.S. Government Printing Office.

Peterson, M. A. and J. L. Walker. 1986. "Interest Group Responses to Partisan Change: The Impact of the Reagan Administration upon the National Interest Group System," in A. S. Cigler and B. A. Loomis (eds.), *Interest Group Politics.* Washington, DC: Congressional Quarterly Press.

Peterson, P. E. 1985. "The New Politics of Deficits," in J. E. Chubb and P. E. Peterson (eds.), *The New Direction in American Politics.* Washington, DC: The Brookings Institution.

Pfiffner, J. 1986. "Political Appointees and Career Executives: Managing Change and Continuity." Prepared for delivery at the annual meeting of the American Political Science Association, Washington, DC.

Pitofsky, R. "Beyond Nader: Consumer Protection and the Regulation of Advertising." *Harvard Law Review* 90 (February 1977): 661–701.

Portney, K. E. and J. M. Berry. 1993. "Centralizing Regulatory Control and Interest Group Access: The Quayle Council on Competitiveness." Prepared for Annual Meeting of the American Political Science Association, Washington, DC.

Quirk, P. 1981. *Industry Influence in Federal Regulatory Agencies*. Princeton, NJ: Princeton University Press.

Quirk, P. 1991. "Domestic Policy: Divided Government and Cooperative Presidential Leadership," in C. Campbell, S.J., and B. A. Rockman (eds.), *The Bush Presidency: First Appraisals*. Chatham, N.J.: Chatham Publishers.

Rabkin, J. "The Judiciary in the Administrative State." *The Public Interest* (Spring 1983): 62–84.

Rabkin, J. 1986. "The Reagan Revolution Meets the Regulatory Labyrinth," in B. Ginsberg and A. Stone (eds.), *Do Elections Matter?* Armonk, N.Y.: M. E. Sharpe.

Rauch, J. "The Regulatory President," *National Journal* (November 11, 1991): 2902–6.

Reagan, M. D. 1985. "Intergovernmental Implementation of Partial Preemption Regulatory Bodies: Can National Policy Effectively Channel State Administration?" Prepared for the annual meeting of the American Political Science Assocation, New Orleans.

Reagan, M. D. 1987. *Regulation: The Politics of Policy*. Boston: Little, Brown & Co.

Reagan, R. 1985. "Remarks of the President to the 12th Annual Conservative Political Action Conference." The Sheraton–Washington Hotel, March 1.

Reagan, R. 1974. Comments during a symposium, in N. Jacoby (ed.), *The Business-Government Relationship: A Reassessment*. Santa Monica, CA: Good-year Publishing Co.

Reich, C. 1970. *The Greening of America*. New York: Random House.

Reich, R. "Public Administration and the Public Deliberation: An Interpretive Essay." *The Yale Law Journal* (June 1985): 1617–42.

Report of the President's Committee on Administrative Management. 1937. Washington, DC: U.S. Government Printing Office.

Ripley, R. and G. Franklin. 1980. *Congress, Bureaucracy and Public Policy*. Homewood, IL: Dorsey Press.

Rock, E. 1987. "Commerce and the Public Interest: James C. Miller at the Federal Trade Commission," in R. Rector and M. Sanera (eds.), *Steering the Elephant*. New York: Universe Books.

Rohr, J. 1986. *To Run a Constitution: The Legitimacy of the Administrative State*. Lawrence, KS: University of Kansas Press.

Roosevelt, F. D. 1938–1940. *Public Papers and Addresses,* 13 vols. New York: Random House.

Roosevelt, T. 1923–1926. *The Works of Theodore Roosevelt.* New York: Da Capo Press.

Rossiter, C. (ed.), 1961. *The Federalist.* New York: The New American Library.

Rothman, S. and R. Lichter. "Elite Ideology and Risk Perception in Nuclear Energy Policy." *American Political Science Review* 81 (June 1987): 383–402.

Rourke, F. E. 1976. *Bureaucracy, Politics and Public Policy.* Boston: Little, Brown & Co.

Rourke, F. E. 1984. "The Presidency and the Bureaucracy," in M. Nelson (ed.), *The Presidency and the Political System.* Washington, DC: Congressional Quarterly Press.

Ruckleshaus, W. "Risk, Science and Democracy." *Issues in Science and Technology* 1 (1985): 19–38.

Sabatier, P. "Social Movements and Regulatory Agencies: Toward a More Adequate—and Less Pessimistic—Theory of Clientele Capture." *Policy Sciences* 6 (September 1975): 301–42.

Salisbury, R. "Institutions and Interest Representation." *American Political Science Review* (March 1984): 64–76.

Sandbach, F. (ed.), 1980. *Environment, Ideology and Politics.* Montclair, NJ: Allanheld, Osmun Publishers.

Sanford, T. 1967. *Storm over the States.* New York: McGraw-Hill.

Schattschneider, E. E. 1975. *The Semisovereign People: A Realist's View of Democracy in America.* Hinsdale, IL: The Dryden Press.

Schnick, A. "Congress and the Details of Administration." *Public Administration Review* 36 (September/October 1976): 516–28.

Schlesinger, A., Jr. 1949. "Broad Accomplishments of the New Deal," in E. Rozewene (ed.), *The New Deal Revolution or Evolution.* Boston: D. C. Heath and Co.

Schmitter, P. C. "Democratic Theory and Neocorporatist Practice." *Social Research* 50 (Winter 1983): 885–928.

Schneider, W. "Clinton: The Reason Why." *National Journal* (November 12, 1994): 2630–32.

Schuck, P. "Why Regulation Fails." *Harpers Magazine* (September 1975): v.251:16–29

Schuck, P. "Public Interest Groups and the Policy Process." *Public Administration Reivew* 37 (March/April 1977): 132–39.

Schumpeter, J. 1942. *Capitalism, Socialism and Democracy.* New York: Harper & Row.

Skowronek, S. 1982. *Building a New American State: The Expansion of National Administrative Capabilities, 1877–1920.* Cambridge, MA: Cambridge University Press.

Smith, M. C. "Robert Lynd and Consumerism in the 1930's." *Journal of the History of Sociology* (Fall/Winter 1979–1980): 99–119.

Sontag, S. "Some Thoughts on the Right Way to Love the Cuban Revolution." *Ramparts* 7 (April 1969): 14–19.

Steiger, J. 1992. Address to the Association of National Advertisers, Hot Springs, VA, October 12.

Stewart, J. and J. Cromartie. "Partisan Presidential Change and Regulatory Policy: The Case of the FTC and Deceptive Practices Enforcmeent, 1938–74." *Presidential Studies Quarterly* (Fall 1982): 568–73.

Stigler, G. "The Theory of Economic Regulation." *Bell Journal of Economics and Management Science* 2 (Spring 1971): 3–21.

Stone, A. 1977. *Economic Regulation and the Public Interest.* Ithaca, NY: Cornell University Press.

Stone, A. 1981. *Regulation and its Alternatives.* Washington, D.C.: Congressional Quarterly Press.

Stretton, H. 1976. "Ideological Bases of Environmentalism," in F. Sandbach (ed.), *Environment, Ideology and Politics.* Montclair, N.J.: Allanheld Osmun Publishers.

The Summary of the Coolfont Conference. Correspondence from Deborah Bleviss to Michael Pertschuk, July 22, 1982.

Thompson, F. J. and M. J. Scicchitano. "State Implementation Effort and Federal Regulatory Policy: The Case of Occupational Safety and Health." *Journal of Politics* (May 1985a): 686–702.

Thompson, F. J. and M. J. Scicchitano. "State Enforcement of Federal Regulatory Policy: The Lessons of OSHA." *Policy Studies Journal* 13 (March 1985b): 591–98.

Tiefer, C. 1994. *The Semi-sovereign Presidency: The Bush Administration's Strategy for Governing Without Congress.* Boulder, CO: Westview Press.

Tocqueville, A. de. 1969. *Democracy in America*, J. Mayer (ed.). New York: Doubleday & Co.

Tolchin, S. and M. Tolchin. 1984. *Dismantling America–The Rush to Deregulate.* New York: Oxford University Press.

Tunstall, S. 1985. "Regulatory Reform and the Reagan Administration: Attempts Toward Reducing Government." Prepared for delivery at the annual meeting of the American Political Science Association, New Orleans.

Victor, K. "Quayle's Quiet Coup." *National Journal* (July 6, 1991): 1677–80.

Viscusi, W. K. "The Impact of Occupational Safety and Health Regulation." *Bell Journal of Economics and Management Science.* (Spring 1979): 117–40.

Vogel, D. 1981. "The New Social Regulation in Historical and Comparative Perspective," in T. McCraw (ed.), *Regulation in Perspective.* Cambridge, MA: Harvard University Press.

Wagner, D. "Bill Bennett's Dilemma." *National Review* (June 1987): 28–31, 60.

Weber, M. 1946. "Politics as a Vocation," in H. Gerth and C. Mills (eds.), *From Max Weber: Essays in Sociology.* New York: Oxford University Press.

Weidenbaum, M. 1978. *The Costs of Government Regulation of Business.* (Joint Economic Committee of Congress). Washington, D.C.: U.S. Government Printing Office.

Weidenbaum, M. and R. DeFina. 1978. *The Cost of Federal Regulation of Economic Activity.* Reprint no. 88. Washington, D.C.: The American Enterprise Institute.

Weidenbaum, M. 1979. *The Future of Business Regulation.* New York: Amacom Press.

Weidenbaum, M. 1984. "Regulatory Reform Under the Reagan Administration," in G. Eads and M Fix (eds.) *The Reagan Regulatory Strategy: An Assessment.* Washington, D.C.: The Urban Institute.

Weingast, B. and K. Hall. 1981. "Congress, Regulation and the Courts: Economic Perspectives on Political Choice," in A. Ferguson (eds.), *Attacking Regulatory Problems: An Agenda for Research in the 1980s.* Cambridge, MA: Ballinger Publishing Co.

Weingast, B. and M. Moran. "The Myth of Runaway Bureaucracy–The Case of the FTC." (May/June 1982): 33–38.

Wenner, L. M. 1982. *The Environmental Decade in the Court.* Bloomington: Indiana University Press.

Wettergreen, J. 1985. "The Constitutional Problems of American Bureaucracy in INS v. Chadha." Prepared for delivery at the annual meeting of the American Political Science Association, New Orleans, LA.

White, F. C. 1993. "The Bush Defeat and Its Lessons," in P. W. Shramm (ed.), *Lessons of the Bush Defeat.* Ashland, OH: John M. Ashbrook Center for Public Affairs.

Wildavsky, A. 1978. *Speaking Truth To Power: The Art and Craft of Policy Analysis.* Boston: Little Brown & Co.

Wilkinson, F. "The Sinkable Carol Browner: New EPA Chief Finds Herself over Her Head." *Rolling Stone* (October 28, 1993): 45–47.

Williamson, O. 1970. *Corporate Control and Business Behavior.* Englewood Cliffs, N.J.: Prentice-Hall, Inc.

Wilson, J. Q. "The Rise of the Bureaucratic State." *The Public Interest.* 25 (Fall 1975): 39–48.

Wilson, J. Q. 1979. *American Government: Institutions and Policies*, 1st ed. New York: D.C. Heath & Co.

Wilson, J. Q. "American Politics: Then and Now." *Commentary* 67 (February 1979); 39–46.

Wilson, J. Q. (ed.). 1980. *The Politics of Regulation.* New York: Basic Books.

Whalen, J. and R. Flacks. "Echoes of Rebellion: The Liberated Generation Grows Up." *Journal of Politics and Military Sociology* 12 (1984): 61–78.

White, L. 1981. *Reforming Regulation: Process and Problems.* Englewood Cliffs, N.J.: Prentice-Hall, Inc.

PUBLIC DOCUMENTS

Environmental Protection Agency, 1990. *Securing Our Legacy: An EPA Progress Report: 1989–91,* Washington, DC: U.S. Government Printing Office.

Federal Trade Commission, 1978. *FTC Staff Report on Television Advertising to Children*, February. Washington, D.C.: U.S. Government Printing Office.

Miller, J. 1984. *Review of Commissioner Michael Pertschuk's Report: "The Performance of the Federal Trade Commission, 1977–1984."* Prepared for the Subcommittee on Oversight and Investigations, Committee on Energy and Commerce, U.S., Congress, House (September).

National Performance Review, Report on Reinventing Government, 1993. *From Redtape to Results—Creating a Government That Works Better and Costs Less.* Washington, DC: U.S. Government Printing Office.

Office of Management and Budget, 1981–1987. *Budget Authority of the United States Government.*

Office of Management and Budget, 1985. *Regulatory Program of the United States Government:* April 1, 1985–March 31, 1986.

Office of Management and Budget, 1986. *Regulatory Program of the United States Government:* April 1, 1986–March 31, 1987.

Office of Management and Budget, 1987. *Regulatory Program of the United States Government:* April 1, 1987–March 31, 1988.

Office of Management and Budget, 1994. "Report on Executive Order No. 12866, Regulatory Planning and Review." *Federal Register* (May 10).

Pertschuk, M., 1984. *FTC Review (1977–1984).* Prepared for the Subcommittee on Oversight and Investigations, Committee on Energy and Commerce, U.S., Congress, House (September).

Presidential Task Force on Regulatory Relief, 1982. *Reagan Administration Achievements in Regulatory Relief for State and Local Government* (August).

Presidential Task Force on Regulatory Relief, 1983. *Reagan Administration Regulatory Achievements* (August 11).

Public Papers of the Presidents, February 18, 1981.

Rosenberg, M. 1986. "Regulatory Management at OMB," in *Office of Management and Budget: Evolving Roles and Future Issues.* Prepared for the Committee on Governmental Affairs, U.S., Congress, Senate, by the Congressional Research Service (February).

Schumann, L., R. P. Rogers, and J. D. Reitzes. 1992. *Case Studies of the Price Effects of Horizontal Mergers.* Washington, DC.: Federal Trade Commission.

U.S. Congress, House, Committee on Energy and Commerce, Hearings before the Subcommittee on Energy and Commerce, 1993. 103rd Congress, 1st sess., March 10.

U.S. Congress, House, Committee on Energy and Commerce, Hearing before the Subcommittee on Transportation and Hazardous Materials, 1992. *Advertising and Labeling Issues with the Bureau of Alcohol, Tobacco, and Firearms, the Environmental Protection Agency, and the Food and Drug Administration.* 102nd Congress, 1st sess. November 21.

U.S. Congress, House, Subcommittee on Commerce, Transportation and Tourism, Committee on Energy and Commerce, 1982. *Federal Trade Commission Reauthorization,* 97th Cong., 2d sess., April 1, 20.

U.S. Congress, House, Subcommittee on Conservation and Natural Resources, Committee on Government Operations, Hearings, 1970. *The Environmental Decade: Action Proposals for the 1970's,* 91st Cong., 2nd sess. February 2–6; March 13; April 3.

U.S. Congress, Senate, Committee on Commerce, 1974. *Federal Trade Commission Oversight.* 93rd Cong., 2d sess., March 1, 7, 14; May 9.

U.S. Congress, Senate, Committee on Environment and Public Works, 1986. *Office of Management and Budget Influence on Agency Regulations* (May).

U.S. Congress, Senate, Committee on Governmental Affairs, 1985. *Renomination of Donald J. Devine to Be Director of the Office of Personnel Management.* 99th Cong., 2d sess., April 1–3; June 5, 6.

U.S. Congress, Senate, Consumer Subcommittee, Committee on Commerce, 1970. *To Amend the Federal Trade Commission Act.* 91st Cong., Dec. 16, 17, 1969; Feb. 3, 5; March 17–19; April 9, 1970.

U.S. Congress, Senate, Subcommittee for Consumers, Committee on Commerce, 1979. *Oversight to Examine the Enforcement and Administrative Authority of the FTC to Regulate Unfair and Deceptive Trade Practices.* 96th Cong., 1st sess., Sept. 18, 19, 27, 28; October 4, 5, 10.

U.S. Congress, Senate, Subcommittee on Administrative Practice and Procedures, Committee on Judiciary, 1969. *Agency Responsiveness to Public Needs: The Federal Trade Commission—Part I.* 91st Cong., 1st sess., Sept. 12, 16.

U.S. Congress, *Study on Federal Regulation,* vols. 1–4, 1977. Prepared for the Senate Committee on Governmental Affairs, 95th Cong., 1st sess.

Persons Interviewed for the First Edition

Although several other individuals in federal agencies and interest groups were interviewed, they requested that their names be withheld. In addition, a number of the individuals were interviewed on more than one occasion.

Arthur Amolsch: Editor, *FTC: Watch*.
Richard Ayers: Senior Attorney, Natural Resources Defense Council.
Daniel Becker: General Counsel, Environmental Action.
Brent Blackwelder: Vice President, Environmental Policy Institute.
James P. Carty: Vice President and Manager, Government Regulation and Competition, National Association of Manufacturers.
Allen Caskie: Assistant General Counsel, American Council of Life Insurance.
Nolan Clark: Former Assistant Administrator for Policy Management, Environmental Policy Agency.
Joan Claybrook: President, Public Citizen.
Douglas Costle: Administrator, Environmental Protection Agency under President Jimmy Carter.
Carol Crawford: Director, Bureau of Consumer Protection, Federal Trade Commission.
Charles Evans: Director of Water Quality, Environmental Protection Agency.
Albert Foer: Attorney, Jackson Campbell & Parkinson, formally Associate Director of Special Project Bureau of Competition, Federal Trade Commission.
Mark Griffins: Director of National Resources, National Association of Manufacturers.
Maureen Hinckle: Lobbyist, National Audubon Society.
Cornish Hitchcock: Public Citizen, Aviation Consumer Action Project.
Barry Kelly: Program Analyst, Environmental Protection Agency Region 10.
Terry Latanich: Former Assistant Director for Service Industry Practice, Bureau of Consumer Protection, Federal Trade Commission.
James Miller, III: Chairman, Federal Trade Commission.
Alan Morrison: Director of Litigation, Public Citizen.

Michael Mullin: Former member of the Senate Commerce Committee staff.

Warren Muir: Former Director of Toxic Substances Program, Environmental Protection Agency.

Timothy Muris: Director, Bureau of Competition, Federal Trade Commission.

John McCormick: Lobbyist, Environmental Policy Center.

Michael Pertschuk: Commissioner, Federal Trade Commission.

Robert Reich: Former Director of Policy and Planning, Federal Trade Commission.

William Ruckleshaus: Administrator, Environmental Protection Agency under Presidents Richard Nixon and Ronald Reagan.

Milton Russell: Assistant Administrator for Policy and Planning, Environmental Protection Agency.

Kathleen Sheekey: Director of Legislation, Common Cause.

Mark Silbergeld: Head of the Washington Office, Consumers Union.

Howard Vine: Director of Corporate Finance and Management and Competition, National Association of Manufacturers.

Persons Interviewed for the Second Edition

Kevin Arquit: Director, Bureau of Competition, Federal Trade Commission.
Richard Ayers: Former Chairman, National Clean Air Council.
Mary Azcuenaga: Commissioner, Federal Trade Commission.
Patricia Bailey: Former Commissioner, Federal Trade Commission.
Barry Cutler: Director of Consumer Protection, Federal Trade Commission.
Salley Katzen: Administrator, Office of Information and Regulatory Affairs.
Victor Kimm: Assistant Administrator, Environmental Protection Agency.
William Kristol: Chief of Staff for the Vice President
James Langenfeld: Director of Antitrust, Bureau of Economics, Federal Trade Commission.
Sharon Lindan: Assistant Director of Legal Affairs, Center for Science in the Public Interest.
David McIntosh: Director, Competitiveness Council.
Seth Mones: Legislative Assistant, Senator Frank Lautenberg (D-New jersey).
Dick Morganstern: Acting Director, Office of Policy, Planning and Evaluation, Environmental Protection Agency.
Deborah Owen: Commissioner, Federal Trade Commission.
Lee Peeler: Advertising Practices Assosicate Director, Federal Trade Commission
John I. Peterman: Director, Bureau of Economics, Federal Trade Commission.
William Prendergast: Office of Congressional Relations, Federal Trade Commission.
William Rosenberg: Assistant Administrator for Air and Radiation, Environmental protection Agency.
Bruce Silverglade: Director for Legal Affairs, Center for Science in the Public Interest.
Janet Steiger: Chairman, Federal Trade Commission.
Christine Triano: Program Associate, OMB Watch.
Luana Wilcher: Director of Water Programs, Environmental Protection Agency.
Denis Yao: Commissioner, Federal Trade Commission.

In addition, several congressional staff members were interviewed on the condition that they remain anonymous.

Index

Acid rain. *See* Clean Air Act (1990)
ACT. *See* Action for Children's Television
ACTION, 120
Action for Children's Television (ACT), 174
ADA. *See* Americans for Democratic Action
Administrative Presidency, 99, 136–39, 367
Administrative Procedure Act (APA), 108, 264
Administrative State, 24, 55
Airborn toxics. *See* Clean Air Act (1990)
Alaska Pipeline Act (1973), 172
AMA. *See* American Medical Association
American Bar Association (ABA)
  report on the Federal Trade Commission, 165–66, 173, 305–6, 311, 368
  regulation of legal profession, 194
American Medical Association (AMA), 207
Americans for Democratic Action (ADA), 174
Americans with Disabilities Act (1991), 289. *See also* Bush, George: regulatory expansion
Amolsch, A. L., 222, 224
Ash Council, 227–30, 232, 248
Ayers, Richard, 345
Azcuenaga, Mary, 308, 326, 327, 329

Bagge, Carl, 9
Bailey, Patricia, 211–12, 314
Barber, Sotirios, 12
Bardach, Eugene, 7
Bernstein, Marver, 62
Bennett, William, 115–16
Berry, Jeffrey, 37, 85
Bingaman, Ann, 329, 375
Bingham, Eula, 103

Bliley, Thomas, 382
Blumenstein, James, 292
Bork, Robert, 35
Boskin, Michael, 350
Boston Harbor, as attack on Dukakis, 334–35
Brandeis, Louis, 142–45, 147–48
Breglio, Vince, 334
Brooks, Jack, 316
Browner, Carol, 355, 377–78, 380, 384
  compared to Ann Burford, 377
Brownlow Committee, 11, 101, 136, 230
Bureaucracy as an inertial force, 45–48, 55
Burford, Ann, 6, 253–55, 257–65, 268, 275, 366
  compared to James Miller, 358–59, 366
  compared to William Reilly, 284, 337–38, 339
  defunding the left, 126
  Reagan personnel policy, 118
Bush, George, 7, 8. *See also* Presidential Task Force on Regulatory Relief
  budgetary allocation to regulatory activities, 285
  and environmental activists, 288, 292, 335, 350
  as the "Environmental President," 286, 311, 333–36, 343, 351
  executive oversight of regulation, 367
  market approach to environmental policy, 344
  1988 presidential campaign, 332, 334–35
  1992 presidential campaign, 292, 300. *See also* Clean Air Act (1990)
  Progressive Republican agenda, 280–81, 286–87
  regulatory expansion, 286, 288, 289, 336, 366
  regulatory personnel policies, 283–85, 307–8, 336

PRAISE FOR THE PREVIOUS EDITION

"Succeeds admirably in painting broad portraits of the progressive, New Deal 'public lobby', and Reagan eras of regulatory politics....Much to ponder here....Arresting." —*Political Science Quarterly*

"A thorough and balanced description of the institutions of social regulation....Its insights regarding the evolving relationship between administrative institutions and ideology are especially valuable." —*Journal of Politics*

"A careful analysis that deserves to be read by all students of regulation....A well crafted evaluation of recent regulatory policy set against the backdrop of significant changes in American politics....One of the better books on the politics of social regulation in some time." —John Hird, *University of Massachusetts, Amherst*

The past three decades have brought remarkable change in American regulatory politics. The re-emergence of public interest movements in the sixties and seventies raised fundamental questions about our market economy and dramatically expanded the government's regulatory role in the protection of public health, the consumer, and the environment. The far-reaching effects of this new regulatory regime in turn precipitated a counter-movement to restrict social and economic regulation spearheaded by the Reagan administration. In their first edition of *The Politics of Regulatory Change*, Richard Harris and Sidney Milkis assessed the long-term consequences of the Reagan administration's attempt to drastically curtail social regulation through an in-depth study of how two of the most influential regulatory agencies, the Federal Trade Commission and the Environmental Protection Agency, were affected by administration reforms. Now with their second edition, Harris and Milkis continue their assessment, creating a completely revised edition that includes coverage of the changes in regulatory politics during the Bush and Clinton administrations. They conclude that the essential elements of the 'public lobby regime' remain intact, even as the successive deregulatory assaults on that regime in the 1980's and 1990's have polarized Washington not simply over public policy but more fundamentally over the just ends of the American political system.

ABOUT THE AUTHORS:

Richard A. Harris is Associate Professor of Political Science at Rutgers University, Camden.
Sidney M. Milkis is Associate Professor of Politics at Brandeis University.

ISBN 0-19-508191-9

9 780195 081916

Cover design by Ann Lowe